BIBLICAL FOUNDATIONS
for BAPTIST
CHURCHES

BIBLICAL FOUNDATIONS
for BAPTIST CHURCHES

A Contemporary Ecclesiology

JOHN S. HAMMETT

Kregel
Academic & Professional

Biblical Foundations for Baptist Churches: A Contemporary Ecclesiology

© 2005 by John S. Hammett

Published by Kregel Publications, a division of Kregel, Inc., P.O. Box 2607, Grand Rapids, MI 49501.

Library of Congress Cataloging-in-Publication Data
Hammett, John S.
   Biblical foundations for Baptist churches: a contemporary ecclesiology / by John S. Hammett.
        p.   cm.
   Includes bibliographical references and index.
   1. Church. 2. Baptists—Doctrines. I. Title.
BV601.H28   2005   262'.061—dc22   2005022167

ISBN 0-8254-2769-X

Printed in the United States of America

05 06 07 08 09 / 5 4 3 2 1

CONTENTS

Illustrations 7
Preface 9
Introduction: Why This Book? 11

PART 1: WHAT IS THE CHURCH?
  1. The Nature of the Church: Biblical Foundations 25
  2. The Marks of the Church: Historical Perspective 51
  3. The Essence of the Church: Theological Conclusions and
     Practical Applications 67

PART 2: WHO IS THE CHURCH?
  4. Regenerate Church Membership: The Baptist Mark
     of the Church 81
  5. Where We Went Wrong and How We Can Get Right:
     Returning to Faithfulness 109

PART 3: HOW IS THE CHURCH GOVERNED?
  6. Baptist Church Polity: The Case for Congregationalism 135
  7. Elders in Baptist Life: Leaders, Not Rulers 159
  8. The Office of Deacon: Servants of the Church 191

PART 4: WHAT DOES THE CHURCH DO?

   9. The Ministries of the Church: Five Crucial Concerns 219
  10. More Than Simple Symbols: Baptism and the Lord's Supper 257

PART 5: WHERE IS THE CHURCH GOING?

  11. In All Directions: New Approaches for a Changing Landscape . . . 299
  12. Into All the World: The Future of the Global Church 335
       Conclusion: A Call for Faithful Churches 351

       Scripture Index 355
       Subject Index 359

ILLUSTRATIONS

I.1:   How to Do Theology 16
1.1:   Summary of Implications of the Church as the People of God ... 36
1.2:   Summary of Implications of the Church as the Body of Christ ... 43
1.3:   Summary of Implications of the Church as the
       Temple of the Spirit 49
4.1:   Regenerate Church Membership as Central to
       Baptist Ecclesiology 107
5.1:   How to Recover Regenerate Church Membership 116
5.2:   J. Newton Brown's Church Covenant 127
5.3:   Saddleback Church Covenant 128
5.4:   Capitol Hill Baptist Church Covenant 129
6.1:   Episcopalian Church Government 139
6.2:   Presbyterian Church Government 141
6.3:   Congregational Church Government 145
9.1:   The Ministries of the Church in Acts 2:42–47 221
9.2:   The Life Development Process 230
9.3:   An Overview of "The Life Development Institute" 231
11.1: Theology of Seeker Church Pastors 306
11.2: Key Characteristics of Modern and Postmodern Eras 324

PREFACE

THIS BOOK HAS BEEN BREWING in my mind for close to twenty years. Along the way, many people have contributed to it in some way. Most important have been the ten churches on two continents and in five states that have been my spiritual homes and the living laboratories in which I have seen many of the principles of this book lived out. To those churches collectively, I dedicate this book.

My theological mentors will be apparent from the footnotes and much of the content of this book. I am grateful for the heritage of Baptist ecclesiology, and have consciously sought to draw upon it. Sadly, much of that heritage was ignored or forgotten in the twentieth century. I thank those who are working to restore it; my debts to them will be seen in my use of their works.

Members of the churches where I have served, and colleagues and students at Southeastern Baptist Theological Seminary, have heard many of these ideas. Collegial and classroom discussions have sharpened my thinking on a number of points, and I am grateful for the interest of my colleagues and students and their encouragement to present the ideas in book form. However, that encouragement would probably have been lost in the midst of academic responsibilities had it not been for the sabbatical granted by the administration and trustees of Southeastern Baptist Theological Seminary for the calendar year 2004. I thank them for the generous gift of time that allowed me to complete my research and put ideas on paper. Those ideas might have stayed on loose pieces of paper and never appeared in print form without the expertise of Phyllis Jackson, Donna Cooper, and Laura White. I thank them for their help in getting the manuscript prepared for publication.

The staff at Kregel Publications, especially editor Jim Weaver, have been more than helpful. I thank them for their willingness to publish a denominational perspective in what is commonly regarded as a postdenominational age.

My wife, Linda, has been the most faithful and fervent prayer supporter of this project a husband could desire, and my children, Suzanne and Michael, have prompted my prayers that this book will play a role in helping to create for them and their generation a host of healthy and faithful churches in which they will serve and be served.

Most of all, I thank the Lord of the church for calling me to be a part of his bride. May this book contribute to the faithfulness of that bride.

WHY THIS BOOK?

IN THE CONTEMPORARY information age, when books gush from publishers, the Internet offers an endless flow of facts, and various forms of media compete for our attention, it seems incumbent on anyone who writes a book to answer the question on the minds of prospective readers: Why should I read this book? This chapter attempts to answer that question and in so doing will give the reader an idea of what lies ahead.

First, I want to show that the church is God's creation, Christ's body, and the special instrument of the Holy Spirit in the world today. Because the church is so important to God, it should be a primary concern to every Christian.

Second, I argue that understanding the doctrine of the church is especially important to contemporary North Americans, because their pragmatic approach to church life, their concern to be relevant to their culture, and their desire to see their churches grow leave them vulnerable to the danger that their churches will be shaped more by those concerns than by the design of the Lord of the church. Indeed, how can churches be what God desires them to be if people do not know what he desires them to be? Thus, this book will seek to ask the foundational theological questions that will help God's people remain faithful to his ideals for the church, as revealed in Scripture.

Third, I want to make a case that, even in our postdenominational age, there is a need for a book on the doctrine of the church from a Baptist perspective. Such a book will, I hope, be of some interest to those who are not Baptists, either out of simple curiosity to understand more about the largest Protestant denomination in North America, or out of a willingness to examine Baptist claims that their doctrine of the church faithfully represents what the Bible teaches. But I especially want to urge Baptists to read this book, because I think few Baptists have a rationale for why they are Baptist, or even realize what it means to be Baptist, and many Baptist churches are hardly recognizable as Baptist churches in any historic sense. Historically, Baptists have been Baptist, not out of blind denominational loyalty, but because of their commitment to what they saw as biblical teaching on the doctrine of the church. That doctrine has been central to Baptist distinctives and was the motivating force behind our origin. It has been largely lost over the past century and is worth recovering, because it addresses critical needs of churches today.

WHY READ A BOOK ON THE CHURCH?

For all those who desire to know God, or for all those who are followers of Christ, the church cannot be a matter of indifference. In the middle of the third century the great North African church father Cyprian said, "You cannot have God as father unless you have the Church as mother."[1] The great Reformer John Calvin called the church "the mother of all the godly."[2] More recently, in an article entitled "The Church: Why Bother?" Tim Stafford has affirmed the same sentiment: "A living, breathing congregation is the only place to live in a healthy relationship to God. That is because it is the only place on earth where Jesus has chosen to dwell."[3] These comments reflect the consistent New Testament teaching that Christianity is not an individualistic enterprise but a corporate commitment. Christians and the church belong together because the church is where the Christian life is born and nurtured. For twenty centuries, most of those who have come to know the true and living God have done so through some form of church ministry. Virtually all Christians have lived out their Christian lives in connection with some form of the church. That is why Hebrews 10:25 admonishes Christians to not give up meeting together; they need the church. It is vitally important to them.

But as significant as the church is to Christians, the most important reason for Christians to be passionate about the church is that the church is

1. Cyprian, "On the Unity of the Church," in *Early Latin Theology*, trans. and ed. S. L. Greenslade, The Library of Christian Classics (Philadelphia: Westminster Press, 1956), 5:127–28.
2. John Calvin, *The Institutes of the Christian Religion*, ed. John T. McNeill, trans. Ford Lewis Battles, The Library of Christian Classics (Philadelphia: Westminster Press, 1960), 21:1011 (4.1).
3. Tim Stafford, "The Church: Why Bother?" *Christianity Today* 49, no. 1 (January 2005): 42–49.

God's passion. It is central to what God has been doing down through history, creating a people for his own possession, a people who will be his people, and for whom he will be their God. Early in the biblical story, we see God calling Abram and promising that through him he would bless all the families of the earth (Gen. 12:1–3). Throughout the Old Testament we see God forming Israel to be his people and, through them, bringing the Messiah into the world. In the Gospels, Jesus gathers a group of disciples, but does not yet call them the church. The story reaches a point of climax and transition with the birth of the church on the day of Pentecost in Acts 2. The coming of the Holy Spirit constitutes the church as God's new creation. The New Testament letters picture the life and growth of the church, continuing until the great purpose of God is fulfilled in Revelation 21:3: "Now the dwelling of God is with men, and he will live with them. They will be his people, and God himself will be with them and be their God." Virtually the whole Bible traces God's work of preparing for the church and working in and through it. The church is of central importance to God.

Paul says that God's intent was that "through the church, the manifold wisdom of God should be made known to the rulers and authorities in the heavenly realms" (Eph. 3:10). He goes on to say that God is eternally glorified in the church: "to him be glory in the church and in Christ Jesus throughout all generations, for ever and ever" (v. 21). Thus any book offering biblical teaching on the church should be of interest to anyone interested in the wisdom or glory of God.

The church is also central to why Christ came. He came to seek and save the lost and then to gather them into a body. He said, "I will build my church, and the gates of Hades will not overcome it" (Matt. 16:18). Paul says, "Christ loved the church and gave himself up for her to make her holy, cleansing her by the washing with water through the word, and to present her to himself as a radiant church, without stain or wrinkle or any other blemish, but holy and blameless" (Eph. 5:25–27). He calls all those who love Christ to love his church as well, and to cooperate with him in his great project of building the church. But how can we cooperate with Christ in the building of the church if we do not understand what he desires it to be? This book presents what Christ calls the church to be.

Further, the church is central to the presence of the Holy Spirit in the world today. The writer of Luke and Acts does not use the term *church* (*ekklēsia*) for the group gathered by Jesus until after the coming of the Holy

Spirit on the day of Pentecost, because it is the presence of the Spirit that gives life to the church. The church is called "a holy temple . . . a dwelling in which God lives by his Spirit" (Eph. 2:21–22). The church is not the only way the Spirit is present in the world, but he is uniquely present in the church.

As such, the church is uniquely empowered by God to minister in the world. A recent survey estimated that Southern Baptist congregations alone provide services such as food pantries and clothing closets to three million people a month.[4] Church members not only fund and voluntarily staff many of the ministries of their churches, but church members also donate two-thirds of the contributions given to nonreligious charities.[5] In so doing they reflect the working of the Holy Spirit in their lives and their churches. Furthermore, according to the projections of Philip Jenkins, the worldwide importance of the church is not decreasing but increasing, and dramatically so in the Southern Hemisphere.[6] The church survived decades of oppression at the hands of communist rulers in Eastern Europe and, though often not recognized as such, was an important factor in the crumbling of the Iron Curtain. Today, the church continues to face persecution in many parts of the world, in part because its power, the power of the indwelling Holy Spirit, is not subject to political control.

All these factors should make the church a matter of intense concern for all those interested in God and what he is doing in the world today.

WHY READ A BOOK ON THE DOCTRINE OF THE CHURCH?

American culture is marked by pragmatism, and most books on the church reflect that orientation. There are dozens of books on how to make a church grow, how to organize and administer church programs, how to revitalize a church's worship, how to get church members involved in missions, how to do almost anything churches do. While I share these pragmatic and practical concerns, in this book I focus on a different set of questions that are more

---

4. This data is from a survey of a representative sample of more than seven hundred Southern Baptist congregations conducted in 2000, called *Southern Baptist Congregations Today: A Survey at the Turn of a New Millennium*. The results of the survey are given in Philip B. Jones, "Research Report: Executive Summary of *Southern Baptist Congregations Today*" (Alpharetta, Ga.: North American Mission Board, SBC, n.d.), 3–4, available via www.namb.net.

5. Tim Stafford, "Anatomy of a Giver," *Christianity Today* 41, no. 6 (May 19, 1997): 19–24.

6. Philip Jenkins, *The Next Christendom: The Growth of Global Christianity* (Oxford, U.K.; New York: Oxford University Press, 2002).

fundamental to a church's long-term health, questions that deal with the doctrine of the church. This is the branch of theology called ecclesiology.

To most people theology is about as appealing as a root canal. Such a view is unfortunate and inaccurate. There are problems with the health of most churches that cannot be corrected by tinkering with the mechanics of their programs. We need to do the important work of theology.

Since the church is God's creation, it must be ordered and operated according to his instructions. Understanding those instructions is the task of theology. It is not a task entrusted to an elite group of scholars, but all Christians are commanded to love God with all their minds. Theology is simply using our minds to know and love God. As one theologian put it, "Theology is too important to be left to the theologians."[7]

This work of theology begins with the study of God's instructions, found in Scripture. This book will seek above all to be biblical in its understanding and presentation of the doctrine of the church. But we have help in understanding the message of the Bible from the twenty centuries of Christians who have gone before us, many of whom sought to understand the same Scriptures that we study. It would be foolish and arrogant to despise the counsel of earlier generations. History has much to teach us in understanding the Bible. At the very least, historical perspective can serve as a safeguard against the perennial danger of allowing our own historical context and culture to distort our understanding of Scripture. For those engaged in the important task of seeking to communicate the gospel to a post-Christian, biblically illiterate culture, the laudable desire to address that culture in a relevant and intelligible way carries with it the danger of allowing the culture to shape and perhaps distort the message. History provides an anchor that can guard against drifting with the currents of culture.

Scripture, informed by historical perspective, thus forms the basis for theology. Theology takes the data of Scripture, utilizes the help of history, and develops doctrine to address the questions posed by life as we seek to live for God in God's world in the contemporary context. Such doctrine then serves as the basis for practical application in concrete, real life situations. The process of theology can thus be pictured as a pyramid, in which theology is built on Scripture, is informed by history, and serves as a platform for ministry.

---

7. W. Ward Gasque, back cover of Robert Banks, *Redeeming the Routines: Bringing Theology to Life* (Wheaton, Ill.: Bridgepoint Books, 1993).

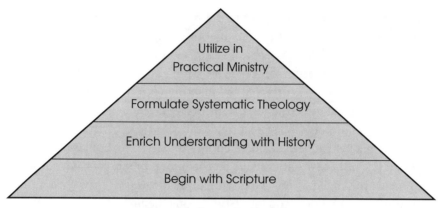

Figure I.1: How to Do Theology

The tendency among most evangelical Christians is to go straight from Scripture to ministry without taking the necessary intervening steps. This book follows the full process, beginning with and emphasizing Scripture as the sole normative source for theology. It, secondarily, draws upon the resources of history, especially Baptist history, to challenge and, at points, to correct contemporary assumptions. It develops the major aspects of the doctrine of the church and includes examples and suggestions of how such doctrine can and should be fleshed out in practical ministry in local church contexts.

The five parts of the book address the major theological issues involved in the doctrine of the church, with each part organized around a central question. The question for this introduction is, "Why this book?" Specifically, why read a book on the church? Further, why read a book on the doctrine of the church? Finally, why read a book on the doctrine of the church from a Baptist perspective?

Part 1 asks the question, "What is the church?" It seeks to answer that question in three chapters. The first chapter examines the New Testament word for church *(ekklēsia)*, considers the major images for the church, and describes the nature of the church as biblically conceived. Chapter 2 utilizes the resources of history, reflecting on the two major formulations of the marks of the church. The classical formulation describes the church as "one, holy, catholic, and apostolic," and the Reformation sees the true church as marked by the preaching of the Word and the right administration of the sacraments.

I consider what these formulations add to our understanding of the church. From this biblical and historical material, chapter 3 offers five theological conclusions on the essence of the church, with each one leading to suggestions for practical application in church life and ministry.

Part 2 turns to the question, "Who is the church?" Here I consider what may be called the Baptist mark of the church—regenerate church membership. Chapter 4 gives the biblical evidence for viewing the church as a body of regenerate baptized believers, traces how that understanding was lost following the conversion of Constantine in A.D. 312, and shows how it was recovered by Baptists and became the centerpiece of their ecclesiology. Chapter 5 recounts the sad story of how that mark of regenerate church membership was lost by Baptists in America in the twentieth century, and considers how and why it should be regained, involving changes in the practices of baptism, church membership, and church discipline.

The question for part 3 is, "How is the church governed?" Chapter 6 presents the case for congregational church government as the form most consistent with New Testament teaching. Chapters 7 and 8 present Baptist teaching on the two offices of church leaders: those called elders or overseers or pastors, and those called deacons. The important issues of the role, responsibility, qualifications, number, and selection of these leaders are given a careful and thorough consideration.

Part 4 looks at the ministries of the church under the question, "What does the church do?" Drawing on the important and paradigmatic description in Acts 2:42–47, teaching, fellowship, worship, service, and evangelism are affirmed as five essential ministries of the church in chapter 9. Under the topic of worship, it discusses the contemporary controversy over worship styles, particularly the use of contemporary music in seeker churches. Chapter 10 presents a Baptist view of the ordinances of baptism and the Lord's Supper, with some specific, practical suggestions for improving how Baptists celebrate these important acts.

"Where is the church going?" is the final question, examined in part 5. Chapter 11 answers that question with the phrase "in all directions." That answer reflects the various responses churches are giving to the challenges presented by our changing cultural context. I give special attention to what I see as the four most important directions churches are taking. Some are reaching out to seekers, and I consider the very important seeker church movement. A number of seeker churches, but also some traditional churches, represent another development unprecedented in church history, that of megachurches. I look at the issues raised by more and more Christians in larger and larger churches, and consider how that development has also provoked what some call the microchurch movement, the use of cell groups, cell churches, and house churches. A related but slightly different concern is reflected in the numerous changes various churches are adopting to reach those identified with postmodern culture, and thus I consider the movement called the emerging church. Also in chapter 11, I look at a small but growing number of churches who are insisting that the way forward is back to the past, to recover emphases and practices that we have left behind. The final chapter, chapter 12, broadens our vision by looking at the church going into all the world and considers some of the questions raised as churches are planted in other cultures.

Each part of the book concludes with a list of study questions to help the reader reflect on the issues raised in the preceding chapters, and an annotated list of resources for further study, to assist those who want to go into further depth on specific issues.

The book concludes, not with a question but a challenge—a challenge to give ourselves to the cause for which Christ gave himself, the development of radiant churches, fully pleasing to him. That requires first understanding what God desires his church to be and then working patiently and lovingly to see that design embodied in our churches. Those interested in responding to such a challenge have ample reason to read a book on the doctrine of the church.

WHY READ A BOOK ON THE DOCTRINE OF THE CHURCH FROM A BAPTIST PERSPECTIVE?

While I have drawn doctrine first and foremost from Scripture, this book does present a clear Baptist perspective on ecclesiology. In so doing, I am countering the widespread postdenominationalism in our culture.[8] Increasingly, people are reticent to identify themselves by a denominational affiliation, preferring to be seen simply as Christian. But in practice, it is hard to

---

8. While there are many indications that denominational loyalty is not as important as it was a generation ago, the point should not be overstated. A recent survey involving more than seven hundred Southern Baptist congregations reported that 90 percent of respondents stated that it was important to the members of their congregation to be affiliated with the Southern Baptist Convention. See Jones, "Research Report," 4.

avoid making some denominational decisions. Even those who join a non-denominational church will find that it either baptizes infants or does not, it operates under a group of elders or it is ruled by the congregation. It would seem reasonable to expect those who attend or join a church to understand their church's rationale for its practices. If I am a Baptist, naturally I would want to understand my denomination's perspective on the doctrine of the church. But such an answer simply prompts a deeper question: "Why be a Baptist?" At times I have asked my students at Southeastern Baptist Theological Seminary or members of churches where I speak to tell me why they are Baptists. I get a variety of answers.

Perhaps the most common answer is, "I am a Baptist because I was raised that way; my parents were Baptists and that is all I have ever known." These individuals like the familiar Baptist literature and mission agencies and traditional programs. But family background alone does not provide a very strong reason for denominational affiliation. The proof of that is the ease with which many Baptists switch denominations. When they consider a church, they are likely to assign greater importance to the style of music and worship, the quality of the preaching, and the variety of the programs than to the denominational label.

Others say they are Baptists because it was in a Baptist church that they first heard the gospel and recognized their need for a personal relationship with Christ, or it was in a Baptist church that they were first taught the Bible, or it was a Baptist church that reached out to them with love. Experiences like these produce a measure of denominational loyalty, but a small measure only, for there are many churches of other denominations that proclaim the biblical gospel, teach the Bible, and reach out in love and, sadly, there are some Baptist churches that do none of these things.

Some realize they have little denominational identity and see that as a good thing. To the question, "Why are you a Baptist?" they answer, "I don't really think of myself as a Baptist, but simply as a Christian." As we noted above, such an answer is characteristic of our postdenominational era and of evangelical Christianity as a whole, which has been largely identified with transdenominational parachurch groups. One such group, Promise Keepers, even identifies denominationalism as a sin akin to that of racism.

I have some sympathy with this answer. Certainly being a Christian is far more important than any denominational commitment, and there have been all too many sinful, arrogant, and divisive expressions of denominationalism.

But, as we noted earlier, in the end, some type of denominational identity is unavoidable. In practice, every church has to answer certain questions. Should we baptize infants or believers only? Are we to be governed by a bishop, by a board, or by the congregation? What type of practices do we believe are appropriate for worship? Is each church connected to others, or does each church have a measure of autonomy? The answers provided to these questions and others like them align an individual and a church, to some degree, with a denomination, or at the least, place them within a denominational tradition. So, while not the most important issue or essential to salvation, the question of denominational affiliation is not irrelevant or unimportant.

To the question, "Why are you a Baptist?" a well-informed Baptist will reply, "because I interpret Scripture as teaching Baptist positions on the traditional ecclesiological questions."[9] Such an answer need not be arrogant, or presume that Baptists have a monopoly on truth, or imply that Baptists are the only true Christians. Rather, it recognizes that since the Reformation, Christians—even Christians of deep piety and genuine love for Christ and commitment to his Word—have not been able to reach agreement on the interpretation of Scripture on certain issues regarding what the church is and how it is to function. These disagreements led to the formation of different denominational traditions. These differences in interpretation endure to this day and present choices every thoughtful Christian must face. Thus any book on the doctrine of the church must present a perspective that is, to some degree, denominational. The perspective presented in this book is Baptist because I agree with how Baptists historically have interpreted the key ecclesiological issues.

To the question with which we began this section, "Why read a book on the doctrine of the church from a Baptist perspective?" there are several answers. For those who are not Baptists, this book will explain the basis for Baptist identity, which has centered around their doctrine of the church. Whether one traces the origin of modern Baptists to the early sixteenth-

---

9. There have been a number of books in Baptist history that have given answers to the question, "Why a Baptist?" One of the earliest and most famous is J. M. Pendleton, *Three Reasons Why I Am a Baptist with a Fourth Reason Added on Communion* (St. Louis, Mo.: National Baptist Publishing, 1856). His reasons all dealt with Baptist ecclesiology. Others, such as Louis Devotie Newton, *Why I Am a Baptist* (New York: Nelson, 1957); Joe T. Odle, ed., *Why I Am a Baptist* (Nashville: Broadman, 1972); Cecil P. Staton, ed., *Why I Am a Baptist: Reflections on Being Baptist in the 21st Century* (Macon, Ga.: Smyth & Helwys, 1999); and Tom Nettles and Russell Moore, *Why I Am a Baptist* (Nashville: Broadman & Holman, 2001), include ecclesiological reasons to some degree, but some also deal with family influence and appreciation for other aspects of Baptist life.

century Anabaptists or the early seventeenth-century English Separatists, the key issue for both groups was the same: their belief in the church as a pure gathered group of believers only. Most other Baptist distinctives grow out of their doctrine of the church. It may well be that some non-Baptists who read this book will be provoked to reconsider their interpretation of scriptural teaching on the church and perhaps revise some of their views.

For those who are Baptists, simple curiosity could be a motivation for reading this book. Most Baptists, and even many Baptist pastors, have never carefully thought through the biblical rationale for historic Baptist views and practices. Indeed, one of the main reasons prompting the writing of this book was the recognition that most Baptists are unaware of their ecclesiological heritage, in part because there have been few books written in the past twenty-five years that address the doctrine of the church from a Baptist perspective. This book can help to confirm and strengthen many in their Baptist identity by showing them the strong basis for that identity.

Other Baptists, especially Baptist pastors, may be led to read this book because they sense that many of our churches are wandering, tossed to and fro by passing fads, suffering from problems that go beyond individual, isolated acts to shoddy doctrinal foundations. In the past century, Baptists as a whole seem to have forsaken many of their historic positions, with little awareness of the slippage. The doctrine presented in this book accurately reflects biblical teaching, is deeply rooted in Baptist history, is intensely practical and applicable in Baptist churches today, and is urgently needed if Baptist churches are to be the radiant bride of Christ. This concern for the welfare of the church motivated the writing of this book; I hope it will motivate many to read it.

STUDY QUESTIONS

1. Which of the reasons given for the importance of the church seems most significant to you? How important is the church? Can someone be a Christian and not be involved in any church?

2. What questions do you have about the doctrine of the church that you hope this book will answer? Write them down and review them after reading this book to see if your questions were addressed.

3. What is your own denominational affiliation? Why? How important is it to you? Could you see yourself becoming a member of a church of a different denomination? Why or why not?

PART 1

WHAT IS THE CHURCH?

CHAPTER 1

THE NATURE OF THE CHURCH

Biblical Foundations

IN THIS CHAPTER, AND THE two that follow, we address the question that must be the starting point for any doctrine of the church, "What is the church?" In everyday language we use the word *church* in a variety of ways. Quite often, we refer to the church as the building where we meet ("We're going to the church."). Some groups apply the term *church* to their denomination (the United Methodist Church). More knowledgeable Christians know that the church is more than a building or denomination—it is people. But simply stating that the church is people, or even God's people, does not go very far. What is the church?

For two thousand years, in hundreds of cultures and languages, divided into a multitude of denominations, thousands if not millions of groups of Christians have assembled under the name of church. Some have certainly been far healthier than others. Some have been closer to what Baptists see as the New Testament pattern than others. What makes a group a church, as opposed to a club, a Bible study, a fellowship group, or even a parachurch group? What is the nature of a church? What marks identify it in the world? What is the theological essence of a true church? Our concern in these first three chapters is to discuss these fundamental and foundational issues. Other issues, which are crucial but relate more to the well-being or health or proper order of the church than to its being or nature, will be treated in the following chapters.

Since Baptists are people of the Book, a Baptist approach to the nature of the church begins with Scripture. In this chapter we, first of all, explore the teaching of Scripture on the nature of the church. Then, respecting the witness of history, we examine in chapter 2 the major historic formulations of the marks of the church. Then, since doctrine is the basis for ministry, we draw upon our findings from Scripture and history to present theological conclusions and practical applications concerning the essence of the church.

THE TERM *EKKLĒSIA*

We begin by looking at the single normative source for all theology, Scripture, and in particular at the word used for church in the New Testament, *ekklēsia.* What was it about this word that led early Christians to apply it to themselves, and what did they mean by it?

Most scholars today agree that the best way to decipher the meaning of a word is by looking at how it is used, rather than looking at its etymology, or origin. Still, the origin of *ekklēsia* is interesting. It is formed from two Greek words, *ek,* "out," and *kaleō,* "to call." Thus, the *ekklēsia* are "the called-out ones." In ancient Greece, the *ekklēsia* was the assembly of the called-out citizens, who came together to conduct the business of the city. But over the years, the element of being called out became less prominent, and an *ekklēsia* was regarded as just an assembly of people.[1] Still, it is worth noting that the element of being called out lies in the background of the biblical word for the church. Paige Patterson points out that it seems unlikely that this idea of being called out was not at least part of the reason why the early Christians chose this word for their gatherings.[2] As we will see below, the New Testament teaching on the church does highlight the idea of being called out, and that idea was implied in the origin and ancient usage of the word.

For New Testament concepts like the church, however, the most important background is not etymology or ancient Greek usage, but the Old Testament. Here, we look to the use of *ekklēsia* in the Septuagint, the Greek translation of the Old Testament. There are two primary Hebrew terms that are used to refer to God's people in the Old Testament: *ʿēdâh* and *qāhāl.* The

---

1. This usage is reflected in Acts 19:32, where a riotous crowd came together and is called an *ekklēsia,* an assembly. Such an assembly is then contrasted with a legal assembly in verse 39 *(ennomō ekklēsia),* one that would be formally convened to conduct civic affairs.
2. Paige Patterson, "The Church in the 21st Century" (privately published paper, n.d.), 5.

translators of the Septuagint used *ekklēsia* to translate *qāhāl* nearly one hundred times, but never to translate *ʿēdâh*. For *ʿēdâh* they usually used the Greek term *synagōgē*, which is used only once in the New Testament to refer to the church (James 2:2).[3] What does this association with *qāhāl*, but not *ʿēdâh*, say about the meaning of *ekklēsia*?

While both *ʿēdâh* and *qāhāl* can be used in a variety of senses (secular as well as religious), the most important distinction seems to be that *qāhāl* "embraces only those who have heard the call and are following it. *ʿēdâh*, on the other hand, is the permanent community into which one was born."[4] In designating themselves *ekklēsia*, the early Christians were taking a word already in use by Greek-speaking Jews to refer to the people of God in the Old Testament, and thus making a claim to some degree of historical connection to that earlier people; they were also using a word that reinforced the idea that the church is made up of those summoned or called by God. They avoided the term *synagōgē*, which was occasionally used to translate *qāhāl*, probably because by the New Testament era, that word was strongly associated with the Jewish law and temple, which made it a problematic term to use for the New Testament church.

When we turn to the actual New Testament usage of *ekklēsia*, we find at least one element of the etymological and Old Testament background confirmed. K. L. Schmidt sees the idea of being called out as central to New Testament teaching on the church: "*Ekklēsia* is in fact the group of men called out of the world by God even though we do not take express note of the *ek*," referring to the etymology of the term.[5] The very term *called (klētos)* is found several times as a virtual synonym for *ekklēsia*. Paul describes the church in Rome as those "called to belong to Jesus Christ" and "called to be saints" (Rom. 1:6–7). The church in Corinth is said to be those who are "called to be holy" (1 Cor. 1:2). On the day of Pentecost, the gift of the Holy Spirit was promised to all those whom God called to himself. The church comes into being, not by any human initiative, but in response to a divine call. Beyond this central idea, there is some variety in the New Testament usage of *ekklēsia*.

The term is found in the New Testament 114 times. Of these, three refer to a secular assembly and two refer to the Old Testament people of God. The

---

3. See the discussion by L. Coenen, "Church," in *New International Dictionary of New Testament Theology*, ed. Colin Brown (Grand Rapids: Zondervan, 1975), 1:292–96.

4. Ibid., 295.

5. K. L. Schmidt, "*ekklēsia*," in *Theological Dictionary of the New Testament*, ed. Gerhard Kittel, trans. and ed. G. W. Bromiley (Grand Rapids: Eerdmans, 1965), 3:531.

remaining 109 verses refer to the New Testament church. More than half of these, sixty-two, are found in Paul's writings. There are twenty references to the church in Revelation, nineteen in Acts, and a few in Hebrews, James, and 3 John. Noteworthy is the surprising lack of references to *ekklēsia* in the Gospels. The only three references are found in two passages in Matthew (Matt. 16:18; 18:17). These are historically and theologically important passages,[6] but they are only two and both seem to look to a future situation. The implication is that the church was not given birth until after Christ's earthly ministry.

The 109 occurrences of *ekklēsia* are usually seen as referring to the church in two senses, local and universal. The overwhelming majority point to local churches, actual assemblies that gather and act. We find them moving quickly toward order and organization, with leadership established (Acts 14:23) and membership recognized, such that Luke can report the numerical growth of the church, from three thousand (2:41) to five thousand (4:4) and beyond (9:31; 16:5).

There is some variation in nomenclature for church leaders. *Elder (presbyteros)* is the term used most often (Acts 14:23; 15:4, 22), but *bishop* or *overseer (episkopos)* is also found (Acts 20:28; Phil. 1:1), along with *deacon* (1 Tim. 3:8). The most commonly used term among Baptists today, *pastor,* is used only once (Eph. 4:11). A discussion of the roles, functions, and significance of these leaders and the related issues of church government would take us well beyond the bounds of this chapter and so will be deferred until part 3. However, it does seem that the church, as portrayed biblically, is not just any group of people, even any group of Christians. It is an organized assembly.

These churches gather to act in a variety of ways. They gather to worship (Acts 13:2–3; 1 Cor. 14:23ff.), which seems to include prayer (Acts 12:5; 13:3; 14:23), reading of Scripture (Col. 4:16; 1 Tim. 4:13), teaching from the lead-

---

6. In Matt. 16:18, Jesus calls Peter *petros,* and says that he will build his church on a rock *(petra).* The relationship of Peter to the *petra* on which the church is built has been the subject of controversy. The traditional Roman Catholic interpretation has seen Peter as the rock, thus establishing the importance of the papacy, but such an interpretation requires that Jesus be referring to Peter, that Peter had a line of successors, that those successors are the bishops of Rome, and that Peter's foundational role was transferred to them. More likely are interpretations that see Peter's confession of Jesus as the Christ as the rock on which the church is built, or Peter himself as the rock, not as the bishop of Rome, but as the leader of the apostles, whose teaching collectively was foundational for the church (see Eph. 2:20). Matt. 18:17 has been important in ecclesiology as the most often cited basis for the practice of church discipline.

ers (Acts 20:28–31; Eph. 4:11; 1 Tim. 3:2), and the Lord's Supper (1 Cor. 11:18ff.). They enjoy fellowship within the local assembly and with other local churches (Rom. 16:16). The church serves widows and the needy (1 Tim. 5:16; 1 Cor.16:1). Believers are involved in spreading the gospel, both personally (Acts 8:2–4) and through those sent by the church (Acts 13:2–3). These ministries emerge without fanfare, exhortation, or command. It is as if such ministries are part of the very nature of the church. Churches are not passive or static; they are dynamic, purposeful assemblies.

In addition to references to the local church, there are at least thirteen references (nine in Ephesians) that seem clearly to refer to the church in a universal sense, as all the redeemed of all the ages. These passages contain some of the most exalted descriptions of the church, seeing it perhaps as it will be at the consummation (Eph. 5:23–27), or even as it is now in the mind of God (Eph. 3:10, 21). A number of these passages contain the biblical teaching on Christ as the head of the church.

Local and *universal* is the most widely used terminology for the twofold meaning for *ekklēsia* found in the New Testament. Some refer to the dichotomy as *visible* and *invisible*. Some even reserve the term *Church* (with a capital *C*) for the universal church, and refer to local assemblies as congregations. However, in view of the predominance of the local church in New Testament usage, it seems more fitting to translate *ekklēsia* as church (with a lowercase *c*), assuming the local church meaning and then noting the exceptions when it has the universal meaning.

Moreover, there may need to be a third sense, in addition to local and universal. For example, when Paul says he persecuted the church of God (1 Cor. 15:9; Gal. 1:13; Phil. 3:6), it wasn't just one church he targeted, though he began with the church in Jerusalem (Acts 8:3). Neither does it seem that any individual could persecute the universal church. What Paul persecuted was the church in general, any church.

Finally, the idea of local church must be seen with some flexibility. While a group small enough to meet in a house is called a church (Rom. 16:5; Col. 4:15), Paul also consistently refers to the church in a *city* in the singular (the church in Cenchrea or Philippi or Corinth, the church of the Thessalonians; see Rom. 16:1; 1 Cor. 1:2; Phil. 4:15; 1 Thess. 1:1), but to the churches in a *region* in the plural (the churches of Galatia or Asia or Macedonia; see 1 Cor. 16:1, 19; 2 Cor. 8:1). Today we see a multiplicity of churches in virtually every city, large or small. To speak of the church in Raleigh, for example, sounds a bit odd, and could only have a rather nebulous meaning for us. What are we to make of the New Testament pattern on this point?

First, we need to remember the historical situation. Christians in any city were a very small minority. In contrast to their pagan neighbors, they felt a sense of oneness with any fellow Christian. It was only centuries later when Christians held a much stronger position in society that differences of interpretation led to division, with churches existing in separation from and, in many cases, in opposition to, other churches. Today, perhaps in response to the sense of hostility many Christians feel from contemporary North American culture, Christians are recovering something of this sense of oneness across denominational lines, particularly in evangelical parachurch groups such as Promise Keepers or Focus on the Family that draw together Christians across denominational lines.[7] In any case, there is nothing in New Testament usage that implies that the oneness of the churches in a city was organizational or institutional, or put any one local assembly under the authority of a larger body.

A second factor involved in the use of church (singular) for all the Christians in a city is that these Christians did in fact seem to gather together (see 1 Cor. 11:18; Col. 4:16) . Even the church at Jerusalem, which numbered several thousand from Acts 2 onward, is reported as gathering and acting together (Acts 11:22; 12:5). There are even four interesting references to what is called the *whole* church in a given city (Acts 5:11; 15:22; Rom. 16:23; 1 Cor. 14:23). Perhaps there were both house church meetings in some of these cities, and occasional larger group meetings of all the Christians in the city. In any case, where geographical distance clearly prohibited meeting together, Paul used the plural, referring to churches in this way twenty-one times.

A third factor that should be remembered is that there is nothing in this pattern of usage of *ekklēsia* that justifies calling a local group a congregation and reserving the term *church* for a larger grouping of congregations. Indeed, since Paul referred to geographically separated congregations as churches and to the smallest house congregations as churches, there is a strong basis for what Baptists have traditionally referred to as local church autonomy, the idea that a local congregation should not be ruled by a larger organization called the church. Rather, each local congregation is fully *ekklēsia* in itself. These various usages of the term *ekklēsia* may be summarized as follows.

---

7. A recent survey reported that 86 percent of Protestant pastors agreed with the statement, "There should be more cooperation among different Protestant denominations," including 79 percent of Baptist pastors. Reported in *Facts and Trends* (January–February 2004): 6–7.

- 2 times *ekklēsia* is used with reference to the Old Testament congregation.
- 3 times it is used for a secular assembly.
- 6 times it is used in a general or nonspecific sense.
- 13 times it is used for the universal church.
- 90 times it is used with reference to a local church or churches, assemblies that have a degree of order and purposefulness in their gatherings.
    - 40 times it is found in the singular, for a local church.
    - 14 times it is used for all the Christians in a city, who apparently met and acted together.
    - 36 times *ekklēsia* is used in the plural for local churches.

In a few cases, it is not immediately obvious in what way the word is being used; most of these fit in the category of general or nonspecific. There could even be differences in opinion in a few cases about whether a particular verse should be seen in a local or universal sense. But the overall pattern is clear and unmistakable. The focus in New Testament usage is on local churches.

IMAGES OF THE CHURCH

Biblical teaching on the church is not limited to passages containing the term *ekklēsia*. Indeed, it could be argued that the primary way the Bible teaches us about the church is through the numerous images or metaphors of the church found throughout the New Testament.[8] The church is pictured as the bride of Christ, as the family of God, as the new creation, and in several other ways. Biblical teaching on the church seems to cluster most fully around three of these images: people of God, body of Christ, and temple of the Spirit. We

---

8. The fullest exposition of this is Paul S. Minear, *Images of the Church in the New Testament* (Philadelphia: Westminster Press, 1960). He lists ninety-six possible images of the church in the New Testament, but many are not well supported by Scripture; some do not seem to be an image and others do not refer to the church at all. Of these ninety-six, Minear recognizes four as "master images." They are "people of God, new creation, fellowship in faith, and the body of Christ" (259). I see the first and last as central images, but combine his second and third in a different way.

will thus consider them in some detail, as they communicate a variety of insights concerning the nature of the church.

The People of God

In 1 Peter 2:9–10, the church is addressed using terminology from the Old Testament. The church is "a chosen people . . . a people belonging to God . . . the people of God," drawing upon the descriptions of Israel in Exodus 19:5–6; Deuteronomy 4:20; 7:6; Hosea 1:10; 2:23; and dozens if not hundreds of places throughout the Old Testament where God calls Israel "my people." This image thus raises the question of the relationship of the church to the Old Testament people of God, Israel.

This question is a key dividing line between two schools of thought. Covenant theology emphasizes the continuity between the Old Testament and the New Testament. There is one and only one people of God. In the Old Testament, that people is Israel; in the New Testament, it is the new Israel, or spiritual Israel, the church. Though the church may enjoy the richer blessings of the new covenant, it stands in continuity with Israel under the overarching covenant of grace, which encompasses all the other covenants God made with people throughout Scripture. By way of contrast, dispensational theology emphasizes the discontinuity between Israel and the church. God works in different ways in different eras, or dispensations. Israel is always Israel and never the church. A defining characteristic of dispensational thought is this distinction between Israel and the church. The church does not replace Israel. There remains a future for ethnic Israel in the plan of God.

Baptist ecclesiology does not stand or fall with either system. Covenantal theology is sometimes associated with infant baptism, but many earlier Baptists and some today could be called covenantal, but do not see infant baptism as a necessary part of the system.[9] Baptist dispensationalists do not conclude that the distinction between Israel and the church means that the

---

9. Two examples of Baptists who see a consistency between covenant theology and Baptist ecclesiology are Paul K. Jewett, *Infant Baptism and the Covenant of Grace* (Grand Rapids: Eerdmans, 1978); and Fred Malone, *The Baptism of Disciples Alone: A Covenantal Argument for Credobaptism Versus Paedobaptism* (Cape Coral, Fla.: Founders Press, 2003). Jewett concludes that covenant theology implies believer's baptism rather than infant baptism (233). Malone says that the covenantal Baptist position he is presenting is the same as that of earlier Baptists such as J. L. Dagg, J. P. Boyce, and Charles Spurgeon (xxxii).

Old Testament has no relevance for ecclesiology or that the church should not be called "the people of God."[10] Both can affirm Baptist ecclesiology.

There are elements of both continuity and discontinuity in the biblical teaching concerning Israel and the church. The continuity is embodied in the image of the people of God and reflected in the biblical promise, "I will be their God and they will be my people." Since the calling of Abram, God has been pursuing the purpose of calling to himself a people. That people is conceived when Abram receives and responds to God's call; it develops eventually into the people of Israel, called to be a special and holy people. Their failure prompts the pledge of a new covenant, which reiterates the promise, "I will be their God and they will be my people" (Jer. 31:33). With the coming of Jesus, a crisis arrives, for he has come to "save his people from their sins" (Matt. 1:21). He does so through the cross and resurrection, but that great victory is not the end of the story. He tells his disciples to wait for the outpouring of the Holy Spirit. Only after that event (Acts 2) is the group of disciples called the church. Only then are they the called-out people of God. It is the indwelling Holy Spirit that makes this people different than the Old Testament people of God. He is the discontinuity; his coming makes the church the new creation of God.

The metaphor I use to illustrate the continuity and discontinuity implied in the image of the people of God is conception, gestation, labor, birth, and growth. The call of Abram is the conception of the church; the Old Testament era is the gestation or preparation for the church; the ministry of Jesus is the time of labor with the expectation of the imminent birth of the church, which occurs with the coming of the Spirit on the day of Pentecost; the entire era following is the life and growth of the church, with the final fulfillment of God's purpose in the eschaton, when we hear a voice from God's throne saying, "Now the dwelling of God is with men, and he will live with them. They will be his people, and God himself will be with them and be their God" (Rev. 21:3).

What does this image add to our understanding of the nature of the church? It connects the church to the Old Testament people of God, and sees the church as involved in God's great purpose of calling to himself a people, while leaving open the question of whether or not there is also a

---

10. For example, W. A. Criswell sees the Old Testament covenants as containing elements that foreshadow the New Testament church, particularly the idea of God calling a people to himself. See W. A. Criswell, *The Doctrine of the Church* (Nashville: Convention Press, 1980), 25.

future purpose for ethnic Israel. The people of God image is also consistent with the idea of the church as the called-out people, for God's people become his people as a result of his call. This image can also serve as a corrective to the strong individualism in American society, for it reminds us that the church is a people, not a collection of isolated individuals. Most important of all, the people of God image reminds us that the church is much more than a human institution. Eleven times the church is called "the church of God."[11] God called it and God relates to it; the church is shaped in every way by its relationship to God.

For example, the God of the Bible is a holy God, and thus his people must be a holy people. God's called-out people are also "called to be saints" (Rom. 1:7), or "called to be holy" (1 Cor. 1:2). The churches are called "the congregations of the saints" (1 Cor. 14:33). More than sixty times God's people are called saints or holy ones *(hagioi)*. This in no way implies that they have attained a state of sinless perfection; "holy" means first of all to be specially set apart for God's purposes. God summons his people out of the world to devotion to him. But the call to be holy in devotion includes a call to be holy in behavior. It seems significant that one of the two places in the Gospels where Jesus discusses the church includes the process by which the church was to take action to exclude an unrepentant sinner (Matt. 18:15–18). Similarly, Paul insists that the church in Corinth must expel the wicked man from the church (1 Cor. 5:13). Because God is holy, the people of God must be holy.

But the holiness of God in Scripture is matched by his love. First John 4:8 says simply "God is love." Indeed, a succinct summary of God's character could be holy love, or loving holiness. Love for God and neighbor is identified by Jesus as the most important commandment (Matt. 22:37–39), but love is especially the mark of the church as the people of God. Early on, Jesus commanded his disciples to love one another, and promised that this would identify them to the world (John 13:34–35). In 1 John, one of the grounds for believing that one is part of the church is love for the brethren (1 John 2:9–10; 3:10, 14; 4:7–8, 19–20). Christians are commanded seventeen times in the New Testament to "love one another" and the record of history indicates early on a widespread obedience to that command. By the late second

---

11. See Acts 20:28; 1 Cor. 1:2; 10:32; 11:16; 11:22; 15:9; 2 Cor. 1:1; Gal. 1:13; 1 Thess. 2:14; 2 Thess.1:4; and 1 Tim. 3:5. By comparison, there is only one reference to "the churches of Christ" (Rom. 16:16).

century Tertullian could claim that even the opponents of Christians noted this, saying, "See, they say, how they love one another."[12] In his classic study, *Evangelism in the Early Church,* Michael Green says that the love of Christians for one another "astonished the pagans" and was a large factor in their evangelistic success.[13] Because the church is the people of the God who is himself love, its members must be characterized by love.

God is also Father. Therefore, the church is his family. He regards not all of humanity as his children, but only those who receive his Son (John 1:12). They receive adoption into God's family through faith in Christ Jesus (Gal. 3:26; 4:4–5). The church of the Thessalonians is twice called "the church of the Thessalonians in God the Father and the Lord Jesus Christ" (1 Thess. 1:1; 2 Thess. 1:1). Members of the church are referred to as "brother" (more than fifty times) and "sister" (six times). Timothy is explicitly told to regard older men in the church as fathers, younger men as brothers, older women as mothers, and younger women as sisters (1 Tim. 5:1–2). Because God is their common Father, they are siblings in his family. Robert Banks thinks that the pervasive use of such terminology makes the family "the most significant metaphorical usage of all" the biblical images for the church.[14]

When the church is called "the people of God," we should not limit our thinking of God to God the Father. Christ the Son is God as well, and the church is his people too. The church is those who respond to God's call by trusting Christ. God's people in Ephesus are called "the faithful in Christ Jesus" (Eph. 1:1); at Colossae they are called "the holy and faithful brothers in Christ" (Col. 1:2). In the book of Acts, the church is referred to as "believers" in Christ, "disciples" of Christ, and, ultimately, as "Christians" (Acts 2:44; 11:26). They are clearly the people of God the Son.

The people of God are also the people of God the Holy Spirit. Indeed, it is the coming of the Spirit that transforms the disciples of Jesus into the church. Perhaps the most distinctive reflection of the church being the Holy Spirit's people is his gift of fellowship. The New Testament term for fellowship, *koinōnia,* is not found in Matthew, Mark, Luke, John, or Acts 1. However, once the Holy Spirit comes in Acts 2, we find fellowship in the first description of the life of the early church (v. 42). In the apostolic benediction of

---

12. Tertullian, "Apology," 39, in *The Ante-Nicene Fathers,* ed. Alexander Roberts and James Donaldson (Edinburgh: T & T Clark, 1868–72; reprint, Grand Rapids: Eerdmans, 1951), 3:46–47.

13. Michael Green, *Evangelism in the Early Church* (Grand Rapids: Eerdmans, 1970), 120.

14. Robert Banks, *Paul's Idea of Community: The Early House Churches in Their Historical Setting* (Grand Rapids: Eerdmans, 1980), 53.

2 Corinthians 13:14, while grace is associated with Christ, and love with God the Father, fellowship is "of the Holy Spirit."

The word *koinōnia* involves the idea of participating in or sharing something in common with another. It can be used to describe a believer's relationship with God (1 John 1:3), but it is also used for the relationship the Holy Spirit creates among believers. He makes them aware that they share new life in Christ, which must radically alter how they relate to one another. In the early church, *koinōnia* was initially expressed in a virtual voluntary community of goods, where "all the believers were together and had everything in common" (Acts 2:44). Fellowship was also expressed in believers living what may be called the "one another" life. There are more than thirty specific commands regarding how believers are to act toward one another, including forgiving one another, encouraging one another, accepting one another, and, most of all, loving one another, which appears seventeen times. We will have more to say about the importance of fellowship as an integral ministry of the church in chapter 9, but fellowship as an intrinsic part of the nature of the church comes from seeing the church as the people of God the Holy Spirit.

---

1. It gives the church a connection to the Old Testament and God's great purpose of calling to himself a people.
2. It underscores the nature of the church as called—called by God to be his people.
3. The church is a people, not a collection of isolated individuals.
4. The church is *God's* people, not a human institution.
   - As God's people, the church is called to be holy and loving.
   - As God the Father's people, the church is a family.
   - As God the Son's people, the church is those who believe in Christ.
   - As God the Spirit's people, the church is those who experience fellowship.

Figure 1.1: Summary of Implications of the Church as the People of God

The Body of Christ

Perhaps the biblical image of the church that comes to mind most readily is that of the body of Christ.[15] But, in fact, this image occurs only in the writings of Paul, and in only four of his letters (Romans, 1 Corinthians, Ephesians, and Colossians). However, in those four letters, the body image is used to illustrate in a vivid and memorable way a number of aspects of the church. Interestingly, the use made of the body image in Romans and 1 Corinthians differs markedly from the use in Ephesians and Colossians, so much so that they need to be examined separately.

In Romans and 1 Corinthians, the body of Christ is a metaphor for the local church, and the emphasis is on the relationships the members of the body have with one another. This is seen most clearly in 1 Corinthians 12:27: "Now you are the body of Christ, and each one of you is a part of it." The local church is not regarded here as merely a part of a larger body of Christ, but as *the* body of Christ in that place. This is another support for a proper understanding of the autonomy of the local church. No local church should be isolated, but no local church needs a larger body to complete it or enable it to function. It is the body of Christ, possessing full ecclesial status.

There is no mention here of Christ as the head of the body. The eye and ear are mentioned (1 Cor. 12:16–17), but only as members in the body. The body image in Romans and 1 Corinthians highlights three aspects of the relationship members of the body enjoy with each other.

The first aspect is that of *unity*. Interestingly, Paul links the body's unity to the two acts that we call ordinances or sacraments.[16] In 1 Corinthians 10:16–17, Paul sees the Corinthians' participation or fellowship in the Lord's Supper as creating and expressing the oneness they enjoy in the body of Christ:

---

15. It should be noted that the body of Christ is an image or metaphor not a literal description of the church as has been the claim sometimes among Catholics. Christ did not lose his own body after the resurrection or ascension, but still possesses a glorified, spiritual body. There are numerous metaphors for the church in the New Testament (temple, bride, etc.), and there is no reason to single this one out as literal.

16. Most denominations use the word *sacrament* for baptism and the Lord's Supper, and there is nothing objectionable about the word itself. The Latin word *sacramentum* originally was used as a term for the oath of loyalty a soldier took to his commander. But since the term *sacrament* over the years became associated with the view that grace is automatically conferred through these acts and that they are essential to salvation, Baptists have generally preferred the term *ordinance* to avoid these connotations. Some Baptists use the term *sacrament* but with a different understanding of its meaning.

"Because there is one loaf, we, who are many, are one body, for we all partake of the one loaf" (v. 17). In this meal, they celebrate and express the common life they have in Christ. Gordon Fee comments on this passage: "there can be little doubt that Paul intends to emphasize the kind of bonding relationship of the worshipers with one another that the meal expresses" and "the solidarity of the fellowship of believers is created by their all sharing 'the one loaf.'"[17] The basis for their unity with one another is their prior union with Christ, but the focus here is on their unity with one another, and Paul naturally turns to the image of the body to express that unity.

Likewise, in 1 Corinthians 12:13, their unity in the body of Christ is related to their common experience of baptism by the one Spirit: "we were all baptized by one Spirit into one body . . . and we were all given the one Spirit to drink." There are several important points in this verse that should be noted. First, contrary to the claims of some, Spirit baptism is an experience common to all believers. The word *all* appears twice in this verse, underscoring that fact. Second, the unity of the body is derived from the unity of the Spirit. Because it is the one Spirit that is acting here, his creation is one body. Third, his action is directed toward the creation of one body. The preposition *into (eis)* can "either be local, indicating that into which all were baptized, or denote the goal of the action, indicating the purpose or goal of the baptismal action (= 'so as to become one body')."[18] The meaning of purpose or goal seems more likely here. Spirit baptism is invisible, and places one in the universal body of Christ, but it is water baptism that is a visible act with a local meaning, placing one in a local body of Christ. Some may object that Ephesians 4:5 says there is one baptism, but the one baptism may have two forms, just as the one church has both a local and a universal form. Spirit baptism identifies us with the universal church and water baptism with the local church. In either case, the result is "one body."

For Paul, the body image is everywhere associated with unity. It is based on a common life in Christ, celebrated in the Lord's Supper. That unity is created by the act of the Spirit, who baptizes believers into one body.

Paul also uses the body image to illustrate *unity in diversity.* Romans 12:4–5 and 1 Corinthians 12:14–20 echo the same message: many members, but one body; diversity of gifts, but one body. The body makes an obvious, clearly

---

17. Gordon Fee, *The First Epistle to the Corinthians,* The New International Commentary on the New Testament, ed. F. F. Bruce (Grand Rapids: Eerdmans, 1987), 466.

18. Ibid., 603, n. 20.

visible, and easily understandable illustration of Paul's point, which perhaps accounts for the popularity of this image. Even so, while easy to understand, the unity of the body is difficult to experience. Paul reminds the Romans that it is only "in Christ" that "we who are many form one body" (Rom. 12:5). It took the supernatural power of a common life in Christ and a common reception of the Spirit to overcome the natural divisions of the ancient world of Greek and Jew, slave and free, and male and female. There can be diversity of race and sex and status, diversity in function and gift, but one body, one Lord, one Spirit, one faith.

It is important, especially for Baptists, to remember both the areas in which diversity is allowed or even esteemed and other areas where unity is required. Baptists have a long history of divisions. I even have a friend who says you're not a real Baptist until you've been through a church split, and, sadly, there are few longtime Baptists who have not experienced such a sad episode. However, most of those splits have come over issues that should not have been allowed to threaten the unity of the body. In many instances, diversity should have been embraced.

More recently, however, we have seen the rise of some in Baptist life who have argued for an acceptance, not just of diversity in race, sex, or status, but also diversity in faith, or doctrine. These Baptists have argued that doctrine divides and ministry unites; that being Baptist means being free from doctrinal constraints. But that is not how Baptists have historically approached the issue of unity, and it is not consistent with the biblical mandate that the "one body" must have "one faith" (Eph. 4:4–5).

Baptists have published dozens of confessions of faith to articulate the "one faith" (Eph. 4:5) as they understood it. While they gladly affirm unity in the universal body of Christ with all those who share life in Christ and the presence of the Spirit, and while many Baptists individually express unity with other believers in numerous community organizations or evangelical parachurch ministries, they see that unity as limited to areas of common doctrinal understanding. To walk together in church fellowship requires a fuller unity and thus a fuller doctrinal agreement. Historically most Baptist churches have included a statement of faith as part of their founding documents, which articulates the common faith that is a legitimate aspect of the church's unity. There must be diversity in many things, but unity in doctrine, especially unity in the doctrine of the church, is necessary for a local church to operate in genuine unity.

The third theme highlighted by the body of Christ image is *mutuality* of love and care among the members of the body. Romans 12:5 says that in Christ's body, "each member belongs to all the others." First Corinthians 12 contains a long explanation of how each part of the body needs every other part, and states that God desires all the members of the body to "have equal concern for each other. If one part suffers, every part suffers with it; if one part is honored, every part rejoices with it" (vv. 25–26). This mutuality is reflected in the more than thirty "one another" passages in the New Testament (such as "love one another," "forgive one another," and many more). The care that members of the church offer to each other is aptly portrayed in the image of the body, whose parts work harmoniously together.

This biblical theme is also reflected in the language earlier Baptists often used in confessions and church covenants to describe what it meant to join together as a church. The widely influential Second London Confession of 1677 says that church members "do willingly consent to walk together according to the appointment of Christ, giving up themselves to the Lord and one to another, by the will of God, in professed subjection to the ordinances of the Gospel."[19] Such language was found even more often in church covenants. Whereas confessions of faith dealt mainly with doctrine, church covenants emphasized the commitment church members make to one another.[20] The most widely used covenant was that adopted by the 1833 New Hampshire Baptist Convention. It described the care members pledged to give to one another in these words: "We do, therefore, in His strength engage, that we will exercise a mutual care as members one of another to promote the growth of the whole body."[21] The convention saw such a pledge virtually as constitutive for the church. It is derived from the image of the body, whose members care for one another as part of their nature.

To summarize, in Romans and 1 Corinthians Paul uses the image of the body of Christ to illustrate the relationships the members of a local church have to one another. The predominant themes are unity of the body, unity and diversity within the body, and the mutuality of care among the members

---

19. William L. Lumpkin, *Baptist Confessions of Faith*, rev. ed. (Valley Forge, Pa.: Judson Press, 1969), 286. This confession was reissued in England for more than a hundred years and came to America almost verbatim as the Philadelphia Confession, the most influential Baptist confession in America well into the nineteenth century.

20. A collection of seventy-nine Baptist church covenants can be found in Charles W. Deweese, *Baptist Church Covenants* (Nashville: Broadman, 1990), 115–99.

21. Ibid., 157.

of the body. In Ephesians and Colossians, the image of the body of Christ is used, but in a totally different context, with different emphases.

First of all, in Ephesians and Colossians, the body is related to the universal church. Five times Paul places the two together: "the church . . . his body" (Eph. 1:22–23; 5:23, 29–30; Col. 1:18, 24). In each case, the description of the church points to and virtually requires the universal sense. However, while the universal church does seem to fit the usage of *ekklēsia* in these two letters, the activities Paul describes (of pastors and teachers equipping God's people, of the body growing as each part does its work; see Eph. 4:12, 16; Col. 2:19) take place in local churches and thus local assemblies are not totally out of view.

Second, in Ephesians and Colossians, a new element is added to the usage of the body image, that of the relationship of the head to the body. In these letters, a major emphasis is on the role and importance of Christ, who is identified as the head of the body five times (Eph. 1:22; 4:15; 5:23; Col. 1:18; 2:19).

What themes emerge from Paul's usage of the body of Christ in these two letters? The teaching on Christ as the head of the body highlights the ideas of his *authority* over the body and his *provision* for the body. His provision for the body leads to its *growth,* which is the third theme encountered here. Each theme deserves more thorough consideration.

Despite recent attempts to remove the idea of authority from the Greek word for head *(kephalē),*[22] the authority of the head over the body seems to be one of the major emphases of Paul's teaching on Christ as the head of the church. Paul's teaching on Christ as the head of the body is found in some of the most exalted Christological passages in all the New Testament. In Ephesians 1:20–23, Christ is described as exalted above all rival powers, for all time, with all things under his feet. This sovereign figure is then appointed "head over everything for the church, which is his body, the fullness of him who fills everything in every way" (vv. 22–23). It is hard to imagine a more majestic description of sovereign authority, but Colossians 1 comes close. There Christ is the image of God, the firstborn, the Creator of all, the one in whom all things

---

22. See the article by Catherine Kroeger, "Head," in *Dictionary of Paul and His Letters,* ed. Gerald F. Hawthorne, Ralph P. Martin, and Daniel G. Reid (Downers Grove, Ill.; Leicester, U.K.: InterVarsity, 1993), 375–77. Unfortunately, her work seems to be directed by her egalitarian view of the roles of husband and wife, and the desire to see the husband's headship as not involving authority rather than by the linguistic and biblical evidence. Her work is subjected to a convincing critique by Wayne Grudem, "The Meaning of *kephalē* ("Head"): An Evaluation of New Evidence, Real and Alleged," *Journal of the Evangelical Theological Society* 44, no. 1 (March 2001): 25–65.

consist (vv. 15–17). This one is also the head of the church, the one who is supreme or preeminent in everything (v. 18). He is even called "the head over every power and authority" (2:10). But lest this authority seem authoritarian and harsh, it is described as a loving, self-sacrificing authority in the beautiful comparison of Christ and the church to a husband and wife (Eph. 5:23–33). Christ's headship certainly involves authority, for the church is called to submit to Christ. But the head exercises his authority on behalf of the church, loving her, giving himself up for her, feeding her, and caring for her.

This theme of Christ as the authoritative head of the church has one immediate practical implication for local churches, especially in the area of church polity. One criterion for evaluating any form of church government should be how well it preserves Christ's unique authority as head of the church. We will return to this point when we consider the issue of church polity and government.

The idea of authority is perhaps the central idea in Christ's headship over the church, but it is not the only idea. Clinton Arnold notes that in the ancient world, especially among first-century medical writers, the head was seen as both the ruling part of the body and the source that provided nourishment and sustenance.[23] This idea of provision is also reflected in Paul's usage. He uses virtually identical language in Ephesians 4:16 and Colossians 2:19 to describe Christ the head as the one "from whom" the body derives what it needs to grow. Indeed, the problem with the Colossians is that they have "lost connection with the Head" (Col. 2:19). This is the same idea as that vividly pictured by Jesus' teaching in John 15 on the vine and the branches. The branches receive all their sustenance from connection with the vine; the body receives all its nourishment via the head. The head makes provision for the body.

Those provisions are designed to aid the church in its growth. In Ephesians, the growth envisioned seems to be not numerical, but spiritual. The goal of growth is referred to as "unity in the faith and in the knowledge of the Son of God," or maturity, "attaining to the whole measure of the fullness of Christ," or even growing "into Him who is the head, that is, even Christ" (Eph. 4:13–16). Knowing Christ their head and becoming like him is the goal of the church's growth. But Paul is careful not to overlook or omit the role of

---

23. Clinton E. Arnold, "Jesus Christ: 'Head' of the Church (Colossians and Ephesians)," in *Jesus of Nazareth: Lord and Christ*, ed. Joel B. Green and Max Turner (Grand Rapids: Eerdmans; Carlisle, U.K.: Paternoster, 1994), 346–66. The same point is made by Gregory W. Dawes, *The Body in Question: Meaning and Metaphor in the Interpretation of Ephesians 5:21–33* (Leiden: Brill, 1998), 122–49.

the members of the body. Part of Christ's provision for the body is gifted leaders: "he gave some to be apostles, some to be prophets, some to be evangelists, and some to be pastors and teachers" (v. 11). These gifted leaders then equip the members of the body to carry out ministry. The end result is that the body is "joined and held together by every supporting ligament" and grows "as each part does its work" (v. 16). The language in Colossians 2:19 is strikingly similar. The body grows when it is "supported and held together by its ligaments and sinews" (v. 19). Paul is again drawing implications from the diversity of parts in the human body for understanding the church. In Romans and 1 Corinthians, the point was that the diversity of gifts in the members and the multiplicity of members do not eliminate the unity of the body. In Ephesians and Colossians, Paul carries the point further. Unity is not only not eliminated by the multiplicity and diversity of the body, but the diverse gifts of the body are necessary for both unity (holding the body together) and maturity (growing up to full Christlikeness).

---

1. The image of the body points to the church's unity, seen especially in the Lord's Supper and baptism.
2. The image of the body aptly illustrates how the church may be one, while its members are diverse.
3. The body image reflects how the members of the church should show a mutuality of love and care to one another.
4. Christ, as the head of the body, is the ultimate authority for the church.
5. As head, Christ also provides for the needs of the church.
6. Christlikeness is the goal of the church's growth; all the members of the church contribute to the growth and unity of the church as all perform their own particular ministries.

Figure 1.2: Summary of Implications of the Church as the Body of Christ

The Temple of the Spirit

The third major image of the church in the New Testament is the temple of the Holy Spirit. The first idea of the church as a building is implied by Jesus' words in Matthew 16:18: "You are Peter, and on this rock I will *build* my church."

Historically, most discussion of this verse has focused on the relationship between Peter (*petros*) and the rock (*petra*) on which the church is built, chiefly because this verse has been used by many Catholics to support the importance of the papacy for the church. But that discussion, while important, should not distract us from another important idea in the text, that of the church as a building. It is elaborated on elsewhere in the New Testament.

The main developer of this idea is Paul. In 1 Corinthians 3:9, he begins by comparing the church to both a field and a building, but it is the latter idea that receives his attention. He states that the foundation of the building is Jesus Christ, with each Christian's work building on that foundation, some in a way that will endure, and others in a way that will not (vv. 11–15). But in verse 16, Paul turns from the foundation upon which we are building to envision the church as a building, and a very special building, God's temple. Elsewhere, Paul speaks of the individual Christian's body as the temple of the Holy Spirit (1 Cor. 6:19); here he addresses the church collectively as the temple of God.

Paul says, "You are God's temple." But why is this temple especially associated with God the Holy Spirit? A response is found in the last part of 1 Corinthians 3:16. The church is not the temple of God by anything inherent in its members, but by virtue of the indwelling Holy Spirit. The word used here for temple, which is also used for the church in 2 Corinthians 6:16 and Ephesians 2:21, is *naos*, which "refers to the actual sanctuary, the place of the deity's dwelling, in contrast to the word *hieron*, which referred to the temple precincts as well as to the sanctuary."[24] This tells us that the key point being made when Paul refers to the church as God's temple is that God indwells or inhabits the church. But the means by which God indwells his people is the Holy Spirit. That is made explicit in Ephesians 2:21–22, where the church is called a holy temple, "a dwelling in which God lives by his Spirit." Thus, the temple of God is the temple of the Spirit.

This leads to the first two implications we may draw about the nature of the church from this image. The first is that just as the physical temple was preeminently the place to worship God, because the temple was recognized as his dwelling place, so the church, as the temple of the Spirit, must be preeminently a worshiping people.

The Old Testament teaches that, in a sense, all that God created is de-

---

24. Fee, *First Epistle to the Corinthians,* 146. Fee notes that the distinction is not universal in first-century Greek, but it is supported by the usage of the Septuagint, which seems to be the key influence on Paul's usage.

signed to bring praise and worship to him. Psalm 19:1 says that the heavens themselves declare God's glory; Psalm 96 calls upon the heavens, earth, sea, fields, and trees to be glad, sing, worship, and tremble before the Lord (vv. 9–12); the whole of Psalm 148 is devoted to enlisting the angels, sun, moon, stars, animals, and even the elements of weather to give praise to God; the last verse of the book of Psalms summarizes: "Let everything that has breath praise the Lord" (150:6). But in a special way God's people are gathered together as his temple for the purpose of worship.

First Peter 2:5 compares believers to "living stones" that are built together "into a spiritual house." The word *house* was used in the Old Testament and by Jesus as a synonym for the temple. When Jesus cleansed the temple, he called it a "house of prayer" (see Isa. 56:7; Jer. 7:11, quoted by Jesus in Matt. 21:13). The church, composed of believers, is not a physical temple like the one in Jerusalem but a spiritual one. However, it serves a similar purpose, for the "living stones" that compose this temple are also a "holy priesthood" who offer "spiritual sacrifices." The adjective *spiritual* indicates that the worship offered by these priests is a Spirit-empowered worship, prompted by the Spirit who indwells them and forms them into his temple. It also indicates that the sacrifices they offer are no longer the animals prescribed by the Old Testament law but sacrifices that reflect New Testament worship. Doing good and sharing with others materially are referred to as sacrifices that please God (Phil. 4:18; Heb. 13:16); so is using our lips to confess God's name (Heb. 13:15). But Paul specifically identifies offering our bodies, or our entire selves, as living sacrifices as our "spiritual" or "rational" worship (Rom. 12:1).

Another point to note in the development of this image is that those offering the sacrifices in the temple of the Spirit are called "a holy priesthood," "a royal priesthood," and "a kingdom and priests" (1 Peter 2:5, 9; Rev. 1:6; 5:10). These verses form the basis for the doctrine of the priesthood of all believers. The New Testament calls those who lead the church elders, bishops, or pastors, but never priests. But by the end of the second century another term for elder, *presbyter*, was contracted to *priest* and applied to clergy. Throughout the Middle Ages, the priesthood and priestly functions were increasingly limited to clergy. Martin Luther is justly identified with the recovery of the priesthood of all believers,[25] but it has been especially

---

25. Timothy George states, "Luther's greatest contribution to Protestant ecclesiology was his doctrine of the priesthood of all believers." Timothy George, *The Theology of the Reformers* (Nashville: Broadman, 1988), 95.

important in Baptist ecclesiology, where it has formed part of the basis for congregational government. Since all believers are priests, and only believers should be members of the church, Baptists have argued that all these believer-priest church members are able and responsible to help the church find God's direction for its life.

In more recent Baptist life, the doctrine of the priesthood of all believers has sometimes become the doctrine of the priesthood of the believer (singular), and has been misinterpreted in terms of individual rights and confused with the idea of soul competence. Soul competence, as believed by Baptists, has been the conviction that each individual is able and responsible before God for his or her relationship with God and does not require the mediation of any human priest to come before God. This applies to every human, and is related to our creation in God's image. The priesthood of all believers applies only to believers and has to do with our common responsibility to minister to one another and to the world. To see it as somehow justifying an attitude of individual self-sufficiency is to misunderstand the doctrine and to forget our need for the church and the church's need for each member's ministry.

In terms of worship, the priesthood of all believers reminds us that worship is never the province of preachers and musicians, with church members as spectators. All believers are called upon to be those offering the spiritual sacrifices of worship. Thus churches should actively seek ways to involve all their members in worship, a challenge that grows as churches get larger. As the temple of the Spirit, the church must be a worshiping community. That is one of its essential, constitutive ministries.

Perhaps the most important and foundational implication of the church as the temple of the Spirit is the idea of relationship. The purpose of the tabernacle and later the temple in the Old Testament was to portray God's dwelling among his people, not just to receive their worship but to bless them and to show his desire for relationship with them. The tabernacle was called the tent of meeting dozens of times, because God's glory filled the tabernacle and there he met with his people. The temple of Solomon was also regarded as a dwelling place of God, a place to which his people could turn and find his presence (2 Chron. 7:15–16). That purpose was furthered in the coming of Jesus, who "tabernacled" or dwelt among us (John 1:14) for a time; but he eventually ascended. In one of the two passages in which Jesus taught on the church, he promised his presence where two or three gather in his name (Matt. 18:15–20). Paul said that when the church gathers, "the power of our Lord

Jesus is present" (1 Cor. 5:4). Yet every time we celebrate the Lord's Supper, we recognize Christ's absence, for we celebrate the Supper only "until he comes" (1 Cor. 11:26). How can we experience the presence and power of Christ when he is ascended and we await his coming? By means of the indwelling Holy Spirit, who is the Spirit of Christ (Rom. 8:9), whose special function it is to make Christ's presence real now, and who makes the church the temple where God meets with us in a special way.

It is only the Holy Spirit who can bring us into relationship with God, for it is the Spirit who sanctifies us and makes us fit to enter relationship with God (1 Cor. 6:11). He makes us, not just a temple, but a holy temple (Eph. 2:21), a fit dwelling place for a holy God.

The image of the church as the temple of the Spirit, as taught in the New Testament, also implies something of the relationship those in the church have with each other. Ephesians 2:21 speaks of the way the church "is joined together" *(synarmologoumenē)*. The root of this Greek word, *harmozō*, is the word from which we get the English word *harmonize*. As used here, the word speaks of the care with which a mason fits together the stones in a building.[26] The same word is used in Ephesians 4:16 to describe how the parts of the body are carefully joined together. In the same way that God arranges the parts of the body just as he wants them to be (1 Cor. 12:18), so God the builder carefully builds his temple, arranging the stones just as he desires them to be. We must remember that the builder of the church is not a pastor or leader but God. Jesus said, "I will build my church" (Matt. 16:18). Both Paul and Peter use the passive voice when speaking of the temple. It "is joined together" and is "being built" (Eph. 2:21; 1 Peter 2:5). The builder, though not specified, is clearly God.

But if this is so, if God is the one who carefully fits the stones together and builds his people into a holy temple, why is there so often friction between the stones, with some not wanting to be fit together with others? Why do churches often seem like temples that are falling apart? One danger, of course, is a faulty foundation. Any church not founded solidly on Christ is at risk of falling apart (1 Cor. 3:10–11); it is only "in him" that the stones are built together (Eph. 2:21–22). It is only by coming to him that we become fit building material (1 Peter 2:4).

There is another reason why many churches have a problem holding their living stones together. We call the church the temple of the Spirit because the

---

26. J. A. Motyer, "Body," in Brown, ed., *New International Dictionary of New Testament Theology,* 1:241.

Spirit is the mortar that holds the stones together. The church is not to be held together by social bonds such as being of the same race or class or income, but by the spiritual bond of a common possession of the Holy Spirit. Church growth strategists tell us that churches grow fastest when they target people most like those already in the church. They are no doubt right; people are usually attracted to those with similar backgrounds and lifestyles. But the New Testament is clear that the church must not become a club of one type of people but a community that transcends those things that divide people in society. In Paul's day, the call was to transcend the barriers between Jew and Greek, slave and free, male and female, and find unity in Christ (Gal. 3:28). Today's barriers include race (white, black, Hispanic), social class (rich, middle class, poor), and even age (young families, senior adults). Contemporary churches need a greater reliance on the Spirit and a deeper experience of his gift of fellowship if they are to be temples fitly joined together.

God fitly joins together the stones in his holy temple with the mortar of fellowship. To switch metaphors, the Holy Spirit is the lubricant that eases friction. Whether seen as mortar or lubricant, true fellowship is the creation of the Holy Spirit and an essential ministry of the church. This too must be a concern as churches grow larger, for fellowship can only happen on a personal, small-group level. The need is for the multiplication of small groups where believer-priests can minister to each other and allow the Spirit to join them together by the bonds of loving fellowship. For example, Willow Creek Community Church, though one of the largest churches in the United States, describes itself "not as a church *with* small groups, but a church *of* small groups."[27] As of November 2000, there were more than twenty-six hundred small groups, seeking to incorporate everyone involved in any of Willow Creek's ministries. Pastors know by experience that those who join a church but do not develop such bonds tend to become easily disattached, because they were never fitly joined together. That work is performed by the Holy Spirit, who links people together on a personal level. He transforms a heap of stones into a holy temple.

While this chapter in no way exhausts biblical teaching on the nature of the church, the major outlines are in place. The following chapter will show how the church in history has filled in that outline, by formulating in two major ways distinguishing marks of the church.

---

27. Verla Gillmor, "Community Is Their Middle Name," *Christianity Today* 44, no. 13 (November 13, 2000): 50.

1. Because it is God's temple, the church must be a worshiping community.
2. In God's temple, all believers form the priesthood; all are involved in the church's ministry.
3. The temple is also the place of relationship.
   - The Spirit mediates our relationship with God, communicating his presence and power and sanctifying us.
   - The Spirit joins together believers as the stones in God's temple through his creation of fellowship.

Figure 1.3: Summary of Implications of the Church as the Temple of the Spirit

CHAPTER 2

THE MARKS OF THE CHURCH

Historical Perspective

WE TURN NOW FROM AN examination of biblical teaching on the nature of the church to a consideration of historical formulations of the marks of the church. We look at two major ways those marks have been formulated in the past. History is certainly not infallible; only Scripture is. But our interpretation of Scripture is not infallible and those who looked at Scripture in other times may see aspects we have missed. Thus, we consider their views, open to learning from them, but free to critique them as well.

THE PATRISTIC FORMULATION: "WE BELIEVE IN ONE, HOLY, CATHOLIC, AND APOSTOLIC CHURCH"

The single most influential statement concerning the church from history comes in the line from the Nicene Creed[1] giving the four classical *notae* of the church: unity or oneness, holiness, catholicity, and apostolicity. These four marks are the starting point for many discussions of the church, and are widely accepted by both Protestants and Catholics.[2] We note that this confessional formula emerged in the context of the church's struggle to

---

1. This line is taken from what is usually referred to as the Nicene Creed, though this line was not in the creed developed at Nicaea in 325, but from an addition to the creed attributed to the Council of Constantinople in 381. Some, therefore, want to call this form of the creed the Niceno-Constantinopolitan Creed, but the shorter title has prevailed in popular usage.
2. See, for example, the recent affirmation by three evangelicals, including one Baptist, in Richard D. Phillips, Philip G. Ryken, and Mark E. Dever, *The Church: One, Holy, Catholic, and Apostolic* (Phillipsburg, N.J.: P & R Publishing, 2004); and the utilization of the four marks in Craig Van Gelder,

define itself against a variety of challengers.[3] This origin raises some questions. Are these four marks as prominent in Scripture as they are in the creed? In other words, did the historical circumstances lead the early church to emphasize the importance of these four adjectives (one, holy, catholic, apostolic) beyond their importance in Scripture? Do these marks relate more to the intrinsic *nature* of the church, or do they just reflect important but secondary *aspects* of the church? And to what sense of the church do they refer? We noted that the word *ekklēsia* refers in Scripture to both local assemblies of believers and the universal body of believers. Are local churches one, holy, catholic, and apostolic, or just the universal church? Finally, how sufficient or comprehensive are these marks in identifying a true and valid church? Are there other marks that need to be added?

The Oneness of the Church

The creedal description of the church originated in the context of controversy and threats to the church's unity. The Nicene Council was called by the emperor Constantine to deal with the threat to the unity of his empire caused by the split in the church over the Arian claim that Christ was an exalted creature, but not fully God. But the concern for oneness goes back far earlier. Controversies troubled the church from its inception, and unity was an ongoing concern.

In the middle of the third century, Cyprian of Carthage wrote an important work, *On the Unity of the Church,* in which he viewed unity in terms of communion with the bishop. Thus unity was a visible matter, easily verified by one's connection to the church headed by the bishop. Initially, loyalty to any one of a number of recognized bishops in the major cities was sufficient, but over a long period of time, the bishop of Rome assumed a more and more central role. He became the symbol and source of the church's unity. To be in communion with him was necessary to be part of the one church. In-

---

The Essence of the Church: A Community Created by the Spirit (Grand Rapids: Baker, 2000), 114–26. Interestingly, Catholic Richard McBrien only notes the four marks in connection with pre–Vatican II Catholic ecclesiology, suggesting a de-emphasis of the marks in contemporary Catholic ecclesiology. See Richard McBrien, *Catholicism,* new ed. (New York: HarperSanFrancisco, 1994), 659.

3. Glenn Hinson says, "This formula took shape chiefly in efforts of the churches to define themselves in relation to the Montanist, Novatianist, and Donatist schisms." E. Glenn Hinson, introduction to *Understandings of the Church,* trans. and ed. E. Glenn Hinson (Philadelphia: Fortress Press, 1986), 4.

deed, in 1302, Pope Boniface VIII claimed that submission to the Roman pontiff was necessary for salvation.

In 1054, the unity of the visible church was called into question by the schism between Christians in the East, who recognized the primacy of the patriarch of Constantinople, and Christians in the West, who continued to see the bishop of Rome as the rock on which the church is founded. Thus the church was divided into Orthodox and Roman Catholic.

While the schism called unity into question, the Reformation made some reformulation of the mark of unity a necessity. The Protestant Reformers continued to affirm their faith in the one, holy, catholic, and apostolic church, but they gave the four marks an interpretation quite different than that of the Catholic Church. They were not in fellowship with the bishop of Rome, but they claimed a spiritual unity with all those who were part of the invisible church, composed of all those truly saved.

Baptists have agreed with the Reformers that the unity of the church is spiritual, not organizational or institutional. It is modeled after the unity of the Father and Son, which is not an institutional or organizational unity, but a spiritual unity, based on a common nature. This is why Ephesians 4:4 can say categorically, "There is one body." All those who belong to Christ share in a oneness rooted in a common relationship with him. But how is this oneness, while undeniably true of the church universal, in any sense a mark of local churches?

Local churches partake of the oneness of the universal church to the degree that they hold to the one Lord and one faith of that one church. In other words, churches that profess and hold to the gospel are one with the church universal and can rightly claim the mark of unity.[4] Such unity should find expression in how the local church interacts with other local churches who also profess the faith of the gospel and are thus one with them. Over the past fifty years or so, Billy Graham crusades have been a catalyst for concrete expressions of such gospel unity in many communities as churches have come together to support the proclamation of the gospel. Other avenues for expressing this unity include churches coming together across denominational lines to support parachurch ministries that are faithful to the gospel, whether they specialize in ministry to youth (groups such as Fellowship of Christian Athletes and Campus Life), ministry to those in prison (Prison Fellowship),

---

4. Richard Phillips develops this idea of the gospel as the boundary of Christian unity. See Richard D. Phillips, "One Church," in Phillips, Ryken, and Dever, *The Church*, 28–33.

or ministry to those with special needs (food pantries, clothes closets, preg-nancy support centers). In fact, as such parachurch groups have exploded in the past fifty years, Christians have met each other in these groups across denominational lines and have discovered that they do share a oneness in the gospel. Craig Van Gelder sees such expressions of unity as crucial for the nature of the church. While he agrees that unity does not require institu-tional oneness, he believes the oneness that is given to the church by God must be expressed "within the historical church" and in concrete forms of communion. To do less, he adds, "is to betray both the nature of God and the nature of the church."[5]

Unity can also be given expression, at least in a limited way, in denomina-tions. Some see denominations as sinful expressions of the division of the church, and no doubt denominations can be guilty of a divisive spirit. But denominations can also exist in a spirit of humility and serve to give some visible expression of unity on a larger than local church level. Baptists have affirmed the propriety of coming together in associations, with one reason for doing so being the desire to show something of a visible unity. In the London Confession of 1644, congregations are referred to "as members of one body in the common faith under Christ their only head."[6] Here it is not the church that is one body, but churches are the members of this one body. They come together to highlight a form of the body larger than a local church, thus giving visible expression to their belief in the unity of the body of Christ on an extra-local church level. Richard Phillips argues that denominations do not detract from the unity of the church, but serve it. Denominations allow us to have a limited organizational unity, and promote spiritual unity among denominations, "since we are not forced to argue our way to perfect agreement but can accept our differences of opinion on secondary matters."[7]

How should we evaluate this mark of oneness? How important is it in biblical perspective? Certainly the unity of the church is a biblical theme. The metaphors of *the* people of God, *the* body of Christ, *the* temple of the Spirit, all point to the unity of the church. As there is unity in the Godhead, so there is unity in his church. Van Gelder says, "The essential oneness of the church . . . finds its source in the oneness of the Triune God."[8] As Paul said to the troubled

---

5. Van Gelder, *Essence of the Church*, 122.
6. Lumpkin, *Baptist Confessions of Faith*, 169.
7. Phillips, "One Church," 27.
8. Van Gelder, *Essence of the Church*, 122.

church in Corinth, "Is Christ divided?" (1 Cor. 1:13). The image of the body is especially utilized to insist on the unity of the church, despite the diversity of members.

Moreover, unity is affirmed as a present reality, not just a pious hope. By God's own nature and by his design, the assembly gathered around Christ, composed of all his people, *is one*. Ephesians 4:4 says, "There *is* one body." It is a fact, not a hope. On the local level, any local church embracing the gospel is one with the church universal; it is one with all other believers on the only level that will endure eternally. In terms of expressing that unity in concrete ways here and now, churches will vary in how fully they express that unity, and there is room for much improvement along those lines. Unity is God's gift to every church in the gospel; expressing it is every church's ongoing task.

Yet in the end, unity is not an end in itself, nor is it the most important element of the nature of the church, nor is it the definitive mark of the church. It is based on the gospel and should serve the gospel. Thus any call to unity that involves a sacrifice of the gospel is not a call to biblical unity. Moreover, even on the secondary issues that historically have divided denominations, unity does not require a sacrifice of conscience in issues where we honestly differ. Unity does not require uniformity. Though the focus of this book is a presentation of ecclesiology from a Baptist perspective, it recognizes and rejoices in the unity Baptists share with all who embrace the gospel and form the one body of Christ.

The Holiness of the Church

Holiness, as perhaps the central attribute of God, was a major concern of the early church. Christians were commanded to be holy, as God is holy. As God's called-out people, they were called to holiness. As the church, they were indwelt by the Holy Spirit. But there was not agreement on how holiness was to be related to the nature of the church.

There were two groups, the Novatians in the third century and the Donatists in the fourth century, who separated from the church over this issue of holiness. They objected to what they saw as the too easy reacceptance into the church of those who had lapsed under persecution, believing the presence of such individuals tainted the church's holiness. Augustine opposed the Donatists, seeing their schismatic spirit as a far greater sin against the church's unity than the sin of the lapsed against the church's holiness. In fact,

Augustine argued that the holiness of the church was the holiness of its head, Jesus Christ. Those in union with him and indwelt by his sanctifying Spirit share in his holiness, but that holiness may not be seen in the lives of the members of the visible church today. The church will one day be perfected in holiness, but in the world today, the church is a *corpus permixtum,* a body composed of both those who would be saved and those who would be lost. According to Augustine, one could not know with perfect assurance who would be saved and who would be lost. Therefore, one had to do as the parable of the wheat and tares suggests: allow the wheat and tares to grow together until the time of the harvest when God will separate the two (see Matt. 13:24–30). Thus, in the present, holiness pertains to the invisible church essentially and to the visible church only partially.[9]

The Reformers disagreed with Augustine on the issue of personal assurance of salvation, but generally followed him in accepting the church as a *corpus permixtum,* a mixed body whose holiness lies not in the personal lives of its members but in its head. Anabaptists and early Baptists differed markedly from the magisterial Reformers on this issue. They pointed out that the parable in Matthew 13 identifies the field in which the wheat and tares grow together as the world, not the church. They sought to be a pure church of visible saints, practicing church discipline and limiting church membership to those who could make a claim to genuine salvation, manifested by a life matching their profession. But even in the most well-disciplined and godly congregation, perfection in holiness is not achieved in this life. Should holiness be deleted from the identifying marks of the church?

Perhaps a resolution of this question can come from a recognition of the twofold meaning of the word *holy* in the New Testament. Holy can mean both a special status, of being set apart, and conduct that is morally pure. In the first sense, all believers are holy, because in salvation they are set apart to God for his purposes.[10] Thus Paul refers to the church in Corinth, though riddled with sin in their personal conduct, as those "sanctified [or holy] in Christ Jesus" (1 Cor. 1:2). Forty times Paul calls Christians "saints" or "holy ones." Holiness is their status, from the moment of justification onward. Holiness, in terms of their moral conduct, is their calling. Paul calls the church in Corinth both "sanctified in Christ Jesus" and "called to be holy" (v. 2).

---

9. For a fuller discussion, see G. G. Willis, *Saint Augustine and the Donatist Controversy* (London: SPCK, 1950), 117–18.

10. Philip G. Ryken writes, "The holiness of the church is a gospel holiness. It is based on the saving work of Jesus Christ." See Philip G. Ryken, "A Holy Church," in Phillips, Ryken, and Dever, *The Church,* 61.

May we say, then, that every church, as part of its nature, is holy in status and called to be holy in conduct? We could, if churches were composed of all Christians. That seems to have been the case with the New Testament churches. Six of Paul's letters are specifically addressed "to all the saints," as if he assumes that only they are members of the church. This is one of the reasons why Baptists historically placed regenerate church membership at the center of their ecclesiology, and practiced careful church discipline; they sought to be holy churches. But most non-Baptist churches baptize and accept into membership infants, acknowledging that they are not regenerate, and few if any Baptist churches, despite their insistence on regeneration prior to baptism and church membership, would claim that they have never mistakenly baptized some who were not truly regenerate. So many if not all visible local churches contain some within their membership who are not saved, and thus not holy, in either status or conduct, and yet few would say that such bodies are not churches.

Craig Van Gelder thinks the holiness of the church is dependent on neither the nature of the church's members nor their behavior. He says, "The redemptive reign of God, present through the indwelling of the Spirit, makes the church holy by nature."[11] But the Spirit does not indwell unbelievers, and thus the holiness of a church is related to the nature of its members. This means that holiness is a partial or provisional mark of a local church. It is holy to the degree that it is composed of those who have been made holy in status by union with Christ (justification) and are being made holy in their conduct by the indwelling Spirit (sanctification). Its holiness is obscured to the degree that unbelievers are present in it, and to the degree that unbelieving conduct is practiced, even by those who are holy in status.

Holiness is a reality now for the universal church, described in Hebrews 12:22–23 as "the church of the firstborn . . . the spirits of righteous men made perfect," but it remains the goal of the church on earth. It is also that for which Christ died, as he "loved the church and gave himself up for her to make her *holy* . . . and to present her to himself as a radiant church, without stain or wrinkle or any other blemish, but *holy*" (Eph. 5:25–27).

The Catholicity of the Church

Most Baptists instinctively react against the word *catholic*, but we need to distinguish between *catholic* (with a lowercase *c*), which is a fine adjective

---

11. Van Gelder, *Essence of the Church*, 117.

simply meaning general, worldwide, or universal, and *Catholic* (with an uppercase *C*) which is part of the title of the Roman Catholic Church, indicating that the church that acknowledges the primacy of the bishop of Rome seeks to be a worldwide, comprehensive church. Mark Dever says the best modern equivalent to the word *catholic* is simply *universal*.[12]

Early on, Christians believed that they all shared the same faith and mission and the "catholic church" meant the "real or authentic church," and was thus associated with orthodoxy.[13] As the church spread, catholic came to mean extending to all areas and types of people. This meaning of catholic is illustrated by the words of Cyril of Jerusalem in his catechetical lectures given c. A.D. 350: "The Church, then, is called Catholic because it is spread through the whole world, from one end of the earth to the other"; he adds, "It is called Catholic because it brings into religious obedience every sort of men, rulers and ruled, learned and simple, and because it is a universal treatment and cure for every kind of sin."[14]

The lack of catholicity was one of the arguments made by the Roman Catholic Church against the Reformers. The Reformation resulted in the development of new churches, but only in a limited geographical sphere. The Reformers responded by claiming a catholicity, not of geography, but of time. They saw themselves in continuity with the church throughout most of its history; the Roman Church of their day had departed from the path of historic orthodoxy and thus forfeited the claim to catholicity. More important, they developed another set of marks for a true church. They never denied the four classical *notae,* but because both they and their Catholic opponents could claim them, and because the Reformers saw the four traditional marks as applying mainly to the invisible church, they saw the need for other marks to give guidance to those looking for a true church. We will discuss those marks shortly.

Is there a biblical basis for the mark of catholicity as an aspect of the nature of the church? While the word *catholic* does not appear in the New Testament, there are a number of aspects of the church that are at least consistent with catholicity. The fact that the church consists of those called out

---

12. Mark E. Dever, "A Catholic Church," in Phillips, Ryken, and Dever, *The Church,* 70.

13. Ibid., 71.

14. Cyril of Jerusalem, "The Catechetical Lectures," in *Cyril of Jerusalem and Nemesius of Emesa,* ed. and trans. William Telfer, The Library of Christian Classics (Philadelphia: Westminster Press, 1960), 4:186.

by God means the church can impose no limitation of age, sex, or race on its members. In Christ's church, there is "neither Jew nor Greek, slave nor free, male nor female" (Gal. 3:28). Any church that erects any limitation other than that erected by God himself, which is "faith in Christ Jesus" (v. 26), violates catholicity.

The metaphor of the people of God shows the catholicity of the church over time, as it is connected to God's ongoing project of gathering for himself a people. Furthermore, the fact that Christ has "purchased men for God from every tribe and language and people and nation" (Rev. 5:9) and commanded us to "make disciples of all nations" (Matt. 28:19) shows his intention that his church be worldwide. Sadly, however, the church has been slow to hear and heed Christ's command. Today, two thousand years later, there are still hundreds of people groups with no disciples. The church is not yet fully catholic geographically. Mark Dever, however, argues that the church's catholicity can be seen in the universality of the gospel as the one way of salvation for all kinds of people: "The church's catholicity is rooted in and bounded by the gospel's catholicity. Anytime, anywhere, anyone can be forgiven his or her sins by faith alone in the one and only Savior, our Lord Jesus Christ. That is the true catholic doctrine of the true catholic church."[15]

Therefore, we may say that while the church does not yet have full catholicity in the sense of existing empirically among every people, it is catholic in offering a universally applicable saving message and possessing a universal missionary mandate. Moreover, the catholicity of the church is an important safeguard against the danger of the church becoming identified with one culture or one race or one type of people.[16]

The Apostolicity of the Church

The apostles came to the fore in discussions in the early church in connection with the question of authority. The apostles were seen as those authorized by Christ to lead the church. From the beginning, the church was under apostolic teaching (Acts 2:42). But as the apostles died, the question of

---

15. Dever, "A Catholic Church," 92.

16. Ibid., 88–92, identifies four problems the catholicity of the church addresses: provincialism, sectarianism, racism, and the distinction between the limited focus of a parachurch and the catholic nature of the church. Along similar lines, Van Gelder, *Essence of the Church*, 119–20, sees the catholicity of the church as affirming that the gospel is translatable into every culture, but normative over all cultures and a prisoner to none.

authority resurfaced, especially as heretics such as the Gnostics arose. Orthodoxy became identified with teaching that was faithful to apostolic teaching. But where could apostolic teaching be found? The apostles and some of their associates had left writings that the church accepted as Scripture, but the canon of the New Testament was still taking shape. Furthermore, the Gnostics cited Scripture in support of their arguments, and even claimed to possess a secret apostolic testimony. Irenaeus, a second-century church father, responded that the true apostolic testimony had been passed down in the churches established by the apostles. The apostles left not only writings, but also an oral tradition that provided the key to the right interpretation of Scripture. This oral tradition was especially entrusted to the bishop, who then passed it down to the succeeding bishop, and so on.[17]

In this context, apostolicity came to be understood in terms of apostolic succession. The church is apostolic in its doctrine because its teachers, the bishops, are the authorized successors of the apostles and share their function of giving the church authoritative teaching. Initially, apostolic succession was claimed for the bishops in several cities, but increasingly focus was placed on the bishop of Rome, who was seen as the successor of Peter, who was appointed by Christ to be the rock on which the church is founded.

The problem with this understanding of apostolicity is that there is no indication that the apostles appointed successors, or that if they had successors, that those successors would have the same function. The Reformers saw the office of apostle as unique and nonrepeatable; thus the mark of apostolicity was understood as faithfulness to the apostolic gospel and the apostolic teaching, preserved for us in the New Testament, which itself authorizes the Old Testament as equally authoritative, God-given teaching.[18] This understanding of apostolicity is confirmed by the qualifications for an apostle in Acts 1:21–22 (which make the office nontransferable), by statements such as Ephesians 2:20 (the church is built "on the foundations of the apostles and prophets"), and by the concern of the early church to remain true to what was originally taught, seen in passages like Jude 1:3 ("contend for the faith that was once for all entrusted to the saints").

To be apostolic in this sense does seem to be closely related to the church's

---

17. Irenaeus, "Against Heresies," 3.2–5, in *The Ante-Nicene Fathers,* 1:415–17.

18. Philip Ryken reflects this perspective. He says, "An apostolic church, therefore, is one that preaches the gospel the apostles preached" and "An apostolic church is Bible-based in its teaching—both testaments." See Ryken, "An Apostolic Church," in Phillips, Ryken, and Dever, *The Church,* 101, 104.

nature. How can the church be God's people, Christ's body, the Spirit's temple, without divine guidance? Christ, as head of the church, is responsible to direct his body, the church. He called and appointed twelve apostles to be his agents in teaching and directing the churches. We see that direction and guidance in their actions in the New Testament, but we also see them claiming authority for their writings to give guidance and direction to all the churches (Col. 4:16; 2 Thess. 3:14). Thus, for a church to be apostolic it must seek above all to be governed by Scripture.

That is what Baptists claim. They seek to be people of the Book, New Testament Christians. However, no church perfectly understands and appropriates the apostles' teaching. Some churches, especially today, challenge or even repudiate apostolic teaching. Thus, local churches are more or less apostolic, depending on their doctrine of Scripture, and their interpretation and application of it. By contrast, the universal church, or at least that portion of the universal church gathered in heaven, possesses full apostolicity. Those in heaven obey the apostolic teaching and understand it as fully as humans can. If they have an interpretive question, the apostolic authors are present to answer. For those on earth, full apostolicity remains the quest, at least among those who see the apostolic teaching as coming with the authority of Christ himself, given to us in the New Testament, and illumined for us by the Spirit as we seek to understand its meaning and practice its precepts.

Evaluation of the Traditional Marks

The four classical marks have been one of the most common approaches taken by theologians to describe the most important attributes of the church, utilized by writers as diverse as Hans Küng, G. C. Berkouwer, and Mark Dever.[19] In fact, Jonathan Wilson thinks submission to these four marks is crucial for the development of an evangelical ecclesiology that is both faithful and improvisational.[20]

---

19. See Hans Küng, *The Church* (Garden City: Image Books, 1976) and G. C. Berkouwer, *The Church*, trans. James E. Davison (Grand Rapids: Eerdmans, 1976). For Dever, see his contribution to *The Church: One, Holy, Catholic and Apostolic*, and his forthcoming chapter in *A Theology for the Church*, ed. Daniel Akin (Nashville: Broadman & Holman, forthcoming).

20. Jonathan Wilson, "Practicing Church: Evangelical Ecclesiologies at the End of Modernity," in *The Community of the Word: Toward an Evangelical Ecclesiology*, eds. Mark Husbands and Daniel J. Treier (Downers Grove, Ill.: InterVarsity and Leicester, U.K.: Apollos, 2005), 63–72).

However, in spite of their widespread acceptance, the four classical marks, while helpful, do not seem to be comprehensive or definitive in outlining what the church is, for a number of reasons. First, the words themselves are ambiguous. That is why both Protestants and Catholics have been able to affirm them; they fill these terms with quite different meanings. Yet even when viewed in ways that seem to mesh to some degree with biblical teaching, these four marks do not seem to highlight all of the aspects of the church that are most central in biblical teaching. Howard Snyder echoes these criticisms and advocates adding "many, charismatic, local and prophetic" as supplements to "one, holy, catholic (or universal), and apostolic."[21]

Furthermore, the marks all seem to be related at least as much to the gospel as to the church. The gospel sets the boundary of the church's unity; it gives the church its holiness as part of the gift of salvation; its universal nature gives the church its catholicity; and the gospel is the heart of the apostolic teaching that the church is to preserve.[22] Thus, perhaps it is more accurate to see the gospel as marking the church more than unity, holiness, catholicity, and apostolicity.[23]

In addition, the classical marks seem less clearly applicable to the local church than to the universal one, but the local church is emphasized more in Scripture and is how believers experience the church today. Even in terms of the universal church, the church is not yet fully catholic. These four marks are possessed partially by local churches today, and are helpful guides and goals for areas of future improvement, but such bodies are still churches, even though not yet perfected in unity, holiness, catholicity, or apostolicity.

THE REFORMATION FORMULATION:
THE WORD AND THE SACRAMENTS

The Reformation precipitated the division of the church into various groups and thus was faced with the need to provide an answer for those who anxiously questioned, "How may I find a true church?" This was more than an academic exercise; it was a matter of the utmost practical importance.

---

21. Howard Snyder, "The Marks of Evangelical Ecclesiology," in *Evangelical Ecclesiology: Reality or Illusion?* ed. John G. Stackhouse Jr. (Grand Rapids: Baker Academic, 2003), 81–88.

22. This seems to be the underlying theme throughout Phillips, Ryken, and Dever, *The Church.*

23. As Millard Erickson says, the gospel is "the one factor that gives basic shape to everything the church does, the element that lies at the heart of all its functions." Millard Erickson, *Christian Theology,* 2d ed. (Grand Rapids: Baker, 1998), 1069.

Many assumed that outside the church there was no salvation. Thus, there could be no appeal to marks that only identified some invisible or universal church. These people needed to know if the church in their neighborhood was a true church in which they might find salvation.

On this question, the magisterial Reformers (Luther, Zwingli, and Calvin) gave much the same answer. Calvin's response is often quoted: "Wherever we see the Word of God purely preached and heard, and the sacraments administered according to Christ's institution, there, it is not to be doubted, a church of God exists."[24] At times, Calvin adds a third mark, that of church discipline, and Luther in one place lists seven marks of a true church, but Luther also says that all the marks boil down to the one mark of the Word: "even if there were no other sign than this alone, it would still suffice to prove that a Christian, holy people must exist there, for God's word cannot be without God's people, and conversely, God's people cannot be without God's word."[25]

These signs relate directly to the struggle the Reformers had with the Catholic Church. The identifying slogans of the Reformation (sola Scriptura, sola gratia, sola fide) are all encompassed in their marks. The pure Word, Scripture alone, must be preached. For the Reformers, the preaching of the Word was almost synonymous with the preaching of the gospel. The gospel message of the Word was salvation by grace alone, not grace plus one's best efforts. And that saving grace was received by faith alone, not via the sacraments as understood by the Catholic Church.

The first mark, the pure preaching of the Word, is close to the idea of apostolicity, as discussed above. The church is apostolic when it listens to the apostolic teaching, found in the written Word of God. That mark is true of the church in heaven, but on earth we are still struggling to understand and rightly preach God's pure Word. Here the narrower meaning of the Word as the gospel is important. Calvin was willing to call a group a true church, even if they did not understand all of God's Word aright, as long as they preserved and preached the pure gospel message.

Here we encounter a true *sine qua non* of the church. If it loses the gospel message, a group of people is no longer a true church. It may be a religious society or a club, but it is not a church, for God's called-out people are called

---

24. John Calvin, *Institutes of the Christian Religion*, 21:1023 (4.1.9).
25. Martin Luther, "On the Councils and the Church," in *Martin Luther's Basic Theological Writings*, ed. Timothy Lull (Minneapolis, Minn.: Fortress Press, 1989), 547. The complete list of seven signs is the Word, baptism, the Lord's Supper, church discipline, called and consecrated ministers, public praise and thanksgiving, and the sacred cross of suffering.

out by the gospel and come in response to the gospel. The power of the gospel is what reconciles them to God, unites them to Christ, and allows them to
be indwelt by the Spirit. There can be no people of God, body of Christ, or
temple of the Spirit without the gospel.

The second mark, the proper administration of the sacraments, is more
problematic. Can a true church exist if the sacraments are not rightly observed?
The Reformers saw the Catholic observance of the Mass, involving the claims
that Christ was recrucified, that it was necessary for salvation, and that it
conferred grace apart from faith, as a repudiation of the gospel. But what of
the differences raised by the Anabaptists and, later, the Baptists, over baptism?
Is the baptism of infants, which Baptists say is not according to the institution
of Christ, sufficient to make a group no longer a church? In nineteenth-century
America, some Baptists thought so. The Landmark Baptists took the
Reformation marks, measured the neighboring Methodists and Presbyterians,
and found them wanting. They termed their assemblies religious societies
but not gospel churches, because they did not practice the ordinances as Jesus
had instructed. They would not practice pulpit exchange with the ministers
of such groups, nor do anything that could be construed as a tacit acceptance
of them as true churches.

There are a number of problems with the claims of the Landmark Baptists, but the most serious is a failure to make a distinction between what is
essential to the church's nature and what is important but not essential. In
other words, they fail to distinguish between issues of being and well-being.
The gospel pertains to the essential nature of the church, and one of the criteria by which an act qualifies as a sacrament among Protestants has been its
appropriateness as a symbol of the gospel.[26] Thus, Miroslav Volf says that
baptism and the Lord's Supper "belong to the essence of the church, for they
have to do with faith and its confession. . . . But the sacraments are an indispensable condition of ecclesiality only if they are a form of the confession of
faith and an expression of faith."[27] It seems therefore that if a practice of the

---

26. Stanley Grenz says that an ordinance, or sacrament, "must be so closely linked to the gospel mes-
    sage . . . that it becomes a symbol for the truth of the good news it embodies." Stanley Grenz,
    Theology for the Community of God (Nashville: Broadman & Holman, 1994), 676.

27. Miroslav Volf, "Community Formation as an Image of the Triune God," in *Community Formation
    in the Early Church and in the Church Today*, ed. Richard Longenecker (Peabody, Mass.: Hendrickson,
    2002), 217–18. Elmer Towns and Ed Stetzer, *Perimeters of Light: Biblical Boundaries for the Emerg-
    ing Church* (Chicago: Moody, 2004), 68, also say that baptism and the Lord's Supper are "essential
    elements without which a true church cannot exist," but they do not comment on whether a par-
    ticular view of baptism and the Lord's Supper is also requisite.

sacraments (or ordinances) amounts to a repudiation of the gospel, then it would strike at the being, or nature, or essence of the church. But if an observance of baptism is not as Jesus instituted, but is not a threat to the gospel, the practice may hinder the well-being of the church, but does not undermine its being or nature. It may be a valid church, but, like all churches on earth, imperfect in some respects.

This position corresponds with the biblical teaching on baptism and the Lord's Supper. They are clearly an essential part of the church's life but do not go to the heart of the church's nature. The Reformers included proper administration of the sacraments in their marks of the church due to the seriousness of their disagreement with Catholic teaching on the Mass, but the sacraments are not as prominent in biblical teaching as are other elements that do belong to the very nature of the church. An improper administration of baptism and the Lord's Supper will hinder the church's health and weaken its ministry, but it does not necessarily invalidate the church, unless the impropriety compromises the message of the gospel.

We may derive three conclusions from our examination of these two major formulations of the marks of the church.

First, both seem to be responsive to and shaped by the historical contexts in which they were formed. The creedal formulation of "one, holy, catholic, and apostolic" helped the patristic church fathers respond to the challenges they faced from various heretical groups in their day, and the Reformation marks reflect the Reformers' conviction that much of the Roman Catholic Church of their day had lost the gospel in their preaching and were practicing the sacraments in a way that obscured rather than portrayed the gospel. This responsiveness suggests that perhaps the development of marks of the church is an ongoing task as churches face new challenges.[28]

Second, both sets of marks serve to some degree as goals toward which churches should strive as well as marks of their genuineness or validity. There is certainly room for improvement in terms of expressions of unity, room for growth toward maturity in holiness, a need for further missionary expansion of the church's catholicity, and a need for sharper understanding of apostolic teaching. There must also be perennial watchfulness that our preaching

---

28. For example, the prominence of parachurch groups in contemporary North American evangelical Christianity calls for thoughtful ways to distinguish churches and parachurch groups. In chapter 9, I suggest that certain ministries assigned to churches are a mark distinguishing churches from parachurch groups.

presents the gospel message clearly, and that our practice of the Lord's Supper and baptism aptly portrays and symbolizes that message.

  Third, both the classical and Reformation marks seem to coalesce around the gospel. It underlies, shapes, and frames the church's unity, holiness, catholicity, and apostolicity; it is the message preached and presented in the sacraments. It is a true sine qua non of a true church.

CHAPTER 3

THE ESSENCE OF THE CHURCH

Theological Conclusions and Practical Applications

WE WILL NOW GATHER ALL OUR data from Scripture and history into five theological conclusions about the essence of the church. Then, since doctrine should govern and guide practice, we will derive practical applications from our theology for life and ministry in local church contexts. We are dealing here only with what we see as essential to the church, not articulating a comprehensive description of it. There are many other issues that relate to the health, well-being, and proper order of a church; we will deal with them in the following chapters. Our present concern is with those things that seem intrinsically connected to the very being of the church.

THE CHURCH: GOD'S ORGANIZED, PURPOSEFUL ASSEMBLY

This one conclusion really contains four theological affirmations, each with practical implications for ministry. First, our study of Scripture shows that the nature of the church centers on God. The church is those called out by God—called to be God's people, Christ's body, and the Spirit's temple. It is not a human invention or a social club. It is God's assembly.

Therefore, the church's first concern must be to please God. To have a growing church is good; to have a church full of pleased people may be desirable, but the church belongs to God, and the point is pleasing him. That means that all programs, events, activities, and priorities must contribute in some way to that goal. Pleasing God begins in the heart, with an attitude that honors God, but it must also include the mind, with the search to understand God's will for the church. Rather than following the latest program or what seems to be working elsewhere or what the people want, our first re-course should be to consult Scripture, seeking to understand God's design for the church.

Second, as God's organized assembly, the church is and must be what God says it is and must be. The church is not just any grouping of people, or even any group of Christians. It is not free to organize itself as it chooses; it is God's assembly. Since God is a God of order (1 Cor. 14:33, 40), we should expect God's assembly to be an ordered one. This is confirmed by New Testa-ment teaching. We find references to authorized leaders of the assemblies from the earliest days. On their first missionary journey, Paul and Barnabas, immediately after planting churches, "appointed elders for them in each church" (Acts 14:23). There was a recognized membership, such that Luke could record the number of those who joined in Acts 2:41 and 4:4, and Paul could make a clear distinction between those outside and inside the church (1 Cor. 5:12–13). The nature and role of the church's leaders and the govern-mental pattern of the church have been understood in a variety of ways in church history, and many conclude that the New Testament teaching on church order or polity is not sufficiently clear and detailed to authorize a single pattern as biblical. Here may be another place where the distinction is between being and well-being. There is enough biblical teaching about order to conclude that some type of order is essential to the church; which pattern is most consistent with New Testament teaching and thus most conducive to the well-being of the church is a matter that has not been equally clear in the history of the church and will receive our full attention in a later chapter.

A third affirmation in the statement above is that the church exists for certain purposes. It is a purposeful assembly. If some Christians gather, but do nothing, they are not a church. The New Testament presents the church in action with such consistent regularity that we may speak of certain minis-tries as essential to a true church. A church that did not proclaim the gospel would not be a church; a church that did not assemble for worship or did not teach its people or did not experience fellowship would not be a church. We will argue later that there are at least five constitutive purposes of the church. Churches perform those ministries with differing degrees of effectiveness, but churches are marked as churches by their possession of a fullness of min-istry, assigned to them by God.[1]

---

1. For more, see the discussion in chapter 9.

Fourth, the church is an assembly. The church is not just people whom God has called out; he has also called them together. We noted earlier that the Greek translation of the Old Testament used the word *ekklēsia* seventy-seven times to translate one of the Hebrew words used for God's people *(qāhāl)*, but never for the other *(ʿēdâh)*. The reason is that the former has the idea of an actual assembly while the latter does not. We also saw that Paul refers to the Christians within a city as the *church* of the city (such as the church in Cenchrea or the church in Corinth) while he refers to the Christians in a province as the *churches* of the province (such as the Galatian churches or the Macedonian churches). One possible reason for this distinction is that the Christians in a city could (and did) actually assemble, while those scattered over a wider area could not. Paul tended to reserve the term *church* for those groups that actually assembled (with the exception of the universal church usage, which appears in Ephesians and Colossians).

The emphasis on assembly has two practical applications. First, it highlights the importance of fellowship for the church. The event usually seen as marking the birth of the church, the descent of the Holy Spirit in Acts 2, is also where we first encounter the word *fellowship (koinōnia)* in the New Testament. It is as if that first group of Christians were bonded together into an assembly by a gift brought by the Spirit, a gift called fellowship. If this is so, then fellowship is no mere diversion from the real work of the church; it is the work of the church, or the work of the Holy Spirit in the church. Churches need to work intentionally and thoughtfully at providing the contexts in which this type of Spirit-given fellowship is nurtured.

As a second application, the church as an assembly serves as a helpful reminder to individualistic North Americans that the New Testament teaching on the church is corporate through and through. The very word *church* and every image for the church is corporate, involving people being assembled together in face-to-face relationships. Thus joining the church should be a momentous step in which the individual surrenders a degree of personal autonomy, accepting the discipline of the body and accepting responsibilities for and commitments to the corporate body. This was reflected in earlier Baptist practice by members covenanting together. Such a commitment was what constituted individuals members of a body.

Paul reflects the link that is established among the members of the assembly when he says, "If one part suffers, every part suffers with it; if one part is honored, every part rejoices with it" (1 Cor. 12:26). Too often today, church members are unaware of or unconcerned about their fellow members' suffering, and envy one another's blessings. But when we realize that those sufferings and blessings are ours, because we are one with other persons as fellow members of one body, bonded together in one assembly, how different the perspective! This corporate perspective of the Christian life is something particularly needed among American Christians. It is implicit in the idea of the church as an assembly, a group bonded together by the Spirit's gift of fellowship.

THE CHURCH: PRIMARILY A LOCAL ASSEMBLY

This second conclusion is true in terms of both biblical usage and personal experience. We noted earlier that out of 114 occurrences of *ekklēsia* in the New Testament, at least ninety refer to a local church or churches. There is a valid usage of *ekklēsia* to refer to all the redeemed of all the ages, the universal church or larger body of Christ, but it is secondary in terms of biblical prominence. Furthermore, the church that Christians attend and in which they minister is a local assembly of God's people.

This would seem so obvious as not to need saying, were it not for the fact that much of what is written on the church focuses on the universal church. The patristic formulation of the church as one, holy, catholic, and apostolic seems to apply more readily to the universal than to the local church, and when the Reformers affirmed the Nicene Creed's statement on the church, they saw it as applying more to the invisible than to the visible church.

By contrast, when the Bible discusses the church, it is overwhelmingly the local church that is in view. This pattern has at least three practical applications. First, Christians who belong to no local church but claim to belong to the body of Christ, referring to the church universal, are living contrary to the biblical pattern, which gives priority to the local church. Second, those who work in or with parachurch groups are not thus exempted from their need to be involved in a local church, both to serve others and to be served by the fuller ministry of the church. Third, we need to recognize the dignity and honor given to the local church. When Jesus says, "I will build my church" (Matt. 16:18), or when Paul says, "Christ loved the church" (Eph. 5:25), or prays "To him [God] be glory in the church" (3:21), these passages may well refer to the universal church. But how is Christ's building of the church seen in the world today? Where do we see Christ loving his church? Where is God being glorified today? The answer in each case is in local churches. Despite all their obvious flaws, God loves real, local churches, not some invisible ideal.

THE CHURCH: BY ITS NATURE A LIVING AND GROWING ASSEMBLY

This conclusion is obvious in the comparison of the church to a body, but is also clearly implied in the image of the church as a building or temple that is made of "living stones" (1 Peter 2:5). In 1 Corinthians 3:9, the church is also compared to a field, where it is God who "makes things grow" (1 Cor. 3:7). This conclusion concerning the essence of the church raises two areas of practical applications.

If the church is living, change is inevitable. Change is part of life, and the church has obviously evidenced change throughout its history. Churches today are noticeably different from churches a hundred years ago, not to mention a thousand years ago. The difficulty is in evaluating any given change. Is it helpful and healthy, dangerous and destructive, or neutral and indifferent? Certainly the Bible does not spell out every aspect of church life, and thus churches are free to be innovative and creative in some aspects. Furthermore, as God's people mature in their understanding of Scripture, there should be change as they grow in obedience. Baptists believe that certain aspects of scriptural teaching concerning the church were misunderstood by the great majority of churches for centuries. Change came as people continued to search the Scriptures. As John Robinson said to the pilgrims as they departed for America, "The Lord has more truth yet to break forth out of his holy Word."

One powerful factor affecting how God's people see Scripture is their cultural context. The culture can at times shed light on the pages of the Bible, or it can blind people to the teaching of the Bible. For example, Baptists believe the Bible has always taught congregational government, but it became popular only as the cultural context began to favor democratic government. The rise of democracy in Western culture may have helped people to see what had always been in Scripture. Other examples are more problematic. For example, it seems undeniable that the growing prominence of business in American life affected churches in the twentieth century. Pastors often began to think of themselves as chief executive officers, with deacons as the board of trustees. This idea of leadership seems to clash with the biblical idea of servant shepherd leadership. Among some seeker churches today, the goal is for the church to feel similar to a shopping mall, and consumerism is shaping church life in a variety of ways.[2] Are these changes simply new ways to relate the gospel in an intelligible way to today's culture, or have our changes accommodated culture in ways that are antithetical to the gospel? Change is inevitable, because the church is alive, not static. But change needs to be thoughtfully evaluated, lest we find ourselves sinfully captive to culture, as has happened all too often in the history of the church. In fact, in a recent book, Alan Wolfe argues that churches in America have been virtually transformed by their interaction with culture. He says, "In every aspect of the religious life, American faith has met American culture— and American culture has triumphed."[3]

Of course, one reason why the church has often accommodated culture, especially in the past hundred years, has been the desire to grow.[4] Growth, especially numerical growth, is assumed among many Baptists to be the most important goal of any church and the most significant barometer of a church's health and success. The New Testament, especially the book of Acts, records dramatic growth in the early church. Three thousand converts were added on the day of Pentecost (Acts 2:41); the number soon grew to more than five thousand men (4:4); Acts 6:7 states that "the number of disciples . . . increased rapidly"; by Acts 9, the church all over Judea, Galilee, and Samaria was growing "in numbers" (v. 31). Later on, the churches planted by Paul "grew daily in numbers" (16:5). But for all the obvious evidence and expectation of growth, it does not seem to have been a stated goal of the New Testament churches. There are no records of Paul reproving a church for not growing, or even giving commands and exhortations concerning personal evangelism. This is all the more striking when we remember that Paul sharply reproved churches for division, heretical teachings, and immoral behavior. There are also sections of Paul's letters filled with numerous commands. Romans 12:9–21 contains about twenty commands regarding a whole host of attitudes and actions, but nothing like "proclaim the gospel," or "share the good news with your friends." First Thessalonians 5:12–22 is another long list of imperatives, with the same omission.

What are we to make of this New Testament pattern of dramatic church

---

2. See Bruce Shelley and Marshall Shelley, *Consumer Church: Can Evangelicals Win the World Without Losing Their Souls?* (Downers Grove, Ill.: InterVarsity, 1992), for some of the effects of consumerism on churches.

3. Alan Wolfe, *The Transformation of American Religion: How We Actually Live Our Faith* (New York: The Free Press, 2003), 3.

4. Ibid., 74–81.

growth, when there is surprisingly little emphasis on it? There are no doubt a number of factors involved, and we will try to give them all due consideration when we return to the issue of evangelism as one of the constitutive ministries of the church. In relationship to the essence of the church, however, there seems to be one important implication. To the degree that the church lives in accord with its own essential being, growth will occur. In some contexts, the growth may be primarily spiritual. For example, in Ephesians 4, the outcome of the body functioning normally is that "we will in all things grow up into him who is the Head, that is, Christ" (Eph. 4:15). In other words, the church will grow in spiritual maturity and Christlikeness. Other situations may be like that reflected in Acts 2, where, as the church lived its life in the power of the Spirit, "the Lord added to their number daily those who were being saved" (v. 47). Certainly, the church bore witness to Christ, as he had promised they would (Acts 1:8), but the growth is seen as the work of God. In fact, the teaching of Paul and the pattern of Acts seem to indicate that churches should focus on obedience to Christ's command, "Follow me"; the results in terms of growth must be entrusted to Christ, who promised those who follow him, "I will make you fishers of men" (Matt. 4:19).

This does not mean that evangelism does not need to be taught, modeled, encouraged, and intentional in the church's life. It does not mean that we must get everything right and then the church will automatically grow. The New Testament churches that grew were very imperfect. But if ultimately it is "God who makes things grow" (1 Cor. 3:7), or it is the Lord who adds to the church (Acts 2:47), we should not wonder if the Lord does not add many new members to sick, deformed, unhealthy churches. The goal of the church is to live the life God has given it. To the degree that it does, it will experience God-given growth.

THE CHURCH: A GOSPEL ASSEMBLY

The gospel message is itself the call that brings the assembly together and connects it to Christ. The gospel is prior to the church and the church exists because of it. Therefore, if the church ever loses the gospel, it ceases to be a church. The Reformers were right to insist on the preaching of the gospel as a mark of the true church. Proper teaching on church polity and worship and other aspects may be essential to the *well-being* of the church; the gospel is essential to its *being*.

Therefore, the church cannot be indifferent to doctrinal orthodoxy. Paul warned the Ephesian elders of the danger posed to their church by those who would "distort the truth" (Acts 20:30). He commanded the churches in Galatia to consider anyone who preached another gospel to them as anathema, or under God's condemnation (Gal. 1:8–9). One qualification for the elders Titus was to appoint was their ability to "encourage others by sound doctrine and refute those who oppose it" (Titus 1:9). By contrast, in the case of those whose preaching of the true gospel was accompanied by impure motives, Paul's response was joy rather than rebuke: "The important thing is that in every way, whether from false motives or true, Christ is preached. And because of this I rejoice" (Phil. 1:18). The purity of their message was more important than the purity of their motives.

Churches may and do differ on things like form of government, mode of baptism, and numerous other issues. The same church cannot be both congregationally governed and episcopally ruled; it cannot practice believer's baptism only and infant baptism. Of course, I believe Baptists are right in their interpretation of these issues; that is why I am a Baptist. But I do not think that makes all those who disagree no longer valid churches, any more than I would think a Baptist church that mistakenly baptizes someone who is not a believer thereby becomes invalid because they have erred on believer's baptism alone. Churches can be and are valid and yet imperfect. But if a church errs on the gospel, they have become not just imperfect, but invalid; they are no longer a church, according to the biblical portrayal of the church.

THE CHURCH: A SPIRIT-EMPOWERED ASSEMBLY

The people of God must have enjoyed something of the power of the Holy Spirit in the Old Testament. Without his ministry, how could anyone have been convicted of sin or have understood God's Word? Yet it is clear that there was also a sense in which the Spirit was not given prior to what John calls Jesus' glorification (John 7:39). After Christ's resurrection and ascension, the Spirit was poured out at Pentecost, changing the group of Jesus' disciples from a group into a church.

As we have already noted, the Gospel writer Luke never uses the word *ekklēsia* prior to Acts 2, but it is found twenty times in the book of Acts after that chapter. The metaphor of the temple of the Spirit implies that the Spirit dwells in a special way in the church. We speak rather readily of the ministry of the Holy Spirit indwelling the individual believer, and rightly so, for it is biblical teaching. But we do not often ponder the teaching that when believers are "built together" they "become a dwelling in which God lives by his Spirit" (Eph. 2:22). Could this be why Paul says that when the church in Corinth is assembled that "the power of our Lord Jesus is present," and that the actions of the church in exercising discipline on an individual have a profound spiritual impact on that person's life? Is it the Spirit's power in the church that accounts for the power of the church to use the keys of the kingdom in ways that call down the power of heaven (Matt. 16:19; 18:18)? Early Baptists had a robust confidence in the power and competence of the church to govern its own affairs; that confidence was linked to the empowering presence of the Spirit in the church.

Some of the earliest church fathers recognized the presence of the Spirit in a special way in the church. The second-century bishop Irenaeus virtually identified the church with the presence of the Spirit: "For where the Church is, there is the Spirit of God; and where the Spirit is, there is the Church and every kind of grace."[5] Augustine went even further to say that the Spirit acts as the animating principle in the church: "What the soul is in our body, the Holy Spirit is in the body of Christ, which is the Church."[6]

More recently, the power of the Holy Spirit has been evident in the movement that emphasizes the Spirit's presence among us, the Pentecostals. Despite its many doctrinal aberrations, serious ones in some cases, Pentecostalism has grown from no adherents prior to 1900 to, a century later, a worldwide movement encompassing more than five hundred million believers in more than ten thousand denominations.[7] After nearly four hundred years of history and the work of thousands of missionaries, Baptists worldwide number about a tenth as many followers. Numbers alone can be very misleading, but might they not also in this case point to the importance of the Spirit as the empowering agent of the church? Whatever their many faults may be, most Pentecostal churches rely upon and call upon the Spirit to empower them in an emphasis that Baptists would do well to ponder and learn from. Without the Spirit, the church is a dead body; his presence makes the church alive. In

5. Irenaeus, "Against Heresies," 3.24.1, in *The Ante-Nicene Fathers.*
6. Augustine, Sermo 267.4.4, in J.-P. Migne, *Patrologia Latina* (Turnholti, Belgium: Brepols, n.d.), 38:1231.
7. These numbers are from David Barrett, ed., *World Christian Encyclopedia,* 2d ed. (Oxford, U.K.; New York: Oxford University Press, 2001), 4. Barrett groups Pentecostals and charismatics together and projects their number to grow to more than one billion by 2050.

an age that increasingly utilizes demographic study and market analyses, we need to remember anew that, as it was with the rebuilding of God's temple long ago, so it is with the building of temples of living stones in churches today: "'Not by might nor by power, but by my Spirit,' says the LORD Almighty" (Zech. 4:6).

STUDY QUESTIONS FOR PART 1

1. Why did the first Christians choose the word *ekklēsia* to describe their gatherings?
2. What implications should we draw from the fact that the New Testament overwhelmingly uses the word *ekklēsia* in a local sense to refer to actual local churches?
3. Which image of the church do you find most helpful? Why? Are there images other than those discussed that you think should be included? What would they add to our understanding of the nature of the church?
4. Do you think most Christians think of themselves in individualistic terms or as part of a group (a people, body, or temple)? How does this affect how one lives the Christian life?
5. How would you respond to the question, "Where can I find the true church?" How would Augustine or Luther have responded?
6. Can you identify common ideas about the church that seem more shaped by cultural influences than biblical teaching? How about practices in your church? Are some more cultural than biblical?
7. Which of the five theological conclusions in the last part of chapter 3 do you think has the most relevance for churches today?
8. What in these chapters encourages you about the church? What in these chapters challenges your previous ideas about the church? What could you apply in a practical way in your life and ministry in your church?

BOOKS FOR FURTHER STUDY

Banks, Robert. *Paul's Idea of Community: The Early House Settings in Their Historical Setting.* Grand Rapids: Eerdmans, 1980. Banks has a very good discussion on the first-century background, on the local and universal church, and on the church as body and family.

Carson, D. A. "Evangelicals, Ecumenism, and the Church." In *Evangelical Affirmations*, edited by Kenneth Kantzer and Carl Henry. Grand Rapids: Academie Books, 1990. In an essay of about forty pages, Carson touches insightfully on a number of key biblical themes relating to the nature of the church.

Clowney, Edmund. *The Church*. Downers Grove, Ill.: InterVarsity, 1995. This is a text on ecclesiology from a Reformed point of view, with helpful discussion of some of the images of the church and the four classical marks of the church.

George, Timothy. "Toward an Evangelical Ecclesiology." In *Catholics and Evangelicals: Do They Share a Common Future?* edited by Thomas Rausch. Downers Grove, Ill.: InterVarsity, 2000. In this essay, George looks at the four classical marks of the church, the Reformation signs of the true church, and discusses how both may be appropriated within an evangelical ecclesiology.

Küng, Hans. *The Church*. Garden City, N.Y.: Image Books, 1976. Though a Catholic, Küng approaches the church in this work from a largely Protestant perspective, organizing much of his discussion around the same three images noted in this chapter.

Minear, Paul S. *Images of the Church in the New Testament*. Philadelphia: Westminster Press, 1960. This is the most thorough study of all the biblical images for the church. Minear catalogs ninety-six, though many do not really seem to relate to the church at all.

Phillips, Richard D., Philip G. Ryken, and Mark E. Dever. *The Church: One, Holy, Catholic, and Apostolic*. Phillipsburg, N.J.: P & R Publishers, 2004. This book presents an evangelical interpretation of the four classical marks in the form of expositions of texts that speak of the church's oneness, holiness, catholicity, and apostolicity. The relationship of the gospel to each mark seems to be an underlying theme of the book.

Saucy, Robert. *The Church in God's Program*. Chicago: Moody, 1972. Saucy gives a very helpful discussion of the meaning of *ekklēsia* in Scripture and looks at several biblical images for the church.

Van Gelder, Craig. *The Essence of the Church: A Community Created by the Spirit*. Grand Rapids: Baker, 2000. Van Gelder combines expertise in missiology, theology, and social sciences to give a helpful discussion of how a proper view of the church's essence should shape the nature, ministry, and organization of North American churches.

PART 2

WHO IS THE CHURCH?

CHAPTER 4

REGENERATE CHURCH MEMBERSHIP

The Baptist Mark of the Church

IN CHAPTER 2, WE CONSIDERED TWO major formulations of the nature of the church developed in church history. In the patristic era, the church was described as one, holy, catholic, and apostolic, thus giving us the four classical marks of the church. The Reformers, seeing the four classical *notae* as applying more to the invisible than to the visible church, gave two additional marks by which one may ascertain if a specific congregation is a true church of God. They stated that wherever one finds the pure preaching of the Word and the right administration of the sacraments, there one may be sure there is a true church.

In this chapter, we look at a third way to look at the church, what we may call the Baptist mark of the church. This mark differs from the previous two formulations in that it does not so much answer the question, "What is the church?" as the question, "Who is the church?" That is, central to the Baptist vision of the church is the insistence that the church must be composed of believers only. That is the distinctive mark of the church for Baptists and others who fall within the stream of those who advocate what is sometimes called the gathered church, or more often today, the believers' church.[1] This

---

1. Donald Durnbaugh, *The Believers' Church: The History and Character of Radical Protestantism* (New York: Macmillan, 1968), ix, traces the origin of the phrase to Max Weber's classic work, *The Protestant Ethic and the Spirit of Capitalism*, in which he used it to describe the Anabaptists and Quakers. It gained more currency with the revival of Anabaptist studies about fifty years ago, and in two conferences that organized around the phrase. The first was held by Mennonites in 1955,

mark may also be called the principle of regenerate church membership. At the first Baptist World Congress in 1905, J. D. Freeman said of Baptists, "This principle of a regenerated Church membership, more than anything else, marks our distinctiveness in the Christian world today."[2] More recently, Justice Anderson has affirmed its centrality for the Baptist doctrine of the church: "The cardinal principle of Baptist ecclesiology, and logically, the point of departure for church polity, is the insistence on a regenerate membership in the local congregation."[3] To put it simply, regenerate church membership is meaningful church membership, involving only those with a genuine commitment to Christ and the congregation of Christ's people. This ideal of regenerate membership has been central to Baptist ecclesiology.

We trace the development and importance of this idea of the church as composed of believers to answer the question, "Who is the church?" Our discussion is divided into two chapters. First, in chapter 4, we briefly review the biblical rationale for this view of the church, look at the historical developments that allowed this idea of the church to become obscured and eventually opposed, even by Reformers like Luther, Zwingli, and Calvin, and, most important, we show how the principle of regenerate church membership became the central principle of Baptist ecclesiology. Then, in chapter 5, we examine how and why North American Baptists over the past one hundred years virtually abandoned this principle, becoming hardly recognizable as historically Baptist. We conclude chapter 5 with some suggestions as to why and how this principle may be recovered in Baptist churches today.

the Study Conference on the Believers' Church. The second was larger and more broadly based, with 150 participants from seven denominational families, and was held at Southern Baptist Theological Seminary in Louisville, Kentucky, in 1967. The papers from that conference were published in James Leo Garrett Jr., ed., *The Concept of the Believers' Church: Addresses from the 1967 Louisville Conference* (Scottdale, Pa.: Herald Press, 1969). There have been seven additional such conferences since 1967, with the most recent in 1990, on the campus of Southwestern Baptist Theological Seminary in Ft. Worth, Texas.

2. J. D. Freeman, "The Place of Baptists in the Christian Church," in *The Baptist World Congress: London, July 11–19, 1905, Authorised Record of Proceedings* (London: Baptist Union Publication Department, 1905), 27.

3. Justice C. Anderson, "Old Baptist Principles Reset," *Southwestern Journal of Theology* 31 (Spring 1989): 5–12.

THE BIBLICAL RATIONALE FOR REGENERATE CHURCH MEMBERSHIP

The biblical basis for seeing the church as composed exclusively of believers is so strong and obvious that the difficulty is in seeing how this idea was ever obscured. The very idea of the church as the called-out ones presupposes that the members of the church have heard and responded to God's call. The image of the church as the people of God assumes that these are people who belong to God. They are referred to more than sixty times as saints, or holy ones *(hagioi),* or people set aside for devotion to God. They are the ones who believe in Christ and are bound to one another by the Holy Spirit. The church is the body of Christ, and believers form one body in Christ (Rom. 12:5). A common possession of Christ is the ground of the church's unity. The church shares "one Lord, one faith, one baptism; one God and Father of all, who is over all and through all and in all" (Eph. 4:5–6). It is difficult to see how the church could be described as the body of Christ or the temple of the Spirit if some of the members of the body or some of the living stones in the temple had no connection with Christ or the Spirit. The very distinction in the New Testament between the church and the world indicates that the church differs from the world, and does so because the church is composed of those who believe in Christ, belong to God, and are bound together by the Spirit. The church is obviously composed of believers.

Some might acknowledge the strength of this argument but seek to limit its application to the universal church. That church, by definition, is composed of believers only, all believers of all time. The local church, they may say, only imperfectly reflects that ideal. We cannot know with certainty the state of anyone's heart and thus we have to accept that local churches cannot be composed of believers only, due to the limitations we have as humans.[4] But four factors weaken this line of thought.

First, simply as a matter of logic, if the universal church is composed of all believers, it seems that the goal of local churches should be to come as close to that same standard as possible. Certainly we may fail, but we need

---

4. Luther objected to the Anabaptist practice of limiting baptism and church membership to those who were believers due to the uncertainty or difficulty of knowing who has faith. He writes, "Have they now become gods so that they can discern the hearts of men and know whether or not they believe?" See Martin Luther, "Concerning Rebaptism," in *Martin Luther's Basic Theological Writings,* 351.

not make a virtue of our limitations. In many areas, biblical standards are above our ability to reach perfectly, but that does not justify lowering those standards. In the same way, we should retain the ideal of a membership of all believers as the goal for local churches, even if we must acknowledge imperfectly reaching that ideal in practice.

Second, it seems as if the New Testament anticipates the possibility that local churches will inadvertently allow false members to creep in, and provides for it. That provision is church discipline, which is applied to "anyone who calls himself a brother" but denies that claim by his life (see 1 Cor. 5:11). He is put out of the church, both in the hope that he will repent and in order to keep the church pure. If the church is not intended to be a pure body of genuine believers, what is the point of 1 Corinthians 5 and other New Testament teaching on church discipline?

Third, the descriptions of local churches in the New Testament assume that these local, visible congregations are composed of believers only. The church of God in Corinth is called "those sanctified in Christ Jesus" (1 Cor. 1:2). The letter to the Ephesians is addressed to "the saints in Ephesus, the faithful in Christ Jesus" (Eph. 1:1). The letter to the church in Philippi is sent "to all the saints in Christ Jesus" (Phil. 1:1). Paul wrote "to the holy and faithful brothers in Christ at Colosse" (Col. 1:2). The church of the Thessalonians is described in both letters as a church "in God the Father and the Lord Jesus Christ" (1 Thess. 1:1; 2 Thess. 1:2). Clearly, Paul thought he was addressing bodies of Christians.

Finally, local churches in Acts gathered only those who believed. On the day of Pentecost, the church in Jerusalem was constituted by those who "accepted his [Peter's] message" (Acts 2:41). Those who were added in subsequent days were those "who were being saved" or those who heard the message of the apostles and believed (v. 47; 4:4). The church in Antioch began when "a great number of people believed and turned to the Lord" (11:21). Near the end of their first missionary journey, Paul and Barnabas visited the churches they had established and encouraged them to stay true to their commitment as believers (14:21–23). The clear implication is that those churches were composed of believers. The church in Philippi began when the Lord opened the heart of a woman named Lydia to respond to Paul's message (16:14). Paul's regular strategy was to enter a city, preach the gospel, and organize those who responded into churches. He operated with the assumption of regenerate church membership.

Thus the objection that regenerate church membership applies only to the universal church seems to run contrary to logic, the biblical teaching on church discipline, and the way local churches are described and gathered in the New Testament.

Others object to regenerate church membership on the grounds that the New Testament reflects a pioneering evangelistic situation. The accounts in the book of Acts record the apostles preaching to adults, and certainly no adult should be baptized and granted church membership apart from regeneration. However, as the church grew, the regenerate individuals composing the church had children. The children of believing parents, they claim, have a special connection with the church because of their parents, and should thus be baptized and brought into the fellowship of the church, even prior to personal faith.[5]

Those who advocate regenerate church membership acknowledge that the children of believing parents have a great blessing and many advantages, but they would note that the children of believing parents must still trust Christ personally to be saved, and that until they are saved, they are not proper subjects of baptism, for baptism in the New Testament is baptism of believers only. And since Baptists agree with most other Christian denominations that baptism is the proper ceremonial rite of initiation into church membership, they object both to baptizing infants and to including them among the church's membership, for both are appropriate only for believers.[6]

Furthermore, the early church did not move to the adoption of infant baptism and a corresponding adoption of infant membership in local churches as soon as their founding members had children. Most scholars agree that the practice of infant baptism did not appear until the latter half of the second century and did not become widespread or standard until the late third or even fourth century. The issue was still being debated as late as Augustine,

---

5. This is one of the classic arguments of those who baptize infants, going back at least as far as Calvin. See John Calvin, *Institutes of the Christian Religion*, 21:1346–47 (4.16. 23–24).

6. In his classic work on Anabaptism, Franklin Littell says that baptism became important to Anabaptists because it was "the most obvious dividing line between two patterns of church organization." See Franklin Littell, *The Anabaptist View of the Church: A Study in the Origins of Sectarian Protestantism*, 2d ed. (Boston: Starr King Press, 1958), xv. Leon McBeth sees a similar development in Baptist life. He says the origin of Baptists is best seen "as a search for a pure church," composed of what they called "visible saints." It was that search that led them to adopt believer's baptism. See Leon McBeth, *The Baptist Heritage* (Nashville: Broadman, 1987), 75. I would add that for both the Anabaptists and Baptists, their commitment to Scripture alone was also crucial for their adoption of believer's baptism.

but his support and rationale for it became decisive. Infant baptism and acceptance of the church as the mixed body composed of saved and unsaved became standard for the next thousand years.

A final objection that could be raised against the idea of regenerate church membership comes from history. We have argued that history can be a useful tool in checking our interpretation of Scripture with those of other times, lest our interpretation be unduly influenced by contemporary cultural forces and assumptions. Some might argue that the fact that the church as a whole, for the bulk of its history, accepted the idea of the church as a mixed body of believers and nonbelievers should call into question the interpretation of Scripture held by those in the believers' church camp. For more than a thousand years, some could argue, the idea of the mixed church had not been seen as incompatible with Scripture by some of the most able interpreters in all of church history. If the doctrine of regenerate church membership is as obvious in Scripture as claimed in this chapter, why did so many notable students of the Bible miss it? Why was it absent for more than a thousand years of Christian history? While these are valid questions, there are three cogent answers to this objection.

First, while it is true that the mixed church interpretation had been accepted for more than a thousand years by the time of the Reformation, it was not true of the first four hundred years of the church's history. During that time, the story was much more mixed. As mentioned above, infant baptism did not begin until the late second century, and with it there was a challenge to the believers' only church. But infant baptism was not immediately or universally accepted. There are also records indicating the serious preparation new believers underwent prior to baptism,[7] and the recurring waves of persecution tended to act as a purifying agent for the church, scaring off those who were not genuinely committed to Christ. The very vehemence with which Augustine argues for the mixed church shows that it was not yet fully or universally accepted in his day.

Second, the long period in which the believers' church interpretation was not adopted coincides with that of relative biblical ignorance. Once the Bible became readily available, the believers' church interpretation was renewed almost immediately. Even Luther, in one of his early writings, contemplated

---

7. The very term *catechism* is derived from the oral instruction given to baptismal candidates prior to baptism in the early church, often over a period of months. It shows the concern of the early church to baptize only those who could make a credible profession of faith.

the possibility of a church for those who wanted to be "Christians in earnest," but did not pursue it, saying he lacked the people ready for it.[8] But others, the Anabaptists and, later, the Baptists found thousands of people ready for it, people persuaded by Scripture that the church should be composed of believers only, people who formed such churches in the face of severe persecution. The English Baptist historian J. H. Shakespeare noted that the availability of the Bible is an important yet often underrated factor in the origin of the Baptists as a pure church of believers only.[9] Once the Bible was opened to people, they soon found the believers' church within its teachings.

Finally, the believers' church has proven itself to be more than a passing fad in biblical interpretation but one that has grown more and more prevalent over the past five hundred years. History rightly guards us against novel interpretations of the Bible, but the believers' church is no longer a novel interpretation. For those who value fidelity to Scripture above tradition, the biblical support for a regenerate church of believers only is so strong and obvious that we wonder how the church could have missed it for so long. The answer to that question lies in a confluence of historical circumstances that powerfully shaped beliefs about a number of issues that in turn led to an acceptance of the church as a mixed body.

THE DEVELOPMENT OF THE *CORPUS PERMIXTUM*

This leads to the second stage of our investigation. How, in view of the strong biblical support for the believers' church, did the opposing idea of the church as a *corpus permixtum*, or mixed body composed of believers and nonbelievers, become so widely accepted?

A key event noted by many in the believers' church tradition is the conversion of the Roman emperor Constantine in 312.[10] Prior to the battle of Milvian Bridge with Maxentius, Constantine supposedly received a vision that he saw as divine

---

8. See Martin Luther, "The German Mass and Order of Service, Martin Luther's Preface," in *Luther's Works,* ed. Jaroslav Pelikan, H. T. Lehmann et al., vol. 53, ed. Ulrich Leupold (Philadelphia: Fortress Press, 1965), 53:63–64.

9. J. H. Shakespeare, *Baptist and Congregational Pioneers* (London: Kingsgate Press, 1906), 2–4.

10. John Howard Yoder describes the fall of the church as the "fusion of church and society of which Constantine was the architect, Eusebius the priest, Augustine the apologete, and the Crusades and Inquisition the culmination." See John Yoder, "A People in the World: Theological Interpretation," in *The Concept of the Believers' Church,* 272. Donald Durnbaugh, *The Believers' Church,* 212–15, sees this idea of the fall of the church with Constantine as one of the defining characteristics of the believers' church tradition.

aid from the Christian God. The genuineness of his conversion is still debated by historians; the genuineness of the change in the Roman Empire cannot be doubted. Rodney Stark says, "For far too long, historians have accepted the claim that the conversion of Emperor Constantine . . . caused the triumph of Christianity. To the contrary, he destroyed its most attractive and dynamic aspects."[11] In 313 the Edict of Milan made Christianity a legal religion, and over the course of the next century, Christianity became the dominant religion. At the time of Constantine's conversion, Christians in the Roman Empire comprised about 10 percent of the population; within a century, that number jumped to 90 percent.[12] Before Constantine, persecution tended to keep membership in the church limited to those who were genuinely believers, and the line between the church and state was clear. After Constantine, the church became the recipient of imperial funds and favor rather than persecution. As a result, membership in the church became a mark of social acceptability, and there was a virtual stampede of candidates for the priesthood.[13] This growing friendliness between church and state led to the eventual union of the two.

Even as the Roman Empire began to break down, the pattern begun by Constantine continued. For example, in 496, Clovis, king of the Franks, agreed to accept Christ, as his Christian wife Clotilde wanted, if God gave him victory over his enemies. Victory came, and Clovis was baptized along with three thousand of his still pagan soldiers. It is hard to see their baptism as the baptism of believers or the church to which they belonged as a church of genuine believers. This pattern of "conversion" became common in the spread of Christianity across Europe. Historian Stephen Neill describes the process:

> The record in place after place tends to be much the same. The first bishop was martyred by the savage tribes; his blood then appropriately forms the seed of the church. Initial successes are followed by pagan reactions, but the church comes in again under the aegis of a deeply converted ruler. The initial Christianization is inevitably very superficial, but this is in each case followed by a long period of building, in which the faith becomes part of the inheritance of the people.[14]

---

11. Rodney Stark, *For the Glory of God: How Monotheism Led to Reformations, Science, Witch-Hunts, and the End of Slavery* (Princeton, N.J.; Oxford, U.K.: Princeton University Press, 2003), 33.

12. Robert G. Clouse, Richard V. Pierard, and Edwin M. Yamauchi, *Two Kingdoms: The Church and Culture Through the Ages* (Chicago: Moody, 1993), 109.

13. Stark, *For the Glory of God*, 33–34.

14. Stephen Neill, *A History of Christian Missions* (Baltimore, Md.: Penguin Books, 1964), 90.

Of course, the churches produced under these circumstances were quite different from those we see in the New Testament. In fact, Stark notes how frequently the church incorporated various popular pagan practices: "the Church made it easy to become a Christian—so easy that actual conversion seldom occurred."[15]

Was there no protest to this decline in commitment? Early on there were the Donatists, whose protest called forth the definitive defense of the church as a mixed body by Augustine. The Donatists wanted a church of genuinely holy people, and were disturbed by the ease with which the church received back into its midst priests and bishops who had denied Christ under persecution or handed over copies of the Scriptures. They separated from the Catholic Church in North Africa, seeing themselves as the preservers of the true and holy church. Augustine argued that the holiness of the church is not a present observable holiness found in the lives of the individual members, but a holiness the church has by virtue of its connection with Christ and the Spirit. He highlighted a parable of Jesus that became often used over the centuries, that of the wheat and tares. In this present age, the wheat and tares grow together; only at the harvest time are they separated. In the same way, the church today consists of believers and nonbelievers. God will separate them only at the final judgment. Of course, the problem with this analogy is that in the parable (Matt. 13:24–30), the field in which the wheat and tares grow is the world, not the church. But Augustine's influence prevailed, and the accepted view of the church became that of the mixed body *(corpus permixtum)* of believers and nonbelievers.[16]

Infant baptism became the norm for those in areas where the church was established; large-scale baptisms incorporated whole tribes into the church in pioneer areas. Baptism was seen as effecting the forgiveness of original sin, regardless of whether the individual baptized had genuine faith or not. The idea of limiting membership in the church to believers only was effectively lost.

Augustine also furthered the union of church and state by appealing to the state for help against the Donatists. He saw their separation from the one true and established church as a sin against the unity of the church, a sin so serious that they should be compelled to reunite with Mother church. He took as his proof text Luke 14:23: "make them come in." Since religious unity

---

15. Stark, *For the Glory of God*, 40.
16. For more on this issue, see Willis, *Saint Augustine and the Donatist Controversy.*

was seen as an aid to political unity and stability, states were eager to act to compel religious unity. Luke 14:23 gave them biblical justification.[17]

Throughout the Middle Ages, the church remained a mixed and often immoral body. Those who desired a purer fellowship usually found their way into one of the monastic orders that developed, at least in part in reaction to the declining level of commitment in the church.[18]

On the eve of the Reformation, Europe could be seen as basically religiously unified in the *corpus christianum,* the one body of Christ. But that unity was to be shattered by the Reformation. Yet, in the case of Luther, Zwingli, and Calvin, there was no change in the fundamental idea of the church. Indeed, all three are called *magisterial* Reformers, because all three saw a role for the *magistrate,* or state, in supporting the church. Though Luther in theory wanted to separate church and state, and at times espoused ideas that would seem to lead to a gathered church of believers only, he never followed these ideas to their logical conclusions. In practice he allowed the godly prince to support and establish the true church and embraced the inclusive or territorial church, where all the members of society were members of the church. Zwingli was emphatic that every member of the state must be baptized and thus become a member of the church, accepting the mixed nature of the church as wheat and tares. And though Calvin clashed with the magistrates in Geneva over a number of issues, he never denied that it was both the right and duty of the magistrates to maintain religious uniformity, nor did he ever disavow the idea of the church as a mixed body.

But in Zwingli's Zurich, some emerged with more radical ideas. Though the flashpoint was the baptism of believers only, the fundamental battle was over the nature of the church. People like Conrad Grebel, George Blaurock, and Felix Mantz began to argue for a church of believers only. They had been taught by their pastor, Ulrich Zwingli, that they should derive their doctrine from Scripture alone. They saw Scripture as teaching a church of believers only and baptism for believers only. The response to their ideas was violent persecution from Catholics, Lutherans, Zwinglians, and Calvinists alike.

What was so dangerous in the Anabaptist view that it called forth such a violent response? The Catholics and magisterial Reformers both assumed

---

17. Clouse, Pierard, and Yamauchi, *Two Kingdoms,* 82.

18. Stark, *For the Glory of God,* 40, calls the official church that developed after Constantine the Church of Power, a mixed body whose leaders were often blatantly immoral. As a reaction to the Church of Power, the Church of Piety arose, mainly in the monastic movement.

without question that a political entity could not remain politically unified without religious uniformity. The church and the state were coterminous; that is, they shared the same membership. And the wars of religion that swept Europe in the wake of the Reformation seemed to support their belief. The 1555 Peace of Augsburg was only able to stop these religiously based wars by mandating that the religion of an area would be that of its prince or ruler (under the formula *cuius regio, eius religio,* which is roughly translated, "whose the region, his the religion"). The idea that there could be multiple churches in a state seemed to them to be a route to anarchy. Luther in particular feared that the Anabaptist view would lead to anarchy and political unrest which would hinder the Reformation and the spread of the gospel. As Paul Avis puts it, the magisterial Reformers were more concerned with redefining the center of the church (Christ and the gospel); the Anabaptists emphasized the importance of defining the circumference of the church (believers only).[19] But defining the circumference meant separating the church from the world. This Anabaptist idea was not just seen as bad theology but as political treason that would lead to chaos in countries they influenced and ultimately hinder the spread of the gospel. Thus the Anabaptists suffered horrible persecution, but the idea of the church as a gathered body of believers would not die. It reemerged with the origin of Baptists.

REGENERATE CHURCH MEMBERSHIP
AND BAPTIST ECCLESIOLOGY

While Anabaptists may have exercised some influence in the origin of Baptists, the clearest seed bed for modern Baptists is seen in English Separatism. Separatism developed in the wake of the Elizabethan Settlement of 1558, which gave the church in England basically the doctrine of the magisterial Reformers but much of the ceremony and external trappings of Catholicism. The Puritans were dissatisfied with what they regarded as these halfway measures and sought to further purify the church. But eventually some of these Puritans began to realize that there would be no radical reform under Elizabeth and concluded that they could no longer remain in the Church of England, as it was a hopelessly corrupted and compromised church. They became Separatists, meeting in congregations or what were called conventicles, separated from the state church, despite the fact that such meetings were illegal.

---

19. Paul D. L. Avis, *The Church in the Theology of the Reformers* (Atlanta: John Knox, 1981), 54–55.

Early Baptists emerged in two forms from two of these Separatist conventicles, and inherited from them their concern for a pure church. In this section, we trace the role regenerate church membership played in the origin of Baptists and show its centrality in Baptist thinking about the church.

Regenerate Church Membership and Baptist Origins

John Smyth (c. 1570–1612) was ordained an Anglican priest, but he became dissatisfied with the Anglican Church and became a Puritan and then a Separatist minister.[20] He and Thomas Helwys were members of a Separatist congregation in Gainsborough, London, that fled to Holland in 1607 to avoid the persecution of the English government. By 1609, Smyth had come to three important conclusions. First, since he, as a Separatist, had concluded that the Church of England was hopelessly corrupt and a false church, he had to further conclude that his baptism from the Church of England was a false baptism. Second, as he studied the New Testament, he concluded that it taught the baptism of believers alone. Third, and perhaps most fundamentally, he concluded that the church should be based on the baptism of professed believers. Such a practice was in accord with Scripture and would produce a pure church. Led by Smyth, his Separatist congregation formally dissolved as a church. He first baptized himself, pouring water over his own head. He then baptized Helwys and about forty others, reconstituting the church on the basis of believer's baptism and a church covenant.

Within a short time, Smyth began to think perhaps he had been hasty in baptizing himself. He tried to persuade the church members to repudiate their baptism at his hands and he himself applied to a Mennonite church for baptism. But Helwys and a number of church members did not share Smyth's concerns. They reluctantly parted ways and decided to return to England, despite the persecution they would face. They established the first Baptist church on English soil in 1611, beginning the line of the General Baptist churches, so called because they believed in a general, as opposed to a particular, atonement.[21] Over the next few decades dozens of General Baptist churches developed across England. A consistent theme in their writings,

---

20. For a thorough study of Smyth's life and thought, see Jason K. Lee, *The Theology of John Smyth: Puritan, Separatist, Baptist, Mennonite* (Macon, Ga.: Mercer University Press, 2003).

21. By the early seventeenth century, Calvinist theologians had articulated the view that Christ's death was designed to accomplish atonement for a particular, limited group, the elect. This was known as particular or limited atonement. The opposing view, which was being advocated by James

especially in their confessions of faith, is their belief in regenerate church membership.

Another line of Baptists emerged from a second Separatist conventicle in England. This group is known to historians as the JLJ church, named after the last names of its first three pastors (Henry Jacob, John Lathrop, and Henry Jessey). Around 1630, controversy began to arise in this church over the issue of infant baptism. Some withdrew as early as 1633, but records are inconclusive as to whether they left because they opposed the baptism of infants or whether their opposition was to any baptism performed by the Church of England. By 1638, records are clear that at least six more members withdrew upon their conviction that baptism was for believers alone. These believers held to Calvinist theology and began the line of Particular Baptists.

Despite the emphasis on baptism, the deeper, more fundamental issue for both the General and Particular Baptists concerned those who should compose the church. Leon McBeth says that these early Baptists "sought a church composed of 'visible saints,' that is, true believers, observing the gospel ordinances and obeying the commands of Christ."[22] Purity had been the motive of the Puritans; the Separatists and Baptists took the search for purity further. For Baptists, a pure church had to be composed of believers alone. True believers would obviously want to obey Christ's command and rightly observe the ordinances, and Baptists saw believer's baptism as the only proper way to practice baptism. Further, baptism was the event in which one gave testimony to faith and repentance. If believer's baptism was made the prerequisite to church membership, then regenerate membership would be preserved. Believer's baptism protected regenerate church membership. We see this principle consistently reflected in Baptist thinking about the church. We look first at their confessions of faith.

Regenerate Church Membership in Baptist Confessions of Faith

While still in Holland, Helwys wrote a confession of faith for his church, regarded as the first English Baptist confession of faith. Here is how that confession treats church membership:

Arminius at the very time Smyth and Helwys went to Holland, claimed that Christ died for all in general. This view was called general atonement. Smyth was trained in Calvinist theology, but apparently he and Helwys adopted Arminian views while in Holland.

22. McBeth, *The Baptist Heritage,* 75.

everie Church is to receive in all their members by Baptisme upon the Confession off their faith and sinnes wrought by the preaching off the Gospel, according to the primitive Institucion. Mat. 28.19. And practice, Acts 2.41. And therefore Churches constituted after anie other manner, or off anie other persons are not according to CHRIST'S Testament.[23]

Charles W. Deweese states that this first confession set the standard for virtually all succeeding Baptist confessions as far as the idea of church membership. The elements of confession of sin, profession of faith, and covenant commitment to the church through believer's baptism "characterize descriptions of the church found in practically all Baptist confessions of faith."[24]

As General Baptists spread in England, they formed associations. By 1651, thirty General Baptist churches in the Midlands region of England had formed an association. They produced a confession called "The Faith and Practice of Thirty Congregations, Gathered According to the Primitive Pattern." It shows the developing consensus among these early Baptists concerning who should compose a properly ordered church: "those which received the word of God preached by the Ministrie of the Gospel, and were Baptized according to the Counsel of God, at the same time or day they were of the visible Church of God, Acts 2.41."

In 1660, forty General Baptist church leaders met in London and drew up a confession of faith that was reaffirmed by the General Assembly of General Baptists in 1663, when it began to be called the Standard Confession. It gives the same, characteristically Baptist view of church membership:

the right and only way, of gathering Churches, (according to Christs appointment, *Mat.* 28. 19, 20.) is first to teach, or preach the Gospel, *Mark* 16.16. to the Sons and Daughters of men; and then to *Baptise* (that is in English to *Dip*) in the name of the Father, Son, and holy Spirit, or in the name of the Lord Jesus Christ; such only of them, as profess *repentance towards God, and faith towards our Lord Jesus Christ,* Acts 2.38. Acts 8:12.

---

23. Lumpkin, *Baptist Confessions of Faith*, 120. Lumpkin preserves the archaic spelling and form of the original. All citations from Baptist confessions are from Lumpkin's collection, unless otherwise noted.

24. Charles W. Deweese, *A Community of Believers: Making Church Membership More Meaningful* (Valley Forge, Pa.: Judson Press, 1978), 12.

One final example from early English General Baptists comes from the work produced in 1678, and signed by fifty-four representatives from General Baptist churches in the Midlands area of England. This document, called the Orthodox Creed, was part of an effort to show the Anglicans that the various dissenting groups (Baptists, Presbyterians, and Congregationalists) were all sound and in agreement on the fundamental doctrines of the faith. Nevertheless, on the issue of the proper subjects for church membership, it preserves the Baptist perspective: "none ought to be admitted into the visible church of Christ, without being first baptized; and those which do really profess repentance toward God, and faith in, and obedience to our Lord Jesus Christ, are the only proper subjects of this ordinance, according to our Lord's holy institution, and primitive practice."

In all these examples, we see the concern to preserve regenerate church membership; believer's baptism is important because it is the principal means by which such membership is preserved. Baptism is seen as the act by which one is admitted into church membership, and baptism is limited to those who are regenerate (i.e., those who profess repentance and faith). The centrality of baptism, in both the denominational name and in confessions, stems from the Baptist conviction that the Bible teaches only the baptism of believers and the use of baptism as the means by which regenerate church membership is preserved.

Particular Baptist confessions reveal the same story. In 1644, seven Particular Baptist churches in London produced what came to be one of the most important Baptist statements of all time. William Lumpkin says of the London Confession of 1644, "Perhaps no Confession of Faith has had so formative an influence on Baptist life as this one."[25] Its description of the church clearly describes a church of regenerate members:

> Christ hath here on earth a spirituall Kingdome, which is the Church, which he hath purchased and redeemed to himselfe, as a peculiar inheritance: which Church, as it is visible to us, is a company of visible Saints, called and separated from the world, by the word and Spirit of God, to the visible profession of the faith of the Gospel, being baptized into that faith, and joyned to the Lord, and each other, by mutuall agreement, in the practical injoyment of the Ordinances, commanded by Christ their head and King.

---

25. Lumpkin, *Baptist Confessions of Faith,* 152.

Since this confession was so formative, we may note briefly several ideas and phrases in this article that are particularly descriptive of the Baptist view of the church. There is an emphasis on visibility. The church referred to here is not the invisible church, but local, visible bodies. The lifestyle of the members of these churches is one of visible godliness. They live as believers ought to live. Baptism is the visible act in which one professes faith. Entering the church involves being joined to the Lord and to the other members in a covenant arrangement. Thus, to be a member of a Baptist church, one, first of all, has to be a genuine Christian, living as a Christian ought to live. Next, there has to be visible profession of faith in believer's baptism. Then, finally, the prospective member is expected to enter into covenant with the church.

The Somerset Confession of 1656 goes even further in emphasizing what William Lumpkin calls a "distinctively Baptist" principle: the duty of the church and its leaders to receive into its membership only those who give evidence of regeneration.[26] Note the tone of urgency and importance in this statement: "in admitting of members into the church of Christ, it is the duty of the church, and ministers whom it concerns, in faithfulness to God, that they be careful they receive none but such as do make forth evident demonstration of the new birth, and the work of faith with power."

Two more confessions demand brief mention. The Second London Confession, published initially in 1677, was adopted by Philadelphia Baptists as their confession by 1742, was renamed the Philadelphia Confession, and remained the most influential confession among Baptists in the New World for close to a century. Concerning the church, it states: "All persons throughout the world, professing the faith of the gospel, and obedience unto God by Christ, according unto it; not destroying their own profession by any errors everting the foundation, or unholyness of conversation, are and may be called visible Saints; and of such ought all particular Congregations to be constituted."

Finally, the New Hampshire Confession of 1833 should be noted because it eventually supplanted the Philadelphia Confession in terms of its importance to Baptists in America. Its statement on the church, with only minor changes, was adopted by Southern Baptists in *The Baptist Faith and Message* of 1925, and was essentially retained in the 1963 and 2000 revisions. Here is the central statement of the 1833 New Hampshire Confession on the church: "a visible church of Christ is a congregation of baptized believers, associated by covenant in the faith and fellowship of the Gospel." Three requirements

---

26. Ibid., 202.

for church membership are implied in these brief words. Candidates must be Christians, they must have received believer's baptism, and they must enter into covenant with the church.

These confessions were not just empty words. A fascinating example of how the confessions were applied is seen in the 1773 *Summary of Church Discipline* of the Charleston Baptist Association.[27] The Baptist Church in Charleston, South Carolina, was the first Baptist church in the South, and was to become widely influential. The Charleston Association was the second Baptist association formed in the New World, and developed this document to guide the practice of Baptist churches in their association and across the South. Chapter 3 is devoted to giving explicit instructions on how to receive persons into church membership.[28] It says, "They must be truly gracious persons," meaning that they must have experienced "an entire change of nature." It states that they "should be persons of some competent knowledge of divine and spiritual things," listing as examples some items that would stump many contemporary pastors. Then they must be examined as to their conduct by the congregation. If it is found that "their practice contradicts their profession they are not to be admitted into church membership." Next, they must receive believer's baptism: "It is allowed by all that baptism is essential to church communion and ought to precede it." The church then votes on the one applying for membership, but only after a period of examination to allow church members to become satisfied that the candidate does meet all the requirements. When the church does vote its approval, the candidate is to be acquainted "with the rules and orders of God's house." Only then, as the candidate enters into covenant with the church, does she or he become a member in union and communion with that church.

In the nineteenth century, discussions of the necessity of believer's baptism by immersion, closed communion, church discipline, and the duties of church membership were common among Baptists and seen as their identifying characteristic concerns.[29] Popular Baptist writer James M. Pendleton,

---

27. This document is reprinted in James Leo Garrett Jr., *Baptist Church Discipline* (Nashville: Broadman, 1962), 27–52; and Mark Dever, ed., *Polity: Biblical Arguments on How to Conduct Church Life* (Washington, D.C.: Center for Church Reform, 2001), 113–33.

28. The quotations in this paragraph are taken from chapter 3 of the document found in Garrett, *Baptist Church Discipline*, 34–39, or Dever, *Polity*, 122–25.

29. See *The Baptist Manual* (Philadelphia: American Baptist Publication Society, 1848). The volume is subtitled: "A Selection from the Series of Publications of the American Baptist Publication Society, Designed for the Use of Families; and as an Exposition of the Distinguishing Sentiments of the Denomination." Most of the articles deal with issues related to regenerate church membership.

in a work that went through many printings, listed four reasons why he was a Baptist: the Baptist insistence on believer's baptism, the Baptist acceptance of immersion as the biblically mandated form of baptism, the Baptist adherence to congregational church government, and the Baptist observance of the Lord's Supper as a memorial for local church members only.[30]

Clearly the vision of the church here is vastly different from the *corpus permixtum* of Augustine and the medieval church, or the territorial churches of the magisterial Reformers. It is a distinctively Baptist vision. Central to that vision is an insistence on regenerate church membership. It is either presupposed by or is prerequisite to a number of important aspects of Baptist ecclesiology.

Regenerate Church Membership as the Center of Baptist Ecclesiology

By this point, the reader may be wondering why we have dealt with this issue in so much detail. There are at least three reasons. One is a biblical reason. Regenerate church membership is clearly taught in Scripture. That point needs emphasis because this teaching was absent from church doctrine and practice for more than a thousand years. A second reason is historical. Regenerate church membership was the root issue behind the origin of Baptists and has been a historic distinctive of Baptists. That fact needs to be recognized and remembered. A third reason is theological. As Justice Anderson said, regenerate church membership is the "cardinal point of Baptist ecclesiology, and logically, the point of departure for church polity."[31] Charles W. Deweese argues that the importance of regenerate church membership is even more far-reaching: "A direct relationship exists between a regenerate church membership and five other areas of Baptist life—church covenants, the ordinances, church discipline, evangelism, and small groups."[32] The following is an attempt to show the connection between regenerate church membership and several key Baptist beliefs about the church.

---

30. Pendleton, *Three Reasons Why I Am a Baptist, with a Fourth Reason Added on Communion.* This was an extremely popular book and reflects widely held Baptist views.
31. Anderson, "Old Baptist Principles Reset,"8.
32. Deweese, *A Community of Believers,* 13.

Regenerate Church Membership and Believer's Baptism

First, regenerate church membership is integrally related to the practice that gives Baptists their name, believer's baptism. Contemporary Baptist theologian Stanley Grenz sees believer's baptism as the "logical outworking" of the principle of regenerate church membership. He sees initiation into the people of God as a three-step process: "This process begins with personal faith in Christ as Savior and Lord, is publicly expressed in water baptism, and culminates in formal church membership."[33] Following this process produces a church that matches the phrase often used to describe the church in Baptist confessions of faith, "a congregation of baptized believers."

A. H. Strong sees a similar link between regenerate church membership and believer's baptism: "Regeneration and baptism, although not holding to each other the relation of effect and cause, are both regarded in the New Testament as essential to the restoration of man's right relations to God and to his people. They properly constitute parts of one whole, and are not to be unnecessarily separated."[34] On the other hand, infant baptism, Strong argues, undermines and eventually destroys regenerate church membership.[35] Those baptized as infants are brought within the membership of the church, regardless of whether or not they have experienced regeneration. Over time, nonregenerate membership becomes common. Believer's baptism safeguards regenerate church membership. If baptism is limited to believers only, and if church membership is limited to those baptized, the church will have only believers (i.e., regenerate people) in its membership. These two requirements—baptism for believers only and baptism for church membership—link baptism and regenerate church membership. This link is recognized in Baptist confessions of faith, which, according to Charles W. Deweese, are "at one in stressing the centrality of believer's baptism in creating a regenerate church membership."[36]

Some Baptists today are questioning the validity of requiring believer's baptism for church membership. They think infant baptism is not taught in Scripture but do not think an improper baptism is a sufficient reason to deny church membership to someone who meets all the other qualifications for

---

33. Grenz, *Theology for the Community of God*, 711–12.
34. A. H. Strong, *Systematic Theology* (Philadelphia: Judson Press, 1907), 950.
35. Ibid., 958.
36. Deweese, *A Community of Believers*, 13.

membership.[37] In my own experience as a pastor, I faced this issue with a couple who wanted to join our church but came from a Presbyterian background. Both were obviously committed Christians, but the husband saw no problem with his infant baptism, and didn't think he ought to be required to be baptized again. A very few Baptists have agreed with this man's position and adopted open membership, in which any believer is accepted as a member, baptized or not. But most Baptists have felt biblical teaching clearly indicates that baptism is for believers only, and that while not necessary for salvation, baptism is an important step of obedience that should not be dismissed in such a cavalier fashion. Mark Dever says,

> Baptism, then, is essential for membership in a church because if one were to be admitted by a church, only to refuse such a clear command of Christ, then such an unbaptized person claiming to follow Christ would simply be immediately disciplined until they either decided to follow Christ's commands, or stopped having the church's endorsement of their claim to follow Him. There will never be anything that Jesus calls you to do that will be easier than baptism.[38]

Baptism is the appointed and commanded means for proclaiming publicly that one is a new creature in Christ. Requiring it for church membership thus safeguards regenerate church membership, which is not a minor, but a major issue for Baptists. In the pastoral situation I mentioned above, we went over the biblical teaching with the man in question, and he eventually agreed that baptism is for believers, was baptized, and joined our church. Whether baptism, as practiced by Baptists in North America today, still serves as an effective safeguard to regenerate church membership is a different question, one that we will examine shortly.

Regenerate Church Membership and Congregational Church Government

A second area in which regenerate church membership has been foundational to Baptist ecclesiology has been in congregational government. Virtu-

---

37. This is the position taken by John R. Tyler, *Baptism: We've Got It Right . . . and Wrong* (Macon, Ga.: Smyth & Helwys, 2003) and by several of the contributors to *Proclaiming the Baptist Vision: Baptism and the Lord's Supper,* ed. Walter B. Shurden (Macon, Ga.: Smyth & Helwys, 1999).

38. Mark Dever, *A Display of God's Glory: Basics of Church Structure,* 2nd ed. (Washington, D.C.: Center for Church Reform/9 Marks Ministries, 2001), 52–53.

ally all Baptist defenses of congregationalism make use of the doctrine of the priesthood of all believers. For example, Millard Erickson says congregational church government is preferable because it "takes seriously the principle of the priesthood and spiritual competency of all believers" as well as "the promise that the indwelling Spirit will guide all believers."[39] Stanley Grenz also asserts that the priesthood of all believers leads to the view that it is the responsibility of "the entire company of believers [to] discern Christ's will for his people."[40] The assumption is that, since all the members of the church are regenerate believer-priests, and thus indwelt by the Spirit, they all have both the ability and the responsibility to hear God's voice and discern God's will for the body. But this rests on the assumption that the church will be composed of those who are regenerate, and thus able to receive Christ's guidance. As J. L. Reynolds noted in 1849, congregational government requires what he called "a Bible constituency." He explained: "If churches are composed only of such as give credible evidence of having been taught by the Spirit of God, they may be safely entrusted with the management of their own interests."[41]

Early Baptists added a further element in their articulation of the basis of congregational polity. It was not just that *individual* believers, because regenerate and thus indwelt by the Spirit, could be trusted to participate in church government; they also believed Christ had given a special gift of what they called "church power" to the *corporate* body gathered according to his instructions, that is, to churches composed of regenerate members.

The First London Confession says every church gathered as a company of visible saints "has power given them from Christ for their better well-being." The Orthodox Creed of 1679 spells out how that power given by Christ to the church is also the basis for the authority exercised by leaders of the church: "We believe that the great king, and lawgiver, Christ, the universal and only head of his church, hath given to his visible church, a subordinate power, or authority, for the well-being, ordering, and governing of it . . . the executive part of which derivative power of discipline and government, is committed to his ministers." Thus the supreme authority over the church is Christ; he gives the church a "subordinate power" that is the basis for congregational government; the church delegates the "executive part" of that power to its leaders.

---

39. Erickson, *Christian Theology,* 1096.
40. Grenz, *Theology for the Community of God,* 723–24.
41. J. L. Reynolds, "Church Polity or the Kingdom of Christ, in Its Internal and External Development," reprinted in Dever, ed., *Polity,* 345.

Perhaps the fullest statement of the doctrine of church competence comes from the extremely influential Second London Confession. It states, "To each of these Churches thus gathered, according to his mind, declared in his word, he [Christ] hath given all that power and authority, which is in any way needful, for their carrying on that order in worship, and discipline, which he hath instituted for them to observe; with commands, and rules for the due and right exerting, and executing of that power."

Congregational church government is founded upon and presupposes a regenerate church membership, because only regenerate members are competent to govern themselves. In recent years there has been a small but perceptible movement among some Baptists toward adopting elder rule, fueled, at least in part, by the difficulties experienced by pastors in dealing with unfit congregations. But the problem is not with *congregationalism* as a system of church government, but with particular *congregations* no longer composed exclusively of regenerate members. Congregational church government demands regenerate church membership.

Regenerate Church Membership and Closed Communion

Regenerate church membership is also involved in the Baptist position on the ordinance of the Lord's Supper, or communion. We will discuss the meaning of this rite in detail in chapter 10; the issue at this point is those who may properly participate in it. Historically, most Christian groups have seen baptism as preceding participation in the Lord's Supper. Since most church members from the fifth to the fifteenth centuries were baptized as infants, this order seemed obvious and was never challenged. There was never a movement to give infants communion prior to their baptism.

Baptists retained the historic order of baptism before the Lord's Supper, but differed in who they regarded as baptized. They saw infant baptism as no baptism at all: they required genuine baptism as a prerequisite to church membership and church membership as a prerequisite to the Lord's Supper. Charles W. Deweese notes that a common theology lies behind both ordinances in Baptist thought: "active faith in Jesus Christ must precede participation in the ordinances."[42] Further, baptism must precede the Lord's Supper because the former marks the entrance of a member into a covenant relationship with the church, while the latter is a reaffirmation and extension of

---

42. Deweese, *A Community of Believers*, 41.

that covenant commitment.[43] The commitment cannot be reaffirmed in the Lord's Supper before it is established in baptism.

The most recent Baptist confession, the 2000 revision of *The Baptist Faith and Message,* echoes earlier language in articulating the link between baptism, church membership, and the Lord's Supper. First, in speaking of baptism, it says, "Being a church ordinance, it is prerequisite to the privileges of church membership and to the Lord's Supper."[44] And if the implication of the linking of church membership and the Lord's Supper is missed, the statement specifies that the Lord's Supper is for "members of the church." This position is called closed or close communion, for participation in the Lord's Supper is closed or limited to church members. Some churches limit participation to members of that particular local church, but more often individuals who are visiting and are members of churches "of like faith and order" (i.e., other Baptist churches) are allowed to participate (a practice sometimes called transient communion or closed intercommunion). However, those who are visiting who are members of other churches but have not been properly baptized (i.e., by immersion, as a believer) would fall outside the requirements for communion given in this statement.

What could cause Baptists to adopt such a view that seems to many today to be harsh and unnecessarily restrictive? In part, it is linked to the importance Baptists place on obedience to Christ in biblical baptism. In part, Baptists could claim to be just following the order that almost all churches follow: baptism first, then communion. But there is another reason that explains the link, not just of baptism and the Lord's Supper, but of church membership and the Lord's Supper.

Baptists believe that baptism and the Lord's Supper are given in a special way to the church, and not just to individual Christians. Therefore, they are somewhat uneasy whenever the Lord's Supper is celebrated in a nonchurch context. As Millard Erickson says in his widely used textbook *Christian Theology,* "The Lord's Supper is an ordinance of the church. It cannot be appropriately practiced by separate individuals in isolation."[45]

This conviction that baptism and the Lord's Supper are for the church is deeply rooted in Baptist thinking about the church. Almost every definition of the church in Baptist confessions mentions the ordinances as a constitutive

---

43. Ibid.
44. "The Baptist Faith and Message," 2000 rev. ed. (Nashville: Lifeway Christian Resources, 2000), 14.
45. Erickson, *Christian Theology,* 1121.

part of the church's life. The Second London Confession specifically states that baptism and the Lord's Supper are "appointed by the Lord Jesus the only Law-giver, to be continued in his Church to the end of the world." The New Hampshire Confession of 1833 defines the church as "a congregation of baptized believers, associated by covenant in the faith and fellowship of the Gospel; observing the ordinances of Christ." The Baptist Faith and Message, in its 1925, 1963, and 2000 versions, follows the New Hampshire Confession verbatim, adding only the number two before the word *ordinances.*

Such an association of the ordinances with the church seems especially justified in the case of the Lord's Supper, for it is the rite that proclaims, not just Christ's death, but the church's unity. In 1 Corinthians 10:16, Paul calls the cup and bread of the Lord's Supper a *koinōnia* (fellowship, participation) in the blood and body of Christ, and teaches that in partaking of the Lord's Supper, the Corinthian Christians express their oneness and solidarity with one another. Gordon Fee comments on verse 16: "there can be little doubt that Paul intends to emphasize the kind of bonding relationship of the worshipers with one another that this meal expresses"; he adds that their *koinōnia* (fellowship) was "a celebration of their common life in Christ."[46] Paul goes on in 1 Corinthians 11:17-33 to scold the Corinthians because their celebrations of the Lord's Supper were not occasions for celebrating their unity but revealing divisions (v. 18). He calls on them to recognize "the body of the Lord" (v. 29) when they partake. Fee argues convincingly that "the body of the Lord" refers here to the church, because the Lord's Supper is the meal where they proclaim that they are one body in Christ.[47] Baptists have understood the Lord's Supper along these lines. In their most influential confession, the Second London Confession, the Lord's Supper is called "a bond and pledge of their communion with him [Christ], *and with each other.*"[48] Contemporary Baptist theologian Stanley Grenz says virtually the same thing: "The Lord's Supper is not only a symbol of present community with Christ but also with one another within Christ's fellowship."[49]

How does all this relate to the issue of closed communion and regenerate church membership? If the Lord's Supper is given to the church, and is designed to deepen and express the unity and communion of the members of the body with Christ and with one another, two conclusions seem inescap-

---

46. Fee, *First Epistle to the Corinthians,* 466.
47. Ibid., 563–64.
48. Lumpkin, *Baptist Confessions of Faith,* 291, emphasis added.
49. Grenz, *Theology for the Community of God,* 701.

able. First, the Lord's Supper is surely only for the regenerate, for only they can experience communion with Christ. Second, it seems that the Lord's Supper is only fully appropriate for regenerate people who do in fact have unity and communion with each other, that is, it is for the members of the local church. Only they can affirm in a meaningful way their unity with the other members of the body. It is true that all Christians are members of the universal church, but the Lord's Supper is celebrated in visible, local churches. In such churches, the regenerate members celebrate their common life in Christ and express their unity in devotion and doctrine as they share in the Lord's Supper. Such regular celebrations can be one of the most important means for preserving and maintaining a vital regenerate membership. Charles W. Deweese goes so far as to say, "The heart and vitality of a regenerate church membership hinge heavily on the intensity with which Christians remain true to their baptismal and Lord's Supper vows."[50] It is also for this reason that one of the first steps of church discipline has been to suspend the disciplined person from the Lord's Supper, for he or she is no longer walking in unity and communion with the Lord and the body.

Not all Baptists have agreed with this rationale for closed communion. In recent years many Baptists have adopted open communion, inviting all genuine believers present in their worship to partake of the Lord's Supper, whether they have experienced believer's baptism or not. While this may seem a more inclusive and welcoming position, others defend the traditional view of closed communion, precisely because they see open communion as undermining the Baptist commitment to regenerate church membership.[51] My purpose at this point is not to argue either for open or closed communion, only to point out that the strong tradition supporting closed communion, still reflected in recent Baptist statements of faith and among some contemporary Baptists, is related to their commitment to regenerate church membership, which is central to Baptist ecclesiology.

Regenerate Church Membership and Church Discipline

One criticism of regenerate church membership has been that, since regeneration is an internal, invisible work of God, it cannot be clearly discerned and is thus an impossible or unworkable requirement for church membership.

---

50. Deweese, *A Community of Believers*, 41.
51. See the fuller discussion of open versus closed communion in chapter 10.

But while regeneration may be an internal and invisible work, Baptists historically have insisted that it has external and visible results. They expected those seeking baptism and church membership to be "visible saints" whose lives supported their profession of faith. Baptists have never claimed to be able to know infallibly whether an individual is regenerate or not, but they have claimed that a church can and must judge whether or not a person's life supports or contradicts her or his claim to be regenerate. The Charleston Baptist *Summary of Church Discipline* states, "if their practice contradicts their profession they are not to be admitted to church membership."[52]

For those who at one time gave visible evidence of regeneration and joined the church but later by their actions betrayed their profession of faith, the Baptist remedy was the practice of church discipline. It was necessary if regenerate church membership was to be an ongoing, visible reality, and not just a theory. It was also possible because churches composed of regenerate church members were competent to practice church discipline. We mentioned above how early Baptists believed Christ gave a gift of "church power" to congregations rightly gathered (i.e., composed of regenerate, baptized believers). Virtually every Baptist confession of faith mentions church discipline as one of the proper exercises of this church power. This power is specifically associated with Christ's words in Matthew 16:19 concerning "the keys of the kingdom" and the exercise of the power of those keys in the "binding and loosing" mentioned in Matthew 18:18, which is the most often cited text in discussions of church discipline. The gift of power Christ gave to the church was the gift of the keys, whose power is used in the exercise of church discipline. Some early documents refer to the power to bind and loose as the "Power of the Keys, or to receive in and shut out of the Congregation," and they specifically see that power as being given to the church in Matthew 18.[53] Benjamin Griffith states, "The Lord Jesus Christ hath committed the use and power of the keys, in matters of government, to every visible congregational church."[54] Griffith emphasizes that the practice of church discipline is based, not on some ability in each individual member, but on their status as a properly gathered church of Christ's people, a pure body of regenerate, baptized believers.

Church discipline and regenerate church membership are related in that

---

52. Garrett, *Baptist Church Discipline*, 36; and Dever, ed., *Polity*, 123.

53. Benjamin Keach, "The Glory of a True Church and Its Discipline Display'd," in Dever, ed., *Polity*, 71.

54. Benjamin Griffith, "A Short Treatise Concerning a True and Orderly Gospel Church," in Dever, ed., *Polity*, 99.

the former can be effectively practiced only by a congregation composed of the latter, and that the former is necessary to maintain the genuineness of the latter. This commitment to the practice of church discipline and with it, a commitment to genuinely regenerate church membership, continued well into the nineteenth century among Baptists in America. In his study of nineteenth-century Georgia Baptists, Greg Wills states, "They placed discipline at the center of church life. . . . Not even preaching the gospel was more important to them than the exercise of discipline."[55] Baptist discussions of the church in the eighteenth and nineteenth centuries almost always included discussions of church discipline,[56] because discipline was directly related to regenerate church membership, which was central to the Baptist vision of the church. However, in the latter part of the nineteenth and throughout the twentieth centuries, church discipline declined almost to the point of disappearance among Baptists, with predictable results to regenerate church membership, results we will detail below.

Figure 4.1 attempts to summarize and make evident the connection between regenerate church membership and other major components of a Baptist doctrine of the church, and so justify regenerate church membership as the central Baptist mark of the church.

Regenerate Church Membership . . .
- is preceded and safeguarded by believer's baptism.
- is the basis for congregational church government.
- is reflected and preserved in the Baptist practice of closed communion.
- is a prerequisite for effective church discipline and is protected by church discipline.

Figure 4.1: Regenerate Church Membership as Central to Baptist Ecclesiology

---

55. Gregory A. Wills, *Democratic Religion: Freedom, Authority, and Church Discipline in the Baptist South 1785–1900* (New York: Oxford University Press, 1997), 8. Wills shows that in this era Baptists disciplined a higher percentage of their members than non-Baptists, and Southern Baptists disciplined a higher percentage than their Baptist brothers and sisters in the North.

56. All ten of the "historic Baptist documents" written from 1697 to 1874 and included by Dever in *Polity* deal with the topic of church discipline.

Though regenerate church membership may justly be called the Baptist mark of the church historically and theologically, in practice the overwhelming majority of Baptist churches in North America today give little evidence of such a practice of membership. How that mark disappeared and how it may be regained is the topic of the following chapter.

CHAPTER 5

WHERE WE WENT WRONG AND HOW WE CAN GET RIGHT

Returning to Faithfulness

THOUGH OFFICIAL STATEMENTS STILL affirm the doctrine of regenerate church membership, statistics indicate a different reality for the great majority of Baptist churches in North America. For example, the largest Baptist denomination in the United States, the Southern Baptist Convention, reported a total of 43,465 churches in their convention as of 2004, with a total of 16,267,494 members. But of those more than sixteen million members, only 6,024,289, or 37 percent, were on average present for the Sunday morning worship service in those churches. Certainly every church has members who are sick or traveling every weekend, but most of the more than ten million absent members are physically well and in town but choose not to gather with God's people and remain absent for years at a time. Yet they remain members in good standing at most Baptist churches. Only God knows their hearts, but they are not living like regenerate believers.

Moreover, the conduct of Baptist church members outside of church attendance is also alarming. Reports find almost no difference in the rate of divorce among Baptists and the culture as a whole. Many Baptists are enmeshed in alcoholism, addiction to pornography, spousal and child abuse, adultery, and virtually every other evil the world offers. One can live a life with no visible difference from the surrounding nonregenerate world and be a member in good standing of a Baptist church. Beyond coming forward at a church service and being baptized at some point in one's life, there are no requirements for ongoing membership in most Baptist churches. Maintaining one's membership in the Rotary or Kiwanis Club is more demanding; they require members to pay dues!

All this invites the disdain of the world. If someone says that the local Baptist church is full of hypocrites who claim to be good church members but live no differently than those outside the church, there is little Baptists can offer in the way of reply. Baptist pastors and church leaders know that if they have a membership of six hundred, rarely are more than two hundred present. And of the four hundred absent, most have been chronically absent for years. In fact, in some churches, there may be dead persons still on the membership roster as members in good standing! Regenerate church membership cannot be seriously maintained as characterizing most Baptist churches in North America today.

How could something that was once so central to Baptist thinking about the church have been so thoroughly abandoned? A variety of explanations from a number of perspectives are possible.

THE DISAPPEARANCE OF REGENERATE CHURCH MEMBERSHIP

From the perspective of social scientists, Baptists offer a good example of the tendency of what they call "sects" to become "churches." The classic work of Ernst Troeltsch, *The Social Teaching of the Christian Churches,* described sects as those groups that take a separatistic and negative approach to the surrounding culture, while churches are those that take a more inclusive, accommodating approach.[1] As Rodney Stark puts it, sects are characterized by "high-intensity" faith; they ask a lot of their members. Over time, later generations tend not to share the intensity of earlier generations. They tend to move toward assimilation with society and economic advancement, meaning they have more to lose from a real commitment to a countercultural faith. Also, leaders of such groups seem to believe that by reducing the level of intensity of commitment, their groups can grow more rapidly.[2] The desire for growth can easily overshadow the desire for purity among many pastors and church leaders, especially in a culture and a denomination that has come to value growth as the greatest, if not the only measure of a church's success.

Some aspects of this analysis do seem to fit what happened among Bap-

---

1. Ernst Troeltsch, *The Social Teaching of the Christian Churches,* trans. Olive Wyon (London: Allen & Unwin; New York: Macmillan, 1950).

2. Stark, *For the Glory of God,* 24.

tists, especially in the South. Christine Heyrman, in a study of nineteenth-century Baptists, Methodists, and Presbyterians in the South, shows that the percentage of southerners who were evangelical church members was quite low in the early years of that century and got larger only as churches relaxed their standards. She concludes that the Bible Belt in the South began, not with a Christian conquest of the culture, but with an adaptation to the culture.[3] But cultural assimilation has always been a struggle for God's people, from the Old Testament Jews who were told not to intermarry, to the Catholics who adopted and "baptized" many of the practices of the pagan tribes they conquered, to modern North American Baptists who easily fit into contemporary society.

Likewise, it is generally recognized that Christians, as individuals and as denominations, tend to rise socioeconomically as they work hard, become less wasteful, and seek to provide better opportunities for their children. But, as Jesus said, "it is hard for a rich man to enter the kingdom of heaven" (Matt. 19:23). Thus a declining rate of growth or commitment tends to accompany a socioeconomic rise.

But alongside the social science explanation there is also an evident theological or ecclesiological explanation. We noted earlier that believer's baptism and church discipline served to protect regenerate church membership. Regenerate church membership began to disappear as these two safeguards were relaxed.

We noted earlier the very strong statements in Baptist confessions of faith concerning the necessity of visible evidence of regeneration prior to baptism and church membership. This indicates something of the seriousness with which they took baptism. It was regarded as an adult decision, not to be made lightly. It was said of Richard Furman's ministry at First Baptist Church of Charleston (1787–1825) that in dealing with children the "greatest care was exercised in guarding against premature professions of piety."[4] But over the years the average age for baptisms among Baptists in North America has steadily declined. Prior to 1966, Southern Baptists did not even keep statistics on the number of preschoolers baptized, but denominational statisticians apparently became aware by then that it was a growing trend. Over the

---

3. Christine Leigh Heyrman, *Southern Cross: The Beginnings of the Bible Belt* (New York: Alfred A. Knopf, 1997), 27.

4. This statement is taken from an anonymous biography of Richard Furman, cited in Garrett, *Baptist Church Discipline*, 21.

next twenty-three years, they saw the number of preschool baptisms triple.[5] It is hard to see how these preschool children could have convinced earlier Baptists that they were in fact regenerate or competent to take on the duties and responsibilities of church membership. For example, among the duties of church members, the *Summary of Church Discipline* lists things like contributing to the financial support of the church's ministry, praying for the other members, visiting the sick, and using their gifts to serve the church.[6] It is hard to see preschoolers fulfilling these duties.

In 1978, Charles W. Deweese noted weak baptismal practices as one of the trends leading Baptists toward a nonregenerate membership. He specified lack of prebaptismal training, the tendency to treat the actual baptism event too lightly, and the movement toward baptizing ever younger children as three problem areas.[7]

The validity of many contemporary baptisms was further challenged by a 1993 study done by the Home Mission Board of the Southern Baptist Convention. In their study of adult baptisms (those over eighteen years of age) in Southern Baptist churches in 1993, they found that the majority of adult baptisms (60 percent) could be called rebaptisms. Some were baptisms of those who had previously been baptized as infants, but 36 percent of these adult baptisms were of those who had been previously baptized in Southern Baptist churches. When asked why they were seeking rebaptism, many said that it was because they had not been regenerate believers when they were first baptized.[8] That means that either these individuals were unusually deceptive or that some churches and pastors baptized these individuals without clear assurance that they were baptizing believers. Many individuals struggle with this issue. They were baptized as children but see no evidence of genuineness in their relationship with Christ until much later. They wonder if they have received believer's baptism or not.

By way of contrast, Baptists in other parts of the world do not have this problem. In Romania, while there is no rule, no one would think of asking for baptism prior to the age of fourteen. The same is true of many Baptist groups in Africa and Asia. I was struck by the practices of Baptist churches I saw in

5. See "Distributions of Baptism by Age and Location," *Quarterly Review* 27, no. 3 (1967): 44; and "Number of Baptisms by Age Divisions—1989," *Quarterly Review* 50, no. 4 (1990): 21.

6. Garrett, *Baptist Church Discipline*, 40–42.

7. Deweese, *A Community of Believers*, 14–15.

8. Phillip B. Jones et al., *A Study of Adults Baptized in Southern Baptist Churches, 1993* (Atlanta: Home Mission Board of the Southern Baptist Convention, 1995), 5.

Brazil. Upon profession of faith, a new convert was placed in a new convert's class for from six to thirteen weeks. The central purpose of this class was to make as sure as humanly possible that the individuals involved had understood the gospel and were making valid professions of faith. After the class, the next step in the process of preparation for baptism was speaking to the congregation. Candidates described their experience of conversion and answered questions from the pastor and congregation concerning what they believed about Christ, their experience of conviction of sin, and their understanding of the gospel. Only then did the congregation vote to baptize the individuals. The contrast with the lack of care concerning baptismal candidates in Baptist churches in North America is striking. Regenerate church membership began to disappear when Baptist churches in North America began to baptize and bring in members who gave no visible evidence of regeneration.

The second protection to regenerate church membership, church discipline, began to disappear from North American Baptist churches in the latter part of the nineteenth century. Studies by Greg Wills and Stephen Haines concur in seeing the decline beginning then; Haines adds that the decline accelerated in the twentieth century.[9] Haines sees individualism, a more optimistic view of humanity, and a general "secularizing of values and procedures" in American churches, along with a revulsion against harsh discipline, as among the causes of the decline in discipline.[10] Wills also sees individualism as undermining the authority of the congregation and business methods "replacing the pursuit of purity with the quest for efficiency."[11] But he also notes the unconscious nature of the process: "No one publicly advocated the demise of discipline. . . . It simply faded away, as if Baptists had grown weary of holding one another accountable."[12]

With no serious consideration of baptismal candidates, many nonregenerate individuals have been baptized and ushered in the front door into Baptist church membership. With church discipline all but extinct, the back door is firmly closed, and those persistently acting in nonregenerate ways are retained on church rolls. The result is that a claim to regenerate

9. Wills, *Democratic Religion*; and Stephen Haines, "Southern Baptist Church Discipline, 1880–1939," *Baptist History and Heritage* 20 (1985): 14–27.

10. Haines, "Southern Baptist Church Discipline," 25–26.

11. Wills, *Democratic Religion*, 9, see also 139–40.

12. Ibid., 9.

church membership is no longer credible for most Baptist churches in North America.[13]

TOWARD THE RECOVERY OF REGENERATE CHURCH MEMBERSHIP

No doubt any attempt to move toward a recovery of membership that is meaningful, that involves genuine commitment and evidence of regeneration, is fraught with dangers. Is such a recovery even a possibility for Baptist churches in North America today? Could one not argue that earlier Baptists were too exclusive and unnecessarily turned people away? Would people not be offended and driven away from Baptist churches today if they were to return to serious questioning of those coming for baptism and a regular practice of church discipline? Is this even a battle worth fighting? These are all serious questions that deserve careful consideration. Any pastor attempting changes in these areas should move slowly, and build trust with his people and their understanding of biblical truth as he proceeds. Particularly, church discipline as redemptive rather than punitive should be clearly explained. Nonetheless, it seems that the time is ripe for change in this area. There is in fact anecdotal evidence of a small but encouraging number of churches adopting new member's classes, requiring commitment to a church covenant, and beginning to practice church discipline.[14] There are four reasons why recovering meaningful membership is a battle worth fighting. After looking at these reasons, we will explore three practical suggestions for beginning such a recovery in a local church.

First, the recovery of meaningful church membership should be the number one priority of Baptist churches today because of the effect it would have on our corporate witness. Imagine being able to respond to the common excuse, "Your church is full of hypocrites," by saying, "Well, we're not perfect

---

13. It is interesting to note that along with the crumbling of regenerate church membership, the weakening of believer's baptism, and the disappearance of church discipline, we are also seeing a widespread rejection of closed communion and the questioning of congregational church government, giving further evidence that all these elements are interrelated.

14. One instructive example is Capitol Hill Baptist Church in Washington, D.C. They invite pastors and church leaders to come for a weekend conference in which they describe the process of recovery of regenerate church membership in their congregation and allow visitors to observe their membership classes and member's meetings and talk with staff about the issues related to regenerate church membership. For more information on such weekends, see www.9MARKS.org.

but we are committed to following Christ," knowing that the lives and minis-tries of church members backed that up. Rather than driving people away, meaningful membership could be the most attractive witness a church could offer. Greg Wills notes that from 1790 to 1860, when Baptist churches main-tained high rates of discipline, they also maintained high rates of growth, growing at a rate twice that of the population, while in later years, as their discipline fell, so did their growth.[15] Could the recovery of meaningful mem-bership allow the light of the gospel to shine through us with greater clarity and beauty? Rick Warren and Mark Dever, though in quite different con-texts, both speak of the evangelistic impact of a congregation comprised of people whose lives are being changed.[16] Our corporate witness would be greatly enhanced by the recovery of meaningful membership.

Second, our corporate health would be strengthened. How can the church live the life we are commanded to live (loving one another, praying for one another, encouraging one another) if most of our people live like they are unregenerate? How can our churches govern themselves responsibly if mem-bers are not walking in fellowship with Christ and one another? Ephesians 4:16 and Colossians 2:19 indicate that the body grows only when each part does its work, but if parts of the body are not regenerate, they will tear down the body rather than build it up.

A third reason for doing the hard work involved in recovering meaning-ful membership is the potential for awakening literally millions of lost church members. At the present, chronically absent church members whose lives give no evidence of regeneration are ignored by most churches. Many may be trusting in their church membership to get them to heaven. A recovery of meaningful church membership would involve a challenge to such members. Sooner or later, they would have to be confronted with the fact that they are not living as followers of Christ and members of his body should. The ad-ministration of loving but firm church discipline, after repeated attempts to bring these individuals to repentance, would be the most serious way a church

---

15. Wills, *Democratic Religion*, 36.

16. Mark Dever, "Pastoral Success in Evangelistic Ministry: The Receding Horizon," in *Reforming Pas-toral Ministry: Challenges for Ministry in Postmodern Times,* ed. John H. Armstrong (Wheaton, Ill.: Crossway, 2001), 255. Dever states, "If you can get a reputation in the community as a church in which people's lives are actually changed, you will begin to see some amazing things." Rick Warren, *The Purpose Driven Church: Growth Without Compromising Your Message and Mission* (Grand Rap-ids: Zondervan, 1995), 247, concurs: "What *really* attracts large numbers of unchurched to a church is changed lives—a lot of changed lives" (emphasis in original).

could attempt to awaken them to their perilous condition. Such an action would be far more loving than the current policy of allowing such members to continue in an apparently lost state without a word of warning.

Finally, recovering meaningful church membership would honor Christ. Ephesians 5:25–27 describes how Christ died for the church, to present her to himself as a holy, radiant church. If such was the goal of Christ's cross-bearing, such must also be the goal of our ministries. Christ is honored when his bride is holy, but that cannot be as long as many of the members making up that bride live like lost people. The Charleston *Summary of Church Discipline* says that when churches allow unconverted people to crowd into them, they "make the church of Christ a harlot."[17] Christ is honored when churches are composed of people whose church membership means first of all a genuine, vital commitment to Christ, and second, a commitment to the people of that local body. Christ is honored when church membership is meaningful.

How can regenerate church membership become a reality in a church with a membership of six hundred but an average attendance of two hundred, and where half of the four hundred absentees have been absent so long that only a few senior citizens even know who they are? How could a pastor or church leader begin to inculcate the idea of meaningful church membership? Where could he start? Let's look at three suggestions.[18]

---

1. Reorganize the church around commitment to a church covenant.
2. Reform the process of baptism and church membership to involve some genuine examination of the candidate's spiritual condition.
3. Reinstitute a carefully explained process of redemptive church discipline.

Figure 5.1: How to Recover Regenerate Church Membership

---

17. Garrett, *Baptist Church Discipline,* 36, or Mark Dever, *Polity,* 122.

18. For more specific suggestions on recovering regenerate church membership, see Mark Dever and Paul Alexander, *The Deliberate Church: Building Biblically in a Haphazard Age* (Wheaton, Ill.: Good News/Crossway), especially section 1, called "Gathering the Church," which deals with church covenants, new member's classes, church discipline, and numerous related topics in a practical, nuts and bolts fashion.

Returning to Church Covenants

Charles W. Deweese notes that Baptists throughout their history "have written and used hundreds, and perhaps thousands, of church covenants."[19] These documents are different from confessions of faith in that conduct is emphasized more than doctrine, though doctrine is often mentioned secondarily. For all their variety, covenants tend to have a remarkable similarity in terms of contents and purposes. Deweese says that a commitment to church fellowship, an acceptance of the authority of the church's discipline, a pledge to support the worship of the church and personal devotion, and a commitment to mutual care for one another appear in virtually all Baptist church covenants.[20]

Furthermore, one of the major purposes for the use of church covenants is precisely to safeguard regenerate church membership. In the past, churches constituted around the commitments involved in adopting a church covenant. Becoming a member involved "owning" the church covenant. Deweese comments, "Baptists have stated forcefully and repeatedly that the covenant idea is essential to the nature, definition, and constitution of a church."[21] Church covenants did not require perfection; indeed, they required nothing that is not explicitly or implicitly commanded in Scripture, but they did make clear that church membership involved a commitment that any regenerate person should accept.

In the late nineteenth and early twentieth centuries the practice of covenanting declined. A number of factors contributed to this decline, among them the sacrifice of the ideal of regenerate church membership to the ideal of numerical growth, the general secularization of American society, and the unwillingness of church members to hold one another accountable. Deweese also suggests that Baptists may have been the victims of the extreme popularity of the 1853 church covenant authored by J. Newton Brown, which was widely adopted by Baptist churches in America (see fig. 5.2). Deweese states:

> Covenantal decline also likely resulted from a growing tendency of churches simply to adopt standardized, uniform covenants printed

---

19. Deweese, *Baptist Church Covenants*, v. In this volume Deweese prints seventy-nine of these covenants as a representative sample.
20. Ibid., 55.
21. Ibid., 97.

in external sources, rather than to write their own individualized statements. Throughout Baptist history covenantal value and dynamic
have correlated closely with the degree of input that churches have
exercised in arriving at the covenants they have used.[22]

He adds, "Baptist presses and publications which have sponsored model covenants have apparently contributed to the weakening of congregational discipline by making it unnecessary for churches to think through, struggle with,
and write down covenantal responsibilities to which they are willing to commit themselves."[23]

A church seeking to recover a meaningful membership of regenerate individuals should begin by discussing among themselves who and what they
are as a church, and what type of commitment Scripture calls them to make
to one another as a body of believers.[24] These discussions would move the
church toward adoption of a church covenant. Several examples of church
covenants are included at the end of this chapter, but churches would do well
to personalize and individualize them, so that the congregation as a whole
owns it as *their* covenant, not one imposed upon them.

Then, when the church has developed a covenant that expresses their commitment to one another and to Christ as his church, the church would vote
to dissolve the present membership and reconstitute around those who sign
their names to the church covenant.[25] This would be preceded by several an-
nouncements of the proposed signing day. The pastor should send a letter to
every member of the congregation with the proposed covenant and the decision of the church to reconstitute around it.

There is a biblical precedent for such action in Nehemiah 9–10. After a time
of renewal and confession in Nehemiah 8–9, Nehemiah 9:38 records the decision of God's people: "we are making a binding agreement, putting it in writing, and our leaders, our Levites and our priests are affixing their seals to it."

---

22. Ibid., 36.

23. Ibid., 89.

24. Deweese, *A Community of Believers*, 28–40, gives a helpful outline of some of the practical steps to
take in the preparation and implementation of a church covenant.

25. Alan Neely, "Church Membership: What Does It Mean? What Can It Mean?" in Shurden, ed., *Proclaiming the Baptist Vision*, 47, commends the example of a Mennonite church that erased their
membership list every three years and asked those who wanted to continue in the fellowship of the
church to sign their name, indicating the renewal of their commitment. I would only change their
practice by making it annual rather than triennial.

After listing all the leaders by name, the text states that the rest of the people joined with them (10:28–29). Their "binding agreement," or covenant, specified the areas of their lives that needed specific commitments. In their context, the key issues were avoiding intermarriage with the surrounding pagans, conducting no business on the Sabbath, and supporting the temple worship (10:30–39). Contemporary covenants would list the areas of commitment contemporary churches see as central to their life together. The people in Nehemiah's day concluded with a summary statement of their commitment: "We will not neglect the house of our God" (10:39). Adopting a church covenant is one way God's people today can say, "We will not neglect our church."

This biblical example gives a beautiful model for contemporary church covenants. The covenant would be their "binding agreement," specifying areas of their commitment to Christ and one another. At the conclusion of a service celebrating the adoption of the covenant, the church leadership could be invited to come and sign their names to a roster attached to the church covenant. Then all who were willing to accept the covenant responsibilities would be invited to come and sign. The same document and roster would be taken to shut-in members who were not able to come but are still committed to the church. Those who sign would become the church's membership. Part of the process for adding subsequent members would involve the signing of the covenant, and existing members would be asked to sign their commitment afresh every year. It could become an annual church renewal event.

Churches should consider this approach for three reasons. First, it is biblical. It follows a biblical pattern and calls for a biblical commitment. Second, it deals with the huge backlog of absentee members in a practical way. Rather than having the church sort through and make decisions who to retain and who to purge from their membership, this procedure places the burden on the individual. The church does not "kick out" or "excommunicate" anyone. It does, however, respect the decision of individuals who choose to not come and sign the church covenant. They have chosen not to be members of the church. Third, it will go a long way toward accomplishing the goal of restoring a regenerate membership. It is not sufficient alone, but it is a good starting point.

What about those who do not come and sign the covenant? In most churches, their number will be considerable.[26] Those individuals should

---

26. For example, when the First Baptist Church of Union, Missouri, reorganized around the signing of a church covenant in 1997, their membership immediately dropped from more than 1,200 to 333, but then it began to grow.

become the object of the congregation's love and concern. They should be visited to ascertain why they did not come. Efforts should be made to reclaim them, but not on any terms. They should be welcomed into Christ's church on Christ's terms, which include commitment to Christ and to his people, which is what the church covenant expresses. Many of these people may not be saved, but it is not the job of the church to pronounce upon that. God alone knows the heart. What the church can and should say is that a Christian who loves Christ and wants to be part of his people should have no trouble committing to the church covenant, and that the church is deeply concerned over the spiritual state of all those who do not manifest a commitment to Christ. Indeed, it is the duty of the church to warn such people of the danger they are in. But it would be less than honest to not acknowledge that chronic church absentees are some of the hardest people to reach. Many, perhaps most, will not respond to efforts to win them. They will simply choose to no longer be part of the church. In truth, they haven't been members since they dropped out. Their decision not to sign simply recognizes what the reality has been.

The adoption of a church covenant, with annual renewal, is a good start, but it is not the only step needed to recover and preserve regenerate church membership.

Reforming Baptism and Church Membership

Early Baptists had a robust confidence that the church was competent to examine a prospective baptismal candidate and find evidence of regeneration prior to administering baptism and welcoming the baptized believer into the church's membership. Today, many churches and no doubt many Christians do not share that confidence. They fear the development of a judgmental attitude that repels those who may be seeking Christ and drives people away, and they know all too well that all human judgment is fallible. Yet there are some measures churches may take to be responsible as well as hospitable in baptizing and welcoming new members.

The first such measure would be a clear separation between welcoming someone who applies for membership and the official granting of membership itself. In most Baptist churches in North America today, what happens when someone comes forward at the end of a service and asks for membership? There may be a few moments of whispered conversation but after a few perfunctory questions the person is presented for a church vote. The problem is the church members have no basis for voting on such a person. No one would think of opposing his or her request for membership and so the vote becomes a meaningless gesture, a relic of an earlier time when churches took membership more seriously. A better approach would be to welcome such a person and rejoice with her or him over the decision made, whether it is to transfer membership or to seek baptism and then church membership, but to delay a vote on the request for membership until a later time, when other requirements for membership have been met.

One such requirement could be the completion of a class. Such classes, called variously "new Christian's classes" or "new member's classes," are becoming more common in Baptist churches today and bear some resemblance to the catechumenate of the early church, a time when new converts were taught the basic elements of the Christian faith before and as preparation for baptism.[27] Among many Baptist groups outside of North America such classes are standard.[28] They serve several important purposes. They provide a natural context for new prospective members to meet others and develop relationships. They provide an opportunity to introduce these individuals to the various ministries of the church. Most important, they provide a context for discussion of each individual's spiritual condition, for a key component of such classes should be a review of each person's understanding of the gospel. Even those coming from other churches need to be given the opportunity of sharing how they came to know Christ and how they understand the gospel, for in some churches the gospel is not clearly explained. For those coming as new converts and requesting baptism, such a review of the gospel is essential. How serious are we about practicing believer's baptism if we do not even ask those seeking baptism if they are believers? And, sadly, in today's theological climate, we need to be a bit more specific, asking them what they believe and how they came to know Christ.

Once prospective new members have completed this class, those who conducted the class can recommend admitting them for baptism and/or church

---

27. Deweese, *A Community of Believers*, 43–48, sees such "prebaptismal classes" as vitally important for regenerate church membership. See the fascinating comparison of these classes to the early church's catechumenate by Clinton E. Arnold, "Early Church Catechesis and New Christians' Classes in Contemporary Evangelicalism," *Journal of the Evangelical Theological Society* 47, no. 1 (March 2004): 39–54.

28. For example, during three years as a missionary in Brazil, I encountered no Baptist church that did not have a new convert's class.

membership, and based on such a recommendation, members can vote with
some confidence. I know of cases where prospective new members were converted in the new member's class, and other cases where prospective new
members came to understand the gospel for the first time in the new member's
class and rejected it. They had responded emotionally to a gospel message in
a worship service, but when they understood the commitment involved in
trusting Christ, they were unwilling. It is far better to know and reject the
gospel, than to be baptized and think one is somehow safe without ever coming to an understanding of the gospel or what it means to place saving faith
in Christ.

An objection often raised to such classes, especially in the case of those
who are new converts and seeking baptism, is the claim that the New Testament pattern was baptism immediately following conversion, with no intervening class. That is in fact the case on most of the occasions recorded in the
book of Acts (2:41; 8:12; 8:36–38, 48; 16:33), but in some cases the time element is not clear (such as in 18:8) or baptism is not mentioned in connection
with conversion at all (4:4; 5:14; 13:48; 14:1; 14:21). In any case, there is no
command regarding the immediacy of baptism anywhere in the New Testament. By the second century, the early church began to institute the
catechumenate to ensure that those they baptized were indeed converted.[29]
That is still the motivation behind new member's classes.

Caution is especially appropriate in the case of very young children. Anyone who works with children knows that five-year-olds will readily ask Jesus
into their hearts, but until very recently Baptists would never have considered baptizing them. Believer's baptism was seen as virtually synonymous
with adult baptism. To request baptism was regarded as a decision requiring
a fair degree of maturity. For a church to grant it was to welcome that person
into the responsibilities of church membership, which would include participation in the governance of the church, which seems inappropriate in the
case of preschoolers. Overseas most Baptists delay baptism until the teenage
years, but it is difficult to avoid arbitrariness in setting any specific minimum
age for baptism.

Some churches have taken a step in the right direction in requiring a class
before baptism, and limiting that class to those seven years of age and older.
For example, this is the practice of the First Baptist Church of Orlando, Florida.
This should be accompanied by clear teaching that God can save any child

---

29. Arnold, "Early Church Catechesis," 42.

whenever he chooses, and that baptism is in no way necessary for salvation. So if some children are saved before the age of seven, delaying their baptism will not somehow endanger their salvation. Instead, it will give their decision time to take root and grow, so that when they are baptized, it will be more meaningful for them. It should also reduce the growing number of rebaptisms, those performed when church members realize later in life that their baptism as a child was not, in fact, believer's baptism.[30] It should also be another helpful step toward recovering regenerate church membership.

Others think even seven is too young an age for baptism. While he states that setting an arbitrary age for conversion is a mistake, William Hendricks also says, "It is highly doubtful that many children below the age of nine can express or have experienced despair for sin as radical separation from God. One cannot be 'saved' until he is aware he is 'lost.'"[31] This raises the issue of the age of accountability or age of moral responsibility. In Judaism, that age was twelve. At the ceremony of the *bar mitzvah*, a child assumed adult spiritual responsibilities.[32] That may be the context for Paul's statement in Romans 7:9: "Once I was alive apart from law, but when the commandment came, sin sprang to life and I died." The commandment came to a twelve-year-old Jewish boy at his bar mitzvah, implying that twelve may be the age of accountability. Jesus first began to manifest his special calling at age twelve (Luke 2:41–50). Furthermore, in groups that practice infant baptism, the ceremony of confirmation is usually around the age of twelve. Finally, most developmental psychologists agree that children reach full moral decision-making ability around the age of twelve. For these reasons, some see twelve as the appropriate minimum age for baptism. This is the course taken by Grace Community Church of Sun Valley, California, whose pastor is the well-known John MacArthur. They believe baptizing a child who is not genuinely regenerate does him a disservice and poses a danger if that child takes his baptism as proof that he is saved. Therefore, they think it is wiser to "wait for more significant evidence

---

30. Art Murphy, children's pastor at First Baptist Church, Orlando, Florida, says, "We have found that most children who make that decision [of baptism] under the age of 7 tend to need to make another decision later," referring to rebaptisms. See Art Murphy, "Leading a Child to Christ," *SBC Life* (June–July 1998), 9.

31. William L. Hendricks, *A Theology for Children* (Nashville: Broadman, 1980), 249.

32. See David Alan Black, *The Myth of Adolescence* (Yorba Linda, Calif.: Davidson Press, 1999), 59–67, for a discussion of the important transitions that occur at the age of twelve. Black draws upon the Jewish traditions surrounding the *bar mitzvah*, the account of Jesus in the temple at the age of twelve, the findings of developmental psychologists such as Piaget and Erikson, and the study of stages of faith by James Fowler.

of lasting commitment," and for "evidence of regeneration that is independent of parental control."[33] Their practice is to wait until a child is at least twelve to look for such evidence.[34]

Whatever choice a church makes about the appropriate age for baptism, our concern here is to encourage a thoughtful approach to receiving children as candidates for baptism and church membership, one that takes seriously the Baptist commitment to believer's baptism and regenerate church membership.

So what does a pastor do when five-year-old Johnny comes forward with his parents during the invitation? Certainly he should pray with the child and his parents, but say to them and the congregation something like this: "We want to celebrate with Johnny and his parents. Today he is taking an important step in his relationship with Jesus. We're going to talk with Johnny and his parents more about this, and at the appropriate time we will be presenting him as a candidate for baptism and church membership. Today we invite you to come by and congratulate him and his parents on the step he has taken today." This affirms the child and allows the church to congratulate him and celebrate his decision, but does not prematurely conclude that the decision made has moved the child from lost to saved, nor does it commit the church to baptizing the child.

But even with these precautions that would seek to make as sure as humanly possible that the church only brings in regenerate members, there will still be a need to deal with members who either are brought in mistakenly in an unregenerate state or begin sometime after joining to live like an unregenerate person. Therefore, there will need to be a third step to restoring meaningful, regenerate church membership.

Redemptive Church Discipline

A strong emphasis on church discipline was a notable characteristic of early Anabaptists and Baptists. It persisted well into the nineteenth century

---

33. Grace Community Church, *Evangelizing Children* (Sun Valley, Calif.: Grace Books International, 2003), 6. Also available via the Internet at www.gracechurch.org/ministries.

34. It is also interesting to note that in a 2001 survey of two thousand worshipers in Southern Baptist churches, of those who affirmed that they had experienced conversion, more indicated that they had experienced conversion at the age of twelve than at any other year. Indeed, the number who experienced conversion at that age were more than twice the number for the ages of eleven and thirteen combined. See "Research Report: Conversion and Witnessing Among Southern Baptists" (Alpharetta, Ga.: North American Mission Board, SBC, 2002), 2, available at http:// www.namb.net/research.

and is still present in Baptist churches outside North America. It appeared pervasively in their confessions of faith as a key exercise of congregational government. It was widely practiced in their churches to maintain purity. It was a popular subject of discussion among their theologians. However, as we noted above, church discipline among Baptist churches in North America declined in the late nineteenth century and nearly disappeared in the twentieth century. It has faced some of the same obstacles as regenerate church membership as a whole: the overall secularization of American society, American individualism, the fear of appearing judgmental, and the desire for increasing numbers. Redemptive church discipline and regenerate church membership have fallen together. Yet there is a strong biblical basis for church discipline[35] and an evident need for it in our churches. Polls on virtually every social index show little difference between the church and the world. Nineteenth-century Baptist theologian John L. Dagg said perceptively over a hundred years ago, "It has been remarked, that when discipline leaves a church, Christ goes with it."[36] How might pastors go about reinstituting discipline in churches today? In a word, they should do so *carefully*.[37]

Restoring church discipline should not be the first step a pastor takes upon entering a church. The people need to see and know that he loves people, lest they think his ideas about church discipline are the product of a hateful heart. He needs to lay a biblical foundation for church discipline by preaching and teaching on the texts dealing with church discipline and illustrate the teaching with examples of traditional Baptist support for this practice. These actions should spark some discussion of the issue. That discussion should lead to incorporating some official statements about church discipline in key documents such as the bylaws and church covenant.

In these documents, it should be clearly stated that becoming a member of the church and signing the church covenant involves an acknowledgment of the church's authority in matters of discipline. Such statements can protect

---

35. Matt. 18:15–20 and 1 Cor. 5:1–13 are the classic texts, but it also appears in Gal. 6:1; 2 Thess. 3:14–15; 1 Tim. 1:20; and 5:19–20.

36. J. L. Dagg, *Manual of Theology: Second Part, A Treatise on Church Order* (Charleston, S.C.: Southern Baptist Publication Society, 1858; reprint, Harrisonburg, Va.: Gano Books, 1982), 274.

37. Deweese, *A Community of Believers,* 74–80, offers nine practical, helpful suggestions as to how contemporary churches might restore the practice of church discipline. The Winter 2000 issue of *The Southern Baptist Journal of Theology* is devoted to a discussion of church discipline, with six very helpful articles. Both these resources recognize both the importance and the dangers involved in implementing church discipline.

the church from lawsuits brought by members who are disciplined. They should also describe the goal of discipline as restoration for the one who is disciplined and protection for the church and its corporate witness in the community. Furthermore, it should be clearly explained that discipline is not for the weak one who falls but repents and wants to grow in Christ but for the strong one who rebels defiantly. It should also state that discipline is not an excuse to take revenge for personal offenses. Some things should be covered over with brotherly love (1 Peter 4:8). Sins that threaten the unity of the church, the purity of the church, or its doctrine are issues that call for church discipline. With such persons, the church should follow the pattern of Matthew 18. The individual who sees the problem should confront the offending brother individually and in all humility. Individual visits can continue as long as the confronter thinks she or he is making progress. But eventually, if the brother is not won over, two or three others (pastors, staff, friends) are to go together to appeal to him again. Only if repeated small-group efforts prove in vain is the issue to go before the church.

It bears repeating that the reintroduction of discipline will not be an easy task. James Leo Garrett Jr. said a generation ago, "Those who would lead in the renewal of discipline must be thoroughly convinced of its terrible urgency."[38] They must also see clearly the wonderful benefits that could come in terms of a powerful corporate witness, spiritual growth, the reclamation of wandering brothers and sisters, the awakening of lost church members to their peril, and the recovery of meaningful church membership.

CONCLUSION

These last two chapters have sought to highlight what may be rightly called the Baptist mark of the church, regenerate church membership. To put it in more everyday language, being a member of a Baptist church ought to mean something. Right now, in most cases it means nothing. I pray that those who read this book will be among those who will faithfully labor to see that change, so that Paul's doxology would be true, that God would be glorified in the church: "Now to him who is able to do immeasurably more than all we ask or imagine, according to his power that is at work within us, *to him be glory in the church* and in Christ Jesus throughout all generations, for ever and ever! Amen" (Eph. 3:20–21, emphasis added).

---

38. Garrett, *Baptist Church Discipline*, 25.

Covenant from J. Newton Brown's
The Baptist Church Manual (1853)

Having been led, as we believe, by the Spirit of God to receive the Lord Jesus Christ as our Saviour; and, on the profession of our faith, having been baptized in the name of the Father, and of the Son, and of the Holy Ghost, we do now, in the presence of God, angels, and this assembly, most solemnly and joyfully enter into covenant with one another, as one body in Christ.

We engage, therefore, by the aid of the Holy Spirit, to walk together in Christian love; to strive for the advancement of this church, in knowledge, holiness, and comfort; to promote its prosperity and spirituality; to sustain its worship, ordinances, discipline, and doctrines; to contribute cheerfully and regularly to the support of the ministry, the expenses of the church, the relief of the poor, and the spread of the gospel through all nations.

We also engage to maintain family and secret devotions; to religiously educate our children; to seek the salvation of our kindred and acquaintances; to walk circumspectly in the world; to be just in our dealings, faithful in our engagements, and exemplary in our deportment; to avoid all tattling, backbiting, and excessive anger; to abstain from the sale and use of intoxicating drinks as a beverage, and to be zealous in our efforts to advance the kingdom of our Saviour.

We further engage to watch over one another in brotherly love; to remember each other in prayer; to aid each other in sickness and distress; to cultivate Christian sympathy in feeling and courtesy in speech; to be slow to take offence, but always ready for reconciliation, and mindful of the rules of our Saviour, to secure it without delay.

We moreover engage, that when we remove from this place, we will as soon as possible unite with some other church, where we can carry out the spirit of this covenant, and the principles of God's word.

Figure 5.2: J. Newton Brown's Church Covenant

Covenant of Saddleback Church, Lake Forest, California

Having received Christ as my Lord and Savior and been baptized, and being in agreement with Saddleback's statements, strategy, and structure, I now feel led by the Holy Spirit to unite with the Saddleback church family. In doing so, I commit myself to God and to the other members to do the following:

1. I will protect the unity of my church
   . . . by acting in love toward other members
   . . . by refusing to gossip
   . . . by following the leaders
2. I will share the responsibility of my church
   . . . by praying for its growth
   . . . by inviting the unchurched to attend
   . . . by warmly welcoming those who visit
3. I will serve the ministry of my church
   . . . by discovering my gifts and talents
   . . . by being equipped to serve by my pastors
   . . . by developing a servant's heart
4. I will support the testimony of my church
   . . . by attending faithfully
   . . . by living a godly life
   . . . by giving regularly[39]

* * *

(Each of the four statements above is followed by quotations from Scripture. After the first are Romans 4:19; 1 Peter 1:22; Ephesians 4:29; and Hebrews 13:17; after the second 1 Thessalonians 1:1–2; Luke 14:23; and Romans 15:7; after the third 1 Peter 4:10; Ephesians 4:11–12; and Philippians 2:3–4, 7; and after the fourth, Hebrews 10:25; Philippians 1:27; 1 Corinthians 16:2; and Leviticus 27:30.)

Figure 5.3: Saddleback Church Covenant

---

39. Warren, *Purpose Driven Church*, 321–22.

Covenant of Capitol Hill Baptist Church, Washington, D.C.

Having, as we trust, been brought by Divine Grace to repent and be-lieve in the Lord Jesus Christ and to give up ourselves to Him, and hav-ing been baptized upon our profession of faith, in the name of the Father and of the Son and of the Holy Spirit, we do now, relying on His gracious aid, solemnly and joyfully renew our covenant with each other.

We will work and pray for the unity of the Spirit in the bond of peace.

We will walk together in brotherly love, as becomes the members of a Christian Church; exercise an affectionate care and watchfulness over each other and faithfully admonish and entreat one another as occasion may require.

We will not forsake the assembling of ourselves together, nor ne-glect to pray for ourselves and others.

We will endeavor to bring up such as may at any time be under our care, in the nurture and admonition of the Lord, and by a pure and loving example to seek the salvation of our family and friends.

We will rejoice at each other's happiness, and endeavor with ten-derness and sympathy to bear each other's burdens and sorrows.

We will seek, by Divine aid, to live carefully in the world, denying ungodliness and worldly lusts, and remembering that, as we have been voluntarily buried by baptism and raised again from the symbolic grave, so there is on us a special obligation now to lead a new and holy life.

We will work together for the continuance of a faithful evangelical ministry in this church, as we sustain its worship, ordinances, discipline, and doctrines. We will contribute cheerfully and regularly to the sup-port of the ministry, the expenses of the church, the relief of the poor, and the spread of the Gospel through all nations.

We will, when we move from this place, as soon as possible unite with some other church where we can carry out the spirit of this cov-enant and the principles of God's Word.

May the grace of our Lord Jesus Christ, and the love of God, and the fellowship of the Holy Spirit be with us all. Amen.[40]

Figure 5.4: Capitol Hill Baptist Church Covenant

---

40. Mark Dever, *Nine Marks of a Healthy Church*, new expanded edition (Wheaton, Ill.: Crossway, 2004), 212–13.

—————— STUDY QUESTIONS FOR PART 2 ——————

1. What are some of the lines of evidence for the view that the New Testament assumes that churches will be composed of believers only? What are some objections to this view? To what degree do you find the objections convincing?
2. Identify the roles played by Constantine and Augustine in the development of the idea of the church as a mixed body of believers and nonbelievers.
3. Why do Baptist historians like Leon McBeth say that the origin of Baptists is best explained as a search for a pure church?
4. How would you compare and contrast the idea of church membership reflected in Baptist confessions of faith with that found in Baptist churches in North America today?
5. Describe the relationship or connection of regenerate church membership with each of the following: believer's baptism, congregational church government, closed communion, church discipline.
6. Of the factors mentioned in chapter 5, which do you think were most influential in the disappearance of regenerate church membership among Baptists in North America? Are there other important factors not mentioned in the chapter?
7. How do you think people in your church would respond to the suggestions for recovering regenerate church membership mentioned in chapter 5? What difficulties would be encountered in implementing them?
8. What did you gain from chapter 5 that could help Baptists answer the question, "Why are you a Baptist?"

—————— BOOKS FOR FURTHER STUDY ——————

Dever, Mark. *Nine Marks of a Healthy Church,* new expanded edition. Wheaton, Ill.: Crossway, 2004. While the entire book is helpful, chapters 6–8 (pp. 146–217) speak directly to the issues of chapter 5, particularly the meaning of church membership and church discipline.

Dever, Mark, ed. *Polity: Biblical Arguments on How to Conduct Church Life.* Washington, D.C.: Center for Church Reform, 2001. This book reprints ten "historic Baptist documents" that date from 1697 to 1874. All deal with issues of polity and the proper order of a New Testament church.

Regenerate membership and church discipline are two of the most prominent themes.

Deweese, Charles W. *Baptist Church Covenants.* Nashville: Broadman, 1990.
Deweese begins this book with a helpful historical introduction to the
nature, function, and importance of church covenants in Baptist life, but
the bulk of the book is devoted to presenting a collection of seventy-nine
representative Baptist church covenants.

———. *A Community of Believers: Making Church Membership More Meaningful.* Valley Forge, Pa.: Judson Press, 1978. In many ways this book provides the perfect companion to chapter 5, for Deweese's two purposes
for this book are to show how Baptist practice today is inconsistent with
their historic doctrine of regenerate church membership and to give practical guidelines to help Baptists restore regenerate church membership.
Though perhaps dated in some respects and difficult to find in print, it is
an extremely valuable resource.

Garrett, James Leo, Jr. *Baptist Church Discipline.* Nashville: Broadman, 1962.
The cover of the book supplies an apt description of its contents: "A historical introduction to the practices of Baptist churches, with particular
attention to the *Summary of Church Discipline* adopted by the Charleston Association." It also helpfully reprints the *Summary of Church Discipline* in its entirety.

Haines, Stephen. "Southern Baptist Church Discipline, 1880–1939." *Baptist
History and Heritage* 20 (1985): 14–27. Through a study of the records of
a representative sample of Baptist churches, Haines documents the decline of church discipline in Southern Baptist churches and discusses some
possible reasons for it.

Lumpkin, William L. *Baptist Confessions of Faith.* Valley Forge, Pa.: Judson Press,
1959. This book presents dozens of the most historically important Baptist
confessions of faith, helpfully grouped and introduced by Lumpkin.

The Southern Baptist Journal of Theology 4, no. 4 (Winter 2000). The entire
issue of this journal is devoted to articles discussing various aspects of
church discipline.

Wills, Gregory. *Democratic Religion: Freedom, Authority, and Church Discipline in the Baptist South, 1785–1900.* New York; Oxford, U.K.: Oxford
University Press, 1997. Wills makes a detailed study of the practice of
church discipline among Baptists in Georgia, illuminating its importance
and tracing its decline.

PART 3

HOW IS THE CHURCH GOVERNED?

BAPTIST CHURCH POLITY

The Case for Congregationalism

IN THE PREVIOUS TWO CHAPTERS, we focused on the issue of regenerate church membership. But the very idea of membership implies some type of organizational structure for the church, one that allows the church to distinguish between members and nonmembers. Paul instructed the Corinthian church to discipline, not those outside the body, but those inside the body (1 Cor. 5:12–13). They clearly knew who their members were. Moreover, as we see the church beginning to grow and expand in the book of Acts, its organizational aspect begins to develop as well, with structures for leadership and governance emerging. This chapter considers the implications of these developments under the question, "How is the church governed?" We begin by noting the importance of this topic for Baptists, then present in this chapter the case for congregational government as the form almost universally affirmed by Baptists. The following two chapters discuss, respectively, the two offices of the church, pastors and deacons.

BAPTISTS AND CHURCH POLITY

While Baptists have never claimed that questions of polity or church government have the same intrinsic importance as issues such as a proper understanding of salvation or a correct view of the person of Christ, they have nonetheless shown a thorough interest in these matters. In *Polity: Biblical Arguments on How to Conduct Church Life,* Mark Dever brings to light ten Baptist documents dating from 1697 to 1874, all dealing with topics relating to church government.[1] To those documents could be added the full-length treatment by J. L. Dagg in *A Treatise on Church Order*,[2] chapters on church government in virtually every theology text written by Baptists from A. H. Strong to Millard Erickson,[3] a number of works sparked by the interest in elders among Baptists,[4] and even a conference devoted to the topic of polity.[5]

Why have Baptists shown such interest in polity? First, because they believe that the Bible does give instruction on these matters. What J. L. Dagg said nearly 150 years ago is still true: "Church order and the ceremonials of religion, are less important than a new heart; and in the view of some, any laborious investigation of questions respecting them may appear to be needless and unprofitable. But we know, from the Holy Scriptures, that Christ gave commands on these subjects, and we cannot refuse to obey."[6] For example, A. H. Strong begins his study of polity by giving fourteen lines of biblical evidence for the fact of organization in the New Testament church.[7] Such evidence still demands investigation.

Second, polity has been of interest to Baptists because it has been one of the Baptist distinctives. Stan Norman, in his survey of the literature on Baptist distinctives, notes the prominence of issues of polity in discussions of Baptist identity, especially the advocacy of congregationalism as the New Testament form of church government.[8]

---

1. Dever, ed., *Polity*. The shortest of the ten reprinted documents runs seventeen very full, single-spaced pages; the longest covers more than one hundred pages. Each contains substantive, detailed discussion of what they referred to variously as church order, discipline, or polity.

2. Dagg, *Manual of Theology*.

3. Strong, *Systematic Theology*; Erickson, *Christian Theology*.

4. See Gerald Cowen, *Who Rules the Church? Examining Congregational Leadership and Church Government* (Nashville: Broadman & Holman, 2003); Dever, *A Display of God's Glory*; Chad Owen Brand and R. Stanton Norman, eds., *Perspectives on Church Government: Five Views of Church Polity* (Nashville: Broadman & Holman, 2004); Steven B. Cowan, ed., *Who Runs the Church? Four Views on Church Government* (Grand Rapids: Zondervan, 2004); and John Piper, *Biblical Eldership*; available from http://www.desiringgod.org/library/tbi/bib_eldership.html, accessed September 24, 2004.

5. "Issues in Baptist Polity," a conference held at New Orleans Baptist Theological Seminary, February 5–7, 2004, hosted by the Baptist Center for Theology and Ministry, drew together Baptist scholars, professors, pastors, and students to hear more than a dozen presentations on this topic.

6. Dagg, *Manual of Theology*, 12.

7. Strong, *Systematic Theology*, 894.

8. R. Stanton Norman, *More Than Just a Name: Preserving Our Baptist Identity* (Nashville: Broadman & Holman, 2001), 119.

Third, an interest in this issue is especially appropriate today because it leads us into a number of ongoing discussions in Baptist life. There has been some movement toward elder rule in a small but growing number of Baptist churches, and the issues of the authority of pastors and a proper understanding of the priesthood of all believers have been sources of controversy in Baptist life in recent years.

Finally, polity should be of interest to all Christians because of its intrinsic importance. It deals with issues that are inescapable in the actual day-to-day functioning of any church, including "the nature and purpose of the church, clergy-laity functions and relationships, and the ministry within and without the church."[9] Polity is also directly related to one of the hottest issues in all of evangelical Christianity, that of the propriety of women serving as pastors or deacons. This and the two following chapters address practical issues concerning how and by whom the church is directed, issues that can affect in profound ways a church's health.

MAJOR FORMS OF CHURCH GOVERNMENT

In recent years, it has been commonly argued that there is no one New Testament pattern of church government; rather, varying patterns are reflected in different parts of the New Testament with no clear blueprint anywhere. Eduard Schweizer states, "There is no such thing as *the* New Testament church order."[10] In support of this view, it is true that there are three major forms of church government that have been developed and utilized by churches, and it is undeniable that there have been healthy churches down through history that have operated under each of these three models.

In fact, there is an interesting correlation between dominant forms of church government and dominant forms of political government. Episcopal polity, with its monarchical ruling bishop, developed in the context of the Roman Empire and was strongly influenced by the imperial model of government, adopting even some of the political terminology of the empire.[11] Presbyterian polity developed in the era when republican forms of

---

9. Norman, introduction to Brand and Norman, eds., *Perspectives on Church Government*, 10.

10. Eduard Schweizer, *Church Order in the New Testament*, trans. Frank Clarke (London, U.K.: SCM Press, 1961), 13 (emphasis added).

11. For example, the term *diocese*, used in episcopal polity for the area supervised by a bishop, was originally the term used for an administrative district in the Roman Empire.

government were becoming popular, and congregationalism, with its democratic ethos, has been extremely popular in North America. Baptists, the largest group practicing congregational government, have found the atmosphere of North America particularly congenial and number around three-fourths of their worldwide adherents in the United States alone.[12] Clearly, biblical teaching has not been the only factor involved in choices concerning church polity.

Yet the lack of an explicit blueprint does not mean that Scripture has nothing to say about church government, or that all forms of church government are equally supported by Scripture. Baptists have consistently seen congregationalism as preferable for a variety of reasons. In this section we briefly describe the other major competing forms of church government, indicate some strengths and weaknesses for each, and then present the case for congregational church government.

Episcopalian Church Government

The first major form of church government to emerge clearly in the postbiblical period was episcopalianism. The episcopal form of government takes its name from the *episkopos,* or bishop, who is the key figure in this system. He has oversight over all the congregations in an area called a diocese. He alone has the power to ordain those who serve in individual congregations. These individuals are called by various titles in different communions: minister, rector, or priest. The bishop assigns these individuals to their respective congregations. More developed forms of episcopalianism add a level above the bishop called archbishop, who is over a number of bishops. Authority flows from the top down: from archbishop to bishop to minister/rector/priest. This is the system followed by the Roman Catholic Church, the Anglican and Episcopalian Churches, the United Methodist Church, and many other denominations.

---

12. The difference between Baptists in North America and in the rest of the world is striking. According to 2002 figures from the Baptist World Alliance, of the nearly forty-six million Baptist church members around the world, more than thirty-three million, nearly 75 percent, live in North America. Certainly many Baptist denominations in the United States have overly inflated membership statistics, while the opposite is true among Baptists in many other countries. Still, it is undeniable that Baptists have flourished in North America. One reason is that Baptist democratic polity fit the democratic spirit of North America.

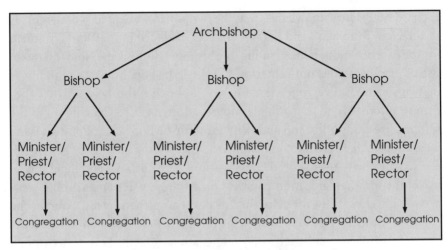

Figure 6.1: Episcopalian Church Government

Advocates of this system can point to the fact that *episkopos* is one of the words used for church leaders in the New Testament. They see the authority of the bishop as supported by the claim that the bishops are the successors of the apostles, who were given authority over the church by Christ himself. Moreover, they claim that bishops function in episcopal government to "represent the true catholicity, continuity and Christianness of the Christian family."[13] They acknowledge that a fully developed episcopal model is not found in the New Testament, but they also say that it grows out of New Testament teaching, began developing immediately in the postapostolic period, is nowhere prohibited by biblical teaching, and has been beneficial for centuries in the life of the church.[14] In fact, Peter Toon argues that the widespread adoption and long time span of usage of this form of polity constitute strong arguments in its favor. If episcopalian polity is wrong, he writes, then the church was blind for nearly sixteen centuries, Christ allowed it to be blind all that time, and only in the Reformation did the church ever get its polity right.[15]

However, closer study of Scripture reveals several serious problems with this view. First, the distinction between *episkopos* and *presbyteros* inherent in episcopalianism is not sustained by New Testament usage. Catholic theologian

---

13. Paul Zahl, "The Bishop-Led Church," in Brand and Norman, eds., *Perspectives on Church Government*, 228.

14. Leon Morris, "Church Government," in *Evangelical Dictionary of Theology*, ed. Walter Elwell, 2d ed. (Grand Rapids: Baker; Carlisle, U.K.: Paternoster, 2001), 256.

15. Peter Toon, "An Episcopalian's Closing Remarks," in Cowan, ed., *Who Runs the Church?* 258.

Richard McBrien acknowledges that the two words were used synonymously in the New Testament, and that we find no evidence in the New Testament for the idea of a monarchical, ruling sole bishop.[16] Second, the New Testament use of *episkopos* does not center on the single bishop, but on a plurality of bishops, who serve together, not to supervise the leaders of other congregations, but to lead a single congregation. As D. A. Carson notes, "the sphere of responsibility and authority for these bishops-elders-pastors is the local church; there is little compelling evidence for the view that a bishop . . . exerted authority over several congregations."[17] Third, the episcopal model leaves the local congregation passive, while the New Testament shows very active churches, fully participating in governing themselves. Fourth, the episcopal model tends to view the church in a denominational sense, as the sum total of all of its affiliated local congregations (i.e., the Episcopal Church, the Methodist Church), while the New Testament sees the church overwhelmingly in a local, congregational sense. The early churches associated with one another, but they were not institutionally joined.

Finally, the hierarchical nature of episcopal church government seems contrary to the humble, serving spirit that is commanded of church leaders (see Mark 10:41–45; 1 Peter 5:3). Despite its early appearance and widespread usage in church history, episcopalianism has the weakest biblical support of any of the three major views on church government.

Presbyterian Church Government

The presbyterian form is followed, in varying degrees, by a wide variety of churches. On the local level, presbyterianism stands for the governance of the church by the presbyters, or the elders. This group is called the *session* in presbyterian churches, the *consistory* in Christian Reformed churches, and simply the *elders* in some independent or nondenominational churches. Within the group of elders there is normally one recognized as the teaching elder, or pastor. In a large church other staff members may also be elders, but usually the majority of the elders are lay members of the congregation. Congregations typically have some role in the selection of the elders, either via direct election or giving approval to those nominated by the existing elders. In either case, however, ruling authority is vested in the elders.

---

16. McBrien, *Catholicism*, 868.

17. D. A. Carson, "Church, Authority in the," in Elwell, ed., *Evangelical Dictionary of Theology*, 250.

Denominations who follow presbyterianism add other organizational levels beyond the local church. Representatives of each session in an area form a presbytery. The presbytery can review decisions or resolve disputes between sessions. The presbytery also holds the official title to the property and buildings of the local congregation. Some denominations have a regional level called the synod, but the highest level is the national level, the general assembly, composed of representatives from the various presbyteries. The general assembly sets overall doctrine and policy for all the local congregations that compose the denomination.[18]

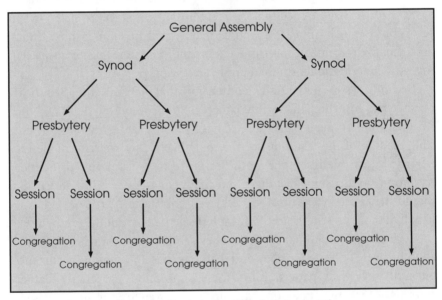

Figure 6.2: Presbyterian Church Government

Advocates of presbyterianism can make a strong case for their view of church government. Elders were clearly the ruling body in Jewish synagogues, which is the background for the church. Moreover, *elder* is the title most often used for church leaders in the New Testament and is equivalent to the other major term, *episkopos.* Elders are seen in the New Testament as acting to lead the church as a group, and advocates of presbyterianism argue that a fair description of the authority of the elders would be that of ruling the

---

18. See "Presbyterianism," in *The Oxford Dictionary of the Christian Church,* ed. F. L. Cross and E. A. Livingstone, 2d ed. (Oxford, U.K.; New York: Oxford University Press, 1974), 1120.

church. Beyond the local church level, Robert Reymond argues that Acts 15 supports the connectionalism in presbyterian polity, because it records actions involving the Antioch presbytery and the Jerusalem presbytery.[19] However, there also seem to be four weaknesses in the presbyterian model.

First, the idea that the elders rule the congregation is questionable. The key text used to establish the rule of elders is 1 Timothy 5:17. The word translated as "ruling" in that verse *(prohistēmi)* can bear a variety of senses, from ruling to managing or directing. Consideration of the whole of New Testament teaching on the nature of spiritual leadership would suggest that elders are not to rule so much as "lead the church into spiritually minded consensus."[20] Baptists have argued that the responsibility of elders reflected in this text is not so much ruling as directing; that is, their function is more "moral and executive rather than governmental and judicial"[21] and thus more in keeping with congregationalism than presbyterianism.

Second, despite Reymond's contention that Acts 13 and 15 indicate presbyteries governing the various congregations composing the churches at Antioch and Jerusalem,[22] the most that can be fairly said is that it is one possible reading of the text, but not the most likely. Presbyterianism elevates what is a possible inference from Scripture to a normative principle.[23] Reymond has to assume that there were many congregations in Antioch, that they formed a presbytery, that the presbytery sent Paul and Barnabas to Jerusalem, that those present in Acts 15 from Jerusalem represent the presbytery of the Jerusalem church, that the letter they sent out was church law, that all churches were obligated to obey, and that Acts 15 is not a unique occurrence, but a divinely given pattern. All of these assumptions are simply that: assumptions that are not mentioned, much less proven in Scripture. James Leo Garrett Jr. calls Reymond's argument for presbyterianism "a network of unproved hypotheses."[24] Acts 15 may give some basis for churches associating with one another, but not for churches being ruled by presbyteries.

---

19. Robert Reymond, "The Presbytery-Led Church," in Brand and Norman, eds., *Perspectives on Church Government*, 107–9.

20. Carson, "Church, Authority in the," 251. A very helpful discussion of 1 Tim. 5:17 and the whole issue of ruling elders is found in the 1874 work by William Williams, "Apostolical Church Polity," reprinted in Dever, ed., *Polity*, 533–35.

21. E. C. Dargan, *Ecclesiology: A Study of the Churches* (Louisville: Chas. T. Dearing, 1897), 24.

22. Reymond, "The Presbytery-Led Church," 96.

23. Carson, "Church, Authority in the," 250.

24. James Leo Garrett Jr., "Response to Robert Reymond's Presbyterian Polity," in Brand and Norman, eds., *Perspectives on Church Government*, 145.

Third, the division of the elders into teaching elders and ruling elders, characteristic of most presbyterian forms of polity, is also a debatable point. It is based primarily on one verse, 1 Timothy 5:17, and is undermined by the requirement that all elders be "able to teach" (1 Tim. 3:2). This verse is far too slender a basis for distinguishing two types of elders.

Finally, while the presbyterian model does make more room for congregational participation than the episcopal one, it still does not seem to do justice to the activity of local congregations seen in the New Testament.

Congregational Church Government

In their confessions of faith and other literature, Baptists have stood virtually unanimously in favor of congregational church government. Beyond Baptists, more than thirty other denominations in the United States alone practice congregational polity.[25] In this model, the congregation exercises the ultimate *human* authority in the church, under Christ's *divine* authority. Christ exercises his headship through the members, as they all seek together to discern Christ's will for the body. Since all the members are regenerate and thus indwelt by the Spirit, all are able to receive guidance from Christ. Thus, congregationalism involves democratic participation, with every member having an equal voice and vote. In such a system, leaders such as pastors or deacons may exercise significant influence and may be entrusted with a measure of authority for acting on behalf of the congregation on certain matters, but, in the final analysis, the highest human authority is vested in the congregation, not the leadership.

Congregationalism also highlights the local nature of the church. Those who affirm congregationalism see no evidence for an authority such as a bishop, presbytery, or general assembly over local churches in Scripture and thus have advocated local church autonomy. But local church autonomy has not meant local church isolation. Baptists, from the earliest days of their history, have evidenced an associational impulse. Norman Maring and Winthrop Hudson see "congregational polity, coupled with an associational principle" as "distinguishing marks" of Baptists down through the ages.[26]

---

25. James Leo Garrett Jr., "The Congregation-Led Church," in Brand and Norman, eds., *Perspectives on Church Government,* 180–81.
26. Norman Maring and Winthrop Hudson, *A Baptist Manual of Polity and Practice* (Valley Forge, Pa.: Judson Press, 1963), 15.

Initially, English Baptists gave a theological grounding to this impulse. The First London Confession of 1644 urged local churches to associate with other like-minded churches "as members of one body in the common faith under Christ their only head." They saw the church as both local and universal, and associations of local churches gave testimony to their belief in the larger body.

Eighteenth-century Baptists in Philadelphia and Charleston reflected consciously on the role and authority of associations, seeing them as a great help in resolving questions relating to doctrine or practice, and recommended by the precedent of the Jerusalem Council in Acts 15. Yet in the end they gave associations no coercive power or jurisdiction over local churches.[27] They saw an important distinction between what they called "church power properly so called," that is, the power of local churches to receive and excommunicate members and select their own officers, and the purely advisory power of an association. The only right reserved to associations was the right to withdraw fellowship from churches judged to be walking disorderly in doctrine or practice.

Nineteenth-century Baptists emphasized even more strongly the local nature of the church and justified associations primarily on pragmatic bases, especially their efficiency in supporting the cause of missions.

By 1925, Southern Baptists included an article on cooperation in their *Baptist Faith and Message* that denied associations any authority over local churches and described them as "voluntary and advisory bodies designed to elicit, combine and direct the energies of our people in the most effective manner." In fact, the degree of denominational unity achieved by various Baptist groups is remarkable in view of the fact that participation in such groups is totally voluntary and that local church autonomy is so zealously guarded.

---

27. Philadelphia Baptists had inherited this idea of the advisory nature of associations from English Baptists, as reflected in the Second London Confession (see article 26, par. 15), which they adopted, but to it they added a 1743 work by Benjamin Griffith, "A Short Treatise," and a 1749 work, "An Essay Respecting the Power and Duty of an Association." The perspective of Charleston Baptists is seen in their 1774 work, *A Summary of Church Discipline.* The earlier work of Griffith and that of the Charleston Baptists are available in *Polity,* 95–112, 116–33.

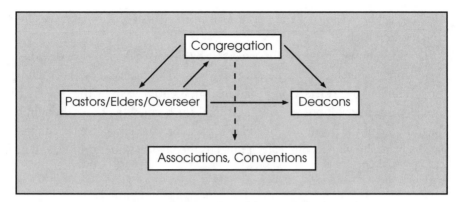

Figure 6.3: Congregational Church Government

In Figure 6.3, the congregation is at the top, representing its final authority and the centrality of the local congregation in the Baptist conception of the church. There is a double line between the congregation and the pastors/elders/overseers, representing the fact that the church has final authority over the elders, but the elders lead the congregation. The deacons serve both the elders and the congregation, and so has lines from both of them. However, since the deacons should not exercise leadership, there is no line from them to the congregation or the elders. Finally, the relationship of the congregation to associations and conventions is not as direct and intrinsic to congregationalism as are its relationship to elders and deacons and so the line to that box is dotted. Yet associations and conventions have a place in congregationalism because they are an appropriate way for churches to show in a visible way their belief in the oneness of the larger body of Christ.

This theory has not always been fleshed out in practice. Powerful pastors and dominating deacons have often sought to control congregations, either alone, in concert with each other, or in competition with each other. In fact, Wayne Grudem sees five varieties of congregationalism: single-pastor government, pastor-deacon government, plural local elder government, corporate board government, and pure democracy government.[28] Another recent book on five views of church polity includes three congregational models: single elder-led, democratic, and plural elder-led, Still another presents single-elder and plural-elder congregationalism.[29]

---

28. Wayne Grudem, *Systematic Theology: An Introduction to Biblical Doctrine* (Leicester, U.K.: Inter-Varsity; Grand Rapids: Zondervan, 1994), 928–36.

All these can be versions of congregationalism if the final court of appeal is the congregation itself.

Congregationalism allows for *leadership* by pastors, elders, and/or deacons, even strong leadership and a measure of delegated authority. It does not allow for *government* by leaders. Congregationalism is *government* by the congregation. Baptists have supported congregationalism, because they have thought it the most scriptural position. The following sections present a case for congregationalism, showing its biblical support, its theological undergirding, and its practical benefits.

BIBLICAL SUPPORT FOR CONGREGATIONALISM

There are numerous lines of evidence in the New Testament that support a congregational model of government. James Leo Garrett Jr. builds the case for congregationalism from six major texts: Matthew 18:15–20; Acts 6:3; 13:2–3; 15:22; 1 Corinthians 5:2; and 2 Corinthians 2:6.[30] One further indirect support comes from the fact that there is no evidence that any body larger than a local congregation ever made decisions for a New Testament congregation. Even the decision of the council in Acts 15 is presented as what "seemed good to the Holy Spirit and to us" and is urged upon them with the words "you will do well" to accept their recommendation (vv. 28-29). But there is nothing in the account that resembles a general assembly determining policy for churches under their authority. The apostles, though they exercised authority in the churches as the authorized representatives of Christ, did not appoint bishops as their successors over churches but appointed bishops and elders to serve within churches. These actions seem in keeping with the congregational principle of local autonomy.

Local autonomy, one aspect of congregationalism, is also supported by the overwhelmingly dominant use of *ekklēsia* to refer to local churches in the New Testament.[31] There is no superior organizational level to which churches are accountable.

---

29. Daniel Akin defends the single elder-led position; James Leo Garrett Jr., the democratic model; and James R. White argues for a plural eldership in Brand and Norman, eds., *Perspectives on Church Government*. In Cowan, ed., *Who Runs the Church?* Paige Patterson presents single-elder congregationalism and Samuel Waldron plural-elder congregationalism. The position of Akin and Patterson could also be called primary elder congregationalism, since they do not deny the viability of plural elders but only maintain that one elder must be primary.

30. Garrett, "The Congregation-Led Church," 158–69.

31. Garrett says *ekklēsia* refers to a local church or churches in 92 or 93 of its 114 occurrences. Ibid., 171.

Another less obvious but highly important support for congregational-ism is seen in the dominant images for the church. None are hierarchical; all are interdependent and breathe the spirit of mutuality. For example, king-dom is not a major biblical motif for the church, but body and family are. Alastair Campbell says that in considering New Testament teaching on pol-ity, it is "of the highest importance" that we recognize the significance of the fact that the early churches "came to birth within households or extended families,"[32] which consist more of brothers and sisters than rulers and sub-jects. In examining Luke's view of church leadership in the book of Acts, Scott Bartchy notes that Luke's ideal for the church was "a well functioning family," a model that leads toward an "antipatriarchal perspective" on leader-ship,[33] a perspective that accords better with congregational polity than any other model.

A third general or indirect support is seen in the fact that most of the letters in the New Testament were addressed to churches, not just to their leaders. Peter, Paul, James, and John seemed to expect churches to take re-sponsibility for their own doctrine. Paul tells the churches of Galatia to reject heretical teaching, even if it comes from an angel or apostle (Gal. 1:8–9). Apparently, he saw doctrinal purity as a congregational responsibility.

But the two clearest examples of congregational government come in the areas of regulating church membership and choosing local leadership.[34] The first area comes to the fore in discussions of church discipline. In Matthew 18:15–17, the final decision for dismissing a member is not assigned to a bishop or elders, but to the church. Historically, Baptists saw this as an exer-cise of the authority given to the church in the gift of the "keys of the king-dom" (Matt. 16:19) and consistently identified the power to discipline their members as one of the proper activities of a congregation.[35] Paul assigns the same responsibility to the Corinthian church in 1 Corinthians 5:9–13. He

---

32. R. Alastair Campbell, *The Elders: Seniority Within Earliest Christianity* (Edinburgh: U.K.: T & T Clark, 1994), 241.

33. S. Scott Bartchy, "Divine Power, Community Formation, and Leadership in Acts," in Longenecker, ed., *Community Formation in the Early Church and in the Church Today*, 97–98.

34. Interestingly, these are also the two activities most commonly highlighted in seventeenth- and eighteenth-century Baptist confessions of faith as belonging to the church. D. A. Carson adds a third general area of congregational responsibility: "They enjoyed responsibility for and authority over a substantial range of questions affecting internal order." Carson, "Church, Authority in the," 251.

35. See, for example, the statement of the *London Confession of 1644*: "Christ has likewise given power to his whole Church to receive in and cast out, by way of Excommunication, any member; and this

describes their action later as "the punishment inflicted on him by the majority" (2 Cor. 2:6), indicating a congregational proceeding. Since the individual involved had repented, Paul now urges them to restore him. Again, the responsibility is placed on the congregation.

In the area of choosing leaders, some see the action of the believers in Acts 1 in choosing a replacement for Judas as indicative of congregationalism, but since this a pre-Pentecost act, and thus prior to the actual birth of the church, it is questionable. Clearer is the example in Acts 6, where the apostles told the "whole group" to choose those who would assist the apostles. This passage, Acts 6:1–6, is commonly seen as the origin of the office of deacon. In Acts 13:1–3, it seems that the church was involved in commissioning Paul and Barnabas to their work as missionaries, and upon their return, Paul and Barnabas reported to the church (Acts 14:27). In Acts 15, the church was involved in the discussion (vv. 4, 12) and decision (v. 22) of the group there. It is true Paul and Barnabas appointed elders for the churches they founded (14:23), and Paul instructed Titus to do the same for the churches in Crete (Titus 1:5), but these are clearly exceptional situations, both because the congregations involved were in their infancy and because an apostle, or in the case of Titus, an associate of an apostle, had unique authority. All these examples of congregational action, along with instructions about the procedure to follow in discipline of an elder (1 Tim.5:19–20), support the final responsibility of the congregation over its leaders.

THEOLOGICAL UNDERGIRDING FOR CONGREGATIONALISM

Some support congregational polity, even though they see the New Testament teaching on church government as incomplete, inconclusive, or indefinite. They do so because they see congregationalism as undergirded by certain important theological principles. Leon Morris says, "Perhaps it would not be unfair to say that the chief scriptural buttresses of this position [congregationalism] are the facts that Christ is the head of the church . . . and that

---

power is given to every particular Congregation, and not one particular person, either member or Officer, but the whole." This statement is clearer than most, but there are similar indications in confessions up to the nineteenth century, when the practice of discipline began to decline. For the connection of this power with the keys of Matt. 16:19, see Benjamin Griffith, "The Glory of a True Church, and Its Discipline Display'd," in Dever, ed., *Polity*, 63–91, a work with the subtitle, "Wherein a true Gospel-Church is described. Together with the Power of the Keys, and who are to be let in, and who to be shut out."

there is a priesthood of all believers."[36] The principle of Christ's headship over the church is seen as supporting congregational government because the other forms of church government place the church in the position of obeying a bishop or presbytery or general assembly, rather than Christ. Of course, it could be argued that the presbytery or bishop is the ordained way for Christ to direct his people, but it has seemed to many that the directness of Christ's authority over the church is compromised by the other forms of government. Congregationalism preserves the congregation's direct responsibility to submit to Christ's headship. Their ability to discern and obey Christ's direction is assured by the second principle supporting congregationalism, the priesthood of all believers.

The priesthood of all believers is seen by many as the strongest support for congregational government. James Leo Garrett Jr., Millard Erickson, and Stanley Grenz all acknowledge its importance. Garrett notes "the important connection between the priesthood of all Christians and Congregational polity."[37] Erickson says, "It is my judgment that the congregational form of church government most nearly fulfills the principles that have been laid down. It takes seriously the principle of the priesthood and spiritual competency of all believers."[38] Grenz states, "proponents claim that democratic congregationalism is the consistent outworking of . . . the priesthood of all believers."[39] The priesthood of all believers affirms that each believer is both able and responsible to seek God directly and receive guidance from him directly apart from any human intermediary. Yet each individual believer is also fallible. Thus, the proponents of congregationalism have seen that the best way for the church to find God's direction is for all the believer-priests to seek God's face and come to a consensus as to his direction for the church. As Grenz says, "This comprises the central principle of democratic congregationalism. The entire company of believers discerns Christ's will for his people."[40]

PRACTICAL BENEFITS OF CONGREGATIONALISM

Congregationalism brings certain practical benefits into a church's life. One such benefit is congregationalism's ability to counter the tendency of

---

36. Morris, "Church Government," 257.
37. Garrett, "The Congregation-Led Church," 185.
38. Erickson, *Christian Theology,* 1096.
39. Grenz, *Theology for the Community of God,* 723.
40. Ibid., 724.

churches to drift doctrinally and thus suffer spiritually. Mark Dever offers this assessment of congregationalism in relationship to this problem: "Friends, the verdict of history is in. While it is clear that no certain polity prevents churches from error, from declension, and from sterility, the more central- ized polities seem to have a worse track record than does congregationalism in maintaining a faithful, vital, evangelical witness." He adds, "Could it be that the gospel itself is so simple and clear, and the relationship that we have with God by the Holy Spirit's action in giving us the new birth is so real that the collection of those who believe the gospel and who know God are simply the best guardians of that gospel?"[41]

Recent history gives a striking illustration of Dever's words. In 1979, cer- tain leaders within the Southern Baptist Convention began a concerted ef- fort to address what they saw as a theological drift in some of that denomination's seminaries and agencies. Over a fifteen-year period, they were able to bring about a remarkable change in the direction of those seminaries and agencies, such that one writer has called it "the Baptist Reformation."[42] Some would dispute the need for their effort or even the motives behind their actions,[43] but one fact seems indisputable. The change in the Southern Baptist Convention could not have occurred had it not preserved in its con- stitution some of the elements of the congregationalism of its churches. The power that changed the course of the Southern Baptist Convention was the power of thousands of grassroots Baptists. They were mobilized and directed by very able leaders, but the determining factor was the actions of thousands of average believers.

Another benefit of congregationalism is that it provides for what is a prac- tical inevitability. Mark Dever asserts that every church is congregational in nature; that is, they can continue to exist only as the people support them. The people can always vote, with their funds and feet if in no other way. Dever says, "The congregation will have their say. That's a simple fact. It is like gravity. It's just a matter of the way things work."[44] But rather than merely acknowledging that a degree of congregational involvement is inevitable and

---

41. Dever, A Display of God's Glory, 38–39.

42. See the account by Jerry Sutton, The Baptist Reformation: The Conservative Resurgence in the Southern Baptist Convention (Nashville: Broadman & Holman, 2000).

43. See, for example, the four widely varying accounts in "The Southern Baptist Convention, 1979– 1993: What Happened and Why?" Baptist History and Heritage, October 1995.

44. Dever, Nine Marks of a Healthy Church, 225.

seeking to minimize it, a wiser course is heartily adopting a full congregationalism and accepting the challenge of developing a congregation that can responsibly and fully participate in governing itself, rather than a congregation that passively accepts whatever the leadership hands down.

James Leo Garrett Jr. says congregational polity is "more capable than other polities of developing loyalty to and support of the congregation" and it is "very likely to produce stronger, more mature Christians than other polities."[45] Correspondingly, a lack of involvement and participation in discerning the direction of the church seem likely to weaken the sense of loyalty and commitment among the members of the congregation.

CHALLENGES FACING CONGREGATIONALISM

Despite the long and virtually unanimous support for congregationalism among Baptists, it is facing a number of challenges today, of both a practical and a theological nature. If genuine congregational government is to endure among Baptists, these challenges must be addressed.

The Need for Responsible, Regenerate Congregations

As we noted in the previous chapter, congregational church government presupposes regenerate church membership, for only a regenerate congregation can govern itself responsibly. But we also noted that regenerate church membership is largely a fiction among Baptist churches in North America today. Most churches have large number of members who have not been present in worship services for years, have shown no signs of commitment to Christ or to the local church, and yet remain as members in good standing and may well show up to vote in crucial church business meetings. With such congregations, many Baptist pastors think of church business meetings with a sense of dread and fear, as something to be avoided as much as possible, for they have seen all too often how what is theoretically supposed to be a search by a congregation of believer-priests for Christ's guidance has degenerated into an angry argument among factions vying for control. For their part, many members of such congregations find business meetings either boring or unedifying and stay away in droves. Either way, congregational church government is frustrated by the lack of congregations able and willing to

---

45. Garrett, "The Congregation-Led Church," 193.

govern themselves responsibly. The need to develop responsible congregations is probably the number one challenge facing Baptists in North America
today.[46]

The Rise of Larger Churches

Another practical challenge to congregationalism is that raised by the trend
toward larger churches. One observer has noted that this is a feature of the
contemporary scene unprecedented in church history: "The recent rise of
larger and larger churches at an increasingly fast rate of growth is unique to
this final quarter of the twentieth century."[47] The same trend has been noted
among Southern Baptist churches. While 53 percent of their churches are
still small (three hundred members or less), the majority of members (65
percent) attend churches with five hundred or more members, and more
than 40 percent of Southern Baptists attend the less than 10 percent of
churches with more than a thousand members.[48]

The difficulties raised for congregational government by churches of such
size are threefold. First is the difficulty of getting such large numbers of people
to come and participate in congregational government. Stanley Grenz says,
"Democratic congregationalism is the active role of all in the corporate de-
termination of Christ's will, not the rule by the voting majority at meagerly
attended church meetings."[49] The larger the church, the greater the practical
difficulty it will face in getting widespread congregational involvement.

Second, even if a large church can get all its members present, it will face
the difficulty of ensuring that all the members are well informed on the issues under consideration. For this reason, Millard Erickson feels that in larger
churches more of the decision making has to be entrusted to leaders chosen
by and responsible to the congregation. He cautions, however, that "the elected
servants must be ever mindful that they are responsible to the whole body."[50]
Even smaller churches typically entrust many minor decisions to their leaders, not feeling the need to be consulted on every specific item. The larger the
church, the greater will be its need for delegation of authority from the con-

---

46. For suggestions as to how to develop responsible congregations, see the material in chapter 5.
47. John Vaughan, *Megachurches and America's Cities: How Churches Grow* (Grand Rapids: Baker, 1993),
     40.
48. "Where We Go to Church," North American Mission Board, Summer 1999.
49. Grenz, *Theology for the Community of God*, 724–25.
50. Erickson, *Christian Theology*, 1097.

gregation to its leaders. But it should be clear that the authority with which they act is delegated from the congregation.

Third is the fact that most megachurches tend to be "heavily pastor centered" and to be pastor-led in practice, even if congregational in theory.[51] John Vaughn argues that churches naturally evolve from congregational to presbyterian to episcopal as they grow in numbers, and sees such a development as positive, for he sees congregational polity as a hindrance in growing a megachurch.[52] James Leo Garrett Jr. observes, "No one seems to be asking whether a megachurch can practice any form of Congregational polity,"[53] yet it seems a very real and important question.

Strong Pastoral Leadership and Church Growth

Another challenge related to the rise of larger churches is the strong pressure for churches to grow numerically and the claim that strong pastoral leadership is essential for such growth to happen. In the last generation a whole school of thought has developed called *church growth*. Those involved in this school of thought study numerically growing churches and try to isolate important factors contributing to growth. One factor they highlight is the importance of strong pastoral leadership, or what is sometimes called a CEO (chief executive officer) model of pastoral leadership.[54]

Strong pastoral leadership is not in itself incompatible with congregational government, but often the CEO model brings with it the corporate concept of hierarchical authority with control being exercised from the top down. As David Crosby notes in his study of church government in the church growth movement, the CEO model fits much more naturally in episcopal or

---

51. Garrett, "The Congregation-Led Church," 190, citing Wilson Hull Beardsley, "The Pastor as Change Agent in the Growth of a Southern Baptist Mega Church Model" (D. Min. diss., Fuller Theological Seminary, 1991).

52. Vaughan, *Megachurches and America's Cities,* 84–85.

53. Garrett, "The Congregation-Led Church," 191.

54. This style of pastoral leadership is advocated by a number of church growth authors, including Peter Wagner, *Leading Your Church to Growth* (Ventura, Calif.: Regal Books, 1984); Lyle Schaller, *The Decision-Makers: How to Improve the Quality of Decision-Making in the Churches* (Nashville: Abingdon, 1974); and Glen Martin and Gary McIntosh, *The Issachar Factor* (Nashville: Broadman & Holman, 1993). Thom Rainer, *Surprising Insights from the Unchurched* (Grand Rapids: Zondervan, 2001) has found strong support for the link between strong pastoral leadership and church growth in his research.

presbyterian polity than in congregationalism.[55] Yet the imperative to grow is so strong in some Baptist circles, and decision making is so often governed by pragmatism rather than theological or ecclesiological considerations, that the perceived advantage of strong pastoral leadership in church growth has led many to an abandonment of congregational government in practice, if not theory. Demonstrating that effective pastoral leadership is consistent with congregational church government is one of the challenges facing congregationalism and its advocates.

The Emergence of Elder Rule

One challenge to congregational rule goes beyond practical difficulties to a theoretical and theological issue. It is the small but noticeable emergence of Baptist churches practicing elder rule. There is nothing intrinsically problematic for Baptists in the use of the term *elder*. The New Testament uses the terms *elder, overseer* (or bishop), and *pastor* interchangeably and so did Baptists for much of their history. The 1859 Abstract of Principles, which still serves as one of the guiding documents for two Southern Baptist seminaries, refers to the scriptural church officers as "Bishops or Elders, and Deacons." There were even those called "ruling elders" among some Baptist churches in the eighteenth century, especially those influenced by the Philadelphia Association. But these ruling elders functioned more as assistants to the pastor, and could be as accurately called "lay elders," for they did not share the preaching and teaching responsibilities of the pastor or minister. In any case, their rule was under the authority of the congregation and thus unlike the authoritative rule of a presbyterian ruling elder.[56] Even that type of ruling elder was generally discarded by Baptists in the nineteenth century.

Today, some Baptist churches are adopting a plurality of elders and utilizing lay elders, while retaining a commitment to congregational government.[57] Elder leadership can coexist with congregational government. Recently, however, other Baptist churches have allowed major decisions on matters of staff,

---

55. David Eldon Crosby, "Church Government in the Church Growth Movement: Critique from a Historic Baptist Perspective" (Ph.D. diss, Baylor University, 1989), 325–32.

56. See the discussion by Charles W. Deweese, "Baptist Elders in America in the 1700s: Documents and Evaluation," *The Quarterly Review* (October–December 1989): 57–65; the analysis by Slayden Yarbrough, "Southern Baptists and Elder Rule," *The Oklahoma Baptist Chronicle* 37, no. 2 (Autumn 1994): 17–32; and the evaluation by Greg Wills, "The Church: Baptists and Their Churches in the Eighteenth and Nineteenth Centuries," in Dever, ed., *Polity*, 19–42.

57. This is the perspective of Dever, *A Display of God's Glory*, 16–43.

budget, and congregational direction to be made by groups of elders with little or no congregational participation. Stanley Grenz calls this development "semi-Presbyterianism."[58] It seems to involve a serious, essential movement away from congregationalism.

To some degree, more decision making by elders may be related to the earlier challenge we mentioned, the rise of large churches. In large churches, the difficulties of getting the congregation together and informing them of the issues, coupled with the necessity of timely decisions, may lead the congregation to delegate a larger measure of decision-making authority to their leaders, but subject to congregational oversight and review. What is troubling about some of the forms of emerging elder rule is the de-emphasis on the role and importance of the congregation. In most of these churches, there is still some degree of congregational involvement or oversight, but whereas traditional congregationalism expected active congregational participation and ensured ultimate congregational control, some of the newer forms of elder rule minimize congregational participation and blur the lines of ultimate authority and control.

Two questions merit examination. First, why is this challenge to the longstanding Baptist commitment to congregational church government arising, particularly, why today, after centuries of congregationalism? Second, how should Baptist churches respond? To the first question, there are numerous suggested answers. Bill Leonard sees an authoritarian mood among some Baptists who emphasize verses that speak of the duty of believers to obey their leaders (Heb. 13:17) and speak of elders ruling the church (1 Tim. 5:17).[59] Such verses certainly may have been muffled by the individualistic, egalitarian culture of America where nobody would think of ordering someone else to obey, and may need more emphasis in our churches today, but Paul never expected uncritical obedience. He only called believers to follow him as he followed Christ and taught the true gospel (1 Cor. 11:1; Gal. 1:8). Moreover, there have been many Baptists who have held a high view of pastoral authority without rejecting congregational government. The two involve no necessary conflict.

James Leo Garrett Jr. thinks Southern Baptists are being influenced by popular independent preachers such as John MacArthur who practice elder

---

58. Grenz, *Theology for the Community of God*, 725.
59. Bill Leonard, "The Church," in *Has Our Theology Changed? Southern Baptist Thought Since 1845*, ed. Paul A. Basden (Nashville: Broadman & Holman, 1994), 177–78.

rule in their churches.[60] The development of radio and television ministries has certainly broadened the reach of popular preachers, and there is no doubt some truth to Garrett's assessment. But there are two more important motivating factors, one on the side of leaders and one on the side of the congregations.

The most important factor motivating pastors to move toward elder rule is the difficulty in working with congregations often filled with members who give no evidence of regeneration and do not seem intent on seeking Christ's will in congregational business meetings. To a pastor who feels his congregation is obstructing his attempts to lead them in godly ways, elder rule might be very appealing.

On the part of congregations who offer no opposition to allowing the elders to make decisions for them, the most important factor is the development of a consumer attitude toward church membership. American culture has been characterized by recent authors as a consumer culture. Rodney Clapp describes it this way: "We are no longer 'students,' but 'educational consumers,' no longer 'worshipers,' but 'church shoppers,' no longer 'patients,' but 'health consumers,' and so on."[61] Bruce Shelley and Marshall Shelley have reflected specifically on how this consumer culture has entered and affected the church. They say, "Many people assume that their needs count for more than their loyalty. If their needs go unmet, they are quick to switch to another church, just as they would doctors, grocery stores or airlines to find better service."[62]

It is interesting to contrast this with the attitude of the early Baptists of the Philadelphia Association. In 1728, a member church of the association asked for their advice on the question of whether or not it was proper to allow a member of one church to move his letter to another church, when his residence had not changed. The association answered in the negative, reflecting the idea that church membership is not a matter of finding a place where one's needs may be met, but finding a place where one can obey God's commands with a clear conscience.[63]

---

60. James Leo Garrett Jr., *Systematic Theology: Biblical, Historical, and Evangelical* (Grand Rapids: Eerdmans, 1995), 2:580.

61. Rodney Clapp, "Consumption and the Modern Ethos," in *The Consuming Passion: Christianity and the Consumer Culture*, ed. Rodney Clapp (Downers Grove, Ill.: InterVarsity, 1998), 7–15.

62. Shelley and Shelley, *Consumer Church*, 166.

63. Excerpts from the minutes of the Philadelphia Association are available in Leon McBeth, *A Sourcebook for Baptist Heritage* (Nashville: Broadman, 1990), 147–55.

This consumer attitude does not tend to develop the type of commitment needed to sustain responsible self-government, but it is increasingly prevalent in many churches. Many members view their commitment to their church much as they view their commitment to shopping at Wal-Mart. They may enjoy the goods and services offered, but they are not remotely interested in working with fellow-shoppers to govern it. If a better deal comes along, or things change and Wal-Mart no longer meets their needs, they will vote with their feet and shop elsewhere.

It is the unconscious adoption of this idea of consumer membership that explains why there has been no complaint from the congregations in the churches that have adopted elder rule. Members seem glad to dispense with business meetings and leave running the church to the elders. Pastors are glad to be able to implement their plans without interference from apathetic or hostile congregations. Thus, the challenge to congregationalism from elder rule may be one some pastors are slow to address.

Baptists should resist elder rule, for two reasons. First, while elder or pastoral *leadership* is crucial, and the use of a plurality of elders can be cogently argued, elder leadership does not negate the case for congregational *government.* In the end, the biblical support and theological undergirding for congregational government is much stronger than the case for elder rule. Second, the motivations behind elder rule (the desire of pastors to avoid dealing with difficult congregations and the idea of consumer membership) do not lead in a healthy direction. The idea of consumer membership is profoundly nonbiblical and does not produce the type of committed members the church needs, and elder rule cuts off the wisdom available for decision making from the whole body of God's people. The biblical support, theological undergirding, and practical benefits of congregationalism are sufficient to justify a call to pastors and churches to address the contemporary challenges, including that of elder rule, and develop congregations committed to responsible self-government.

CHAPTER 7

ELDERS IN BAPTIST LIFE

Leaders, Not Rulers

A BAPTIST PERSPECTIVE ON CHURCH LEADERS

An emphasis on congregational government should not be interpreted as a denial or denigration of the crucial role church leaders play in the life and health of a church. One of Paul's first steps in the churches he founded was to provide for leaders (Acts 14:23; Titus 1:5). Scripture gives specific examples, directions, and qualifications for those who are to lead churches, and practical experience verifies their importance. No church can be healthy with poor leaders.

The first leaders of the New Testament churches were the apostles. They, along with prophets, evangelists, and pastor-teachers, are mentioned in Ephesians 4:11–12 as those given by Christ to the church to equip the saints to do the work of ministry. But apostles, prophets, and evangelists are not generally recognized as offices pertaining to the local church. There is almost nothing in terms of instructions or qualifications for them, as there are for elders and deacons, and they are not mentioned as officers of any local churches in the New Testament.

Apostles and prophets are most commonly seen as extraordinary ministries, serving an important foundational purpose (Eph. 2:20), but are not intended to be ongoing offices in the church. After Acts 6, the original twelve apostles begin to fade into the background. In the council described in Acts 15, they do not hand down a decision, but act in concert with the elders and the whole assembly (v. 22). Some see missionaries today as serving an apostolic function, but that is quite different than a local church office. Some varieties of polity ground the authority of bishops in a supposed succession from the apostles, but there is no evidence in the New Testament that the apostles ordained, appointed, or envisioned successors. Indeed, when one of the twelve, James, is martyred (Acts 12:1–2), there is no move to replace him. It seems the early church recognized the apostolic office as a passing one.[1]

There were numerous prophets associated with the New Testament churches, but none were seen as officers of any particular church. Prophets in the New Testament were commonly involved in ministries of exhortation and interpretation of Scripture, and so some today refer to pastors as prophets and see prophecy as preaching, but no one affirms the office of prophet as normative for local churches today.

The term *evangelist* occurs only three places in the New Testament (Acts 21:8; Eph. 4:11; 2 Tim. 4:5). Many have exercised such a ministry, perhaps the most famous being Billy Graham, but it too is not recognized as an ongoing office in the local church.

Terms such as *minister* and *priest* are used to refer to offices of leadership in some churches today, but in the New Testament, they are used to refer to all believers. First Peter 2:9 calls the church a "royal priesthood," and John says Christ has made all his followers "a kingdom and priests" (Rev. 1:6). And while the word *minister* is often used to refer to those serving as pastors or elders, it too can describe the work to which all Christians are called (Eph. 4:12; 1 Peter 4:10).

In Baptist life, there have been two categories of those called leaders or officers in the local church. The first office has been called by a variety of terms. Scripture most often refers to this office as elder and, less frequently, overseer or bishop. Contemporary Baptists prefer to use the term *pastor*. The second office is universally referred to as deacon, but often with divergent understandings of the proper responsibilities of those occupying that office.

A variety of factors, including the rise of elder rule and the feminist movement, have occasioned a good deal of discussion concerning the functions and qualifications of leaders in Baptist life in recent years. Those controversies, plus the intrinsic importance of leadership, call for a thorough discus-

---

1. See the interesting discussion of the surprisingly small role played by the apostles, especially the original twelve, in the early Christian movement in Bartchy, "Divine Power, Community, Formation, and Leadership in the Acts of the Apostles," in Longenecker, ed., *Community Formation in the Early Church and in the Church Today*, 98–101.

sion of this topic. This chapter considers the office designated by the terms *elder, overseer*, or *pastor*. Chapter 8 examines the office of deacon.

ELDERS/OVERSEERS/PASTORS

The Issue of Terminology

As the heading above indicates, we are first faced with the issue of terminology. What are we to call this office? For many people, the terms *elder (presbyteros)* and *overseer* or *bishop (episkopos)* carry associations with presbyterian and episcopal polity, though they were widely used by Baptists in the eighteenth and nineteenth centuries.[2] Today, the term most often used in Baptist life is *pastor (poimēn)*. Is there any importance to what we call this office?

There is at least some value in understanding how these terms have been used (or misused) historically. Despite the strong evidence that the three are interchangeable terms for one office, there was a movement, beginning early in the second century, toward the development of what is called the monarchical bishop as an office separate from and higher than the office of elder.[3] That pattern endured until the Reformation. Calvin recognized what many earlier exegetes had seen, that Scripture uses the terms *elder* and *bishop* interchangeably.[4] However, presbyterianism, as it developed, began to distinguish two different types of elders, based on 1 Timothy 5:17. Those called ruling elders were usually laypeople, involved in the governance of the church but not in the teaching and preaching of God's Word. There was usually only one teaching elder in a church, an ordained man, the one chiefly responsible for the ministry of teaching, more often called the pastor or minister than teaching elder. For a time, there was some debate among Baptists as to the validity

---

2. See, for example, the interesting resolution passed by the Sandy Creek Baptist Association on October 24, 1829: "Resolved, That we, as a body, will discontinue, and recommend to the churches and preachers discontinue, the title of reverend prefixed to a minister's name, and substitute, as a more scriptural appellation, the title of Elder." G. W. Purefoy, *A History of the Sandy Creek Baptist Association from Its Organization in a.d. 1758 to a.d. 1858* (New York: Sheldon and Co., 1859), 143.

3. The earliest evidence for this usage is found in the early second-century letters of Ignatius (35–107) to a variety of churches. See J. H. Strawley, *The Epistles of St. Ignatius, Bishop of Antioch* (London: SPCK; New York: Macmillan, 1900). The bishop is seen as the head of the church in a city, with the elders or presbyters under him. As the office developed, a bishop came to oversee the congregations in an area called a diocese. Those exercising leadership in a single congregation came to be called "priests," which is a contraction of the term *presbyter*, or *elder*.

4. Calvin, *Institutes of the Christian Religion*, 21:1060 (4.3.8).

of having ruling and teaching elders in the church, but the practice was never widespread, because it was seen as having a very slender and debatable biblical basis; it virtually disappeared after 1820.[5]

How are these terms used in Scripture? The word *elder* is used most often in the Gospels for the Jewish leaders, with whom Jesus often clashed. They were usually the more mature men (since elder does mean older) and were the leaders of synagogues. The term was taken over for the leaders of the early church, especially the church in Jerusalem. In all, the word *elder* is used as a term for a church leader in the New Testament seventeen times, ten of those times in the book of Acts, with eight of those with reference to the church in Jerusalem.[6] Perhaps it seemed the most natural term for these early Jewish believers to use for their leaders. *Overseer* or *bishop* is found only four times as a noun with reference to a church office; a verbal form is used once to describe the function an elder serves.[7] *Pastor* is used as a noun only once for a church office (Eph. 4:11), but twice the verbal form is used to designate the responsibility of an elder (Acts 20:28; 1 Peter 5:2). More often, *pastor* or *shepherd* is used to refer to Jesus, the great and chief shepherd of the sheep (John 10:11; Heb. 13:20; 1 Peter 2:25; 5:4).

The evidence for the interchangeability of the three terms is seen most clearly in Acts 20 and 1 Peter 5. In Acts 20, Paul sends for the *elders* of the church at Ephesus (v. 17). When they arrive, he says the Holy Spirit has made them *overseers* of the flock (v. 28) and he charges them to *pastor*, or shepherd the church of God. In 1 Peter 5, Peter addresses the *elders* (v. 1), telling them they are to *pastor* or shepherd the flock and that they are to serve as *overseers* (v. 2). The synonymous use seems obvious and has been widely recognized as such by exegetes.[8] Baptist confessions of faith utilize all three terms for this

---

5. See the discussion by Greg Wills, "The Church: Baptists and Their Churches in the Eighteenth and Nineteenth Centuries," in Dever, ed., *Polity*, 33–34. Evidence of the debate can be seen in Samuel Jones, "Treatise of Church Discipline (1805)," in Dever, ed., *Polity*, 145–46.

6. With reference to the elders of the church in Jerusalem, see Acts 11:30; 15:2, 4, 6, 22–23; 16:4; 21:18; with reference to elders of other churches, see Acts 14:23; and 20:17. Elsewhere in the New Testament, see 1 Tim. 5:17, 19; Titus 1:5; James 5:14; 1 Peter 5:1; 2 John 1; and 3 John 1. Some would add 1 Peter 5:5, but others would see the term there as simply referring to an older man.

7. Acts 20:28; Phil. 1:1; 1 Tim. 3:2; and Titus 1:7. First Peter 2:25 uses *episkopos* to refer to Christ. The verb *episkopeo* is used for the work of an elder in 1 Peter 5:2, and *episkope* is used for the office of bishop or overseer in 1 Tim. 3:1.

8. One of the most recent and detailed demonstrations of this fact is the revision of a 2002 doctoral dissertation produced at Southern Baptist Theological Seminary by Benjamin Merkle, *The Elder and Overseer: One Office in the Early Church*, Studies in Biblical Literature, ed. Hemchand Gossai, vol. 57 (New York: Peter Lang, 2003).

church office. Clearly, the term to be used for the leaders of the church does not seem to have been a major concern of the writers of Scripture.[9] Of greater concern is what they do.

The Role and Responsibility of Elders

There are scattered references to the tasks or responsibilities of elders throughout the New Testament. The most important texts are Acts 20:28–31; Romans 12:8; Ephesians 4:11–16; 1 Thessalonians 5:12; 1 Timothy 3:1–7; 5:17; Titus 1:5–9; Hebrews 13:7, 17; and 1 Peter 5:1–4. These texts describe the four primary responsibilities assigned to this church office.

The first may be called the ministry of the Word. While all Christians are commanded to teach and admonish one another (Col. 3:16), those who are elders are to be especially gifted and responsible for teaching the church. Acts 20:31 and Titus 1:9 reflect the charge laid on elders to preserve sound doctrine; Ephesians 4:11 links the office of pastor with that of teacher; 1 Timothy 3:2 has "able to teach" as one of the elder's qualifications; 1 Timothy 5:17 describes certain elders who work at "preaching and teaching," and Hebrews 13:7 identifies leaders as those "who spoke the word of God to you." Whether it is called preaching, teaching, prophecy, or exhortation, the ministry of the elder is emphatically a ministry that includes the communication of God's Word. It is primarily by means of his preaching and teaching that the elder exerts the influence of leadership in the congregation.

Communication of God's Word is also involved in his second area of responsibility, which is commonly termed pastoral ministry. This is directly related to the charge laid on elders to shepherd the church (Acts 20:28; 1 Peter 5:2). One of the duties of a shepherd is to feed the flock; for Christians, our food is the Word of God (1 Peter 2:2; Matt. 4:4). So the shepherd must provide his flock with healthy biblical food. Another duty of the shepherd is to protect the sheep (John 10:11–13). One danger to the flock highlighted in the New Testament is the danger of false doctrine (Acts 20:29–31). By teaching the truth, the shepherd provides them with protection. This protection is also spoken of in more general ways as "watching over" the flock. The word used in Hebrews 13:17, *agrupneō*, has the idea of constant wakefulness or unceasing vigilance. This care would be expressed concretely in acts like pastoral

---

9. For convenience sake, we will use the term *elder* in the chapter, recognizing that the office to which the term refers is usually called "pastor" in most Baptist churches.

visitation, personal counseling, and ministry in times of sickness (see esp. James 5:14) and grief. Shepherds who love their sheep notice when their sheep are hurting and seek to be with them to care for them. Making that pastoral responsibility even more solemn is the reminder that leaders "must give an account" for those under their care (Heb. 13:17).

The third area of responsibility assigned to this office is that of oversight or leadership. This is why the term *overseer (episkopos)* is appropriate. This officer gives overall administrative oversight and leadership to the church. Three other biblical terms seem to be related to this area of responsibility.

In Titus 1:7, the elder is called to be an *oikonomos,* or steward of God. This word was used of the servant in a household who managed affairs on behalf of the master (Luke 12:42). As it is a position of considerable trust, the key requirement of a good steward is faithfulness to the master (1 Cor. 4:2). This responsibility fits well with the ideas of oversight and leadership.

A second term, found in Hebrews 13:7, 17, and 24, seems to add a tone of authority to the leadership pastors are to exercise. It is true that the individuals involved here are not explicitly described as elders, pastors, or overseers. The word used for them, a form of the verb *hēgeomai,* is simply translated "leaders" and can be used for a variety of leaders, including military and political ones. But the work they are described as doing (speaking the Word of God, watching over the flock) points to them serving in the role of elders and pastors. The note of authority is found in the command in verse 17: "Obey your leaders and submit to their authority."

The third term relates to the nature and extent of pastoral or elder authority. This much disputed question is one of the central differences between presbyterian and congregational polity.[10] The key term in this dispute is the verb *prohistēmi,* which is used six times of church leaders.[11] It can be used in a variety of senses, from the authoritative leadership one would exercise in an army, to the idea of assisting or helping, to the idea of leadership in a family. With reference to church leaders, it seems to carry a very general

---

10. See the criticism of congregationalism and defense of the authority of elders in Alexander Strauch, *Biblical Eldership: An Urgent Call to Restore Biblical Church Leadership,* 2d ed. (Littleton, Colo.: Lewis & Roth, 1988), 116–27.

11. Rom. 12:8 does not specifically link it to an office, but speaks of how those who lead should do so. First Thess. 5:12 is also a general reference. First Tim. 3:4–5 gives the ability to lead or manage one's family as a qualification for an overseer; 1 Tim. 3:12 uses it in the same way as a qualification for a deacon. First Tim. 5:17 speaks of leading as an activity of the elders.

sense.[12] But the difficulty of determining the nature and extent of the authority involved can be seen in the various ways the term has been translated,
especially in 1 Timothy 3:4–5 and 5:17, the two texts that most explicitly and
directly connect this activity to the elder. The King James Version, Revised
Standard Version, and New American Standard see the elders in 1 Timothy
5:17 as those who "rule" the church, while the New International Version sees
them as those who "direct the affairs" of the church. But on 1 Timothy 3:4–5,
all except the King James Version see the overseer as the one who is to "manage" or "care for" the church; only the King James Version uses "rule."

The issue of the nature and extent of pastoral authority cannot be decided on purely lexical evidence; the key terms are too general. Therefore, we
look to the larger context of overall biblical teaching. On that topic, we find a
delicate tension. On the one hand, church members are called upon to recognize their leaders' authority, submit to them, and obey them (see 1 Thess.
5:12; Heb. 13:17). As Daniel Akin points out, "this mind-set is foreign to our
radically autonomous, democratic and egalitarian culture."[13] On the other
hand, the way leaders exercise their authority in the New Testament is never
dictatorial, but with a humble spirit, open to the input of others, and seeking
to "lead the church into spiritually minded consensus."[14] This pattern fits
congregational government with elder leadership. Moreover, the support for
congregational government in the New Testament also qualifies the nature
of pastoral authority. Thus, the leadership exercised by elders is very important and should be obeyed by the church, though not uncritically or apart
from congregational input. Elder leadership with congregational government
is in keeping with the meaning of *prohistēmi* and the biblical description of
the leadership responsibility of the elder.[15]

There is a fourth responsibility of the elder, one that is easily overlooked

---

12. For more information, see L. Coenen, "Bishop, Presbyter, Elder," in *New International Dictionary
of New Testament Theology*, 1:188–201, esp. 189, 193, 197–98 on *prohistēmi*; and B. Reicke,
"*prohistēmi*," in *Theological Dictionary of the New Testament*, 6:700–703.

13. Daniel Akin, "The Single Elder-Led Church," in *Perspectives on Church Government*, 72.

14. D. A. Carson, "Church, Authority in the," in Elwell, ed., *Evangelical Dictionary of Theology*, 251.

15. I am glad to note a growing movement toward this position among Baptists. While they differ on
the plurality of elders, Mark Dever, Daniel Akin, James R. White, Paige Patterson, and Samuel
Waldron all seem to affirm the compatibility of congregational government and elder leadership.
See Dever, *A Display of God's Glory*; Akin, "The Single Elder-Led Church"; White, "The Plural
Elder-Led Church," in *Perspectives on Church Government*; and Paige Patterson, "Single-Elder Congregationalism," in Cowan, ed., *Who Runs the Church?* and Waldron, "Plural-Elder Congregationalism," in Cowan, ed., *Who Runs the Church?*

because it is so basic, yet it seems to be the responsibility most clearly related to the qualifications for the office in 1 Timothy 3 and Titus 1. That responsibility is to serve as an example to the flock (1 Peter 5:3). Leaders are to be set apart, not just to honor them but to recognize them as setting forth the pattern of faith and life that the congregation is to emulate (Heb. 13:7). This leads naturally into the next topic, the qualifications of an elder.

The Qualifications of Elders

The qualifications for this office are given primarily in 1 Timothy 3:2–7 and Titus 1:6–9, with a much briefer description in 1 Peter 5:2–4. Since these lists comprise some of the most detailed and pointed teaching on church order in the New Testament, they deserve careful examination.

The first notable aspect of these lists is their ordinariness. As D. A. Carson notes, "almost every entry is mandated elsewhere of *all* believers."[16] Whatever is involved in being an elder, it is not a calling to a higher standard of Christian living. How could it, when every Christian is commanded by Christ to "be perfect" (Matt. 5:48) and when the goal and destiny of every Christian is Christlikeness (Rom. 8:29)?

But if these character traits are commanded of all Christians, what is their significance here? The key to understanding the meaning of these lists of character traits is remembering that one of the responsibilities of leaders is to set the example for the flock (1 Peter 5:3). The character required to be an elder is the character necessary to be an example to the flock. Such a person would not need to be perfect (such persons are in very short supply among fallen humanity) but would need a degree of maturity and proven character that would enable him to serve as an effective example, including an example of how to confess and repent when he does stumble.

Second, it is also striking how different these qualifications are from modern lists of qualifications for a position. There is no mention of the need for training or educational requirements, little in the way of skills or experience or certification. Character is the central issue.

A third aspect that should be noted is that while there are a number of similar qualifications and some exact parallels between 1 Timothy 3 and Titus 1, there are also a number of differences between the two lists. For example, Titus says nothing about the fact that an elder should not be a recent convert

---

16. Carson, "Church, Authority in the," 249 (emphasis in original).

(1 Tim. 3:6); Timothy does not include the characteristics of being "upright, holy and disciplined" (Titus 1:8). These differences imply that Paul was not trying in either list to be exhaustive, but giving a representative list of character traits an elder should embody. Nonetheless, while the lists are not intended to be exhaustive, they are fairly comprehensive. They cover five major areas.

Moral Qualifications

The first may be called moral qualifications. The person in view in these lists is a person of integrity and good judgment, free from vices such as drunkenness, greed, and a quick temper, and one who is worthy of respect. The initial words in the two major lists, "above reproach" (1 Tim. 3:2) and "blameless" (Titus 1:6), serve as summaries. For the flock, he would be a worthy example; for the outside world, he would be someone who would command their respect.

Marital and Family Qualifications

The second area of qualifications, and perhaps the most controversial, comes in the area of marital and familial qualifications. First Timothy 3 and Titus 1 both say an elder must be "the husband of but one wife." Interpretations of this phrase vary from the idea that "he must be married," to "he must not be a polygamist," to "he must not be remarried," to "he must not have been divorced."[17] With the prevalence of divorce in recent American society (and sadly, even within Baptist churches), the last interpretation has become perhaps the most debated interpretation. Some say that a person who is divorced cannot be considered "blameless" and cannot qualify as a husband of but one wife. Thus divorce disqualifies one from serving as an elder.[18] In some circles, such an interpretation is viewed as virtually required if one believes in the literal interpretation of the Bible. Others make a distinction based on the circumstances of the divorce. For example, if the divorce occurred before

---

17. These are the options listed by Gordon Fee, *1 and 2 Timothy, Titus,* Good News Commentary (New York: Harper and Row Publishers, San Francisco, 1984), 43–44. Fee himself advocates a position close to mine; that is, the elder must be exemplary in marriage and family life.

18. This is the view of Warren Wiersbe, *Be Faithful* (Wheaton, Ill.: Victor Books, 1986), 42. John Piper, *Biblical Eldership,* interprets the phrase to prohibit remarriage after a divorce. Divorce per se does not disqualify one; remarriage after divorce does.

conversion, some say, it is wiped away, because in Christ, the divorced person is a new creation.

All these interpretations, however, overlook the central point of these lists. The question that should be asked is this, "Can this person serve as an example to us in the area of marriage and family?" While some would object that this approach avoids or undermines the literal interpretation of Scripture, literally, the passage says nothing about divorce at all. Had Paul wanted to exclude divorced persons, he simply could have said, "he must not be divorced." Also, if someone wants to be fully literal, he would have to conclude that a single person could not qualify as an elder (thus disqualifying Paul and Jesus), nor could a married person with less than two children, since 1 Timothy 3 and Titus 1 both mention the elder's relationship with his children. But no one disqualifies either single persons or those with less than two children. Further, we do not see the other qualifications in this same way. No one argues that a person who got drunk while in college is permanently disqualified, nor someone who at one time struggled with his temper. Rather, we interpret these in terms of his present character. Finally, to those who differentiate preconversion and postconversion divorce, the issue is not forgiveness, but fitness. All our sins, pre- and postconversion, are equally forgiven. That's not the issue. Can this person serve as an example in this crucial area of life? That is the question.

In practice, such an interpretation would exclude some who have been married to only one woman and have more than two children, but are lousy husbands or dads. Perhaps they meet the letter of the lists of qualifications, but cannot serve the purpose behind the lists. Someone who has recently been through a divorce would likewise not be in a position to be an example to the flock. However, someone who at some time in the past suffered through a divorce, but in the years since has established a solid track record as a husband and father would not be automatically disqualified. In terms of those who are single, or married but with little experience in parenting, such persons are not automatically disqualified, but limited. They may be exemplary in all their current family relationships, but if they have no marital or parental relationships, it is difficult to see how they can be an example in those areas. Perhaps even more difficult is the question of a man who is otherwise qualified, but whose children are not noteworthy for their obedience to him (1 Tim. 3:4; Titus 1:6). What degree of obedience is required to meet this qualification? Obviously, Scripture gives no objective standard by which to measure degrees of obedience. The best solution is to recall again the purpose of the qualifications: Can this person serve as an example to the congregation in the area of parenting? If not, it would not be either wise or loving to place him in a position of leadership over the body. He needs, rather, to focus his energy on his own family.

Areas of Giftedness

In addition to his role as an example to the flock, an elder also has teaching and leadership responsibilities. Therefore, there are also some qualifications in terms of giftedness that are included in the lists. First Timothy 3:2 says an elder must be "able to teach." Titus has the same idea but expresses it in terms of an elder's ability to "encourage others by sound doctrine and refute those who oppose it" (Titus 1:9). Together, they imply that the elder must have some degree of ability or giftedness in the area of communicating God's Word, and must have an understanding of sound doctrine. Some elders may have a greater degree of giftedness in teaching or a greater depth of understanding of doctrine, but all elders should be competent in both areas. An elder should also give some evidence of giftedness in leadership, revealed in his management of his own family (1 Tim. 3:5).

Spiritual Maturity

One of the qualifications, unique to Timothy but implicit in the idea of an elder, is that of spiritual maturity. In the words of 1 Timothy 3:6, he must not be "a recent convert" *(neophytos)*. Titus has no similar language but an elder would be assumed to be a man of some years, an older man. Again, Scripture attaches no specific number to this qualification, but it is a qualification that seems to be often overlooked. Most of the prospective pastors I train as a seminary professor are relatively young men. Many are not recent converts, having grown up in Christian homes and having been converted as children. Still, many lack the maturity and judgment that come with age, and sometimes their inexperience has gotten them into trouble. Since there is no specific standard, it is hard to determine how young is too young, but this qualification serves as a warning. It is ideal when a young pastor can serve as an associate under an experienced pastor for his first few years of ministry. When that is not possible, young pastors should pursue informal mentoring relationships with older pastors in their community.

Limited to Males

There is one final qualification pervasively assumed throughout these lists. It too has become controversial in recent times. These lists assume that elders will be males. The nouns, pronouns, articles, and endings on adjectives all point to males as those in mind. An all-male eldership has been the overwhelming norm in Baptist life, and has recently been officially affirmed by Southern Baptists in *The Baptist Faith and Message 2000*,[19] but there have also been some Baptists who have begun to affirm and argue for female elders. Countless gallons of scholarly ink have been spilled in discussions of this issue, and a full review of it is beyond the scope of this book's objectives. Nevertheless, it does pertain directly to the qualifications of elders, and thus a brief recap of the key issues in this debate is in order.

Two overall perspectives have emerged among evangelical Christians over the past twenty years or so. One is called egalitarianism. It affirms the full equality of men and women, and sees the ability to serve in any role open to men as intrinsic to genuine equality for women, especially roles in the home and church.[20] The other perspective, though sometimes called traditionalism or, mistakenly, patriarchalism, is properly called complementarianism. It affirms full equality between men and women, but sees equality as compatible with differing, complementary roles for men and women in the home and church.[21] When complementarians point to passages such as the lists in 1 Timothy 3 and Titus 1 or other texts relating to differing roles in the church

---

19. Article 6 of that document states, "While both men and women are gifted for service in the church, the office of pastor is limited to men as qualified by Scripture."

20. Some of the key works enunciating this perspective are Gilbert Bilezikian, *Beyond Sex Roles: A Guide for the Study of Female Roles in the Bible* (Grand Rapids: Baker, 1985); Alvera Mickelsen, ed., *Women, Authority and the Bible* (Downers Grove, Ill.: InterVarsity, 1986); Gretchen Gaebelein Hull, *Equal to Serve: Women and Men in the Church and Home* (Old Tappan, N.J.: Revell, 1987); and Mary Stewart Van Leeuwen, *Gender and Grace* (Downers Grove, Ill.: InterVarsity, 1990). All these are representative of what is called evangelical feminism. Less evangelical but foundational to much egalitarian thought, is the important work of Paul Jewett, *Man as Male and Female* (Grand Rapids: Eerdmans, 1975). The works of more radical feminists are legion. One collection showing their approach is Letty Russell, ed., *Feminist Interpretation of the Bible* (Philadelphia: Westminster, 1985).

21. The landmark work for this perspective is John Piper and Wayne Grudem, eds., *Recovering Biblical Manhood and Womanhood: A Response to Evangelical Feminism* (Wheaton, Ill.: Crossway, 1991). It includes a comparison of the statement on "Men, Women and Biblical Equality," from the egalitarian group, Christians for Biblical Equality, with the Danvers Statement, the doctrinal statement of the complementarian group, The Council on Biblical Manhood and Womanhood (see 403–22, 469–72).

(such as 1 Tim. 2:9–15) or home (Eph. 5:22–33), egalitarians respond that such texts are culturally conditioned, were addressed to specific situations, or are, for one of a number of reasons, limited in their application, such that the limitations placed on the roles open to women in those texts do not apply today. Complementarians have argued that the passages themselves give no hint of limitation, but rather seem to be based on eternally valid principles going back to the very creation of male and female.

I remain a complementarian because I fail to see any convincing argument that empties the key texts of their significance. First Timothy 2:9–15 contains some phrases that are difficult, but the phrase prohibiting women from teaching and exercising authority, occurring as it does immediately prior to the qualifications for elders whose responsibility it is to teach and exercise authority, seems clearly intended to prohibit women from serving as elders. Other roles, such as teaching men in Sunday School classes, serving in various positions on the staff of a local church, and many other roles, were not a part of New Testament church life and thus are not directly addressed. The propriety of women serving in such roles is debatable and depends on the specific job description and the church's understanding of these roles; what seems clear is the prohibition of women serving as elders.

But what seems clear to me does not seem clear at all to others. In fact, they cannot see why I cannot see that the complementarian position stands in contradiction to the spirit of Christ and the tendency of the whole New Testament. When equally earnest Christians, equally seeking to understand Scripture, come to such opposing convictions, one wonders if there may be some unrecognized influences affecting the interpretation of Scripture.

One such influence is obviously the feminist movement. It has been one of the most profoundly important movements of the past hundred years, affecting the Western world on a variety of issues. Biblical scholarship does not occur in a vacuum but is fully exposed to the currents of history. The question is, has the feminist movement been like a light on Scripture, enabling us to see its true teaching more clearly, without patriarchal or chauvinist assumptions, or has the feminist movement been more like a light in our eyes, blinding us to what has been obvious to past generations?

A curious feature of modern society is our tendency to believe that newer is better. In terms of history, this means we tend to believe that we understand things better than our predecessors. Thus, we often underestimate the importance of historical rootedness. This is especially important in the area of theology. The Holy Spirit's ministry of illuminating the Scriptures is not a recent development. Thus, I am reluctant to believe that the overwhelming majority of exegetes and students of Scripture down through the centuries are wrong. I do not think history or tradition is infallible. I am a congregationalist, despite the fact that most Christians for centuries were not. But the burden of proof lies on the historically newer interpretation. The egalitarian interpretation cannot bear that burden. It has been unduly swayed by the secular spirit of modern, political feminism.

Another factor, helpfully noted by Stephen Clark in his book, *Man and Woman in Christ,* is the changing idea of equality and identity involved in the transition from a traditional to a technological society.[22] Clark argues that the organizing principle of traditional society was relational. What determined one's identity were one's relationships; that is, whose daughter am I, from what clan or tribe do I come, who are my ancestors? People were valued for things intrinsic to them, for *being* something as opposed to *doing* something. In technological society, the organizing principle is functional. What determines identity is what one does; that is, I am a teacher, a doctor, a mechanic. Identity is achieved rather than ascribed. Value depends on what one can do.

This distinction casts a helpful light on the egalitarian-complementarian debate. I have noticed in reading both sides that they seem to be talking past each other and rarely connecting. The egalitarian side does not believe that complementarians can really believe in genuine equality if there is a distinction in the roles open to men and women. This is rooted in the functional idea of identity. If a woman is denied the chance to achieve something simply because she is a woman, equality is undermined because it is seen in a functional framework. Equality means equal opportunity to achieve. Those in the complementary camp seem to be operating with a relational understanding of equality. Men and women can be equal and yet have different roles, because value and equality is a matter of being, not doing.

This distinction can also help resolve one difficulty that has troubled many on both sides of this debate. That difficulty is the question that arises in the minds of many when they read what seem to be prohibitions against women serving as elders: Why? It is obvious that there are many gifted women who are excellent teachers; many are very capable leaders. Why should they be prohibited from serving as pastors? It seems capricious.

---

22. Stephen B. Clark, *Man and Woman in Christ* (Ann Arbor, Mich.: Servant Books, 1980). In what follows I am drawing from Clark's argument on pp. 467–506.

There seem to be two responses to this question. First, we cannot or should not need to know all the reasons why God commands us to do as he says. There was no reason why Adam and Eve should not have eaten of the tree of the knowledge of good and evil. The fruit was ripe, delicious, and desirable. It was within reach. God had created it and put it there. The only reason for not eating of it was because God had commanded them not to do so. Obedience involves trusting, sometimes without knowing the reason.

However, in this case, there are reasons why Scripture prohibits women from serving as pastors, but they are not functional reasons. God may gift a woman in teaching and leadership, and yet ask her to serve in a context other than that of an elder, not because of any functional inability, but for relational reasons. God may have a purpose for asking males and females to relate in a certain way. Perhaps those relationships reflect something of the relationship of the Father and Son (1 Cor. 11:3). Perhaps they reflect something of God's original intention in creating men and women (Gen. 2:18; 1 Tim. 2:13). But these reasons don't make much sense to us, because they are not functional reasons. Similarly, we all know many women who seem far more capable of leading their families than their husbands. Yet one of the purposes why God assigns husbands to be the head of the family is to illustrate something of the relationship between Christ and the church (Eph. 5:23–24).

If all this is true, that is, that the egalitarian view is undergirded by a technological, functional view of life, and the complementarian view is based on a relational view of life, how do we decide which view to adopt for male-female relationships in the church today? We live in a world that is clearly dominated by a functional understanding of life, and while a functional view is perfectly acceptable in some arenas of life, faithfulness to Scripture requires adopting a relational view in the church and within the Christian family. God desires his people in these two areas to show relationships that reflect something of his nature and his relationship with us.

Scott Bartchy, though writing on a different topic, makes a helpful observation concerning the society in which the church originated. He states that there were two primary institutions in the Greco-Roman world that provided the metaphors for human relationships: politics and kinship. In the political realm *egalitarianism* was a key term, referring to things like "equal access to vote, positions of public leadership, and the ownership of property."[23] In kinship, the key term was *patriarchy*. But the New Testament, particularly

---

23. Bartchy, "Divine Power, Community, Formation, and Leadership," 97.

Luke in the book of Acts, while antipatriarchal, was not egalitarian. Bartchy says that the goal of Luke's portrayal of the development of the church in Acts "was not the creation of an egalitarian community in the political sense, but a well-functioning family in the kinship sense."[24] Egalitarianism is a political term, dealing with equal rights, and is an idea we can applaud in the political realm. But the church is a different type of entity, more like a family than a state. Issues of individual or personal rights are secondary to the health and well-being of the family, and that family may be healthiest when men and women fill complementary roles.

Therefore, since it seems to be the teaching of Scripture, since it is the overwhelming view historically speaking, and since it seems to accord with the relational view of life that the church as a family is called to exhibit, I affirm a complementarian view of male and female roles. In the church, that means that the office of elder is limited to males. How far that limitation extends to other roles not mentioned in Scripture (Sunday School teacher, youth group leader, minister of music, etc.) is a matter for debate on which we should be willing to allow a degree of diversity, since the answer seems to depend in large measure on individual factors such as the understanding of the role by the individual church, and thus must be decided on a case-by-case basis.

A Divine Call

One final matter in terms of the qualifications of the elder concerns a qualification that many think is vital, but is not found in any list. It is the matter of a divine call to ministry. Daniel Akin includes "a call to ministry and aptness to teach" as among the qualifications for the office of elder,[25] but only the second is found in the biblical lists. Nonetheless, for many Baptists, a special divine call is the most important and indispensable qualification. Commonly, the first question put to a young man seeking ordination has to do with his conversion and call to ministry. The list of those emphasizing the importance of a call to ministry includes Baptists like John Dagg, Charles Spurgeon, and W. A. Criswell.[26] Most mention the necessity of an *inward* call, which Gerald Cowen calls "a profound conviction that God has chosen one

---

24. Ibid., 98.
25. Akin, "The Single Elder-Led Church," 54.
26. See the discussion in Dagg, *Manual of Theology*, 241–54; and Cowen, *Who Rules the Church?* 17–32.

to serve Him in a special way," and an *outward* call, which is corporate confirmation of the individual's conviction, often expressed in ordination, as fellow believers affirm their belief that he is gifted and qualified to serve.[27]

Those who emphasize the necessity of a divine call want to highlight God's initiative in the lives of those who become pastors and the serious commitment involved in entering pastoral ministry. Certainly the importance of pastoral ministry is seen in the extensive qualifications that are given for the office. Certainly those who are involved in pastoral ministry should do so with the conviction that they are doing the will of God. But should that not be the goal of every believer, in all areas of life?

While there is no problem in saying that God has called some to pastoral ministry every Christian should see his or her vocation, be it medicine, business, or farming, as a calling from God.[28] The idea that there is a special divine call, unique to pastoral ministry, is not clearly found in Scripture. There is an Old Testament precedent in the calling of prophets and a New Testament precedent in the calling of apostles, but there is no clear example of the calling of pastors or elders. A survey of the terms *called* and *calling* in the New Testament finds the overwhelming proportion refer to a call common to all believers. All believers are "called to belong to Jesus Christ" and "called to be saints" (Rom. 1:6–7; 1 Cor. 1:2). Indeed, the very word *church (ekklēsia)* implies that believers are those called out by God. Paul exhorts the Ephesian believers to "live a life worthy of the calling" they had all received. Of the eleven occurrences of the word *calling (klēsis)* in the New Testament, none refer to a special calling of an individual; all but one (Rom. 11:29) seem to refer to a calling issued to all believers. Furthermore, ministry is not a work reserved for some, but the responsibility of all. First Peter 4:10 says all believers are to minister, faithfully using whatever gifts they have been given.

If, then, all believers are called to minister, how is a young man to determine if he is called to pastoral ministry? It is the same way all Christians find their area of ministry. They are to seek to serve and see if their gifts (teaching,

---

27. Cowen, *Who Rules the Church?* 29–31.

28. This was involved in Luther's idea of the priesthood of all believers: "It is pure invention that pope, bishop, priests, and monks are called the spiritual estate while princes, lords, artisans, and farmers are called the temporal estate. . . . All Christians are truly of the spiritual estate, and there is no difference among them except that of office. Paul says in 1 Corinthians 12[:12–13] that we are all one body, yet every member has its own work by which it serves the others." Martin Luther, "To the Christian Nobility of the German Nation Concerning the Reform of the Christian Estate," in *A Reformation Reader: Primary Texts with Introductions,* ed. Denis Janz (Minneapolis, Minn.: Fortress Press, 1999), 91.

leadership) equip them for pastoral ministry. They should possess a desire and willingness to serve in this way (1 Tim. 3:1; 1 Peter 5:2). They are to seek confirmation from those who know them best, especially concerning whether or not they meet the qualifications. And they are to listen for the still, small voice of the Holy Spirit that guides God's people.

What about the idea of a calling to full-time vocational ministry? First, the term *full-time* might be misleading. Does it not imply that others are part-time Christians? Should not all Christians do all they do in obedience to God's will? Does not God call for all of every Christian's life? Calvin says, "the Lord bids each one of us in all life's actions to look to his calling." He adds, "no task will be so sordid and base, provided you obey your calling in it, that it will not shine and be reckoned very precious in God's sight."[29] So all Christians are to obey God's calling in all of life's activities. All Christians are called to be full-time Christians.

As to the second aspect, vocational ministry, it is certainly valid to pay pastors (1 Tim. 5:17), and pastoral ministry is so important to the life and health of a church that churches normally seek to pay their pastors and thus relieve them of working another job to provide for themselves and their families. But God's calling is always a calling to minister, not to receive a paycheck. Anyone gifted and called to pastoral ministry should begin to seek avenues to be involved in teaching and leading, whether they are paid to do so or not. All Christians are called to minister because they are gifted, whether paid or not.

Paul provides a good example here. In Acts 18:3–4, Paul worked as a tentmaker with Priscilla and Aquila. Apparently he concluded that doing so, and thus providing for his needs, was the will of God for his life. It was God's calling for that time in his life. He ministered on every Sabbath, using his gifts in evangelistic ministry. But when Silas and Timothy came from Macedonia (with financial support for Paul), he gave himself to full-time ministry (Acts 18:5). He ministered part-time when he had to and full-time when he could. Those gifted in pastoral ministry should not wait until a church hires them full-time but should to seek to exercise their gifts as time and circumstances allow immediately. If a church recognizes the value of someone's ministry and wants to provide for him so that he can devote his full time to that ministry, that is wonderful, but hundreds if not thousands of Baptist churches have been planted and led by pastors who farmed or taught

---

29. Calvin, *Institutes of the Christian Religion,* 21:724–25 (3.10.6).

school or worked in other ways to provide for their families. Their call to pastoral ministry was no different from that of those called to serve churches that had the means to support them. Nor were they being disobedient to their calling in working in other ways to provide for their needs. God's call to all believers includes a call to provide for their needs. For some, that call is answered *through* their calling to pastoral ministry; for others, that calling is answered *alongside* their calling to pastoral ministry.

In short, while it is useful to speak of a call to full-time vocational ministry to describe a calling to a type of ministry that normally is of such value to a local church that they want to enable someone to devote his full time to it, it is open to misunderstanding and thus may require some qualification. All Christians are called to minister and to live out God's calling on their lives full-time. For some individuals, their gifts and qualifications are recognized by God's people as equipping them for pastoral ministry. As they seek God's will, they hear his call to that type of ministry. In most cases, churches will want to enable them to devote their full time to their ministry. Thus, their call to provide for their needs coincides with their call to minister. For others, their call to pastoral ministry involves serving small or new congregations that have no means to support them. They answer God's call to provide for their needs through other avenues, and answer God's call to minister as their time and circumstances allow.[30]

This discussion of the qualifications of the elder has been long but necessary. While I am a convinced congregationalist, it is obvious that churches can be healthy with any pattern of polity, if they have good and godly leaders. Even more important than the pattern of our polity is the character of our leaders. Congregations should ponder these qualifications carefully, and evaluate candidates for leadership graciously but biblically.

The Number of Elders

We raise the issue of the number of elders because, while most Baptist churches today have one pastor or elder, some see strong support in Scripture for a plurality of elders.[31] Beyond the fundamental theological question

---

30. This will also be true of most churches that adopt a plurality of elders. Normally, a number of them are not paid and are sometimes called "lay elders." They work other jobs to provide for themselves and their families, and minister as elders as their time allows.

31. Advocates of a plurality of elders include White, "The Plural Elder-Led Church," 255–96; Grudem, *Systematic Theology*, 928–36; Dever, *A Display of God's Glory*, 16–28; and Piper, *Biblical Eldership*,

of which pattern seems most in keeping with Scripture, the idea of a plurality of elders raises other practical questions of implementation. If a church has a plurality of elders, are they all equal? Would they take turns preaching on Sundays? Would they all be financially supported by the church? For larger churches with multiple staff members, would all the members of the pastoral staff be considered elders? All these questions merit consideration, but the first matter to consider is the teaching of Scripture on this issue.

When one looks at the verses containing the words *elder, overseer,* and *pastor,* a consistent pattern of plurality emerges. The church in Jerusalem is spoken of eight times in the book of Acts as having elders;[32] the church at Ephesus had elders (Acts 20:17); the churches to which James wrote had elders (James 5:14), as did the churches to which Peter wrote (1 Peter 5:1). Perhaps the strongest support is found in Acts 14:23: "Paul and Barnabas appointed elders for them in each church." *Elder* is used in the singular only three times; once in a generic sense (1 Tim. 5:19) and twice for an individual (2 John 1; 3 John 1). There is no verse describing anyone as *the* elder of a church. *Overseer* is only used as a term for a church officer four times. Three times it is used in a generic sense (1 Tim. 3:1–2; Titus 1:7). The one place where it refers to the officers of a specific church it is used in the plural, for the overseers of the church in Philippi (Phil. 1:1). The one place where *pastor* is used for a church office it is in the plural, though not referring to a specific church (Eph. 4:11).

Moreover, when church leaders are referred to in other ways, the pattern is the same. The church of the Thessalonians was commanded "to respect those who work hard among you, who are over you in the Lord" (1 Thess. 5:12). Clearly the reference is to a group, not to an individual. Likewise, the letter to the Hebrews refers three times to the "leaders" of the group to which that letter was sent (13:7, 17, 24). Looking at this evidence, E. C. Dargan states, "It appears to be well-nigh certain that in the apostolic churches generally there was a plurality of elders."[33] John Piper states categorically, "All New Testament churches had elders."[34]

In addition to this strong biblical support, there are also theological and

6. According to Greg Wills, the texts reprinted in *Polity,* ed. Mark Dever, give ten examples of earlier Baptists who also believe the New Testament churches practiced plural eldership. See Wills, "The Church," 34.

32. See Acts 11:30; 15:2, 4, 6, 22–23; 16:4; 21:18.

33. Dargan, *Ecclesiology,* 57.

34. Piper, *Biblical Eldership,* 6.

practical reasons for plurality in leadership. Theologically, the doctrine of human depravity warns us against entrusting too much power or authority to any one individual. Practically, plural leadership would seem to offer many advantages. Mark Dever says of his experience:

> Probably the single most helpful thing to my pastoral ministry among my church has been the recognition of the other elders. The service of the other elders along with me has had immense benefits. A plurality of elders should aid a church by rounding out a pastor's gifts, making up for some of his defects, supplementing his judgment, and creating support in the congregation for decisions, leaving leaders less exposed to unjust criticism. Such a plurality also makes leadership more rooted and permanent, and allows for more mature continuity. It encourages the church to take more responsibility for the spiritual growth of its own members and helps make the church less dependent on its employees.[35]

James White sees a plurality of elders as advantageous in fostering maturity as elders learn from each other, in providing a check for the errors of any one man, in better providing for the full spectrum of needs in a congregation, and as helping in the exercise of discipline.[36]

In view of the strong case for a plurality of elders, how is it that the great majority of Baptist churches today have one pastor? A variety of factors are probably involved. First, it should be noted that the single-elder model has not been universal in Baptist life. In the early nineteenth century, Samuel Jones's "Treatise of Church Discipline" noted several of the advantages of plurality in leadership,[37] and W. B. Johnson, the first president of the Southern Baptist Convention, argued from Scripture and practical benefits for a plurality of elders in each church.[38] But over time, the single-pastor model became dominant. It seems likely that the rapid growth of Baptist churches, from 150 in 1770 to 12,150 in 1860, outstripped the supply of qualified men.[39] In some churches, deacons have taken the role of elders and provide some of the benefits of plurality in leadership. In fact, many nineteenth-century Baptist

---

35. Dever, *A Display of God's Glory,* 24.
36. White, "The Plural Elder-Led Church," 282–83.
37. Samuel Jones, "Treatise of Church Discipline," in Dever, ed., *Polity,* 146.
38. W. B. Johnson, "The Gospel Developed," in Dever, ed., *Polity,* 190–95.
39. These numbers are from Mark Noll, *America's God* (Oxford, U.K.: Oxford University Press, 2002), 166.

churches saw the pastor and deacons as constituting the church's eldership.[40] In the twentieth century, the business model entered Baptist life and perhaps conditioned people toward adoption of the single pastor, patterned after the chief executive officer of the business world. In the absence of an explicit command in Scripture concerning the number of elders, the single-elder model became dominant.

There were and are others who seek to make a case for the single elder/pastor from Scripture. Gerald Cowen argues that the support for plural elders from Scripture is not as clear as may first seem.[41] For example, it is true that the church in Jerusalem had a plurality of elders, but that congregation numbered several thousand from its first day. Clearly so many could not meet in one place at one time, but met often in homes. Each home group would need a pastor-elder. Still they considered themselves one church, the church of Jerusalem. It was one church, composed of many groups with a plurality of elders. The same may have been true of the church in Ephesus, Philippi, and other cities. In fact, it is a fascinating fact that the New Testament never speaks of churches (plural) in a city (singular). One can find references to the churches in Syria and Cilicia (Acts 15:41), the churches of the Gentiles (Rom. 16:4), and "the churches of Judea" (Gal. 1:22), but it is always the church in Jerusalem, Antioch, Ephesus, and every other city. In Titus 1:5, Paul even commands Titus to appoint elders in every city. Perhaps there were elders (plural) in every city, but an elder (singular) for every congregation.

This is one possible reading of the evidence. The situation today is quite different, with churches in the same city, even those of the same denomination, seeing themselves as separate churches, with separate pastoral leadership. Thus, it can be argued that the plural eldership of the church in Jerusalem and other New Testament churches was a plurality for a different context than the one in which churches function today. However, the most that can be said for this argument is that it is a *possible* explanation for *some* of the texts, but even at that, it is an argument from silence. We are not told how many elders each house group had, but we do know that these groups were called churches (Rom. 16:5; 1 Cor. 16:19; Col. 4:15), and that it was Paul's practice to appoint elders (plural) in every church he planted (Acts 14:23), and that the church to which James wrote had a plurality of elders who are

---

40. Wills, "The Church," 34, says such a view was adopted by the Tyger River Baptist Association of South Carolina in 1835, and reflected the practice of many churches.

41. Cowen, *Who Rules the Church?* 14–16.

described as ministering jointly (James 5:14). If one elder had responsibility for a particular small group, it would have seemed more natural for James to have described that single elder as visiting a particular sick member.

Perhaps the classic case for the single pastor is that given by A. H. Strong in his influential theology text.[42] Negatively, he begins by noting that there is no requirement for a plural eldership. The New Testament nowhere prescribes any number, and the fact that many churches had plural elders may be due simply to their size. On the positive side, he points to some indications that some churches had only one pastor. He sees Acts 12:17; 15:13; 21:18; Galatians 1:19; and 2:12 as indicating that James "was the pastor or president of the church at Jerusalem, an intimation which tradition corroborates."[43] He further claims that the use of overseer in the singular in 1 Timothy 3:2 and Titus 1:7 supports the idea of a single pastor, and believes the reference to the "angel of the church" in the seven letters to the churches in Revelation 2–3 should be interpreted as referring to the pastor of each church. Finally, Strong claims that plural eldership is natural and beneficial only in cases where the size of the church requires it.

What can be said in evaluation of Strong's case for the single elder-pastor? First, he is correct in saying that there is no biblical *requirement* for plural elders. Thus, having either a single pastor-elder or a plurality of elders is not a matter of obedience to a clear command of Scripture, for there is no such command. A decision on this question is thus a matter of drawing out the implications of Scripture, and allowing a degree of diversity may be advisable.[44] Nonetheless, Strong's arguments for a single pastor are quite weak. James may have had a certain prominence in the church at Jerusalem, but that church did have a plurality of elders. The use of overseer in the singular in 1 Timothy 3:2 and Titus 1:7 is clearly generic, giving the qualifications for any elder. It really has no relevance to the issue of plurality. As to the angels of the seven churches of Revelation 2–3, it is barely possible that *angelos* in these instances refers to a pastor or elder, but it would be the only place in the New Testament or anywhere else in Greek where *angelos* bears that meaning. It is a very unlikely interpretation. By contrast, the case for a plurality of elders, outlined above, seems quite strong. In fact, it would

---

42. Strong, *Systematic Theology*, 915–16.

43. Ibid., 916.

44. For example, Akin, "The Single Elder-Led Church," says he could pastor a single elder-led church or a church with a plurality of elders or co-pastors because the New Testament allows flexibility on this matter (73).

be fair to characterize the New Testament as assuming a plurality of elders. After all, that was the pattern they would have inherited from synagogues, which employed a council of elders.

Daniel Akin, while acknowledging that it is easier to make the biblical case for a plurality of elders, nonetheless maintains that a viable case for the single elder can be made from Scripture. He points to the possibility of a single elder in house churches and contends that there is a biblical pattern for "a plurality of leaders with a senior leader over them."[45] He also notes the New Testament emphasis is on the character of leaders, rather than the number of leaders, and thus there should only be one elder in the many churches he suspects would have only one qualified man. Finally, he adds the observation that, in practice, only one can and must lead. Yet, in the end, Akin concludes that "a plurality of God-called men in leadership, led by a senior pastor/teacher" is the preferable model.[46]

In a similar fashion, Paige Patterson, while defending the position called "single-elder congregationalism," states that the position as he understands it could also be called "primary-elder congregationalism," because he acknowledges that some churches in the New Testament had a plurality of elders, and so may churches today, when necessary.[47] But he argues strongly that a plurality of elders cannot be mandated because there is no commandment relating to the number of elders. In the absence of such a command, he believes we should decide the issue of plurality based on what we see of leadership patterns elsewhere in Scripture. He says "the general pattern that emerges in the Bible is that God calls a leader from among the people." As he adds later, "it is difficult to find any place where God called a committee."[48] He believes that pattern is substantiated by the practice of church history and true to "the psychology of leadership," in that every human endeavor seems to require a leader. Thus, while many churches may need more than one elder, one among the elders "should be the primary leader and preacher-teacher for the flock."[49]

---

45. Ibid., 66. He sees evidence for this pattern in Exod. 18:19–22.

46. Ibid., 67–73.

47. Paige Patterson, "A Single-Elder Congregationalist's Closing Remarks," in Cowan, ed., *Who Runs the Church?* 283.

48. Patterson, "Single-Elder Congregationalism," in Cowan, ed., *Who Runs the Church?* 150, 152. He sees that pattern in the sole leadership of Moses, the individual judges and prophets, Peter's leadership among the apostles, the position of James in the church in Jerusalem, and the "messengers" to the churches in Revelation 2–3.

49. Ibid., 152.

For my own part, I think the consistency of the example of a plurality of elders in New Testament churches and the practical benefits that result from such a plurality constitute a strong recommendation for the advisability of adopting a plurality of elders in local churches. But I would not raise that recommendation to the level of a command. That would be going beyond New Testament teaching. I can imagine at least two situations in which I would not seek to adopt a plurality of elders, at least not immediately. The first would be a church where there were no other men qualified to serve as elders. The pastor's task in such a setting would be to mentor some who would become qualified. The second situation would be the more common scenario of a very traditionally minded church. I would not divide a church over the issue of a plurality of elders. If there was significant resistance, I would not push for immediate adoption but would teach and train the congregation in the hopes that over time the resistance would lessen. In the meantime, I would be looking for individuals in the church who fit the qualifications for elder and begin using them as elders, even without that title. That is, I would solicit their input on various ideas and seek to involve and mentor them in a variety of areas of ministry. They could provide some of the benefits of a plurality of elders without incurring the objections some would make to formal adoption of a plurality of elders. But in other cases, it may be both possible and desirable to move a church toward an open adoption of a plural leadership. For those considering moving a church toward a plurality of elders, a number of practical questions of implementation must be faced.[50]

"Where do I begin" would be a common question for pastors. Perhaps a prior question would be, "Should I begin?" Transitioning a church from a traditional practice to a smoothly functioning plural leadership will probably take at least two to three years.[51] A pastor would need to be convinced of the biblical basis and important practical benefits of such a change to make the long-term commitment transitioning would require. It may be wiser for

---

50. I have been aided in thinking through the issues in transitioning a church to a plural eldership by a book by Phil A. Newton, *Elders in Congregational Life: Rediscovering the Biblical Model for Church Leadership* (Grand Rapids: Kregel, 2005). Pastor Newton draws upon his own experience and that of several others with whom he has had contact. John Piper also reflects on the process his church followed in "Rethinking the Governance Structure at Bethlehem Baptist Church" (http://www.desiringgod.org/library/topics/leadership/governance.html, accessed September 24, 2004).

51. John Piper's church took close to four years to adopt plural eldership (see Piper, *Biblical Eldership*, 2). Four years also elapsed between Mark Dever's installation as pastor of Capitol Hill Baptist Church and their adoption of elders (conversation with Mark Dever, September 17, 2004).

those anticipating a short pastorate or unconvinced that plural leadership has New Testament sanction and practical value to not attempt a transition. Even those who are convinced and desire change would be advised to proceed slowly and build trust among the members of the congregation initially.

For those who decide to proceed with change, assessment of present practice and policy is a good starting point. Most Baptist churches have some affirmation of congregational government in their governing documents (constitution, bylaws, charter, confession of faith, etc.), but in practice, many are deacon ruled, staff ruled, or pastor ruled. In fact, Jeff Noblitt, pastor of First Baptist Church of Muscle Shoals, Alabama, was moved to transition his church to plural leadership when he realized the temptations he faced as pastor in a church where the pastor was accepted as a virtual dictator.[52] Other churches may be accustomed to rule by powerful deacons. A wise pastor will identify where he is likely to encounter problems and opposition at the outset.

The second step is a long-term focus on preaching and teaching. Phil Newton recommends studying in depth all the major texts on leadership with the existing church leadership in a context that allows for give and take, questions, and discussion on how a church can follow biblical guidelines.[53] Eventually such teaching must also be presented to the church body as a whole. Here too there must be opportunities for questions to be asked and feedback to be received.

Eventually, a specific proposal for changing the leadership structure of the church would be presented to the church. It would be best for this proposal to emerge from the existing church leadership and be presented to the church as a draft for their dialogue, discussion, input, and revision. Putting proposals in writing would force the church to think through some issues systematically.

For instance, what would the new leaders be called? Jeff Noblitt initially called them "Pastor's Council," to avoid the reaction he feared would come to the term *elders*. Eventually, his church came to accept that term, and biblically, it is the most appropriate term. But far more important than their title are their qualifications and responsibilities.

Their qualifications we have discussed at length above. We have also considered the responsibilities of elders in general, but need to speak more spe-

---

52. Newton, *Elders in Congregational Life,* 139.

53. Ibid., 152–59, presents a well thought-out plan for leading a church in working through the biblical teaching.

cifically of the responsibilities of the elders in relationship to the one called the pastor. Of course, in the Bible a pastor is simply an elder; the terms are interchangeable. But in practice, most Baptist churches have one man that does most of the public preaching and teaching and is known as *the* pastor. What would these new elders do? Would they take turns preaching?

We noted above the four responsibilities assigned to elders in the New Testament: the ministry of the Word, overall leadership of the church, pastoral ministry, and setting an example. All elders should be qualified and capable of involvement in all four. One of the qualifications is "able to teach." But there are many settings and areas of teaching. If one of the elders, the one called the pastor, is especially gifted in preaching and teaching the Word, there is no reason why he should not handle the bulk of the public preaching and teaching. In fact, it could be argued that 1 Timothy 5:17, while not validating a distinction between teaching elders and ruling elders, does recognize "a distinction in gifts and function within the eldership."[54] John Piper thinks it "very likely [that] one will be the 'preaching elder' while not excluding others from that responsibility."[55] Similarly, if an elder is particularly gifted in administration or visiting the sick, there is nothing wrong if he focuses his efforts in that area. All elders share in all the responsibilities of the elders, but they need not all share equally in all these responsibilities.

How do the other elders relate to the one called the pastor? Is he the senior elder, or the teaching elder? In New Testament terminology, the pastor is an elder, and all the elders are pastors. In terms of contemporary Baptist usage, the pastor is the one primarily responsible for the public preaching of the Word. He is usually paid and thus able to devote his full time to pastoral ministry. He is also the one most of the church members look to for leadership and ministry. By virtue of his intense involvement, experience, and giftedness, he may exercise leadership among the elders, but he should not seek to be the senior elder in the sense of ruling over them, lest he and the church lose one of the major advantages of a plurality of elders, namely, the help other mature and godly men give in decision making and leadership of the church. The pastor should see himself as one of the elders, accountable to them and under their corporate authority, even as they as a whole are under the ultimate authority of the congregation.

Another question could be asked concerning the relationship of the elders

---

54. White, "The Plural Elder-Led Church," 282.
55. Piper, "Rethinking the Governance," 17.

to the other staff members in churches with multiple staff. Are all staff members elders? Not automatically. Not all the jobs on a modern church staff require those who would qualify as elders. For example, many fine youth ministers, Christian education ministers, and music ministers could perform their ministries well, without necessarily meeting all the qualifications for elders. However, staff members exercising general pastoral oversight and leadership should probably qualify as elders to hold their positions. Which staff members function in that way would differ from church to church and from job description to job description. The other staff members, though they may have responsibility for a specific area of ministry, are accountable first to the elders, as those charged with general oversight of all the ministries of the church; second, to the congregation as a whole; and, ultimately, to the Lord.

How many elders should a church have? A church should set no fixed number, but wait to see how many the church recognizes as qualified and how many are willing to serve. However, the larger the church, the larger the number of elders it will need to shepherd the flock.

Another important issue would be the process for selecting elders. Scripture gives little explicit help on this matter. Paul and Barnabas appointed elders in the churches they planted (Acts 14:23); Titus was to appoint elders "in every town" in Crete (Titus 1:5). Aside from those two instances, elders and overseers appear in the churches of Jerusalem, Ephesus, Philippi, and elsewhere with no explanation. However, two biblical principles would seem to apply. The biblical support for congregational church government would argue for a role for the congregation in the process. The biblical teaching on the leadership role for the elders would support their involvement in and oversight of the process. Below are some suggestions for a process that incorporates these two biblical principles and that has been found workable in local church contexts.

Certainly, the pastor would want to preach very carefully on the qualifications for elders prior to any selection process. After careful examination of the qualifications, all members of the congregation would be invited to pray and submit nominees. Perhaps requiring that such nominations be accompanied by a rationale explaining how the person nominated meets the biblical qualifications would be advisable to lessen frivolous nominations or the idea that such nominations are a popularity contest.

Someone or some group would then have to screen the nominees. Initially, the screening committee might consist of the pastor and the deacons, or a special committee chosen for the purpose; later, the existing elder body would be the obvious choice. This group would receive and evaluate the nominees, with the pastor, or an elder, giving leadership and oversight. Some members of the committee may know of circumstances that would make some nominees ineligible. Those the group considered as at least possibly qualified would be contacted concerning their willingness to serve. Those willing would then be asked to complete some material, evaluating their own qualifications. They would be asked doctrinal questions, indicating their understanding of God, the gospel, the church, and other basic doctrinal issues. They would be asked to evaluate their own marriage and family relationships, and other aspects of the qualifications. The group would review each nominee's responses. All those seen as willing and qualified would be brought before an ordination council. Such a council is often formed of local pastors but could be formed of a local church's elders as well. This council would ask further questions relating to the fitness of the nominees to serve as elders. The council would then issue a recommendation to the church, in favor of or opposed to ordination.

The names of those nominated and recommended for ordination and service as elders of the church would then, for the first time, be made known to the church at large. Those who were initially nominated but not recommended would never be mentioned publicly. A period of time (two to three weeks) would be given for any church member to give a reason to the committee why a nominee is unqualified and should not be accepted. The committee would investigate any such charge. If found valid, the nomination would be withdrawn. If there were no challenge, or any challenges were found to be invalid, the congregation would be asked to affirm or reject the nominee. While all prospective leaders should receive a clear consensus of approval, it would probably be wise to specify a percentage (e.g., 75 percent of those voting) required for a nominee to be selected.

All those selected would be ordained. This ordination would not signify that the individual was entering "full-time vocational ministry" but would be the church's affirmation of his qualifications to serve as elder and recognition of his entering into ministry as one of their elders. A wise pastor would also set a priority on training new elders, especially in their first year or so of service.

A final matter in the selection of elders would be the issue of terms of service or rotation. By virtue of his character, an elder should always serve as an example to the flock, but there is no biblical barrier to the possibility that an elder could take a time apart from active service in the church leadership. There are pluses and minuses to mandatory rotation from active service after a set length of time. Some advocate rotation on the ground that it keeps any one individual from accumulating too much power, but internal account-ability among the elders should prevent that occurrence. More cogent is the observation that circumstances in an individual's life may change. Family or career responsibilities may change and affect one's ability to minister as an elder. Provision should be made for such situations. In opposition to manda-tory rotation are the observations that some elders' skills and abilities in min-istry may improve over time, that we don't force pastors to rotate out of their ministry, and that mandatory rotation could mean the replacement of quali-fied elders by unqualified or less qualified men. John Piper sees the issue of terms of service as balancing the need to have the most qualified men in positions of leadership with the need "to guard against burn out and stagna-tion."[56] On the whole, a church should have a provision for rotation of elders, and encourage elders to take a sabbatical from active service from time to time, but leave the final decision on an individual's rotation to the individual in consultation with the elders.

Finally, there should be a statement in a church's constitution or bylaws mandating an annual review of the church's leadership structure, to be done by the elders and reported to the congregation. This would include matters such as rotation of one or more elders off active service and the solicitation of nominees for new elders, if needed. It would also be an appropriate time for reviewing the paid staff of the church, and considering if further staff need to be added. It would also provide an opportunity to review the church's policies as to the qualifications and responsibilities of the elders, to inform new members and refresh longtime members on these matters.

All these proposals should be incorporated within the church's governing documents. Since some may believe that a plural eldership implies elder rule, it may be wise to state explicitly that ultimate authority for church decisions resides in the congregation, acting under Christ's lordship and headship, and that the authority exercised by the elders is delegated to them by the congre-gation and is ultimately subject to congregational review. It may even be help-ful to delineate some of the specific decisions that are reserved for the

---

56. Piper, *Biblical Eldership*, 11.

congregation (approval of budgets, hiring of staff, approval of elders, any decisions affecting the church as a whole) and those that are delegated to the elders. On the whole, though, it would be wise and healthy to keep the congregation as involved as practically possible, while recognizing the impossibility of congregational involvement on every minor item. Congregational involvement would seem to be an incentive to congregational commitment, which is another reason to preserve congregational government alongside a plurality of leadership.

Moving a church to a plurality of elders could be problematic. It is still very much a minority view in Baptist life today, and Baptist churches like change as little as most other churches. There is no biblical command that requires churches to adopt a plural eldership and thus there is no problem with a pastor moving slowly on this issue or even working informally with a group he sees and relates to as elders, even if they are not recognized as such by the church. Some remain convinced that the single-elder model has a solid biblical basis or that there should be a primary elder if a church has a plural eldership. On the whole, the weight of the biblical evidence supports plural eldership, and the practical benefits offered by a plurality of elders seem considerable. Thus, churches should move toward a plural elder model with two conditions: (1) that the church have men who meet the qualifications for elder, and (2) that the church be accepting of such a change.

CHAPTER 8

THE OFFICE OF DEACON

Servants of the Church

THE OFFICE OF DEACON HAS been universally accepted among Baptists, but their understanding of the nature and responsibilities of deacons has undergone a number of shifts over the years. In some ways, those shifts have paralleled shifts in the understanding of pastors or elders. Now with a resurgence of interest in examining the role of elders, the time seems ripe for a corresponding reconsideration of the role of deacons, especially in the area of leadership.

THE BIBLICAL BACKGROUND

While *deacon* is the universal term for this office, the word *diakonos* and related terms in the New Testament are much more often translated by terms like *servant* or *minister*.[1] The verb *diakoneō* is found thirty-six times in the New Testament, reflecting the same uses of the term as secular Greek: to wait on someone at a table, to care for someone's basic needs, or to serve in a general sense.[2] The related noun *diakonia* is usually translated as service, and *diakonos* as servant. Only in two texts is the meaning clearly that of deacon (Phil. 1:1; 1 Tim. 3:8–13). Most see Acts 6:2–4 as related to the origin of

---

1. It is interesting to note that recent translations like the New International Version or New American Standard render *diakonos* and the related terms by "minister" much less often than the King James Version, perhaps recognizing that "minister" in contemporary English use connotes more of an ecclesiastical office, whereas *diakonos* in New Testament use is more a general word for "servant."
2. K. Hess, "Serve, Deacon, Worship," in Brown, ed., *New International Dictionary of New Testament Theology,* 3:545.

deacons, and some see Romans 16:1 as a basis for the office of deaconness, but that is a matter that will require further examination below.

The major importance of knowing the broader background of *diakonos* is in understanding the role deacons were designed to play. There was no counterpart to deacons in Judaism, and with the scanty material in the New Testament, theologians have taken the normal meanings associated with *diakonos* as indicating the types of activities appropriate to deacons, namely, caring for material needs and general serving. Nothing in the background suggests that it is a role of leadership or authority.

The Origin of Deacons

Most see Acts 6 as describing the origin of deacons or, at least, the prototypes of deacons.[3] Though some object that Luke nowhere applies the term *diakonos* to the men chosen to coordinate the distribution of food to widows, there are several good reasons for the traditional view. First, the related noun *diakonia* and a form of the verb *diakoneō* are found in Acts 6:1–2. Second, the qualifications and activities of the men selected in Acts 6 seem commensurate with the more detailed information in 1 Timothy 3:8–13. Third, if Acts 6 is not linked to the origin of deacons, we have an office with no precedent in Jewish society, with no origin described in Scripture, and yet an office that was widely and readily accepted by New Testament churches.

The Qualifications of Deacons

The qualifications of deacons are found principally in 1 Timothy 3:8–13. The seven chosen in Acts 6 were to be "full of the Spirit and wisdom" (Acts 6:3), and that is consistent with the description in 1 Timothy 3, but the latter list of qualifications is more complete. There are important similarities and differences between the qualifications for deacons and those for elders, found in 1 Timothy 3:2–7 and Titus 1:5–9.

All three passages portray a dignified man of good reputation. All three exclude drunkenness and greed. Titus 1:9 and 1 Timothy 3:9 both have a concern that the individual know sound doctrine. First Timothy 3 requires a de-

---

3. Saucy presents arguments for and against seeing the origin of the office in Acts 6, and concludes by calling the seven selected in that text as "prototype deacons." Robert Saucy, *The Church in God's Program* (Chicago: Moody, 1972), 154–55.

gree of maturity for both elder and deacon, though the requirement is worded differently, with the warning that the elder must not be a new convert (v. 6), while the deacon must be tested first (v. 10). Titus 1:6 says an elder must be blameless, a requirement for deacons in 1 Timothy 3:10. All three have the same qualification in terms of marriage ("husband of one wife") and a similar requirement in the area of parenthood, with 1 Timothy 3 using the same verb, *prohistēmi,* or manage, for both elder and deacon (see vv. 5, 12).

There are also noticeable differences. The list of qualifications for the deacon is considerably shorter and less detailed than that for the elder. The office of elder seems to have somewhat more stringent requirements. Also, there are certain functions associated with the elder that are not associated with the deacon. The elder must be "able to teach" (1 Tim. 3:2) or "encourage others by sound doctrine and refute those who oppose it" (Titus 1:9). The deacon must know doctrine, but he is not charged with teaching it to the church. This is not to say that an individual deacon cannot be gifted in teaching; Stephen was one of the seven and yet may have been a gifted teacher. But the gift of teaching is not intrinsic to the office of deacon. Also, the office of elder is explicitly linked with the function of oversight, both in the fact that elder is synonymous with overseer and in specific phrases identifying the elder as the one who must "take care of God's church" (1 Tim. 3:5); he is the one who "is entrusted with God's work" (Titus 1:7). Finally, there is one requirement for deacons that has no counterpart for elders. It is found in the description in 1 Timothy 3:11 of the *gynaikas,* a much debated and controverted word that requires separate discussion. Some see it as referring to deacons' wives and is thus another qualification for deacons; that is, they must have wives of a certain character. Others see the word as indicating a third office, that of deaconness. We will examine the arguments for and against both views shortly.

THE ROLE AND RESPONSIBILITY OF DEACONS

One reason for considering the qualifications of deacons so carefully is that they provide a clue to the role and responsibility of deacons. We have no description in the New Testament of deacons acting as deacons, with the single exception of Acts 6, which, while controverted, is still widely used as a model for the ministry of deacons. Aside from that episode, we have no example of deacons at work. In what follows, we will draw clues for the role and responsibility of deacons from the associations that gather around the word *diakonos* itself, from the description of the actions of the seven in Acts 6, and by implication from the qualifications in 1 Timothy 3.

The associations around the word *diakonos* we have already mentioned. The word is closely associated with humble, some would say even menial, service. That does not make such service unimportant, for even the offering of a cup of cold water in Christ's name brings reward (Matt. 10:42). Christian leaders are called upon to exercise leadership in a humble spirit, but leadership itself is not an activity normally associated with *diakonos*. Thus, it seems likely that deacons are not called to give leadership to the church in the same way as are elders. If the two offices were identical, why would two be needed? *Diakonos* indicates more of a support role than *episkopos* or *presbyteros*.

The example in Acts 6 fits the distinction between the ministry of leaders (elders/overseers/pastors) and the important but different ministry of other servants (deacons). The rationale for the selection of the seven is given in the apostles' words, "It would not be right for us to neglect the ministry of the word of God in order to wait on tables" (Acts 6:2). The distribution of food was important; it threatened to divide the early church. But the apostles could not do everything, and their calling was "the ministry of the word of God."

The relationship of the ministries of elders and deacons has been seen in the same light. The elders are called to the ministry of the Word of God and to overall leadership of the church, while the deacons are called upon to deal with the material needs of the people, the care of the sick and poor, and the temporal affairs of the church in general. These were the functions assigned to the deacons, especially in the churches that emerged from the Reformation. Calvin says simply, "The care of the poor was entrusted to the deacons."[4] One of the very earliest Baptist confessions, the 1611 Short Confession of John Smyth, says that deacons "attend to the affairs of the poor and sick brethren," and many other Baptist confessions echo similar ideas.

Another common duty or role of deacons in Baptist life is derived from the phrase "wait on tables." Benjamin Keach said, "The Work of Deacons is to serve Tables, viz. to see to provide for the Lord's Table, the Minister's Table, and the Poor's Table."[5] The reference to the Lord's Table indicates that deacons often assisted pastors or elders in the celebration of the Lord's Supper. R. B. C. Howell, in one of the most influential books on the diaconate of the nineteenth century, states concerning the duties of deacons: "The table of the Lord must fre-

---

4. Calvin, *Institutes of the Christian Religion*, 21:1061 (4.3.9).
5. Benjamin Keach, "The Glory of a True Church," 66.

quently be spread. The necessary furniture for the purpose, as well as the elements, must be provided and superintended."[6] Deacons also assisted in the distribution of the elements, though leading in the administration of the ordinances was seen as a responsibility limited to elders. The reference to the minister's table, or the minister's remuneration, reflects the growing role deacons would have in the financial affairs of the church in the nineteenth and twentieth centuries. The reference to the Poor's Table indicates the same responsibility mentioned by Calvin, that the deacons administered the ministry of the church to the needy.

The example in Acts 6 can also be applied in a more general way. The pastors or elders of the church are given the job of teaching the Word of God, providing pastoral ministry to the members, and giving overall leadership to the church. That is a job too demanding for any one person, and it can be challenging even for a body of elders. The deacons are there to assist the pastors and relieve them of any duties that would prevent them from doing those things that most require their energy, time, and attention. John Piper says, "From our study it would seem that the office of deacon exists to assist the leadership of the church by relieving the elders of distractions and pressures that would divert them from the ministry of the word and prayer and the general, visionary oversight of the church."[7] Those "distraction and pressures" may vary from church to church. At one church, there may be so much hospital visitation that pastors have no time to study and prepare to teach God's Word. Deacons could assist in that area of ministry. In another church it may be an aging building that requires considerable maintenance. Deacons could relieve pastors of the need to deal with those matters. Perhaps one reason why, in the providence of God, we are not given an explicit job description for deacons is to allow them the flexibility to serve in a variety of roles that allow the elders to focus on those things that most utilize their gifts and most match their calling. This is reflected in descriptions of the deacons' role as caring for the secular or temporal affairs of the church, so that pastors may be "relieved from secular burdens, and be left to the spiritual service of the church."[8] While every service offered to Christ is a spiritual service, there are some ministries more properly done by elders and others that may be handled by other godly servants, namely, deacons.

---

6. R. B. C. Howell, *The Deaconship* (Philadelphia: American Baptist Publication Society, 1846), 82.

7. John Piper, "Rethinking the Governance."

8. Dagg, *Manual of Theology*, 266.

Further hints are supplied as to the role and responsibility of the deacon in the qualifications listed in 1 Timothy 3:8–13. First, simply the fact that he is listed alongside the elder with a varying list of qualifications implies that his duties are different. We noted above that there is no requirement for an ability to teach, implying that teaching God's Word is not part of the job of the deacon. Managing God's work or the church is not explicitly mentioned, implying that the deacon is not one who exercises oversight of the church as a whole, but he is required to manage his household well, so the role may involve limited oversight of a particular area. Not being greedy is mentioned (v. 8), and so the role of the deacon may have something to do with the finances of the church. That has in fact been one of the responsibilities consistently associated with the office of deacon. In early twentieth-century Baptist life, management of business and financial affairs identified the ministry of most Baptist deacons. A very popular book on deacons stated, "The business of the church and its finances constitutes the special and distinct assignment of the deacons."[9] Perhaps this ministry also accounts for the fact that deacons must first be tested (v. 10), to prove their trustworthiness before handling funds. His skill in managing his household (v. 12) would also support the role of management of the temporal affairs of the church.

But most of the qualifications listed for deacons are similar to those of elders. This implies that deacons may share at least one of the functions of elders, that of setting an example of Christlike character. Anyone identified as an officer of the church in some way represents the church publicly and is thus required to possess a degree of maturity. It also indicates that the office of deacon is not a small, unimportant ministry that anyone can render. Though it may involve humble service, if it is to be limited to men who are required to have this type of blameless character, it must be important. Indeed, the ministry of a deacon can profoundly affect the lives of individuals and the health of the church, and thus it must be exercised in a Christlike way.

However, these biblical clues have not been the only factors influencing Baptist perceptions of the role and responsibility of deacons. Howard Foshee says that in the late 1800s, "the business-world concept of 'board of directors' was, unfortunately, transferred to the church."[10] With the board of directors idea, the distinction between the overall leadership role of the elders and the

---

9. P. E. Burroughs, *Honoring the Deaconship* (Nashville: Sunday School Board of the Southern Baptist Convention, 1929), 69.

10. Howard Foshee, *The Ministry of the Deacon* (Nashville: Convention Press, 1968), 32–33.

serving role of the deacons began to blur. In practice, many deacon boards practiced something close to elder rule. Beginning in the 1950s, there were several books calling deacons to involvement in ministry more than management.[11] The most common expression of this commitment to ministry has been the Deacon Family Ministry Plan, in which deacons take some responsibility for a degree of pastoral ministry to a number of families in the church. According to one researcher, by 1990, one-third of Southern Baptist churches had adopted the Deacon Family Ministry Plan.[12] Yet even the Family Ministry Plan has the potential of perpetuating the confusion of the roles of pastor and deacon.

The best way to clarify the role and responsibility of deacons would be the establishment of a plural eldership. That would force churches to think through the relationship of the two offices and would result in a renewal of the servant aspect of diaconal ministry, with leadership left to the elders. As to specifics, it seems advisable for churches to follow the pattern of Acts, in which the roles and responsibilities of deacons are left flexible, to enable them to address whatever is hindering the ability of their church's elders to accomplish their ministry.

THE NUMBER AND SELECTION OF DEACONS

There is no biblically mandated number of deacons a church should have, though Gerald Cowen observes that if the church in Jerusalem only chose seven for a church with several thousand members, by comparison most Baptist churches have too many deacons.[13] Once again, the wisest course is to specify no number or ratio the church must maintain, but to be guided by two factors: the needs of the church and the number of qualified candidates, with the second being the more important of the two. A church can do well with a small number of deacons, but to have unqualified deacons invites problems. Moreover, there is no need for annual elections of deacons. Rather, new deacons should be selected as needs arise and as existing deacons need to

---

11. Robert Naylor, *The Baptist Deacon* (Nashville: Baptist Press, 1955), was a very important book in this regard, emphasizing the importance of deacon involvement in servant ministries like visitation of the sick. The emphasis continued in the 1968 book by Foshee, *The Ministry of the Deacon*, and the still more recent book by Robert Sheffield, *The Ministry of Baptist Deacons*, ed. Gary Hardin (Nashville: Convention Press, 1990).

12. Bruce Grubbs, introduction to *The Ministry of Baptist Deacons*, 10.

13. Cowen, *Who Rules the Church?* 114.

withdraw from active service. A mandatory rotation of deacons is not neces-sary, though deacons should be allowed to step down without any sense of failure or disqualification if they feel called to a different area of ministry, simply need to rest, or if the elders feel that a rotation would be in the best interest of the church and the deacon.

Deacons would be selected, then, only when vacancies arise or new areas of need are identified. As to the method of selection, Acts 6 points to congre-gational action. In a manner similar to that with elders, nominations could be made by any member, submitting names along with a rationale showing how the individuals nominated match the biblical qualifications. This pre-supposes, of course, that these qualifications have been explained to the mem-bers. As with the elders, there needs to be a body that screens the names. The best body would be a group of elders. In churches without elders, the pastor and a couple of the senior deacons would probably be the best choice. They would examine the names of those nominated, eliminate those who obvi-ously did not meet the qualifications, and talk to the remaining individuals concerning their willingness, their evaluation of their fitness, and their sense of call to this ministry. A list of all those found to be qualified and willing would then be submitted to the congregation.

At this point, many churches make a needless mistake. If they have more names of qualified and willing candidates than their bylaws or constitution prescribe, they often ask members to select only some of the names submit-ted. For example, suppose a church's bylaws prescribe four new deacons, but eight qualified and willing applicants are found. Members are often asked to pick four of the eight. The result is that the election becomes more of a popu-larity contest than an affirmation of deacon candidates, and those not elected quite often become bitter and resentful. Rather, the church should vote yes or no for each name and take the number of deacons approved by the church. If all are qualified, there is no reason why all should not serve. Few churches have an overabundance of willing and qualified servants.

DEACONESSES

The final issue we must consider in connection with the office of deacon is the propriety of the corresponding office of deaconess. This is a difficult question for several reasons. There are good arguments on both sides con-cerning the interpretation of the key texts, there is evidence on both sides from church history, there are pragmatic issues pro and con, and one can argue for or against the office based on how one understands the office of deacon. This is an area of growing diversity among Baptists. I will try to present both sides of the issue and give the position I feel best fits the evidence, but acknowledge that it is a complex question.

The biblical evidence for the office of deaconess rests primarily on two texts. The first is 1 Timothy 3:11. In the midst of a chapter devoted to giving the qualifications for church offices, we find a verse listing the qualifications for those simply called *gynaikas*. The word means women, but can also be translated wives, and is translated that way in many English translations (KJV, NIV, TEV, ESV). In the context of 1 Timothy 3, however, many feel that it refers to a special group of women, deaconesses.

The Interpreter's Bible treatment of this verse helpfully summarizes the arguments on both sides.[14] In favor of seeing the verse as referring to deaconesses are the following:

1. It appears in a context dealing specifically with church order.
2. The word *hōsautōs*, "in the same way," is used in verse 8 to introduce the qualifications for deacons; its usage in verse 11 indicates the introduction of a new category parallel to deacons.
3. The virtues required in verse 11 are similar to those required for deacons, arguing for a similar office.
4. If verse 11 refers to deacons' wives, why is there no reference to the wives of elders?
5. If the writer meant to refer to wives, he would have added the pronoun *their*, but it is missing.

In support of the view that *gynaikas* refers to the wives of deacons are the following points:

1. If the writer meant deaconess, why use *gynaikas*?[15]

---

14. Fred D. Gealy, "The First and Second Epistles to Timothy and the Epistle to Titus: Introduction and Exegesis," in *The Interpreter's Bible*, ed. G. A. Buttrick (New York; Nashville: Abingdon, 1955), 11:417–18. Gealy lists six commentators who support the deaconess interpretation and six who support the deacon wife interpretation.

15. Alexander Strauch, *The New Testament Deacon: The Church's Minister of Mercy* (Littleton, Colo.: Lewis & Roth, 1992), 116–17, points out that when discussing the offices of overseer (v. 2) and deacon (v. 8), Paul uses the title. If he begins discussion of the office of deaconess in verse 11, why is there no reference to the title for the office?

2. The list of qualifications is much shorter than that for deacons or elders, too short for a new office.
3. There is an office for women, discussed at length in 1 Timothy 5:9–16.
4. Deacons' wives fits the flow of thought in verses 8–13 (deacons, their wives, their marital and family life).
5. Deacons' wives would inevitably be involved in their ministries to some extent and, therefore, needed to be women of character, not prone to gossiping or drunkenness.

Of the two sets of arguments, the arguments in favor of deaconess appear to be the weaker. As to why the wives of elders are not mentioned, Alexander Strauch sees the reason lying in the differing roles of elders and deacons. An elder is charged with the responsibilities for teaching and leading, responsibilities Paul does not give to women (1 Tim. 2:12), but a deacon is charged with responsibilities his wife may and should share.[16] In fact, the only one of the five arguments for deaconess that cannot be cogently explained by the opposing view is the last, the absence of the pronoun *their* before *wives,* and that is an argument from silence. On the other hand, three of the arguments for seeing *gynaikas* as wives (arguments 1, 4, and 5) are quite strong and without convincing rebuttal from the opposing side. Therefore, it seems that 1 Timothy 3:11 is not a biblical basis for the office of deacon, but rather, adds another qualification for the office of deacon. To be qualified for the office of deacon, a man must have a wife of character, who can be trusted to assist her husband in the diaconal ministry.

The second controverted text is Romans 16:1, in which Phoebe is referred to as a *diakonos* of the church in Cenchrea. Here the appropriate title for the office is used, but most English versions of the Bible translate the word as "servant" rather than "deaconness." The arguments here are fewer in number, but more evenly balanced. In favor of translating the word as "servant" are the facts that (1) of the twenty-nine times *diakonos* is used in the New Testament, servant is overwhelmingly the normal translation, and (2) at the time Romans was written, there is no record of any church, with the possible exception of Jerusalem (Acts 6), that had recognized deacons. The church at Philippi did (Phil. 1:1), as did the church at Ephesus (1 Tim. 3:8–13), but both of those epistles are later than Romans. How could Paul speak of Phoebe as filling an office that was not yet recognized? But the church would be fa-

---

16. Ibid., 127.

miliar with references to people being called "servants." Paul had used the word to refer to rulers (Rom. 13:4), and had used it for himself and Apollos (1 Cor. 3:5) and Tychicus (Eph. 6:21; Col. 4:7), and in each instance it is translated "servant." However, in support of the deaconess interpretation it must be noted that none of these other texts refer to a *diakonos* of a specific church, as does Romans 16:1. It suggests some type of official service. Moreover, the description of her ministry in Romans 16:2 fits well with the type of ministry associated with deacons. On this text, I take a mediating position. To me, the linkage of Phoebe with a specific church suggests some type of recognition, but to call her a deaconess seems to anticipate later developments and is without clear biblical precedent.

Thus, in terms of biblical evidence there is little clear support for the office of deaconess. However, that should not completely end the discussion, for we have a number of positions in contemporary churches not mentioned or contemplated in the New Testament. It would be difficult to find explicit biblical support for the idea of a youth minister, or minister of education or music, yet we have found such positions useful. Deaconess may be a similarly useful position, even if it is not a biblically mandated office. After weighing the arguments for and against deaconesses in 1 Timothy 3:11, John Piper concludes, "It seems that the decision will not be made with confidence simply from this text alone but will be made on the basis of the wider consideration of what it is appropriate for women to do according to all the New Testament teaching."[17] If deacons perform such "appropriate" ministries, then there is no automatic bar to calling such servants, when female, deaconesses.

There is some evidence of deaconesses in the early church. The earliest clear discussion comes from a third-century document called the *Didascalia*. But A. G. Martimort argues that "the ancient institution of deaconesses . . . was encumbered with not a few ambiguities."[18] For the first five centuries, deaconesses were found in only a limited number of Eastern churches, and not at all in Egypt, Ethiopia, Rome, Africa, or Spain.[19] Their chief function was "assistance at the baptism of women, at which, for reasons of propriety, many of the ceremonies could not be performed by deacons."[20] As infant

---

17. Piper, "Rethinking the Governance," 30.

18. A. G. Mortimort, *Deaconesses: An Historical Study,* trans. K. D. Whitehead (San Francisco: Ignatius Press, 1986), 250.

19. Ibid., 5–6.

20. F. L. Cross and E. A. Livingstone, eds., "Deaconess," in Cross and Livingstone, eds., *The Oxford Dictionary of the Christian Church,* 381.

baptism became increasingly the norm, this function was no longer needed, and deaconesses virtually disappeared.

Among Baptists, there has been a mixed appraisal of deaconesses. The first English Baptist confession of faith, penned primarily by Thomas Helwys, specifically refers to "Deacons, Men and Women who by their office releave the necessities off the poore and impotent brethre concerning their bodies, Acts 6.1–4."[21] However, most confessions are silent as to the gender of deacons. Church records reveal that deaconesses were not uncommon among early Baptists, but were found mainly among the General Baptists. The Particular Baptists, by far the larger branch of Baptists, allowed women less active roles.[22]

There were notable advocates of deaconesses among nineteenth-century Baptists in America. R. B. C. Howell argues that Scripture "authorizes, and in some sense, certainly by implication, enjoins the appointment of deaconesses in the churches of Christ."[23] He calls them "female assistants to the deacons," whose duty it was to minister to females, to help the sick and helpless, and to assist females in being baptized. He also acknowledged that some churches have failed to appoint deaconesses and that, in some such cases, women of intelligence and piety have voluntarily undertaken the necessary duties, becoming "substantially deaconesses," making "amends for the want of proper ecclesiastical action."[24] J. R. Graves, while Howell's opponent on most issues, agreed with him on this issue, seeing "no good reason why saintly women should not fill the office of deaconess to-day in most churches. In fact, they often perform the duties of the office without the name."[25] A third example comes from First Baptist Church of Waco, Texas, whose records show that they recognized six deaconesses in 1877, during the pastorate of B. H. Carroll, who was later the founder of Southwestern Baptist Theological Seminary.[26]

But such churches were never the norm. Charles W. Deweese notes, "Although deaconesses have existed in every century of Baptist life, the position has never been widespread."[27] Deaconesses began to decline, especially in the

21. The spelling is that of the original, reproduced in Lumpkin, *Baptist Confessions of Faith*, 121–22.

22. Leon McBeth, *Women in Baptist Life* (Nashville: Broadman, 1979), 140.

23. Howell, *The Deaconship*, 131.

24. Ibid., 134.

25. Graves's statement is found in McBeth, *Women in Baptist Life*, 142. McBeth's source is an article in the February 22, 1879 newspaper, *The Baptist*.

26. McBeth, *Women in Baptist Life*, 143.

27. Deweese, *A Community of Believers*, 102.

twentieth century as the role of the deacons began to change from ministry to management. With the business model dominating church life, most churches hesitated to put women on the "Board of Directors."[28] Churches that did so were viewed as moderate or liberal, for placing women in positions of leadership was seen as violating 1 Timothy 2:12. But today there is something of a revival of interest in deaconesses, even among churches that see the eldership as limited to males. They can utilize deaconesses because they see the role as one of service rather than leadership. Since John Piper understands the office of deacon to involve neither teaching nor leading men, he concludes, "It appears then that the role of deacon is of such a nature that nothing stands in the way of women's full participation in it."[29] Mark Dever testifies that his church has felt itself free to recognize deaconesses, because they clearly distinguish the deacons from the elders, with the latter assigned responsibility for leadership and limited to males.[30]

What is one to make of this debate? Certainly the contemporary feminist movement has sensitized us to the importance and value of women being involved in ministry. Indeed, in many churches, women have served in the role of deaconess without the title. With 60 percent of American church members female, the need for females to minister to other women in many areas is obvious. Moreover, there are considerable historical precedents and some possible biblical passages to support the recognition of deaconesses, such that churches cannot be charged with explicitly violating Scripture if they utilize deaconesses in a serving role. However, as noted above, the passages cited (Rom. 16:1; 1 Tim. 3:11) are not clearly pointing to an office of deaconess. First Timothy 3:11, assumes that the wives of deacons are part of the qualifications for the diaconate and will help them in their ministry, particularly in their ministry to other women. Thus, the need for ministry to women by women has an obvious group designed to meet that need, the wives of deacons, whose character qualifies them and their husbands for such ministry.[31] In addition, Romans 16:1 is simply indicating the recognition of Phoebe's ministry as a servant in her church. She is like millions who have followed her, who have served because they were gifted and empowered by the Spirit, and saw areas where their service was needed. Regardless of whether they

---

28. Ibid., 103.

29. Piper, *Biblical Eldership*.

30. Dever, *A Display of God's Glory*, 13–14.

31. I have seen this idea put into practice in a Baptist church we were a part of in Mundelein, Illinois. Husbands and wives were elected and served very effectively as deacon teams.

have a formal office and title or not, such godly servants quietly and simply serve. They deserve the same commendation as Phoebe.

ORDINATION

Baptist churches traditionally ordain their leaders, both elders and deacons. But why? What does ordination mean and what does it accomplish? For such a widespread practice, there is a surprisingly sparse biblical basis.

Possible Old Testament precedents include events like the commissioning of Joshua as Moses' successor (Num. 27:18–23), or the consecration of Aaron and his sons (Exod. 28–29; esp. 28:41) and the Levites (Num. 8:5–22), but none of these are real parallels to contemporary ordinations. There is no suggestion in the New Testament that Moses is in any way a model or type of a pastor or deacon, and ordination is not seen as transferring power to lead a nation. As to the consecration of priests, the New Testament teaches a priesthood of all believers and calls upon them all to be a set-apart, or holy, people.

In the New Testament, there is no record of anything like a formal ordination of the twelve apostles. They were simply called and appointed by Christ (Mark 3:14; Luke 6:12–13). The apostles themselves neither ordained nor appointed successors; thus any theory of ordination as involving apostolic succession or transfer of apostolic authority is problematic at best. The evidence for something like ordination is limited to Acts and the Pastoral Epistles.

In Acts 6:1–6, we find the closest parallel and clearest basis for ordination to a church office. If, as argued above, Acts 6 does narrate the origin of deacons, verse 6 describes their ordination. They were selected by the congregation and received public recognition, followed by apostolic laying on of hands. Alan Culpepper notes several similarities between this account and the commissioning of Joshua as Moses' successor in Numbers 27:18–23. In each case, there is an appointing, a reference to the Spirit, a public presentation, and a laying on of hands.[32] However, there is also an important difference. The seven appointed in Acts 6 were not replacing or succeeding the apostles, as Joshua was Moses. Rather, the seven who were ordained were to assist the apostles, as the Levites were to assist Aaron and his sons.

Laying on of hands is also found in Acts 13:3, where Paul and Barnabas were set apart for the ministry to which God had called them, but laying on of hands is not mentioned in Acts 14:23 or Titus 1:5, where elders are ap-

---

32. Alan Culpepper, "The Biblical Basis for Ordination," *Review and Expositor* 78, no. 4 (1981): 478.

pointed. The word used in Titus 1:5, *kathistēmi,* is used in Acts 6:3 for the appointment of the seven, is found three times in Hebrews for the appointment or ordination of priests (5:1; 7:28; 8:1), and does seem associated with an official type of appointment. The word used in Acts 14:23, *cheirotoneō,* can mean choose or elect by raising hands, raising the question of congregational involvement. The context seems to indicate that Paul and Barnabas appointed the elders in this case, but the active role of the congregation elsewhere in Acts argues for at least "the concurrence of the congregations."[33] In any case, laying on of hands, which some see as the "actual act of ordination,"[34] is not mentioned in these two texts.

Laying on of hands is mentioned twice in connection with Timothy (1 Tim. 4:14; 2 Tim. 1:6). It seems that both Paul and the presbytery laid hands on him, and that act was associated with a gift, perhaps an empowering of the Spirit for ministry. However, such giving of gifts is not mentioned in other contexts of ordination, and is not included in the instructions regarding elders in 1 Timothy 3 or Titus 1. In any case, it is not clear if Timothy was ordained as a pastor/elder at all. He may have been commissioned as Paul and Barnabas were in Acts 13, to a special ministry, but not to a regular church office. Thus, using the descriptions regarding the laying of hands on Timothy as a pattern for contemporary ordinations is problematic. A final reference in 1 Timothy 5:22, warning Timothy to not be hasty in the laying on of hands, is probably a reference to ordination of elders, since it is found in a section dealing with elders. Other references to laying on of hands have to do with conferring of the Spirit (Acts 8:17–18; 19:6), healing (Mark 6:5; Acts 9:12, 17; 28:8), and blessing (Matt. 19:13–15; Mark 10:16).[35]

Over the course of church history, ordination grew in importance. It

---

33. Richard Longenecker, "The Acts of the Apostles," in *The Expositor's Bible Commentary,* ed. Frank Gaebelein (Grand Rapids: Zondervan, 1981), 9:439.

34. Saucy, *The Church in God's Program,* 163.

35. It is interesting to note that there was once a fairly strong sentiment among some early Baptists that laying on of hands should be given to all baptized believers. The Philadelphia Baptist Association adopted the Second London Confession verbatim, but felt compelled to add two articles. One dealt with singing in worship, and the other with the laying on of hands, which they referred to as an ordinance of Christ "to be submitted unto by all such persons that are admitted to partake of the Lord's Supper." The purpose of this act was for "a farther reception of the graces of the Spirit, and the influences thereof; to confirm, strengthen, and comfort them in Christ Jesus." However, other churches and associations, such as the Charleston Association, often adopted the Philadelphia Confession, but dropped this article. See the discussion in Lumpkin, *Baptist Confessions of Faith,* 348–53.

eventually became viewed as a sacrament, conferring grace and the gift of the Holy Spirit on the recipient. Also, since ordination was asserted to go back in unbroken succession to the apostles, ordination also conferred on one a share in the authority Christ granted to the apostles. Thus, as Glenn Hinson puts it, by virtue of their ordination, "the clergy were thought to differ *essentially* and not just functionally from the laity."[36]

This understanding of ordination came under sharp attack in the Reformation, because it contradicted the idea of the priesthood of all believers, it created a false dichotomy between clergy and laity, and it lacked biblical warrant. Even so, the idea that the ordained are a special class persists, even among many evangelical groups, and militates against the biblical idea that all believers are called to ministry. Raymond Bailey even makes the following radical suggestion: "Perhaps the doctrine of the priesthood of believers could best be demonstrated by doing away with ordination altogether. It may well be that the greater diversity of ministries does not call for more ordinations but for the abolition of the practice as counter-productive to the mission of the church in the modern world."[37] He suggests that we could observe baptism as the ordination of every believer for service and thus find a way to affirm all believers in their call to ministry. At the same time, he acknowledges that ordination may be too firmly entrenched in our traditional practices to be abandoned.[38]

The most famous Baptist of the late nineteenth century, C. H. Spurgeon, refused ordination, due to the sacramental understanding common in England. Yet there is a biblical basis for recognizing leaders in some way, and a properly understood practice of ordination could serve some positive purposes.

First and most important, ordination allows a church to affirm the gifts, character, and calling of those it recognizes as qualified to serve as elders and deacons. This seems to be something of a biblical principle, that God confirms individual leading by corporate affirmation. For example, it wasn't the case that Paul and Barnabas heard God's call to go out as missionaries and went out; they and their church heard that call together and the body then affirmed that call and sent them out (Acts 13:1–3). Corporate affirmation, if

---

36. E. Glenn Hinson, "Ordination in Christian History," *Review and Expositor* 78, no. 4 (1981): 485 (emphasis in original).

37. Raymond Bailey, "Multiple Ministries and Ordination," *Review and Expositor* 78, no. 4 (1981): 533.

38. Ibid., 534.

taken seriously, could be a powerful means of confirming God's call to ministry in the lives of many prospective pastors and deacons.

This idea of corporate affirmation leads to two suggestions in the actual practice of ordination. First, the laying on of hands should not be limited to those ordained, but open to any member of the congregation. If ordination is not about communicating sacramental grace, but affirming someone's gifts, character, and calling to ministry, what is to prevent any believer from laying hands on a brother whom he or she can affirm? Such a practice has biblical precedent (Num. 8:10), it accords with the meaning of laying on of hands,[39] and it is in keeping with a congregational understanding of ordination, in which it is the church, not some ordained elite, that acts to ordain. Second, if ordination is primarily a way to affirm that one has the gifts, character, and calling requisite for a particular ministry, and if all believers are called to ministry, then something similar to ordination ought to be widespread in the church. Since ordination has legal implications and could cause some misunderstanding if widely practiced because it is associated almost exclusively with pastoral ministry, perhaps on these additional occasions it should not be called ordination. Commissioning, or blessing, or affirming would all serve the same purpose—to give corporate affirmation of individual calling. It would also reinforce the idea that all believers are called to some form of ministry.

A second positive result of a careful practice of ordination would be that it would allow for appropriate recognition of the church's leaders. Such recognition seems presupposed by scriptural commands regarding leaders, who must be recognized if they are to be respected and highly regarded (1 Thess. 5:12–13), obeyed (Heb. 13:17), or called to pray for the sick (James 5:14). Recognition of leaders fits with the admonition to do all things decently and in order (1 Cor. 14:40).[40] It is also fitting to recognize them and set them apart, not because they are somehow part of an elite class, above the laity, but because they perform an important ministry in and for the church, a ministry that merits the support and prayers of the body.

39. See Culpepper, "The Biblical Basis for Ordination," 481: "The laying on of hands by the church was primarily a blessing and an expression of prayer for the one being appointed to minister in that congregation."

40. Suggestions for the elements to be included in an orderly ordination service can be found in Bill Leonard, "The Ordination Service in Baptist Churches," Review and Expositor 78, no. 4 (1981): 549–61. For an example of an ordination sermon, see John S. Hammett, "Ordination Sermon," Proclaim! 32, no. 3 (2002): 39–40.

A third positive result of a careful practice of ordination could be the protection of churches from ill-prepared, unqualified, or heretical pastors. This *could be* the result, but the current practice of ordination in many Baptist churches is so casual that it affords little protection. One proof of this casual attitude is the fact that no one, at least in my experience, has ever been denied ordination. Ordination councils are commonly called to examine a candidate and may question him concerning his call to ministry, his character, and doctrine, but the outcome of such a council is never in doubt. Indeed, often the ordination service is already scheduled to take place an hour or so after the council meets, presupposing that the ordination will proceed. Of course, the responsibility cannot be placed finally upon the ordination council. After all, they only make a recommendation to the church. The church is the ordaining body, and thus it is the church that should make a genuine evaluation of a young man's character and gifts. Only then can their affirmation be genuine. But most churches seem grateful or even proud that they have those in their midst who have been "called to the ministry," and would sooner casually approve their application for ordination than question their calling, character, or doctrine.

Here the topics of parts 2 and 3 of this book come together. Only a congregation of regenerate members would be able to evaluate a prospective leader; only a congregation that accepts its responsibility as the governing body of the church would be willing to evaluate prospective leaders. Under congregational government, churches have little right to complain about their leaders, for it is the churches that certify their calling, character, gifts, and doctrine when they ordain them. If they practice ordination wisely, they will have little cause to complain of their leaders, for they will have protected themselves from leaders who merit complaints.

Finally, a very pragmatic reason for continuing the practice of ordination in the United States has to do with the country's legal system. The U.S. tax code was developed in a time when ordained ministers were seen as assets to their communities, contributing to the general welfare. Thus, there are considerable tax advantages made available to ordained ministers. Also, in some states ordination is required for performing legally valid marriages. Such pragmatic, legal reasons perhaps would not be sufficient to justify ordination in and of themselves, but neither are they unimportant or unworthy of consideration. Thus, the advantages of ordination clearly outweigh the dangers, as long as its meaning is clearly and carefully explained.

CONCLUSION

These issues surrounding church government have required three lengthy chapters, and the main points may have gotten lost in the details. Thus, by way of summary and conclusion, I briefly describe how a church governed in the manner described in these chapters would look. It is an idealized description, but it incorporates ideas and practices that have roots in Scripture and Baptist heritage—ideas and practices that are being utilized in some Baptist churches today.

A congregationally governed church begins with a congregation of regenerate members. These members all sign a covenant commitment to the church each year, pledging themselves to live, pray, and work for the welfare of the church. They feel a sense of ownership of the church and attend business meetings in a prayerful spirit, seeking to play their part in discerning God's guidance for their body. They are actively involved, using their gifts to serve the body and affirming others in their ministries.

This church is led by a group of elders, selected by the congregation after careful reflection on the biblical qualifications for that office. One (or more) of the elders is paid a salary by the church and thus is able to devote his full time to pastoral ministry. He is called the pastor, but sees himself as one of the elders, responsible along with the other elders for the overall leadership of the church. However, because he is particularly gifted and trained, he does most of the public preaching and teaching and handles most of the day-to-day pastoral and administrative duties. He is grateful, however, that he has other elders who have been longtime members of the congregation, are men of character, and are also gifted in the areas of leadership and teaching. They deliberate with him over the decisions facing the church, and share with him in shepherding the congregation, with each elder taking leadership in areas where he feels he has the most to contribute. Some may share some of the teaching responsibilities; some may focus on pastoral ministry with the sick and hurting; others may give attention to the financial health of the church, or the youth or children's ministries, or evangelism. As a body, they are entrusted by the church with the authority to make most of the day-to-day decisions regarding individual situations, and they take that responsibility seriously, devoting time in each of their regular meetings to prayer over these matters. However, they value the congregation's input and bring matters affecting the congregation at large to the regular church business meetings.

Such matters would include things like the church's budget, the addition of paid staff, the selection of elders and deacons, and matters of church discipline. The leadership of the elders is respected and generally followed, but there is also a genuine belief that the Lord leads his church through his people, and so the feedback and contributions of members are often incorporated in final decisions.

Along with the elders who give overall leadership, the church has a number of deacons who assist the elders. They make sure the church buildings and grounds are properly maintained, coordinate many of the church's ministries, and serve where the church's needs and their gifts dictate. They are chosen as the church recognizes the need for them and discerns qualified individuals among their members. Their wives serve alongside them, and indeed, a wife of godly character is one of the qualifications for selection as a deacon. These wives serve especially in teaching and ministering to the women of the congregation, in accordance with their gifts. Some are especially gifted in counseling; others keep in close contact with shut-in members of the congregation; still others make sure moms are happy with the nursery and children's ministries.

Ministry is by no means limited to elders and deacons. All members are challenged to recognize that they are called to minister, and they are urged to discover and develop their gifts. The church leaders take the initiative to recognize and affirm publicly those who are using their gifts through commissioning services for those going on short-term mission trips, public recognition and prayer for those who work in the nursery or with the youth, and encouragement of those with the appropriate gifts and character to seek ordination.

A church that operates in a fashion similar to this is consistent with Scripture and offers many advantages. It is not the only possible healthy model. Many Baptist churches will operate with one pastor/elder and a traditional board of deacons, and such churches can still be healthy, vital bodies. In other churches the staff may be the elders; still others may go beyond the model suggested above to elder rule; some may have deaconesses who serve along with deacons. Indeed, there are healthy and vital Presbyterian, Pentecostal, Methodist, and Lutheran churches with virtually none of the elements of the model above. God can bless and use imperfect instruments, for that is all we find on earth. More important than the model of government is the character of the leaders. Still, some models are less imperfect than others. The model

outlined above incorporates four principles that reflect faithfulness to biblical teaching, and offer safeguards to a church's health, especially over the
long term.

The first and most important of these principles is congregational government. Baptist pastors may be attracted to elder rule because it seems far
easier to deal with a group of elders than with a stubborn congregation, and
some verses seem to support a strong authoritative role for the elders. But
elder rule misreads Scripture and is at best shortsighted, for one of the pastor's
goals must be for the members of his congregation to mature spiritually. In
the end, they are the ones who must give financially to support the ministry
he envisions; they must act if the church is to love and reach and disciple
people as he desires. They are far likelier to give and act on plans they have
had a part in developing. And, if the members are maturing spiritually, why
would a church or its pastors want to cut themselves off from the wisdom
they may contribute? By far the most important goal of a pastor, and the goal
that will contribute most to the long-range health of a church, is the development of a congregation that is able and willing to govern itself. In most
churches, the development of such a congregation may be a multiyear project,
but wise leaders will nurture such congregations and lead them to practice
congregational government.

A second key principle is a plurality of leadership. This is recommended
by the scriptural examples of elders (plural), by the doctrine of depravity
(which warns against the concentration of power in any one individual), and
by the realities of ministry (no one pastor has the wisdom and gifts sufficient
for leading an entire congregation). This plurality is best exercised in a body
of elders, but where recognition of elders could divide a congregation, a wise
pastor could still develop plural leadership informally, taking a number of
godly men into his confidence, seeking to involve them in ministering among
the congregation, and utilizing their counsel in making decisions and rec-
ommendations to the church. In some churches, the staff or the deacons virtually serve as elders. Such a model may work, but too often, the individuals
involved are not qualified for elder-type responsibilities. And if the deacons
are serving as elders, the responsibilities that properly belong to deacons may
be neglected.

That leads to the third principle. There need to be two categories of leaders
in a church. Some give overall leadership, provide pastoral ministry and
teaching, and set an example of Christian conduct. Another category of leaders

also help set an example, but serve in a support ministry, enabling those charged with overall leadership to focus on overall concerns and not become enmeshed in specific detailed concerns. Among these support leaders, there need to be men and women, for more than half of the church's members are women and they have some needs best met by other women. Some women serve in such a capacity, without any title, motivated simply by their love for Christ and their desire to minister in his name. But the Bible makes specific provision for women to lead in this way, as the wives of deacons. Some churches may want to call such women deaconesses, other churches may choose to not recognize them formally at all. Regardless, the point is that every church needs women who will minister in such a way to other women.

The final principle involved in healthy church government is not a specific organizational point but the cultivation of an atmosphere that will affect every aspect of the church's organization. That atmosphere to be cultivated is one of challenge, encouragement, and affirmation in the area of every member ministry. For the church to be and do all it is called to do and be, every member needs to be involved in ministry. A healthy church will be one where individuals hear the challenge to minister, receive the encouragement and equipping they need to minister, and are affirmed in their ministry. This includes a careful practice of ordination to pastoral ministry, but goes far beyond just pastoral ministry, just as the church's ministry extends far beyond just pastoral ministry. Exactly how far a church's ministry extends and what it should include is the topic of the next chapter.

—————————— STUDY QUESTIONS FOR PART 3 ——————————

1. What are the arguments, pro and con, for episcopal, presbyterian, and congregational church government?
2. Do you agree with Mark Dever's assertion, "The congregation will have their say"? Do congregations really want to govern themselves? How important is it to you to have a voice in your church's direction?
3. What would be some of the benefits in having a plurality of elders in a local church? What difficulties might it involve?
4. Write a job description for the office of pastor or elder, drawing upon the relevant New Testament texts and the discussion in chapter 7.
5. Write the qualifications for the office of elder in concrete terms, indicating where you agree and disagree with the position taken in this book.

6. Which of the qualifications for the office of elder do you see as most important? Do you think churches take these qualifications seriously when looking for a pastor? Are there members in your congregation who meet these qualifications and thus could be elders?

7. What roles have you seen deacons exercise in churches? What roles do you think they should exercise?

8. Does 1 Timothy 3:11 give a basis for the office of deaconess? Give your understanding of this verse and its relevance to the office of deacon.

9. Who actually ordains someone to ministry—the ordination council, those who lay hands on him, or the whole church? What does ordination mean or signify?

10. How important are all these organizational matters? Do they really affect a church's health? Would you have any problem joining a church that practiced presbyterian or episcopal polity? Why or why not?

——————————— BOOKS FOR FURTHER STUDY ———————————

Brand, Chad Owen, and R. Stanton Norman, eds. *Perspectives on Church Government: Five Views of Church Polity.* Nashville: Broadman & Holman, 2004. The three major forms of polity are presented here, along with three congregational models. The chapters on the single elder-led church by Daniel Akin and the congregation-led church by James Leo Garrett Jr. are particularly good. Unfortunately, the Presbyterian and Episcopalian contributors do not make the best cases for their positions.

Cowan, Steven B., ed. *Who Runs the Church? Four Views on Church Government.* Grand Rapids: Zondervan, 2004. This book is another in the popular Counterpoint Series, this one giving four approaches to church government, advocated and critiqued by four able scholars. Peter Toon presents episcopalianism, L. Roy Taylor, Presbyterianism, Paige Patterson, single-elder congregationalism, and Samuel Waldron, plural-elder congregationalism.

Cowen, Gerald. *Who Rules the Church? Examining Congregational Leadership and Church Government.* Nashville: Broadman & Holman, 2003. This book gives a judicious examination of New Testament teaching on the call, role, authority, and qualifications of the pastor-elder. Cowen advocates pastoral leadership in the context of congregational government and emphasizes the importance of a divine calling for the pastor-elder.

Dever, Mark. *A Display of God's Glory,* 2nd ed. Washington, D.C.: Center for Church Reform/9 Marks Ministries, 2001. This is a brief but helpful treatment of what Dever calls "the basics of church structure: deacons, elders, congregationalism and membership." Like Cowen, he makes a good case for congregational government; unlike Cowen, he advocates a plurality of elders and allows for the possibility of deaconesses, if their role is clearly distinguished from that of the elders.

Dever, Mark, ed. *Polity: Biblical Arguments on How to Conduct Church Life.* Washington, D.C.: Center for Church Reform, 2001. Though cited previously, this book deserves mention here too, for its ten historical reprints give examples of historic Baptist teaching on the topics of this chapter, and the introductory essay by Greg Wills gives a helpful overview.

Newton, Phil A. *Elders in Congregational Life: Rediscovering the Biblical Model for Church Leadership.* Grand Rapids: Kregel, 2005. This book argues for the validity of plural eldership in Baptist churches, and more important, offers detailed practical suggestions for moving toward implementation of such polity in a Baptist congregation.

"Ordination for Christian Ministry." *Review and Expositor,* Fall 1981. I hesitate to list this resource because it will only be available to those with access to theological libraries, but seven articles in this journal are devoted to the issue of ordination, treating biblical, theological, and practical issues. I do not agree with the perspectives of all the articles, but on the whole, they give helpful information on a topic rarely treated elsewhere in any depth.

Piper, John. *Biblical Eldership.* Available at http://www.desiringgod.org/library/tbi/bib_eldershi.html, accessed September 24, 2004. Piper's study cites virtually all the relevant texts on eldership, and gives a detailed treatment of the qualifications of elders. Particularly helpful are the eleven biblical principles of local church governance he derives from Scripture.

———. "Rethinking the Governance Structure at Bethlehem Baptist Church." Available at http://www.desiringgod.org/library/topics/leadership/governance.html, accessed September 24, 2004. Much of the material in this document is similar to that in *Biblical Eldership,* only this document reflects the decision-making and policy-making process used by Bethlehem Baptist as they moved to adoption of a new governance structure, with a plurality of elders, and deacons and deaconesses serving in supportive roles.

Piper, John, and Wayne Grudem, eds. *Recovering Biblical Manhood and Womanhood: A Response to Evangelical Feminism.* Wheaton, Ill.: Crossway, 1991. This book contains several essays relating to the controversy over the proper roles women may fill in churches. The final chapter contains a helpful comparison of the views of the egalitarian organization, Christians for Biblical Equality, and those of the complementarian organization, the Council on Biblical Manhood and Womanhood. Also, the notes to the various essays will lead the reader into the voluminous literature on this issue.

Strauch, Alexander. *Biblical Eldership: An Urgent Call to Restore Biblical Church Leadership.* 2d ed. Littleton, Colo.: Lewis & Roth, 1988. This book has been one of the most influential arguments for a plural eldership. It consists mainly of an exposition of all the relevant passages on elders in the New Testament. Most of his points are sound, with the exception of his denigration of congregational government.

Webb, Henry. *Deacons: Servant Models in the Church.* Rev. ed. Nashville: Broadman & Holman, 2002. This is the most recent in a series of books produced by Southern Baptists to guide their churches and deacons in their understanding of a deacon's ministry. It has been widely influential, going through several editions since 1980. Its chief shortcoming is a lack of adequate discussion of the distinction between the ministry of the elder and that of the deacon.

PART 4

WHAT DOES THE CHURCH DO?

THE MINISTRIES OF THE CHURCH

Five Crucial Concerns

IN THIS CHAPTER, WE LOOK AT THE church in terms of its visible activities. Theologians differ in the number and names they give for these activities. Millard Erickson sees four functions as "essential to the spiritual health and well-being" of the church: evangelism (both local and global), edification (which includes fellowship and teaching as means of edification), worship, and social concern.[1] Stanley Grenz speaks of a threefold mandate of the church: worship, edification, and outreach, all manifesting the church as community.[2] Edmund Clowney describes the church's activities in terms of service: "The church is called to serve God in three ways: to serve him directly in *worship;* to serve the saints in *nurture;* and to serve the world in *witness.*"[3] John Newport approaches this topic by considering the purpose of the church (to express Christ's lordship in the church and world) and then enumerating nine ways in which the church carries out that twofold purpose, including worship, service, fellowship, discipline, organization, edification and education, and proclamation and testimony.[4] In his very popular book, *The Purpose Driven Church,* Rick Warren encourages churches to allow their activities,

---

1. Erickson, *Christian Theology,* 1060–68.
2. Grenz, *Theology for the Community of God,* 638.
3. Edmund Clowney, *The Church,* Contours of Christian Theology (Downers Grove, Ill.: InterVarsity, 1995), 117 (emphasis in original).
4. John Newport, "The Purpose of the Church," in *The People of God: Essays on the Believers' Church,* ed. Paul Basden and David Dockery (Nashville: Broadman, 1991), 23–38.

programs, and structure to be driven by five purposes: worship, ministry, evangelism, fellowship, and discipleship.[5]

The approach taken in this chapter comes closest to Warren's, but differs in three ways. First, I describe the same five activities, but with differing terminology. I call teaching, fellowship, worship, service, and evangelism the five *ministries* of the church that serve the overall *purpose* of glorifying God. In using the word *ministries*, I in no way intend to imply that these activities belong in some special way to the officers of the church. As argued in the previous chapter, all members of the church are ministers. Nor do I mean to suggest that these five ministries exhaust all that a church might do in terms of ministry, though they do seem fairly comprehensive categories. Rather, I want to maintain that these five ministries are biblically mandated for all churches; that is, all churches must undertake these ministries to be biblical churches.

Second, I differ from Warren in relating these ministries directly to the nature of the church. I argue that these five ministries form a distinguishing mark of the church and are intimately related to the church's nature. Warren's interest in the purposes of the church is how they help revitalize and direct a church's life. He sees them as equally applicable to each person's life.[6]

Third, I differ in the derivation of these ministries. Warren states that his church derived their five purposes from the study of many passages of Scripture, but especially from two texts that seemed to them to summarize all the church is to do and be: Matthew 22:37–40, which gives the Great Commandment to love God with all your heart and your neighbor as yourself, and Matthew 28:19–20, which gives the Great Commission to go and make disciples of all nations.[7] I see Acts 2:42–47 as a more appropriate text for deriving these ministries, since it refers explicitly to the early church's life and does so in a way that is deliberately descriptive. (See Fig. 9.1 for the phrases from this passage that show the presence of these five ministries in the life of the early church.) Warren does see Acts 2:42–47 as another way to present the church's purposes, but does not note what I see as its paradigmatic importance.[8]

---

5. Warren, *Purpose Driven Church*, 103–6.

6. See Warren's extremely popular book, *The Purpose Driven Life* (Grand Rapids: Zondervan, 2002), which gives these same five purposes as answering for each individual the question, What on earth am I here for?

7. Warren, *Purpose Driven Church*, 102–3.

8. For Warren, see Warren, *Purpose Driven Church*, 119. For the paradigmatic nature of Acts 2:42–47, see Richard Longenecker, who calls Acts 2:42–47 a "thesis paragraph on the state of the early church," and sees the repeated use of the imperfect tense as indicating that these verses give the habitual, ongoing practices of the early church. Longenecker, "The Acts of the Apostles," 9:288ff.

"They devoted themselves to the apostles' teaching."	The Ministry of Teaching
"They devoted themselves . . . to the fellowship. . . . All the believers were together and had everything in common. . . . They broke bread in their homes and ate together with glad and sincere hearts."	The Ministry of Fellowship
"They devoted themselves . . . to the breaking of bread and to prayer. Everyone was filled with awe. . . . They continued to meet together in the temple courts . . . praising God."	The Ministry of Worship
"Selling their possessions and goods, they gave to anyone as he had need . . . enjoying the favor of all the people."	The Ministry of Service
"And the Lord added to their number daily those who were being saved."	The Ministry of Evangelism

Figure 9.1: The Ministries of the Church in Acts 2:42–47

THE MINISTRIES OF THE CHURCH AS A MARK OF THE CHURCH

In chapter 2, we discussed the classical marks of the church (the church is "one, holy, catholic, and apostolic") and the Reformation marks of the church (a true church is marked by the right administration of the sacraments and the pure preaching of the gospel). Those marks, properly understood, still have some value today, especially the mark of the preaching of the gospel. In fact, as Millard Erickson asserts, the gospel lies at the heart of the ministry of the church.[9] A church that loses the gospel ceases to be a church.

But while those marks may have sufficiently distinguished true churches

---

9. Erickson, *Christian Theology,* 1069–76.

from their rivals in the past, the five ministries of the church serve as a help-ful mark to distinguish churches from parachurch groups today. Parachurch groups number in the thousands and form one of the most pervasive fea-tures of American Christianity in the post–World War II period. Groups such as Focus on the Family, Campus Crusade for Christ, and World Vision Inter-national have staffs numbering in the thousands, with budgets in the mil-lions of dollars, and are well known to millions of American church members. And while not rivals of churches, parachurch groups have existed in some tension with churches.[10] On the side of the churches, the tensions are often associated with the perception that parachurch organizations take money and workers away from churches; on the side of the parachurch groups, the charge is sometimes made that churches are dead and that there would be no need for parachurch groups if churches did their ministries as they should.[11]

A recognition of the ministries of the church as a mark of the church could be a helpful first step in lessening these tensions. Basically, the distinction between the church and the parachurch organization is that of generalist and specialist. The church has an assignment from God to provide teaching, fellowship, worship, service, and evangelism to people of all ages, sexes, and races. They cannot just do teaching, or just do missions, or just work with prisoners, or just work with college students. A distinguishing mark of the church is its calling to minister in a holistic way to all types of people. They are generalists. The parachurch has the luxury of specializing in a particular type of ministry to a selected group of people. As Rick Warren observes, "most of the parachurch movements begun in the past forty years tend to specialize in one of the purposes of the church. . . . I believe it is valid, and even helpful

---

10. See, for example, the title of the study of this topic by Jerry White, *Church and Parachurch: An Uneasy Marriage* (Portland, Ore.: Multnomah Press, 1983). For a more detailed treatment of the relationship of church and parachurch, see John Hammett, "Selected Parachurch Groups and South-ern Baptists: An Ecclesiological Debate" (Ph.D. diss., Southern Baptist Theological Seminary, 1991). For two varying assessments of the relationship of church and parachurch, see Philip Jensen and Tony Payne, "Church/Campus Connections: Model 1" and Mark Gauthier, "Church/Campus Con-nections: Model 2," in *Telling the Truth: Evangelizing Postmoderns*, ed. D. A. Carson (Grand Rapids: Zondervan, 2000), 199–213. Jensen and Payne think parachurch groups are churches if they gather to proclaim God's Word to a group of God's people; Gauthier advocates a partnership between churches and parachurch groups.

11. See the discussions in Wesley Willmer, J. David Schmidt with Martyn Smith, *The Prospering Parachurch: Enlarging the Boundaries of God's Kingdom* (San Francisco: Jossey-Bass Publishers, 1998), 170–80; and International Commission on Evangelical Cooperation, *Cooperating in World Evangelization: A Handbook on Church/Para-church Relationships*, Lausanne Occasional Paper no. 24 (Wheaton, Ill.: Lausanne Committee for World Evangelization, 1982).

to the church, for parachurch organizations to focus on a single purpose. It allows their emphasis to have greater impact on the church."[12] The church should not envy the parachurch's ability to specialize nor feel inferior if they cannot do a ministry as well as the parachurch group. Specialization does allow a higher degree of proficiency, but requires a narrower breadth of ministry. A medical general practitioner is not threatened by the heart specialist. On the contrary, she is happy to be able to refer a patient with a heart problem to him. The heart specialist, on the other hand, should not look down on the general practitioner nor think that he is able to care for all the needs of the patient. Rather, he should send the patient back to the general practitioner for ongoing care. Both cooperate for the health of the patient.

This supplies a helpful metaphor for the relationship of church and parachurch. A pastor need not feel threatened if his men get more excited about going to a Promise Keepers conference than going to the men's prayer breakfast; the parachurch group has the benefit of specialization. But neither should the college students in Campus Crusade conclude that their church is dead and that their Campus Crusade meeting is where real spiritual life is found. If that is so, why are there no senior adults or families with preschoolers there? No, Campus Crusade has the luxury of catering to the type of worship college students enjoy. Churches are called upon to minister to all types of people with all types of needs. Where possible, churches should freely take advantage of the specialized services offered by parachurch groups, and even seek to recognize church members who work for such groups as extensions of their church's ministry. At the same time, the church cannot abdicate any ministry to a parachurch group, for Christ has entrusted it to the church. For their part, parachurch groups should "understand the primacy of the church in the day-to-day spiritual lives of most Christians"[13] and thus seek to operate as genuine arms of the church. John Stott has said we may grade parachurch groups on this basis: "independence of the church is bad, cooperation with the church is better, service as an arm of the church is best."[14] The ideal would be for parachurch groups to operate consciously in a servant partnership with churches.[15]

---

12. Warren, *Purpose Driven Church*, 126.

13. Willmer et al., *The Prospering Parachurch*, 178.

14. John Stott, "Theological Preamble," to *Cooperating in World Evangelization*, 13.

15. For more detail on what such a model would involve, see Hammett, "Selected Parachurch Groups," 235–40, or John S. Hammett, "How Church and Parachurch Should Relate: Arguments for a Servant-Partnership Model," *Missiology: An International Review* 28, no. 2 (2000): 199–207.

The most important point is that churches must provide these ministries. It is a part of their calling. A church that has no teaching ministry, or that has no evangelistic impact, or whose members never experience fellowship, is an unhealthy church, one whose well-being is severely damaged and whose very being as a church is called into question. Elmer Towns and Ed Stetzer say, "a church is no longer a true church when it abandons the functions of a church."[16]

Moreover, churches are called to provide such ministries to all types of people. The only qualifications a church can make for membership is regeneration and a life lived in conformity with a profession of faith in Christ. Beyond that, churches are called to welcome all types of people. Students of church growth tell us that churches grow most rapidly when they attract people who are like those who are already members. That may well be so, but if it is, it is a mark of our fallenness, for in Christ, there "is neither Jew nor Greek, slave nor free, male nor female" (Gal. 3:28). A distinguishing mark of the church in the world today must be its openness to all types of believers and its provision of all the types of ministries it is charged to provide.

THE MINISTRIES OF THE CHURCH AND THE NATURE OF THE CHURCH

The challenge to provide teaching, fellowship, worship, service, and evangelism to all types of people is a daunting one, but one that is not in the least capricious or beyond the ability of churches to meet. In particular, this section shows how the ministries of the church are inherent in the nature of the church.

For example, take the ministry of teaching. It is certainly important to the church. It is required of all elders that they be "able to teach" (1 Tim. 3:2), and in the one place where the noun *pastor* is used for a church officer, it is joined to *teacher* (Eph. 4:11: "pastors and teachers"). Even the early name for Christians, *disciples*, means learners or students, and all Christians are called "to teach and admonish one another" (Col. 3:16).

How is the ministry of teaching inherently connected to the nature of the church? It is inherent in the nature of the God to whom the church is related. The church is the people of God, and that God is the God of truth. The church is the body of Christ, who is himself "the way, the truth and the life" (John

---

16. Towns and Stetzer, *Perimeters of Light*, 70. They specifically mention preaching and observing the ordinances as mandatory biblical functions of the church.

14:6). The church is the temple of the Spirit, who is the Spirit of truth, given to guide us into all truth (16:13). But truth is not self-evident. Because of the fall, our minds are darkened. The fallen world hates the truth, and the evil one is the father of lies. Therefore, the church must provide a ministry of teaching. It is called to be "the pillar and foundation of the truth" (1 Tim. 3:15). Furthermore, the church must have a teaching ministry because the church is called into being by the gospel. This gospel is a message, not an opinion. It has content and provides an outlook on life, a worldview. There-fore, believers must be taught the message, for that message is "the power of God unto salvation" (Rom. 1:16).

A similar argument can be made for fellowship. The word *church (ekklēsia)* is used most often in the New Testament, not for an invisible ideal but for actual gatherings of believers, who meet with each other and sense that they belong together because God has called them together. The images for the church underscore the connectedness of the members with one another. The church is the people of God, not his individuals. The church is the body of Christ, not separated parts. Most of all, the church is the temple of the Holy Spirit and it is the Spirit who is especially associated with fellowship. The implication seems to be that fellowship, the Spirit, and the church belong together, for part of the very nature of the church is that it is indwelt by the Spirit, whose presence creates fellowship. That is why the apostolic benediction of 2 Corinthians 13:14 specifically ascribes fellowship to the Spirit: "May the grace of our Lord Jesus Christ, and the love of God, and the fellowship of the Holy Spirit be with you all." Moreover, the "living stones" that make up the church (1 Peter 2:5) are only living stones because they have been given new life by the Spirit (John 3:5–8; 6:63). The building composed by these living stones is indwelt by God's Spirit (Eph. 2:20) and is held together by the Spirit, for he is the Spirit of unity (Eph. 4:3). For the diverse members of the church to experience fellowship, all that is necessary is that they live in accordance with their nature as a Spirit-indwelt, Spirit-energized, and Spirit-unified body.[17]

Worship is also integrally related to the nature of the church. The most characteristic thing most churches do is gather for worship. They do so be-cause they are primarily a divine institution, not a human creation. Their first allegiance and orientation is to God, and the natural response to God is worship.

---

17. For more on fellowship, see Bruce Milne, *We Belong Together: The Meaning of Fellowship* (Downers Grove, Ill.: InterVarsity, 1978).

Elements and styles of worship have varied widely over the years and across cultures. The early church continued worshiping in the temple for a short time, but soon moved to worship on the first day of the week with distinctively Christian elements, especially the Lord's Supper. Over the centuries, the Roman Mass developed into the centerpiece of worship, but as practiced in the late medieval period, the people became spectators of the priest more than worshipers of the Lord. Dissatisfaction with worship was one of the fuels of the Reformation, which led to a renewed emphasis on the preaching of the Word in worship. The Reformation marks of the church simply point to the two major aspects of worship: the administration of the sacraments and the preaching of the Word. The Reformers were saying a true church is marked by true worship. Today churches around the world worship in a myriad of ways, but the diversity of practice should not blind us to the significant fact that all churches worship. It is their nature as God's people to respond to him in worship.

The close relationship of the church's ministry of service to its nature is implied in the image of the body of Christ. Because they are followers of Christ, who "did not come to be served, but to serve" (Mark 10:45), his people must serve. The first epistle of John sees serving in practical, material ways as the test of Christian genuineness: "If anyone has material possessions and sees his brother in need but has no pity on him, how can the love of God be in him?" (1 John 3:17). This was immediately and radically true in the New Testament, so much so that many have thought the early church practiced something like communism. But there was no economic system or plan; there was just Christian compassion, expressed in service. And through the centuries, Christians have been disproportionately represented among those who heal the sick, feed the hungry, and serve the world. They do so because they are moved by Christ's compassion and because they are Christ's body, his means for serving the world today.

Finally, the ministry of evangelism is intrinsically related to the church's nature. There is of course the Great Commission, which mandates the making of disciples in all nations (Matt. 28:19–20) and thus indicates that the ministry of evangelism must extend to all cultures. But there is an even more foundational reason why the church cannot avoid involvement in evangelism. It is that all the other ministries of the church involve to some degree a proclamation of the gospel. The ministry of teaching involves an explanation and defense of the gospel. Genuine Christian fellowship portrays the power of the gospel in human relationships and has long been one of the most effective means of drawing people to faith in Christ. The gospel is central in Christian worship. The Lord's Supper proclaims Christ's death until he comes. Baptism is a confession of faith in the gospel and illustrates death to sin and resurrection to newness of life involved in a response to the gospel. Service makes the love of God described in the gospel manifest in human life. The gospel is constitutive of the life of the church. By simply living its life, the church proclaims the gospel. That is reflected in Acts 2:42–47, where the church is described as teaching, enjoying fellowship, worshiping, and serving. There is no explicit mention of the church evangelizing, but the passage concludes: "And the Lord added to their number daily those who were being saved" (v. 47).

Sadly, there have been periods when the light of the gospel has been dimmed by corruption and the mandate for international evangelism ignored, but the darkness has never finally conquered the light. Particularly in the past two hundred years, the church has taken the gospel around the world and Christianity has become the first and only truly worldwide religion. In fact, the spread of the gospel into other cultures has raised the question of to what degree ecclesiology has been shaped by Western culture and to what degree it preserves biblical imperatives, a question to which we will return in a coming chapter, when we look at the church in other, non-Western cultures. For now, we simply note the inevitability of evangelism whenever the church lives out its nature.

THE MINISTRIES OF THE CHURCH IN LOCAL CHURCH LIFE

Thus far, we have discussed the ministries of the church as they relate to the nature of the church and as they constitute a mark that distinguishes churches from parachurch groups. This next section aims to examine each one of these ministries in terms of its importance in the life of a local church, with some practical suggestions for implementing, developing, or enhancing these ministries in a local church context.

The Ministry of Teaching

Acts 2:42 records the devotion of the early church to "the apostles' teaching." Though the apostles are gone, their teaching remains for us in the form of the New Testament. And since the apostles also accepted the Old

Testament, we may place it alongside the New Testament as the material for the ministry of teaching. Thus, the teaching ministry of the church is the ministry of the Word of God, or the Bible teaching ministry of the church.

The importance of this ministry is evident in Scripture. As we noted above, the early name for a follower of Christ, disciple, means learner. One of the disciples' favorite titles for Christ was Rabbi, or teacher,[18] and teaching was one of his characteristic activities, along with preaching and healing (see Matt. 9:35, for example). He commissioned his followers to make disciples, which involves "teaching them to obey everything I have commanded you" (Matt. 28:20). The early church continued the emphasis on teaching, from the devotion to the apostolic teaching noted in Acts 2:42, to the requirement that church leaders be those "able to teach" (1 Tim. 3:2), to the title given to their leaders of "pastors and teachers" (Eph. 4:11), to the command given to all believers "to teach and admonish one another" (Col. 3:16).

In Baptist life, the ministry of the Word has been central. Early Baptist worship centered around Bible exposition, often extending over several hours.[19] As time has gone by, the length of services has decreased, but preaching and biblical exposition have always been central. Recently, however, with the advent of seeker-sensitive services, some have advocated adapting preaching to speak more clearly to nonbelievers. Rick Warren urges preachers to adapt their style to their audience. In weekend services, designed for seekers, Warren begins with a point of common ground, something all people share, often what are called felt needs, and then moves to how those needs are addressed in Scripture. He calls this topical exposition, and believes it works best for evangelism, while he practices a traditional verse-by-verse exposition in preaching to believers, as the best method for edifying believers.[20] He sees both of these methods as biblical exposition.

Mark Dever sees a problem with this perspective. While he advocates being sensitive to the presence of non-Christians in worship services, speaking in language they can understand, and even crafting titles and introductions to sermons that are attractive to nonbelievers, still he insists, "the main weekly Lord's Day gathering of a church is primarily for Christians, not non-

---

18. According to Robert Stein, *The Method and Message of Jesus' Teaching* (Philadelphia: Westminster Press, 1978), 1, Jesus is called Teacher forty-five times in the Gospels and Rabbi fourteen times.

19. For a fascinating description of Baptist worship dating from 1609, involving prayer, the reading of Scripture, and exposition of a text by as many as four or five speakers, see McBeth, *Baptist Heritage*, 91–92.

20. Warren, *Purpose Driven Church*, 294.

Christians," and therefore the main goal of preaching should be the edification of believers.[21]

Both Warren and Dever can make a good case for their views. Warren's research convinced him that if nonbelievers were ever going to visit a church, it would be on Sunday morning. Therefore, he designed that service for seekers and placed services for believers at a midweek meeting.[22] But Sunday morning is also the most likely time that church members will attend, and at even the most seeker-oriented churches, the overwhelming majority of those present on Sunday mornings will be believers. Since Sunday morning is a time when the church gathers, Dever argues, evangelism can be a part of that meeting, but the main point is glorifying God through feeding his flock.[23] Any pastor that wants to teach his church will have the greatest chance of doing so through his Sunday sermons. Therefore, pastors should be accommodating and sensitive to the presence of nonbelievers in their congregations, but address themselves primarily to the purpose of teaching the flock in Sunday services. Such teaching will also indirectly address the purpose of evangelism, for it will equip church members to live "seeker-sensitive lives" that will result in effective evangelism outside the walls of the church.[24]

Certainly, the ministry of teaching begins with the preaching of the pastor. His messages should lead his flock into Bible study that results not only in increased Bible knowledge but also heart and life transformation. But there is also a need for smaller, more specialized classes. In fact, every church should develop as part of its teaching ministry a series of classes specifically designed to teach believers what they need to grow into mature disciples.

In the twentieth century, the Southern Baptist Sunday School Board aggressively promoted Sunday Bible study classes for all ages as a central part of the Bible teaching ministry of churches. They were so successful that more than 95 percent of Southern Baptist churches adopted Sunday School classes. But while such classes take students systematically through the Bible, they do not follow a conscious design to bring believers to mature discipleship. One

---

21. Mark Dever, "Evangelistic Expository Preaching," in *Give Praise to God: A Vision for Reforming Worship*, ed. Philip Graham Ryken, Derek W. H. Thomas, and J. Ligon Duncan III (Phillipsburg, N.J.: P & R Publishing, 2003), 131–33.

22. Warren, *Purpose Driven Church*, 245–46.

23. Dever, "Evangelistic Expository Preaching," 131.

24. Dever says: "We talk here not about having seeker-sensitive sermons or services, but about having seeker-sensitive lives." See Mark Dever, "Pastoral Success in Evangelistic Ministry," in Armstrong, ed., *Reforming Pastoral Ministry*, 258.

helpful exception is the process developed by Rick Warren at Saddleback Community Church in California. They use a diagram of a baseball diamond, with first, second, third, and home bases. Church membership is going to first base, and involves completion of a new member's class and commitment to a membership covenant. But they make it clear that reaching first base is not the goal. Second base in their process involves a class that focuses on the development of four habits important to the life of a disciple: Bible study, prayer, tithing, and fellowship. As new members grow toward maturity, they can take the next step, which involves commitment to a ministry. At this level (third base), there is another class that helps members identify areas of giftedness and possible ministry. The final step in their process is enlisting members in evangelism, providing training to teach them how to share the message of Christ at home and on mission trips.

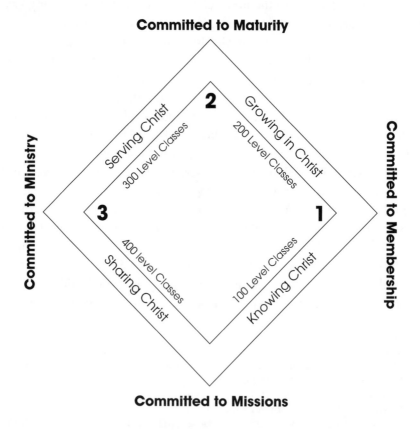

Figure 9.2: The Life Development Process

---

100 Level Classes

To lead people to Christ and church membership

200 Level Classes

To grow people to spiritual maturity

300 Level Classes

To equip people with the skills they need for ministry

400 Level Classes

To enlist people in the worldwide mission of sharing Christ

Figure 9.3: An Overview of "The Life Development Institute"

Another helpful example comes from Capitol Hill Baptist Church in Washington, D.C. On Sunday mornings, they offer five tracks of what they call core seminars. The first track, called Basics, includes their membership class, basic disciplines of the Christian life, how to share the gospel, and a brief course on doctrine. Altogether, it lasts six months. The second track gives an overview of the Old and New Testaments over a six-month time frame. The third track gives attendees a six-month introduction to church history and systematic theology. The fourth track is a year-long sequence of studies on spiritual disciplines, courtship, dating, marriage, and parenting. The fifth track is also a year in length and covers evangelism, discipling, apologetics, worldviews, and missions. Each track is continually offered. Students move through at their own pace, in accordance with the own needs and interests, but as they progress through the various tracks, they are systematically acquainted with the major issues involved in growing to maturity as a Christian.[25]

Neither example is perfect nor suited to every church, but they represent two attempts to provide a comprehensive, thoughtful sequence of teaching on issues that lead to Christian maturity. Beginning such a process will require a large commitment of time from pastors and church leaders. Decisions will have to be made concerning what sequence of classes can best provide the necessary ingredients for growing members into disciples. Materials for the classes will have to be developed. Pastors and elders will either have to teach

---

25. More information on these core seminars is available at http://www.capitolhillbaptist.org.

these classes or train others to teach them. But such a commitment must be made if churches are to provide the type of teaching ministry that produces disciples. The alternative is to continue with a haphazard assortment of Sunday School and other classes that may or may not provide what members need to grow. This is not to suggest that Sunday School classes should be abolished. They provide ongoing avenues for teaching, fellowship, service, and evangelism. But they should be supplemented by a thoughtful sequence of more specifically focused, short-term classes, designed for discipleship.

But even small group classes should not exhaust the teaching ministry of the church. There will be some who need individual mentoring and there should always be informal teaching going on, as believers teach one another. On this level, every member of the church should be involved in the teaching ministry of the church, both as learners and as teachers.

On the whole, churches in America do not seem to be doing a very good job of teaching. Polls consistently reflect a shocking degree of biblical illiteracy among church members; Baptists seem to have more members who drop out than move toward maturity. The very idea of teaching, which involves the notions of truth and error, runs counter to the relativistic culture of our day. We tend to gravitate more toward the experiential than the mental, and some suggest that our very ability to think has been corrupted by the pervasive influence of the image-oriented medium of television. Pastors who seek to be good teachers struggle to find the time to study amidst their myriad responsibilities. Yet, despite these obstacles, the church cannot abdicate its calling to be "the pillar and foundation of the truth" (1 Tim. 3:15). The nature of the church, its commission to make disciples, and its allegiance to the God of truth, compel churches today to give renewed attention to the ministry of teaching.

The Ministry of Fellowship

Fellowship is a common word among Baptist churches. Many even have buildings called Fellowship Halls. They are often the site of a favorite Baptist activity, a meal called a fellowship supper. But, beyond food, what does the church's ministry of fellowship involve? Is it just another term for Christian socializing?

We may begin by noting several interesting implications arising from the word for fellowship in the New Testament, *koinōnia*. The first is that there is no counterpart for this word in the Old Testament and there is no occurrence of the word in the New Testament prior to Acts 2:42. So genuine fellowship seems to have been an impossibility prior to the coming of the Holy Spirit on the day of Pentecost. Further, John 7:39 indicates that the Spirit was not given until Jesus was glorified. The implication is that any genuine experience of fellowship on the human level must be preceded by fellowship with God, who embodies fellowship in his triune nature, created humans for fellowship, and bestows fellowship on his people. Fellowship with God was made possible when Jesus was glorified (i.e., crucified, buried, raised, and ascended). Those who experience fellowship with Jesus become indwelt by his Spirit. The Spirit then joins believers together and grants them fellowship with one another.

A second implication arises from the root meaning of fellowship as participating or sharing something in common with another. It seems that one way the Spirit grants believers fellowship with one another is by revealing to them all they share in common in Christ. This explains how otherwise diverse believers can experience oneness in Christ; what they have in common outweighs their differences. Their oneness is then expressed in a corporate life of love and service to one another.

To summarize, we may say that the fellowship that is a ministry of the church is a gift of God, based on fellowship with him. It mirrors the divine fellowship that occurs eternally in the relationship that the members of the Trinity enjoy with one another, and fellowship is a need implanted by God in humans, as a consequence of their creation in his image. Fellowship consists in a common sharing or participation in the blessings of salvation, a commonality we perceive due to the action of the indwelling Holy Spirit, who thus creates fellowship. Fellowship is expressed in the common life and intimate relationships believers share in the church. This is what fellowship is. We now press on to two further questions. How important is the ministry of fellowship to a local church? How may local churches faithfully cultivate the ministry of fellowship among their members?

To understand the importance of fellowship, we need to recall the radical nature of Christ's call. It takes precedence over all human ties. Responding to such a call can be difficult, for humans are social creatures, and conversion in some contexts will involve a loss of previous relationships. Made in the image of a God who is a triune community, human beings are created for community. So in calling us, God calls us corporately, to be not isolated believers, but part of his people. The fellowship we experience as part of his people is not just an enjoyable optional luxury, it is part of God's essential provision for us, from which we draw strength and vitality. One has called fellowship "the blood that flows through the veins of the church giving it health and vibrancy."[26] It may justly be regarded as a means of sustaining and sanctifying grace.[27]

In fact, the centrality of fellowship in the life of the church is reflected in the dozens of "one another" commands in the New Testament.[28] It is only in obeying these commands that the church can fulfill its purpose. For example, consider the classical marks of the church: one, holy, catholic, and apostolic. For the church to experience oneness, members must "live in harmony with one another" (Rom. 12:16). Holiness is developed as members "build each other up" (1 Thess. 5:11) and "spur one another on toward love and good deeds" (Heb. 10:24). The catholicity or universal nature of the church is expressed when members "accept one another" (Rom. 15:7), regardless of race, age, sex, or class. The apostolicity of the church is ensured as members of the body "teach and admonish one another" (Col. 3:16).

Its importance is further seen in its intimate relationship to the other ministries of the church. We have already mentioned how fellowship is expressed in the teaching ministry of the church, as members teach and admonish one another. Fellowship also provides the motivation for the ministry of service. In fact, the most frequent usage of *koinōnia* in the New Testament is for the sharing of material needs (Rom. 12:13; 15:26–27; 2 Cor. 9:13; 1 Tim. 6:18; Heb. 13:16). Serving one another in terms of the practical, material needs of life is itself an expression of fellowship. The ministry of worshiping God is hollow if fellowship with others is broken. First John repeatedly relates fellowship with God and proper fellowship with others (1:5–7; 2:9; 3:10, 14; 4:7–8, 11–12, 19–21). Love for God, expressed in worship, and love for God's people, expressed in fellowship, cannot be separated. Bruce Milne boldly says, "No man can be reconciled to God without being reconciled to the people

---

26. I am indebted to my student Jeremy Oddy for this comparison in an unpublished paper, "Christian Fellowship: A Study of Koinonia in the Church."

27. This should not be confused with saving grace, which is received by faith alone. Fellowship is a means of sustaining or sanctifying grace in that it is one of many activities by which God strengthens believers. See the discussion in Grudem, *Systematic Theology*, 950–51.

28. I have counted at least thirty-one different commands. "Love one another" is found at least seventeen times; "encourage one another" four times; "forgive one another" four times; "serve one another" three times. Most of the others are found once or twice.

of God within whom his experience of God's grace sets him."[29] Even the ministry of evangelism is enhanced or undermined by the quality of fellowship manifested in the lives of church members. Ray Stedman says the early church shared the gospel by both proclamation *(kerygma)* and fellowship *(koinōnia)*.[30] This is supported by Michael Green, who says of the early Christians in his study *Evangelism in the Early Church:* "Their community life, though far from perfect . . . was nevertheless sufficiently different and impressive to attract notice, to invite curiosity, and to inspire discipleship. . . . Paganism saw in early Christianity a quality of living, and supremely of dying, which could not be found elsewhere."[31] By contrast, Howard Snyder suspects that the reason many churches are not effective in evangelism today is because "their communal experience of the gospel is too weak and tasteless to be worth sharing. . . . But where Christian fellowship demonstrates the gospel, believers come alive and sinners get curious and want to know what the secret is. So true Christian community *(koinōnia)* becomes both the basis and goal of evangelism."[32]

Fellowship is essential to fulfilling the ministries of the church because fellowship is the church acting corporately to fulfill its corporate mandate. Kenneth Boa sees seven characteristics of the church's corporate ministry: corporate love and compassion, corporate identity and purpose, corporate nurture and service, corporate discernment, corporate forgiveness and reconciliation, corporate authority and submission, and corporate worship and prayer.[33] Fellowship addresses all of these purposes, directly or indirectly.

Finally, on a practical level, sociologists Rodney Stark and Roger Finke note the importance of fellowship for both the initial impetus to join a church and the continuing involvement of new church members. On the basis of more than twenty-five studies, they claim that it has been fairly well established that those who join a new group are generally "those whose interpersonal attachments to members overbalanced their attachments to nonmembers."[34] Moreover, one's commitment level after joining is strongly

29. Milne, *We Belong Together*, 19.

30. Ray Stedman, *Body Life* (1972; reprint, Glendale, Calif.: Regal, 1977), 114–15.

31. Green, *Evangelism in the Early Church*, 274–75.

32. Howard Snyder, *Community of the King* (1977; reprint, Downers Grove, Ill.: InterVarsity, 1978), 124–25.

33. Kenneth Boa, *Conformed to His Image: Biblical and Practical Approaches to Spiritual Formation* (Grand Rapids: Zondervan, 2001), 426.

34. Rodney Stark and Roger Finke, *Acts of Faith: Explaining the Human Side of Religion* (Berkeley, Calif.: University of California Press, 2000), 117.

affected by the commitment level of those closest to her. That is, if her closest friends are not committed to the church, neither will she be.[35] If those joining a church do not develop a significant number of fellowship relationships fairly soon after they enter the church, they become excellent candidates for dropping out. Many people may join a church because of the pastor, but those who become active in the church will normally not leave when the pastor leaves because they develop friendships with others in the church. By contrast, church dropouts leave because they lack meaningful relationships. For a church to be a New Testament church at all, it must offer the ministry of fellowship to its members. For it to be a healthy church, its ministry of fellowship must be healthy. It is indispensably important to every aspect of the church.

Unfortunately, much of American culture presents obstacles to the development of fellowship. America is widely recognized as having one of the most individualistic cultures in the world. We honor the person who goes his own way, and value the virtue of self-reliance. But such attitudes are anathema to the development of fellowship. America is also a very mobile society, and fellowship requires time for relationships to develop. Sometimes families have to move for a variety of reasons, but the value of the fellowship the family experiences in the church should be a factor that may question the wisdom of some moves. More recently, the influence of the consumer society has adversely affected how Americans approach church membership. Many American Christians see themselves, consciously or unconsciously, as consumers of religious goods and services provided by churches. They "pay" for the goods and services by their presence, participation, and giving, but they always retain the right to go elsewhere if they find a producer (church) that offers better goods and services. They justify leaving their church because "it isn't meeting our needs."[36] How different is the perspective of the New Testament! The church is like a family, and one cannot retain the right to transfer families; the church is like a body, and one amputates a part of the body only under extreme circumstances. Joining a church is an expression of a commitment to the fellowship, not a commitment to having one's needs met.

What, then, can churches do to cultivate this important ministry? One simple but often overlooked imperative is the necessity of the preceding min-

---

35. Ibid., 147.
36. For more on the impact of consumerism, see Shelley and Shelley, *Consumer Church*.

istry of teaching the truths of the gospel. Bruce Milne says, "Only the truths of apostolic Christianity, embraced and whole-heartedly adhered to, effectively break up the sinful isolation of the human heart and create the possibility of true relationship at depth with others."[37] As we said above, fellowship with God, created through embracing the gospel, is prerequisite to fellowship with members of the body. First John 1:7 says it is only as "we walk in the light, as he is in the light, [that] we have fellowship with one another."

Embracing the gospel creates the possibility of fellowship, but churches can do more to move members from the possibility of fellowship to its reality. Rick Warren encourages churches to develop a plan to assimilate members and connect them to fellowship, thinking through the questions prospective new members have: Do I fit here? Does anybody want to know me? Am I needed? What is the advantage of joining? What is required of members?[38] The first place such questions can be addressed and the first step in bringing a new member into full fellowship is a new member's class. Happily, such classes are becoming increasingly common in Baptist churches. We discussed earlier the importance of such a class for the development and maintenance of regenerate church membership. It is also crucial in the development of a healthy ministry of fellowship. Such a class should elicit from new members a commitment to fellowship, embodied in signing the church covenant.

The new member's class is also their first involvement in what is perhaps the central necessity for fellowship; that is, a context for developing relationships. Most people's first level of involvement is in the large-group worship service of the church. But that service is not primarily designed for fellowship; it is vertically oriented to worship of God, not fellowship with others. Therefore, churches need to create other contexts in which fellowship can develop, where people can talk and share their lives. Often, fellowship develops when people work on something together. Choirs, mission teams, even some committees develop fellowship as they work together. But most often fellowship is nurtured in small groups. Sunday School classes can be one type of small group for developing fellowship, but in most cases, time constraints and the proper emphasis on teaching limit the depth of fellowship in such classes. My own experience of fellowship has been richest in home-based small groups. Such small groups can be built around common interests, a common struggle, or a common geographical location, but the goal will be

---

37. Milne, *We Belong Together*, 94.
38. Warren, *Purpose Driven Church*, 312.

to share a common life in Christ. According to Rick Warren, *"Small groups are the most effective way of closing the back door of your church."*[39] Constant creation of new small groups is the single most important step a church can take to stimulate the ministry of fellowship in their midst. This is especially true in a growing church, for as the church grows larger, relationships and fellowship suffer, unless they are sustained in small groups.[40]

One final step in cultivating ongoing fellowship is proper celebration of the communion meal, the Lord's Supper. But since that meal relates to the ministries of worship and teaching as well as fellowship, and since the understanding of the Lord's Supper has been a dividing point for many denominations, we will give it, along with baptism, separate consideration in the following chapter.

The Ministry of Worship

The ministry of worship is rooted in both the nature and historical background of the church. The church is God's people, called to declare the praises of the one who called them out of darkness and into his wonderful light (1 Peter 2:9–10). As the temple of the Holy Spirit, the church is to do that for which temples are erected, namely, worship God. Furthermore, the historical background in which the church was born assured that it would be a worshiping community. They continued, at least initially, to meet in the temple and continued to offer the prayers that were a part of temple worship (Acts 2:42, 46). However, as Robert Saucy notes, there is no record of the early disciples offering up sacrifices, which was the main act of worship in the temple; they saw the sacrificial system as fulfilled in Christ.[41] Instead, their worship would soon include a commemoration of his one sacrifice. They also had in their background worship in the synagogue, which included three main elements: corporate praise, prayers, and the reading and instruction in the Law and Prophets (as reflected in Luke 4:16–21 and Acts 13:15–42).[42] It was this pattern that is reflected most strongly in early Christian worship. Will Willimon says, "By the end of the first century, Christians were to have a liturgy directly derived from synagogue worship."[43] While the pattern was drawn from their background in Judaism, the

---

39. Ibid., 327 (emphasis in original).
40. See the discussion in Stark and Finke, *Acts of Faith,* 157–60.
41. Saucy, *The Church in God's Program,* 177.
42. Ralph P. Martin, *Worship in the Early Church* (Grand Rapids: Eerdmans, 1964), 24–26.
43. William H. Willimon, *Word, Water, Wine and Bread: How Worship Has Changed Over the Years* (Valley Forge, Pa.: Judson Press, 1980), 16.

content was revised by their experience of Christ, the coming of the Holy Spirit, and the Christian message. David Peterson argues that New Testament worship is distinctively different from that of the Old Testament in that worship is no longer associated with a particular place, such as the tabernacle or temple, nor with a particular time, such as Passover, but worship is all of life, as Paul describes it in Romans 12:1.[44]

There is no definition of worship in Scripture, but the origin of the word provides a clue. *Worship* comes from the Anglo-Saxon word *weorthscipe*, which became *worthship* and then *worship*. To worship God is to ascribe worth to him. Psalm 29:2 says, "Ascribe to the LORD the glory due his name; worship the LORD in the splendor of his holiness." The most common biblical words for worship (*šāḥâh* in the Old Testament and *proskuneō* in the New Testament) associate worship with bowing down, humble prostration, and awe-filled reverence before God. This indicates the profoundly God-centered nature of true worship. But the New Testament also describes other characteristics of true worship.

Perhaps the most often quoted text concerning worship comes from John 4:24, where Jesus says that those who worship God must do so "in spirit [*pneuma*] and in truth [*alētheia*]." While there are differing opinions on the meaning of *pneuma* and *alētheia* in this verse, I find persuasive the argument that *pneuma* refers here to the Holy Spirit and *alētheia* includes the idea of doctrinal truth.[45] This leads to further characteristics of true worship. True worship is Spirit-empowered. And since the Spirit comes to exalt Christ (John 16:14), true worship will be Christ-focused. The reference to truth implies that true worship is bounded and shaped by truth, truth as embodied in Christ and as preserved in Scripture. Thus, true worship will be biblically grounded. The concern for truth or doctrine, while necessary to honor God rightly, also points to secondary purposes for worship on the human side. The primary purpose of worship is to honor God, but as worship is portrayed in the New Testament, it also serves the purpose of edifying believers and evangelizing nonbelievers. First Corinthians 14:26, speaking specifically of the occasions when believers come together, insists that everything "must be done for the strengthening [or edifying] of the church." David Peterson goes further and says that in the New

---

44. David Peterson, *Engaging with God* (Grand Rapids: Eerdmans, 1992), 284–88.

45. For a discussion of the views of various commentators on this phrase, see David Nelson, "In Spirit and Truth: The Holy Spirit and the Interrelation of Doxology and Doctrine with Implications for Evangelical Congregational Worship" (Ph.D. diss., Southeastern Baptist Theological Seminary, 2001), 118–37.

Testament, worship is all of life, while the focal purpose of the time when the church gathers and sings, prays and hears the Word is edification.[46] But this may be separating worship and edification too neatly. David Nelson sees worship as multidimensional. The doxological dimension calls for a focus on God; the didactic dimension indicates that worship can have a teaching function (see Col. 3:16); the hortatory dimension expresses the edifying aspect of worship (see 1 Cor. 14:26; Eph. 5:18–21); and the evangelistic dimension speaks of the proclamation of the gospel in worship, which, according to Scripture, is done whenever we celebrate the Lord's Supper (1 Cor. 11:26).[47]

These different dimensions help to explain some of the elements of worship. For example, prayer in worship expresses our adoration of God but also allows us to seek God's help in edifying believers and winning nonbelievers. Hearing the preaching of God's Word honors God but is also a major means of edifying the church. Even the music we sing to praise God can serve to teach or remind us of the truth about God.

The following may serve as a summary of the chief characteristics of true worship.

True worship is:

- God-centered, that is, God is the supreme object of our worship, his glory is our supreme concern in worship, he is the audience to whom our praise is directed.
- Spirit-empowered, that is, the Spirit is the one who initiates, enables, and prompts us to worship.
- Christ-focused, that is, Christian worship is directed to the God who revealed himself to us in Christ, the same Christ to whom the Spirit bears witness, the Christ who is the truth.
- Biblically grounded and shaped, that is, all that we do in worship must be in harmony with these biblical characteristics of true worship.
- Multifaceted, that is, while the purpose and focus of worship is honoring God, some aspects of worship also inevitably edify believers and proclaim the gospel to nonbelievers.[48]

---

46. Peterson, *Engaging with God*, 287.
47. Nelson, "In Spirit and Truth," 167.
48. This diagram bears some resemblance to the definition offered by D. A. Carson, "Worship Under the Word," in *Worship by the Book,* ed. D. A. Carson (Grand Rapids: Zondervan, 2002), 26, but he focuses on the doxological element of worship.

Unfortunately, the worship of the church has not always exemplified these characteristics. In the medieval church, the celebration of the Lord's Supper became increasingly the center of worship, to the neglect of other elements. Further, the role of the priest's mediation was emphasized so as to make the congregation virtually spectators rather than participants. The Reformation's change in theology also produced a change in worship. The preaching of the Word became a central part of worship, a fact that was reflected in church architecture, which placed the pulpit in a central location.

Early Baptist worship was often several hours long and featured extensive exposition of Scripture along with prayers and a contribution taken for the poor. Baptism was a part of worship, as was the Lord's Supper. Some celebrated the Lord's Supper every week, but most eventually adopted the pattern of Zwingli and the church in Zurich of quarterly observance. The most important contribution of Baptists to Protestant worship in the seventeenth century involved the singing of hymns. The key figure was Benjamin Keach, who argued for the appropriateness of hymn-singing in a 1691 work called *The Breach Repaired in God's Worship, or Singing of Psalms, Hymns and Spiritual Songs proved to be an Holy Ordinance of Jesus Christ*.[49] By the end of the seventeenth century, hymn-singing began to catch on among English Baptists. In America, Keach's son, Elias, was a key figure in the Philadelphia Baptist Association, whose confession of faith specifically endorsed hymn-singing, and singing has become a central element of Baptist worship.

By and large Baptist churches have been nonliturgical in the sense that there have been few written prayers, confessions, or responses. Baptist hymnals have printed selections of Scripture for responsive reading in worship services, but few churches use them. This is an area where most Baptist churches could improve. Paul commanded Timothy to devote himself "to the public reading of Scripture" (1 Tim. 4:13), but aside from the sermon text, Scripture is seldom read in many Baptist churches. Terry Johnson and Ligon Duncan III comment: "Not reading the Scriptures is on the same order as not having a sermon or omitting congregational singing."[50] A careful, thoughtful reading of Scripture serves both to honor God and to edify believers by exposing them to the whole counsel of God. But to do so requires

---

49. For more on Keach, see J. Barry Vaughn, "Benjamin Keach," in *Baptist Theologians*, ed. Timothy George and David Dockery (Nashville: Broadman, 1990), 49–76.

50. Terry L. Johnson and J. Ligon Duncan III, "Reading and Praying the Bible in Corporate Worship," in *Give Praise to God*, 143. Johnson and Duncan also include eleven pieces of counsel concerning the public reading of Scripture.

careful planning to choose texts that range throughout Scripture and to choose readers who can read Scripture with understanding and feeling.[51]

Baptist worship has typically followed the Reformation emphasis on the preaching of God's Word, though the time expended on reading and expounding it has dropped from several hours in the early days of Baptist life to perhaps thirty minutes in today's worship. It is another example of the multidimensional nature of worship. We honor God in hearing his Word preached, because God's Word recounts the wondrous deeds and nature of God. Also, in preaching the Word the pastor teaches the whole congregation, and they are thus edified. And, since Baptist pastors often include the gospel message in their preaching, it can serve an evangelistic function. However, since the New Testament emphasis is on congregational edification in worship (see 1 Cor. 14:26), evangelism should not be the primary aim.

Prayer has also been a consistent feature of Baptist worship, in obedience to the commands in 1 Timothy 2 and elsewhere that place prayer in the context of public worship. As mentioned above, we have almost universally eschewed written prayer in favor of spontaneous prayer. Still, careful planning could improve the element of prayer in Baptist worship. Baptist pastors and worship leaders spend hours preparing sermons and rehearsing music, but seem to feel that it is somehow wrong to think through what they should include in public prayer. Prayer is our direct address to God, and a thoughtful prayer should lead worshipers to adore, confess, intercede, and thank God. Preparation doesn't make sermons or music less heartfelt; neither should it have any effect on prayer but to make it a more helpful and positive aspect of worship.[52]

Guiding Baptists in their choice of the elements of worship, at least to some degree in the past, has been what is called the regulative principle. This principle has held that worship should only include those elements that Scripture explicitly or implicitly endorses. It is contrasted with the normative principle, which advocated the view that whatever is not prohibited is permissible in worship. A Baptist preference for the regulative principle would be expected in view of their desire to be biblical in all they do, and support for the regulative principle is explicit in the Second London Confession (or, as it was known in America, the Philadelphia Confession), which states: "the accept-

---

51. R. Kent Hughes, "Free Church Worship," in *Worship by the Book*, 176, gives some helpful suggestions on public reading of Scripture.

52. Ibid., 175. Hughes also gives helpful resources and suggestions for planning to lead congregational prayer, as does Johnson and Duncan, "Reading and Praying the Bible in Corporate Worship," 165–66.

able way of worshiping the true God is instituted by himself, and so limited by his own revealed will that he may not be worshiped according to the imaginations and devices of men, nor the suggestions of Satan, under any visible representations, or any other way not prescribed in the Holy Scriptures."[53] However, as Jerry Marcellino notes, this principle alone is not altogether helpful, for no evangelical would say that he desires to worship in a way contrary to the Word of God; the difficulty is in the application of the principle.[54] Marcellino himself sees seven elements as proper in worship: the preaching/ teaching (and, I would add, reading) of the Word, prayer, baptism, communion, an offering, sharing of testimony, and singing.[55]

It is this last element, singing, that has sparked the controversy in evangelical churches today called "the worship wars." This "war" is between contemporary and traditional styles of worship, and is marked most noticeably by differing musical styles. Contemporary music replaces organ and piano with guitar and drums, replaces hymns with praise choruses, and replaces choirs with praise teams.[56] Often such churches adopt casual dress, and seek in other ways to present fewer obstacles and more attractiveness to those they call "seekers." K. H. Sargeant says, "Seeker church leaders design new, contemporary forms of worship to mirror the musical and cultural preferences of contemporary society."[57] Rick Warren says frankly, "You must match your music to the kind of people God wants your church to reach."[58] He sees no theological obstacle involved in musical style, as long as the lyrics are Christian. Others are not so sure.

Charles Colson is concerned that the medium affects the message. For example, he says, "rock music, by its very form, encourages a mentality that is subjective, emotional, and sensual—no matter what the lyrics say." He adds,

53. For more discussion of the regulative principle, see J. Ligon Duncan III, "Does God Care How We Worship?" in *Give Praise to God*, 17–50; and Derek W. H. Thomas, "The Regulative Principle: Responding to Recent Criticism," in *Give Praise to God*, 74–93. See also Ernest C. Reisinger and D. Matthew Allen, *Worship: The Regulative Principle and the Biblical Practice of Accommodation* (Cape Coral, Fla.: Founders Press, 2001).

54. Jerry Marcellino, "Leading the Church in God-Centered Worship: The Pastoral Role," in *Reforming Pastoral Ministry*, 142.

55. Ibid.

56. A survey of more than seven hundred Southern Baptist churches conducted in 2000 found that more than half of those categorized as contemporary in worship style had experienced conflict over worship. See Philip B. Jones, "Research Report," 4.

57. Kimon Howland Sargeant, *Seeker Churches: Promoting Traditional Religion in a Nontraditional Way* (New Brunswick, N.J.; London, U.K.: Rutgers University Press, 2000), 55.

58. Warren, *Purpose Driven Church*, 280.

"Churches that use mostly contemporary music in their services should consider the effects of a steady diet of simple choruses and pop-style worship songs while neglecting the classic hymns of the faith."[59]

Others see contemporary worship and its music as detracting from the focus on God, which should be at the heart of worship. Marva Dawn says, "Style is not the issue. . . . The question is whether our worship services immerse us in God's splendor. . . . The value of the liturgies established by the Church over time (in new settings and old) is that they do not depend on any leader's personality; instead they keep the focus on the God who is the Subject of our worship."[60] As well, she sees much of contemporary music as "filled with stuff that trivializes God and forms narcissistic people," while hymnals contain music that has been sorted over time so that most of traditional music "is quite good theologically and musically."[61]

Others offer more reserved cautions. Jerry Marcellino acknowledges that we cannot say that all styles other than traditional are wrong; he believes that to do so would involve "cultural bigotry."[62] Elmer Towns and Ed Stetzer make the same point from history: "Any Christian who reads history would know there is no one right way."[63] But both are concerned that we exercise some caution in the use of contemporary music. Marcellino recommends that we ask ourselves questions such as: Is the music "essentially free of strong worldly associations"? Does it conform to the criteria of Philippians 4:8 (true, noble, right, pure, lovely, admirable, excellent, praiseworthy)?[64] Towns and Stetzer expand the question we should ask in this fashion: "What impact does this music have on the culture via association, memory, emotions, understanding, and music? These are not easy questions—but they are essential."[65]

A final element contributing to the worship wars is the underlying issue of purpose. Is the worship service to be designed to attract seekers or to honor God? Seeker churches not only modify music, but adjust the types of buildings they build and the type of participation they ask of worshipers, and they

---

59. Charles Colson and Nancy Pearcey, *How Now Shall We Live?* (Wheaton, Ill.: Tyndale House, 1999), 470, 471–72.

60. Marva Dawn, *A Royal "Waste" of Time: The Splendor of Worshiping God and Being Church for the World* (Grand Rapids; Cambridge, U.K.: Eerdmans, 1999), 158.

61. Ibid., 150.

62. Marcellino, "Leading the Church in God-Centered Worship," 143.

63. Towns and Stetzer, *Perimeters of Light,* 98.

64. Marcellino, "Leading the Church in God-Centered Worship," 143.

65. Towns and Stetzer, *Perimeters of Light,* 107–8.

add the use of drama and multimedia, all to attract nonbelievers. R. C. Sproul sees such changes as "methods used to entertain and justified by a misguided sense of evangelism."[66] One of the most detailed examinations of the well-known Willow Creek Church concluded that "although Willow Creek's statement of faith affirms exhortation, exaltation, and extension as aspects of the purpose of the church, the central and driving function of the church is evangelism."[67] Similarly, while Rick Warren says that the key issue for churches in the twenty-first century will be church health, rather than church growth, what receives the most detailed treatment in his book, and what he is best known for, is reaching seekers.[68]

In their defense, Warren and Hybels and many others in the seeker church movement can say that they do have a time for believers to worship, but that their Sunday morning gathering is for evangelism, and shouldn't be judged as a worship service. Willow Creek and Saddleback both have believers' services as well as seeker services. Rick Warren says frankly that he preaches differently at the two types of services.[69] Bill Hybels notes how Willow Creek recently reorganized itself to address the needs of believers: "We've set up all our leadership structures and goals to grow a full-functioning Acts 2 community, as opposed to just an evangelizing machine that doesn't drive the roots down deep and do all the other things it's supposed to do."[70]

Sargeant's research seems to show that seeker churches are increasingly recognizing the need for separate services for believers, where worship of God and edification of believers is central. He says, the "model of holding separate services for seekers and believers is more popular among newer churches and is therefore more likely to become more prevalent in the future as more seeker churches are founded."[71] Still, more than 60 percent of the churches affiliated with the Willow Creek Association have no separate believers' service,[72] and, while I know of no hard data, my reading of the literature suggests that there are many more churches whose worship has been

---

66. R. C. Sproul, foreword to *Give Praise to God,* xii.
67. G. A. Pritchard, *Willow Creek Seeker Services: Evaluating a New Way of Doing Church* (Grand Rapids: Baker, 1996), 282.
68. In Warren, *Purpose Driven Church,* while there are statements on balancing the purposes of the church (17, 128–29), there are whole chapters devoted to attracting seekers (chaps. 9–16).
69. Ibid., 294.
70. Bill Hybels, quoted in Gillmor, "Community Is Their Middle Name," 50.
71. Sargeant, *Seeker Churches,* 25.
72. Ibid.

influenced by that of Willow Creek and Saddleback that have no separate believers' service. For them, worship planning may involve walking some very fine lines. Treating unbelievers with love and respect should be standard for any church, traditional or contemporary, and removing unnecessary barriers to unbelievers, such as accepting casual dress and explaining church terminology, likewise would not seem to affect worship.

But the basic question of the orientation in worship remains problematic. Is the service designed to be relevant to seekers or to glorify God? Is the sermon addressed to the felt needs of people in general, or is it designed to feed and challenge Christians? Most churches try to do both, and in so doing there is some cause for concern. Even in seeker churches, the overwhelming percentage of attendees are Christians, and services designed for seekers may not accomplish all that worship is meant to accomplish for believers. And, if my experience in churches, large and small, is any guide, many of the believers who attend on Sunday will attend only on Sunday, and will regard that service as their time to worship God. Seeker church services may be subtly changing the view of these Christians as to what worship is.

As churches adopting seeker-sensitive services report more and more stories of growth, more and more pastors are attracted to them.[73] Not only are the numbers of seeker churches growing, the churches themselves are growing. While 80 percent of all churches in America are stagnant or declining, 75 percent of the churches adapting some of Willow Creek's methods (those in the Willow Creek Association) are growing.[74] In fact, most large, rapidly growing churches seem to have adopted at least some aspects of seeker church methodology. The whole phenomenon of seeker churches merits more thorough examination, particularly the question of the effect of its adaptation to American culture on the message it proclaims, and we will look at it as a whole later. For now, our concern is limited to the question of how are we to evaluate seeker worship.

To some degree, it is hard to avoid the conclusion that part of the problem of the critics of seeker churches is a difference in musical taste and style. I have been a member of numerous Baptist churches, with worship styles from very traditional to very contemporary, and most styles in between. I

---

73. For example, the number of churches in the Willow Creek Association, a network of churches utilizing at least some of Willow Creek's ideas, grew from 146 churches in 1992 to more than 5,000 by 2000. See ibid., 22.

74. Ibid., 23.

have found that it is possible to worship God and to keep God in the center of worship in a variety of ways. In contemporary worship, there are some hymns I certainly want to retain and some choruses I find insipid. At the same time, there are also many hymns I do not miss at all and some choruses that have beauty and theological depth. I can find no biblical basis for concluding that one style of music is necessarily more conducive to worship than another. I think the warnings and tests suggested by Jerry Marcellino and Elmer Towns and Ed Stetzer, noted earlier, are helpful here, and all our music should pass the test of Philippians 4:8. But I cannot condemn contemporary music as a necessary hindrance to authentic worship.

At the same time, seeker services do raise a danger in their confusion of worship and evangelism. While worship as portrayed in Scripture does not focus exclusively on honoring God (there is concern for edifying the body and the gospel is proclaimed via baptism and the Lord's Supper), there does seem to be a degree of conflict between services designed for worship and those designed for seekers. A seeker service is designed with the needs of unbelievers in mind, while worship's primary concern must be the glory of God. Despite the disclaimers of some seeker church leaders that these services are for evangelism, and despite the fact that many that are being reached for Christ through these services, these seeker services are perceived and received by many as worship services, and as such may be having a harmful influence on Christian worship as a whole. The Cambridge Declaration, produced by the Alliance of Confessing Evangelicals, decries what it sees as the erosion of God-centered worship:

> The loss of God's centrality in the life of today's church is common and lamentable. It is this loss that allows us to transform worship into entertainment, gospel preaching into marketing, believing into technique, being good into feeling good about ourselves, and faithfulness into being successful. . . . God does not exist to satisfy human ambitions, cravings, the appetite for consumption, or our own private spiritual interests. We must focus on God in our worship, rather than the satisfaction of our own personal needs. God is sovereign in worship; we are not. Our concern must be for God's kingdom, not our own empires, popularity or success.[75]

---

75. "The Cambridge Declaration: A Statement by the Alliance of Confessing Evangelicals" is available at http://www.alliancenet.org.

Most seeker church pastors do not intend any of the consequences attributed to the loss of the centrality of God in the paragraph above. Research shows that they are overwhelmingly conservative in their theological convictions,[76] and I have a great deal of respect and appreciation for many in the seeker church movement. In particular, I find much to applaud in Rick Warren's approach. Yet in their zeal to reach the lost, they may have contributed to a reorienting of worship away from the centrality of God. Moreover, it needs to be asked if seeker-sensitive worship can accomplish the more important long-range goal of developing believers who can live seeker-sensitive lives. After all, Paul's statement about becoming "all things to all men" (1 Cor. 9:22) was not given as instruction for Christian worship but as a model for Christian living.

The description of the worship of the early church in Acts 2 gives more helpful guidance on worship. First, it is worth noting that God-centered worship service need not be antithetical to evangelism. The early church's worship manifested God's presence among them and was noted by the surrounding world (Acts 2:43, 47; 5:12–14; 1 Cor. 14:24–25). Yet evangelism was a byproduct of worship, not the design of worship.

Second, whatever the style of worship, it should elicit the same twofold response we see in Acts 2. On the one hand, the early worshipers felt a sense of awe (Acts 2:43) as they saw God at work among them. Thus, worship should be so God-centered that it will produce, not necessarily comfort, but reverence, awe, and submission. In worship we should encounter the One before whose greatness we feel our smallness. Contemporary worship does not always do this well. Some of its music does exalt God's greatness in marvelous ways, but the casual atmosphere of most contemporary worship can lead to a casual attitude toward God rather than an attitude of awe. But alongside the sense of awe, there was a joyful sense of praise in early Christian worship (Acts 2:47). Praise comes as we recognize that the great God, before whom we bow in awe, has, in his great mercy and amazing love, provided forgiveness and life in Jesus Christ. He has called us his children and bids us stand, give him praise, and rejoice in his love for us. And it is on this count that much of traditional worship can be faulted. An excessive emphasis on reverence can dull any exuberant expression of praise, while advocates of contem-

---

76. Sargeant found that 98 percent of the seeker church pastors surveyed identified themselves as "evangelical," and 99 percent agreed that "the Bible is the inspired Word of God, true in all its teachings." Sargeant, *Seeker Churches*, 20–21.

porary worship believe worship should be joyful, exciting, and enthusiastic. These two keynotes can be compared in this way:

Characterized by reverent awe.	Characterized by joyful praise.
Honors God for his holiness.	Rejoices in God's love.
God is transcendent and above us.	God is immanent and with us.
"Be still and know that I am God."	"Shout for joy to the Lord, the King."

The key is balancing these two keynotes of worship. Contemporary worshipers may need to take care that they not obscure God's holiness. One of the earliest studies of Willow Creek found that 70 percent of the sermons emphasized God's love, while only 7 percent dealt with God's holiness.[77] Admittedly, this survey was of the seeker service, not the believers' service, and comes from the early 1990s, but it represents the danger contemporary worship can face. Traditionalists need to guard against the opposite danger, that of joyless worship that does not actively engage worshipers in praise, but leaves them to sit in silence.

One final element of worship, central to worship for much of the church's history, we have not yet considered. That is the role of the sacraments, or as they are more commonly called among Baptists, the ordinances of baptism and the Lord's Supper. They are vital acts of worship, but are often underappreciated and poorly understood and celebrated among Baptists. Their importance requires a thoroughness of consideration that would unduly lengthen this chapter. Therefore, they will be treated at length in the following chapter.

The Ministry of Service

Acts 2:45 records the radical way the early believers served one another. To meet the financial needs of one another, they sold possessions and even

---

77. Gregory Pritchard, "The Strategy of Willow Creek" (Ph.D. diss., Northwestern University, 1994), 769.

parcels of land. But it seems likely their service extended beyond the boundaries of their own congregation. The love of Christ, as well as his command, would prompt them to serve their neighbor, whether church member or stranger. Paul commanded the early churches in Galatia to do good to all men, though he did underscore the special place for "those who belong to the family of believers" (Gal. 6:10). Perhaps the service they rendered to all helps explain why Acts 2:47 says the early church was "enjoying the favor of all the people."

Service is also a necessary ministry of the church. The New Testament is replete with texts describing how the love of Christ impels Christians to serve others, following the example of their Lord, who did not come to be served, but to serve (see Rom. 13:8; Gal. 5:13; 1 John 3:16–18). As the body of Christ, motivated by his love, the church from the earliest days has provided service. Caring for the needs of members of the body is implicit in the very idea of the church as Christ's *body* (see 1 Cor. 12:26), but because the church is the body of the Christ who came for all the world, the service of the church extends to all the world. The idea of service is also implicit in the image Christ applied to his followers, who are to be "the salt of the earth" and "the light of the world" (Matt. 5:13–14). The salt and light exist to serve that which is in some sense opposed to them. Even the ministry of worship is incomplete without the accompanying action of service. Miroslav Volf says, "There is something profoundly hypocritical about praising God for God's mighty deeds of salvation and cooperating at the same time with the demons of destruction, whether by neglecting to do good or actively doing evil."[78] The specific task of pastor-teachers is to "prepare God's people for works of service" (Eph. 4:12). While that word *service* is broad enough to cover all that the church does in ministry, it certainly includes the church's ministry to basic human needs, or what is sometimes called social action.

Caring for the poor has a long heritage in the church. Paul testifies that he was eager to do so (Gal. 2:10). The patristic church was known for its willingness to serve. An anonymous second-century letter describes Christians in these terms: "They marry and have children just like everyone else; but they do not kill unwanted babies. They offer a shared table, but not a shared bed."[79]

---

78. Miroslav Volf, "Reflections on a Christian Way of Being-in-the-World," in *Worship: Adoration and Action*, ed. D. A. Carson (Grand Rapids: Baker, 1993), 211.

79. From the anonymous Letter to Diognetus, cited in Tim Dowley, ed., *Introduction to the History of Christianity* (Minneapolis, Minn.: Fortress Press, 2002), 67.

In the sixth century, Pope Gregory I earned the title "Gregory the Great" in part because of the extensive provision he led the church to make for the poor. One of the main motivations for the various monastic movements throughout the medieval period was Jesus' command to the rich young ruler to sell his possessions and give to the poor (Matt. 19:21), a command several rich Christians obeyed literally, including Francis of Assisi.

By the time of the Reformation, the care of the poor and sick was seen as a standard ministry of the church, typically entrusted to deacons. The earliest description of Baptist worship includes "an exhortation to contribute to the poore, wch collection being made is also concluded wth prayer."[80] Up until the 1930s, churches provided the major portion of social welfare in the United States. Schools, hospitals, soup kitchens, and other care of the poor and sick were all seen as a sphere of ministry of the church.

Perhaps the most extreme example of the commitment to service is seen in the development of the so-called social gospel, whose foremost advocate was a Baptist named Walter Rauschenbusch.[81] Moved by the appalling poverty that he saw in the Hell's Kitchen area of New York, Rauschenbusch called for a radical commitment to the gospel, which for him involved a commitment to social action on behalf of the poor. Because his theology was suborthodox on many points (he denied the inerrancy of Scripture and the deity of Christ, for example) and because he was firmly opposed to American capitalism, Rauschenbusch did not gain a wide following. In fact, many conservatives of his day criticized him as a communist, and the term *social gospel* was associated with liberal theology. Still, the cause he championed was carried on by many who did not share his theology.

The poverty of the Great Depression overwhelmed the resources of the churches. The government stepped in with the creation of the modern welfare state and increasingly has taken over the role formerly held by the church in the areas of caring for the poor and sick. Still, anyone who has served on the staff of a church knows that poor people still look to churches for help, and most churches are involved in some way in ministries providing assistance to those in need. One survey estimates that Southern Baptist congregations alone minister to three million persons per month through food and

---

80. This reference is from 1609 and is cited in McBeth, *Baptist Heritage*, 91. McBeth, in turn, is citing Champlin Burrage, *The Early English Dissenters in Light of Recent Research* (New York: Russell and Russell, 1967), 2:176–77.

81. For more on Rauschenbusch, see Stephen Brachlow, "Walter Rauschenbusch," in *Baptist Theologians*, 366–83.

clothes closets, not to mention those who volunteer as tutors in after school programs and in providing meals and transportation for the elderly.[82] The services that churches provide voluntarily and free of charge would cost government agencies millions of dollars. Such service is motivated by the love of Christ.

Still, this is an area in which Baptists, and most evangelical Christians, need to improve. Baptists are found mostly in suburban and rural areas. They are least found in urban areas, where social needs are the greatest and social ministry is imperative. Some Baptists emphasize evangelism to the exclusion of social action, seeing attempts to improve society as an inevitably losing battle, akin to rearranging deck chairs on the *Titanic*. Others have admitted some legitimacy to social action as a helpful adjunct to evangelism. But expressing Christ's love in practical acts of service is not merely a means to the end of evangelism, but is legitimate in its own right. While the result of service may be an openness to the other ministries of the church, including the message of the gospel,[83] the service itself must be offered unconditionally if it is to model Christ's love.

One helpful strategy for encouraging acts of service is through small, purpose-oriented groups. We have mentioned small groups as important contexts for the ministries of teaching and fellowship, but service can be a helpful way to prevent small groups from just being inward-looking holy huddles. Groups together can tackle projects and ministries that could be overwhelming to an individual, and one catalyst for forming a small group can be a shared desire on the part of several to serve in a specific area of need.

The Ministry of Evangelism

The last ministry we find in the description of the church in Acts 2 is not really described as a ministry of the church but as the activity of God. As the church devoted itself to teaching its members, developing fellowship, enjoying worship, and serving the community, the text says that "the Lord added to their number" (v. 47). Richard Longenecker notes in his commentary on Acts that the title *the Lord (ho kurios)* appears first in the sentence, emphasiz-

---

82. Jones, "Research Report," 3–4.
83. In his very helpful book, *The Church of Irresistible Influence*, Robert Lewis gives a very practical strategy for building bridges of service between the church and its community, bridges that will lead unbelievers into the church. See Robert Lewis with Rob Wilkins, *The Church of Irresistible Influence* (Grand Rapids: Zondervan, 2001).

ing its importance.[84] Nor is this an unusual emphasis. While evangelism is everywhere present in almost every chapter of the book of Acts, human actors are overshadowed by divine activity. In Acts 6:7, "the word of God spread." In Acts 9:31, the church "grew in numbers" as it was "encouraged by the Holy Spirit." When Gentiles came to believe, the church saw it as God granting to them "repentance unto life" (11:18). When Barnabas went to Antioch, he saw the converts there as "evidence of the grace of God" (v. 23). As Paul and Barnabas preached, "the word of the Lord spread through the whole region" (13:49). When they returned from their missionary journey, Paul and Barnabas reported that God "had opened the door of faith to the Gentiles" (14:27). Verses like these do not deny human involvement, but they underscore the divine initiative.

Moreover, while there is obvious human involvement in sharing the gospel message, there is almost a total absence of commands concerning evangelistic involvement in the New Testament. Most books on evangelism give obedience to Christ's command as one of the chief motives for evangelism, and give the Great Commission, Matthew 28:19–20, as biblical support. But what is not often noted is that the command in the Great Commission is to make disciples, which includes but is not exhausted by evangelism, and that the command is one of a handful regarding evangelism.[85] Texts like Romans 12:9–21 and 1 Thessalonians 5:12–22 contain dozens of commands, but none that say anything like "share the gospel with others" or "be zealous in evangelizing." Likewise, the qualifications for elders in 1 Timothy 3:1–7 and Titus 1:6–9 show concern for character and abilities to lead and teach, but there is no mention of giftedness in evangelism. Yet this is not to say that evangelism is absent from the pages of the New Testament. On the contrary, evangelism is everywhere evidenced in the New Testament, but it is hardly ever commanded.

Of course, it is possible that the New Testament writers assumed that the early Christians knew and would obey Christ's command in the Great Commission, but the evidence seems otherwise. Michael Green says in his classic study, *Evangelism in the Early Church*, that the three motives energizing the evangelistic activity of the early believers were a sense of love and gratitude to God, a sense of responsibility and stewardship before God the Judge, and a sense of the dangerous condition of the lost. Green adds, "It is important to

---

84. Longenecker, "The Acts of the Apostles," 9:291.
85. See John Hammett, "The Great Commission and Evangelism in the New Testament," *Journal of the American Society for Church Growth* 10 (Fall 1999): 3–14 for elaboration of this point.

stress this prior motive of loving gratitude to God because it is not infrequently assumed that the direct command of Christ to evangelize was the main driving force behind the Christian mission," but in fact Christ's command is quoted very rarely in Christian literature of the second century and is referred to only once in the New Testament writings themselves (Acts 10:42).[86]

My point in noting the way the New Testament speaks of evangelism is not to minimize the importance of obedience and intentionality in evangelism. A recent survey of a thousand churches having a successful ministry of evangelism found that a common factor in these churches was "intentionality in evangelism."[87] Rather, the implication we are to draw from the New Testament is that evangelism *should be* a natural product of a healthy church. In fact, if one thinks of God as the head of the heavenly adoption agency, looking into families seeking to adopt new spiritual children, why would he place them in dysfunctional families where they will not receive proper teaching, fellowship, worship, and service? But when churches are healthy, evangelism seems to pop out irrepressibly, even in the absence of the latest methodologies. Rick Warren says, "What *really* attracts large numbers of unchurched to a church is changed lives—a lot of changed lives. People want to go where lives are being changed, where hurts are being healed, and where hope is being restored."[88] Mark Dever, from a very different style of church, makes much the same observation: "If you can get a reputation in the community as a church in which people's lives are actually changed, you will begin to see some amazing things."[89]

Though hindered in their early years by persecution, and stunted at times by hyper-Calvinistic theology, for most of their history Baptists in America have been an evangelistic people. From 1740 to 1848, Baptists grew from less than one hundred churches to more than eleven thousand churches, with more than eight hundred thousand members. Such growth was not just the result of a growing population in the United States; in fact, Baptists were growing more than three times as fast as the population.[90] By and large, these

---

86. Green, *Evangelism in the Early Church*, 236–55, 239.

87. Thom Rainer, "The Great Commission to Reach a New Generation," *The Southern Baptist Journal of Theology* 1 (Winter 1997): 40–50.

88. Warren, *Purpose Driven Church*, 247. Emphasis in original.

89. Dever, "Pastoral Success in Evangelistic Ministry," 255.

90. These numbers are from Noll, *America's God*, 162, 166, 181. Noll cites Robert Baird, *Religion in the United States* (Glasgow: n.p., 1844); and John Winebrenner, *History of All the Religious Denominations* (Harrisburg, Pa.: n.p., 1848) as his sources.

Baptists were serious about their church membership, for if they took it lightly, churches regularly practiced church discipline.

However, as we discussed earlier, in the twentieth century, church discipline nearly disappeared, standards for baptism and church membership were relaxed, and the continuing growth in numbers did not necessarily reflect effective evangelistic ministry. A significant portion of new members eventually became inactive, and many active new members were not new converts but transfers from other churches, a process sometimes called "the circulation of the saints." In recent years, some Baptist denominations have been in decline, and the largest Baptist denomination, the Southern Baptist Convention, has been growing at a rate well under 1 percent per year despite a strong denomination-wide emphasis on evangelism.

If the understanding of the New Testament teaching on evangelism sketched out above is correct, perhaps the reason for the lack of evangelistic effectiveness lies in weaknesses in other ministries. And if this is so, then the solution is not simply a stronger emphasis on and louder calls for commitment to evangelism. Rather, the solution is the development of healthier churches with stronger ministries of teaching, fellowship, worship, and service that, in turn, produce changed lives. It is with such changed lives that intentional emphases on evangelism and practical training in evangelism produce results.

One final aspect of evangelism merits special mention. It is the extension of evangelism to the ends of the earth, or what is usually called international missions. This, too, has been a ministry very close to the hearts of many Baptists. The man usually regarded as the father of the modern missionary movement, William Carey, was a Baptist, and Baptists in America formed their first national organization primarily to support missions. Today, the Southern Baptist Convention supports more than five thousand missionaries, the largest force of any Protestant denomination. They are supported by 50 percent of the Convention's regular budget, plus an annual offering devoted exclusively to missions, totaling more than $136 million in 2003.

Over the past two centuries, the missionary enterprise supported by Baptists and many others around the world has borne fruit and made Christianity the first and only truly worldwide religion. There are still many unreached peoples and areas that have been resistant to Christianity, but the accomplishments of the missionary movement have been remarkable yet largely unreported. Some seem to think that the influence of Christianity is waning and that America is becoming a post-Christian nation. That may or may not be true of America, but it is definitely not the case worldwide. As Philip Jenkins has shown, the center of Christianity may be moving from the Northern to the Southern Hemisphere, but demographic evidence suggests that Christianity will continue to grow for the foreseeable future.[91] We will look at the implications of the globalization of the church in more detail in chapter 12.

In conclusion, these are the five mandated ministries of the church. They are God's assignment to churches, inherent in the nature of the church. This holistic assignment also distinguishes the church from parachurch groups that serve more specialized functions. By contrast, churches are called to provide all five of these ministries to all types of peoples. That is their challenge and their glory. Only as they keep all five in balance can they be as healthy and fruitful as God intends them to be.

---

91. See the fascinating analysis in Jenkins, *The Next Christendom*.

CHAPTER 10

MORE THAN SIMPLE SYMBOLS

Baptism and the Lord's Supper

WE TURN NOW TO TWO important acts that have occasioned much discussion, controversy, and division among churches in the course of history, particularly following the Reformation. The first, baptism, provided the name for Baptists, due to their distinctive practice of it. The second, the Lord's Supper, remains the central act of worship in Catholic churches and to a lesser degree in some other denominations.

Yet for all their importance, there seems to be a lack of interest in, and even a sense of embarrassment by, these corporate acts of commitment among Baptists. To some degree, this may be due to the fact that Baptists have regarded these acts as symbolic and thus intrinsically less important than the realities they symbolize. Americans, on the whole, seem less appreciative of ritual and symbolism than those of many other cultures. Some in Baptist life have expressed regret at the divisions caused by different perspectives on these acts and seem ready to revise traditional Baptist views to be more inclusive of others.[1] The minimizing of these rites is also reflected in the often sloppy, haphazard, dry celebration of them in Baptist churches. Rarely are they high

---

1. For example, in Shurden, ed., *Proclaiming the Baptist Vision*, G. Todd Wilson advocates open membership, dropping the traditional insistence on believer's baptism as a condition for membership in a Baptist church. There is even broader movement away from the traditional insistence on believer's baptism as a condition of partaking in the Lord's Supper (the position called closed or close communion) as Fisher Humphrey's treatment of the Lord's Supper shows. See G. Todd Wilson, "Why Baptists Should Not Rebaptize Christians from Other Denominations," in Shurden, ed., *Proclaiming the Baptist Vision*, 5:41–48; and Fisher Humphreys, "A Baptist Theology of the Lord's Supper," in Shurden, ed., *Proclaiming the Baptist Vision*, 117–28. A similar position is advocated by Tyler, *Baptism*.

times of worship in Baptist life; rather, they are performed as part of the tradition (in the case of communion, as infrequently as possible) with little expectancy or joy. There is, thus, considerable need to rethink the Baptist views of baptism and the Lord's Supper, and considerable room for improvement in Baptists' celebration of them.

INTRODUCTORY ISSUES

The Proper Terminology

We face an initial problem of terminology in discussing baptism and the Lord's Supper: what should we call them? Books variously refer to them as rites, rituals, ceremonies, and acts, but the word most often used throughout Christian history has been *sacrament*. *Sacramentum* was the word chosen in the Latin translation of the New Testament for the Greek word *mystērion*, which, ironically, was never used in the New Testament in connection with either baptism or the Lord's Supper. As a secular term, a *sacramentum* was an oath of loyalty made by a Roman soldier to his commander and thus was not totally alien to the meaning of baptism or the Lord's Supper. However, as the Catholic Church developed its theology and began to apply the word to certain practices, especially the Lord's Supper, the meaning attributed to *sacrament* began to evolve.

Perhaps the most well-known definition of sacrament is that given by Augustine: a visible sign of an invisible grace. More problematic was the growing assertion that the sacraments conveyed God's grace to the recipient. By the time of the Reformation, the sacraments were thought to communicate grace in an almost mechanical way. The phrase used to refer to this view is *ex opere operato*, "from the work done." The meaning is that the sacrament conveys grace by the mere fact that is it properly done, apart from faith on the part of the recipient. For example, the Council of Trent, meeting in 1547, promulgated this decree: "If anyone says that by the sacraments of the new law grace is not conferred *ex opere operato*, but that faith alone in the divine promise is sufficient to obtain grace, let him be anathema."[2] This, of course, was written to counter the claim of Luther and the Reformers as a whole that we receive grace by faith. Even today, a prominent Catholic theology text defines sacrament as "a sign through which the

---

2. Canon 8 from the "Canons on the Sacraments in General," in Janz, ed., *A Reformation Reader*, 359.

Church manifests and celebrates its faith and communicates the saving grace of God."[3]

Protestants often use the word *sacrament* though without the idea that it automatically conveys grace apart from faith. R. S. Wallace defines a sacrament simply as "a religious rite or ceremony instituted or recognized by Jesus Christ."[4] Baptist theologian A. H. Strong refers to baptism and the Lord's Supper as sacraments, "in the sense of vows of allegiance to Christ, our Master,"[5] and used with that understanding, the term is perfectly acceptable. However, due to its long association with the idea of conveying grace, most Baptists have chosen *ordinance* as the term for baptism and the Lord's Supper, signifying that these acts are ordained by Christ for the church.

Neither term can claim biblical warrant, and, indeed, there is no biblical term used for these rites. Thus, one can use *rite, ritual, ceremony, act, sacrament*, or *ordinance*; what matters is the meaning one attaches. However, since Baptist confessions of faith show a strong preference for *ordinance*, that will be the term primarily used in this chapter.

The Proper Number

Baptism and the Lord's Supper have been almost universally recognized as ordinances given to the church by Christ; among the churches growing out of the Reformation, they have been regarded as the only true sacraments.[6] Among Catholics, while these two have been strongly affirmed, they have not been the only sacraments. Augustine used the word *sacramentum* for the Lord's Prayer and the Creed, another medieval theologian specified as many as thirty sacraments,[7] and contemporary Catholic theologian Richard McBrien says that one of the essential aspects of Catholicism is its "sacramental vision" in which virtually anything can become a "carrier of the divine presence."[8] The traditional formulation, which dates from at least the twelfth century, sees seven sacraments: baptism, confirmation, the Eucharist or the Lord's Supper,

---

3. McBrien, *Catholicism*, 1250.

4. R. S. Wallace, "Sacrament," in Elwell, ed., *Evangelical Dictionary of Theology*, 1047.

5. Strong, *Systematic Theology*, 930.

6. The only exceptions are the Quakers and the Salvation Army, which observe no sacraments.

7. F. L. Cross and E. A. Livingstone, eds., "Sacrament," in Cross and Livingstone, eds., *Oxford Dictionary of the Christian Church*, 1218.

8. McBrien, *Catholicism*, 10.

penance, matrimony, holy orders, and extreme unction (also called last rites or anointing of the sick).

The two criteria by which the Reformers (and Baptists) have limited the number of ordinances to two have been: (1) they must have been directly instituted by Christ, and (2) they must be directly related to the gospel; that is, they must "depict in a symbolic manner the central story of Jesus and our union with him."[9] On these grounds, they have maintained that only baptism and the Lord's Supper qualify. The Council of Trent claimed that Christ instituted all seven of the Catholic sacraments, but attempts to find such occasions in the New Testament have led to disagreements among Catholic theologians themselves.[10] Robert Saucy is more blunt, claiming that it is impossible to find a biblical basis for any ordinances other than baptism and the Lord's Supper.[11] Some Baptists have argued for foot-washing as an ordinance. It was instituted by Christ, but has been seen as relating more to how Christians should serve one another than to the gospel, and thus has never been widely accepted as an ordinance.

The Proper Administrator

The question of the proper administrator of the sacraments is raised mainly by the idea that ordination gives to the one ordained special rights or powers. For example, in Roman Catholicism, it is only when a properly ordained priest says the words, "This is my body," that God performs the miracle of transubstantiation, whereby the bread and wine become the actual body and blood of Christ. As officers of the church, the priests are the ones that manage the grace conveyed through the sacraments. Therefore, they are the ones who must perform the sacraments.

The Reformers, and Luther in particular, championed the principle of the priesthood of all believers. Yet they maintained the propriety of only pastors administering the sacraments for the sake of order. Luther says, "what would happen if everyone wanted to speak or administer, and no one wanted to give way to the other? It must be entrusted to one person, and he alone should be allowed to preach, to baptize, to absolve, and to administer the sacraments."[12] Baptists have generally followed Luther on this issue. There is

---

9. Grenz, *Theology for the Community of God,* 676.

10. Cross and Livingstone, "Sacrament," 1218.

11. Saucy, *The Church in God's Program,* 192.

12. Martin Luther, "On the Councils and the Church," in Luther, *Basic Theological Writings,* 551.

no theological reason why someone must be ordained to administer the ordinances, but it does seem prudent and orderly. At the same time, we view the ordinances as entrusted to the church, not to the church's leaders. Therefore, the church can designate whomever it chooses to administer the ordinances, whether that person is ordained or not.

The Proper Setting

There is widespread agreement that the administration of the ordinances belongs to local churches. This agreement is based on a number of factors. First, the command to baptize (Matt. 28:19–20) was given to the apostles, not as independent individuals, but as the authorized leaders of the early church. New Testament descriptions of baptism and the Lord's Supper seem to assume that these activities normally take place in the context of a church, or in the case of some baptisms, at the beginning stage of a church's establishment (as in Acts 2:41; 8:12; 16:15).[13]

More important, as will be argued below, the meanings of baptism and the Lord's Supper link both to the church. Stanley Grenz says, "the meaning of the sacred practices lies in their use as acts of commitment within the context of the community of Jesus' disciples"; they are the means by which "we initially affirm and repeatedly reaffirm our inclusion in the community."[14] Millard Erickson notes that virtually all Christians agree that baptism is connected "with one's initiation into the universal, invisible church as well as the local, visible church."[15] In the case of the Lord's Supper, the connection is even clearer. The key text on the Lord's Supper, 1 Corinthians 11:17–34, speaks of the church meeting or coming together *(sunerkomai)* for this purpose five times in this brief passage. Clearly, it is an act "to be celebrated by the assembled church" rather than "a solitary observance on the part of individuals."[16]

In addition to biblical and theological reasons, there are practical reasons why most parachurch groups and interdenominational groups leave the ordinances to local churches. In such gatherings, there will normally be a variety of understandings of these acts. Observing them would promote confusion

---

13. The only clear example of a baptism that does not seem connected in any way to an established or beginning church is that of the Ethiopian eunuch in Acts 8:36–39, but there are a number of elements in this account that mark it as an exception, rather than the rule.
14. Grenz, *Theology for the Community of God*, 673.
15. Erickson, *Christian Theology*, 1099.
16. Strong, *Systematic Theology*, 961.

rather than worship. Also, most parachurch groups seek to minister along-side *(para)* churches rather than in competition with them. The ordinances are normally seen as belonging to the church.

This does not mean that there can be no ordinances observed except in a church building. Outdoor baptisms are practiced by many churches in lakes and provide a wonderful opportunity for public testimony. But the ordinances involve commitment to a body of believers (in baptism) and renewal of that commitment (in the Lord's Supper) and thus cannot be properly observed in a context unrelated to a church. They are not appropriate for loosely related groups like those found, for example, on a youth retreat, or a small portion of the church, like a home Bible study. However, in situations where a church member is unable to attend public worship, the Lord's Supper may be carried to such a one by representatives of the church and would in fact be an important way for such a one to affirm that, though separated physically from the body of believers, she or he remains committed and one with them in spirit. But the normal setting for observation of the ordinances is the gatherings of the church.

The Proper Perspective

The final issue in this preliminary overview is that of perspective. Before we turn to the individual ordinances and the meaning of each, we should notice an interesting dualism of perspectives that colors one's interpretation of the ordinances. Some see the ordinances as places where God acts. He ministers help and encouragement; he seals and confirms. He is there in blessing, and the ordinances can be means of grace—not the grace that saves, but that which strengthens and upholds a believer. If not carefully qualified, this position can veer toward an *ex opere operato* view and thus we must maintain that the ordinances do not automatically dispense grace but must be met with faith.

On the other hand, Baptists typically emphasize the human actions involved in the ordinances. At baptism, we emphasize that those who are coming are coming to testify of their faith in Christ. They are the actors. They are buried; they are raised. Likewise in the Lord's Supper, we remember Christ's body broken and his blood spilled for us. We proclaim Christ's death. The focus is on what we do. The danger here is missing a blessing God may have for us, because we never look for it.

Both perspectives have a part in the ordinances. In addition to the traditional Baptist emphasis on action, this chapter also points out how God is active around us in the ordinances and how we may seek to partner with him.

BAPTISM: THE ORDINANCE OF COMMITMENT

In some ways it is ironic, yet understandable, that the opponents of Baptists chose to identify them by the term *Baptists*. It is ironic because the more fundamental idea prompting the origin of Baptists was their idea of the church; it is understandable because their practice of baptism was the most obvious and visible expression of their idea of the church. Baptists differed most visibly in the *subjects* and *mode* of baptism. That is, they baptized no infants, but only those of an age to make a credible decision of faith, and they baptized them by immersion, not sprinkling. But underlying these visible differences was their view of the meaning of baptism. It is to that topic that we turn our attention first.

The Meaning of Baptism

The meaning of baptism in the New Testament seems to center around the idea of identification with Christ. Romans 6:3–4 and Colossians 2:12 say that in baptism we are buried with Christ and raised with Christ, in keeping with our union with him. Robert Saucy notes the importance of the repeated references in the book of Acts that link baptism and Jesus' name (2:38; 8:16; 10:48; 19:5). "Into the name" was a technical term indicating a transference of ownership. Thus, in baptism one openly confessed that he belonged to Jesus; that is, he was henceforth to be identified with Jesus.[17]

Identification with Christ also meant identification with his acts. Because we are identified with Christ in his death and resurrection, we experience purification. This is seen in the command of Ananias to Paul, "Get up, be baptized and wash your sins away, calling on his name" (Acts 22:16). Purification is seen not just in terms of forgiveness but also empowering. The point

---

17. Saucy, *Church in God's Program*, 193–94. Richard Longenecker, "The Acts of the Apostles," 9:283, concurs, noting that though the preposition used with baptism varies from *on* (*epi*, Acts 2:38) to *in* (*en*, Acts 10:48) to *into* (*eis*, Acts 8:16; 19:5), the use of the phrase "the name of Jesus" indicates that the person is calling on Jesus, signaling commitment to and identification with Jesus.

of Paul's argument in Romans 6 about union with Christ in his death and resurrection is that in that union we have died to sin and can no longer live as slaves to it. We have the power to "live a new life" (Rom. 6:4). The context and argument is similar in Colossians 2:11–12. In union with Christ the sinful nature is put off and buried with Christ in baptism; we are raised with Christ to live a new life.

Alongside identification and purification, baptism signals incorporation. To be identified with Christ means to be identified with his body. This is described in Acts 2:41, where those who were baptized were added to the church. There is also a fainter connection in 1 Corinthians 12:13, where Paul affirms that all were baptized into one body, but baptism in this context seems not to be water baptism but the common reception of the Spirit, as the parallel phrase in verse 13 shows: "and we were all given the one Spirit to drink."[18] But even if the reference is to Spirit baptism and not water baptism, it shows that Paul associated baptism with incorporation into Christ's body.

The more difficult question is the precise relationship of baptism to identification with Christ, purification from sin, and incorporation into the body. Typically, Baptists have seen baptism as symbolic; that is, it does not effect or accomplish identification, purification, or incorporation, but symbolizes that they have occurred. We come to be included in Christ when we hear the gospel and believe (Eph. 1:13); our hearts are purified by faith (Acts 15:9); we receive the Spirit who incorporates us into the body when we believe (Gal. 3:2). Thus, we have seen faith as the reality and baptism as the symbol of faith, the appointed way one proclaims and testifies to faith. But in the latter half of the twentieth century, a number of British Baptists argued for a more "sacramental" understanding of baptism; that is, a view that sees baptism as that which "mediates the experience of salvific union with Christ, i.e., that one submits to baptism as a penitent sinner in order to experience the forgiveness of sins and the gift of the Holy Spirit, rather than as a confirmed disciple in order to bear witness to a past experience of union with Christ."[19]

---

18. Fee, *First Epistle to the Corinthians*, 605–6, argues persuasively that Paul in 1 Cor. 12:13 refers "to their common experience of conversion, and he does so in terms of its most crucial ingredient, the receiving of the Spirit"; thus, the baptism "in the Spirit" indicates the element in which they have been baptized.

19. Stanley Fowler, *More Than a Symbol: The British Baptist Recovery of Baptismal Sacramentalism*, Studies in Baptist History and Thought (Carlisle, U.K.: Paternoster Press, 2002), 2:6. Fowler has been the most persistent defender of this position. This is his most complete presentation and defense of it.

Perhaps the key work for this view has been G. R. Beasley-Murray's *Baptism in the New Testament* (1962). Beasley-Murray painstakingly exegetes all the relevant New Testament passages on baptism and states, "the idea that baptism is a purely symbolic rite must be pronounced not alone unsatisfactory but out of harmony with the New Testament itself."[20] He does not deny that baptism is a symbol, but it is "a symbol with power, that is, a sacrament."[21] It is evident that Beasley-Murray is not using the word *sacrament* in the sense of an oath of allegiance but with a strong connection to grace. He argues, "in the New Testament precisely the same gifts of grace are associated with faith as with baptism."[22] He concludes, "It behoves us accordingly to make much of baptism. It is given as the trysting place of the sinner with his Saviour; he who has met Him there will not despise it."[23]

What are we to make of the argument of these British Baptists? In one way they are raising the issue of what God does for believers in baptism. Many would affirm that God always acts in response to faithful obedience to his commands, and in this sense, baptism may be a means of grace.[24] But does God act in baptism to bring the blessings of salvation?

Acts 2:38 and 1 Peter 3:21 are perhaps the verses that make the closest connection. In Acts 2:38 baptism is "for the forgiveness of your sins." First Peter 3:21 makes the blunt statement: "baptism now saves you." But, as Saucy notes, in these passages "faith is either imputed or explicitly stated along with baptism."[25] For example, the command to be baptized is prefaced in Acts 2:38 by the command to repent, which is often seen in the New Testament as inseparable from faith (see Mark 1:15; Acts 20:21). In 1 Peter 3:21, the apostle immediately qualifies his statement on baptism, saying that what saves is not an external act but the condition of the heart. As Richard Longenecker says, "it runs contrary to all biblical religion to assume that outward rites have any value apart from true repentance and an inward change."[26]

---

20. G. R. Beasley-Murray, *Baptism in the New Testament* (Grand Rapids: Eerdmans, 1962), 263.

21. Ibid.

22. Ibid., 272 (emphasis in original). Specifically, he cites forgiveness, cleansing, justification, and union with Christ as "the effect of baptism" in Acts 2:38; 22:16; 1 Cor. 6:11; and Gal. 3:27.

23. Ibid., 305. He does say that "necessary" is not the best way to describe baptism, for in the end, it is Christ who saves, not baptism.

24. This seems to be the sense in which Wayne Grudem calls baptism "a means of grace." See Grudem, *Systematic Theology*, 950–54.

25. Saucy, *Church in God's Program*, 197.

26. Longenecker, "The Acts of the Apostles," 9:284.

Moreover, any overall reading of the New Testament reveals clearly the priority of faith in salvation. Baptism is discussed once in Romans, Galatians, and Ephesians, and in none of the other Pauline epistles, save 1 Corinthians. By contrast, faith is everywhere. Even in Acts, baptism is not always mentioned alongside salvation. After the mass baptism in Acts 2, it is not mentioned again until Acts 8. There are numerous references to people being saved during Paul's first missionary journey (Acts 13–14), but there is no mention of any of them being baptized. They very well might have been, but it is not recorded, whereas their faith is repeatedly noted.

Still, this is not to deny that God's activity in baptism may relate in some way to salvation. Saucy says that while saving faith always precedes baptism, God may use the act of baptism "to confirm the realities of salvation."[27] Wayne Grudem believes the Holy Spirit may work through baptism to increase faith, increase our realization of the power of Christ's life in us, give us additional assurance of salvation, and help us realize more fully the blessing of the Holy Spirit.[28] Though his views on baptism differ in some respects with those of Baptists, John Calvin's definition of a sacrament describes God's work in baptism in a way that seems consonant with the New Testament evidence. A sacrament "is an outward sign by which the Lord seals on our consciences the promises of his good will toward us in order to sustain the weakness of our faith; and we in turn attest our piety toward him in the presence of the Lord and of his angels and before men."[29] I would state the last part more strongly to include the idea of testifying to faith and identifying with Christ and his body, but the first part states God's action in baptism well. God promises to save all those who come to him by faith in Christ; in baptism, God seals that on our conscience. He does so because believing in Christ is an internal, invisible matter, and humans, as sense-bound creatures, need an external action to make that decision concrete. That is why we often ask people to respond to the gospel in some physical, external way. We say that "walking down the aisle" or "saying the sinner's prayer" does not save, yet we continue to include them in our practice of evangelism, because they give us a way to mark that invisible decision of the heart. I do not oppose either of these other practices, but I do think baptism is the "outward sign" appointed in Scripture by which we

27. Saucy, *Church in God's Program*, 198.

28. Grudem, *Systematic Theology*, 953–54.

29. Calvin, *Institutes of the Christian Religion*, 21:1277 (4.14.1).

make faith visible. It is the "supreme occasion" for confessing faith in the gospel.[30]

A lovely analogy is provided by marriage. Faith may be compared to the love that binds two people together. It develops internally and leads two people to make a commitment to one another. The wedding is the occasion where that love is publicly celebrated, confessed, and confirmed. It does not create the love, but it expresses and seals it in a beautiful and solemn way. Likewise, baptism does not create faith or union with Christ, but it confesses, celebrates, and confirms it.[31] To the invisible seal of the Holy Spirit, it adds a public, visible, God-sanctioned seal.

In summary, baptism is best understood as the rite of commitment. It is the ordained occasion when one confesses that she or he has made a faith commitment to Christ. That commitment to Christ is lived out in a commitment to Christ's church and leads to a life lived out in union with him. When faithfully and rightly observed, baptism may also be a means of grace, not in the sense that it saves, but in the sense that it is the occasion where God acts to seal and confirm the blessings and promises of the gospel. Rightly observing baptism involves understanding its meaning, which is foundational to the next question we must consider in relationship to baptism.

Who May Be Baptized?

The proper subjects for baptism is the topic that has most dominated discussions of baptism in the past five hundred years. By the time of the Reformation, infant baptism had been practiced for more than a thousand years. It was one of the ways in which church and state were united; every citizen of the state was made a member of the church via infant baptism. The union of church and state was seen as essential to societal order and cohesion, and so infant baptism had theological, political, and social ramifications.

---

30. G. R. Beasley-Murray, "Baptism," in *New International Dictionary of New Testament Theology,* 1:147.

31. Grenz, *Theology for the Community of God,* 685, also notes the usefulness of marriage as an analogy. Like all analogies, it should not be pushed too far, but it provides an interesting perspective for a number of questions related to baptism. For example, would it be too farfetched to say that a professing Christian who is living without the benefit of baptism is comparable to one living with another person without the benefit of marriage? On the issue of how old someone should be to receive baptism, is the decision to follow Christ a less weighty one, requiring less discretion, than the decision of marriage? This analogy does not necessarily answer these questions; no analogy fits perfectly, but it should provoke our thinking about baptism.

Reformation theology had challenged the sacramental theology that saw the Lord's Supper as channeling grace to the recipients in an automatic *(ex opere operato)* manner, insisting that God's grace is given to those who come to God by faith. Apart from faith, the sacraments have no value. Such a view raised natural questions about the validity of infant baptism, for it is difficult to demonstrate that infants are believers when baptized. It is true that Luther argued that infants can and do have faith,[32] but few have found his argument convincing. More common ways to link faith and the baptism of infants have been to see their baptism as looking to future faith, or to see their baptism as justified by the faith of others (either the parents or the church) exercised on their behalf. In the first case, the difficulty is that this makes the value of their baptism conditional and raises the question, what of the baptism of those infants who do not come to faith? Was it, after all, a mistake to baptize them? What did God do when they were baptized? In the second case, the idea that someone may have faith on behalf of another seems contrary to one of the core beliefs of evangelical Christians: that Christianity involves a personal relationship with Christ, not a relationship via proxy.[33]

Moreover, the Reformation concern to base all of theology on Scripture alone also raised questions about infant baptism. The earliest Anabaptists and later Baptists challenged infant baptism because they could not find it in Scripture. Indeed, one of the most common reasons for conversion to Baptist views down through history has been the perceived biblical support for the Baptist position on baptism. With such theological and biblical questions, how had infant baptism become dominant? What arguments can be adduced in its favor?

There are hints at a developing practice of infant baptism by the end of the second century, with Origen claiming apostolic warrant for it in an oral tradition. However, other churches still required a period of instruction (the catechumenate) prior to baptism, and thus were practicing something close to believer's baptism. As on many other issues, the influence of Augustine

---

32. Martin Luther, "Concerning Rebaptism," in Luther, *Basic Theological Writings*, 353ff. Yet Luther says that even if infants don't have faith, infant baptism is valid, for faith can come later. Baptists have always responded with the fact that many of the infants baptized never come to faith, and since we cannot know which will and will not come to faith, we should wait until faith becomes evident.

33. Jewett says that the idea that a sponsor can have faith for a child "is wholly without warrant in the Scripture and repugnant to the fundamental truth that no one can receive and rest upon Christ for salvation by proxy" (Jewett, *Infant Baptism*, 184).

was decisive on this issue. Around 400, he gave the classic justification for infant baptism, as that which washes away the stain of original sin. Moreover, Augustine taught that infants who die without receiving infant baptism are forever barred from heaven. Thereafter, infant baptism became the norm.[34]

By the time of the Reformation, infant baptism was deeply ingrained in society and was the unquestioned assumption of the church. In fact, Luther, who on other issues challenged tradition in the name of Scripture, used tradition to argue for infant baptism against the Anabaptists: "Were child baptism now wrong God would certainly not have permitted it to continue so long, nor let it become so universally and thoroughly established in all Christendom."[35] As mentioned above, Luther also postulated the existence of infant faith, but the major arguments for infant baptism have come from Zwingli, Calvin, and the Reformed branch of Christendom.

One often-mentioned support for the idea of infant baptism is the household baptisms mentioned in Acts 10:44–48; 16:33–34; 18:8; and 1 Corinthians 1:16. Since the whole household was baptized in each case, advocates of infant baptism (or paedobaptists) argue that it is probable that at least some of the households included infants. But G. R. Beasley-Murray has shown that a close examination of the texts in question raises doubts about the presence of infants, for the members of the households are described as hearing the message of the gospel, receiving the Spirit, speaking in tongues, praising God, and most important of all, as believing.[36] If the infants believed, then they were certainly appropriate candidates for baptism, but the context strongly implies that infants were not present.

Another argument is sometimes made from the account in the Gospels of children being brought to Jesus (Matt. 19:13–15; Mark 10:13–16; Luke 18:15–17). But here, too, careful attention to the text shows that the parents brought their children to be blessed by Jesus, and to have him touch them and pray for them, but not to be baptized.

However, the "most persuasive and fundamental argument for paedobaptism" comes from Reformed teaching on the covenant of grace.[37] Some

---

34. See the discussion of Augustine's influence in Beasley-Murray, *Baptism in the New Testament*, 306, 366; and Jewett, *Infant Baptism*, 16–18.

35. Luther, "Concerning Rebaptism," 367.

36. Beasley-Murray, *Baptism in the New Testament*, 312–16.

37. This is the judgment of Donald Bridge and David Phypers, *The Water That Divides: The Baptism Debate* (Downers Grove, Ill.: InterVarsity, 1977), 41. The classic formulation of the covenant argument is found in Calvin, *Institutes of the Christian Religion*, 21:1324–1359 (4.16).

paedobaptists acknowledge that there is no clear example of infant baptism in the New Testament, but they note that the New Testament describes a missionary situation, in which the church was evangelizing adults. Infant baptism, they say, addresses the situation that arises when these adult Christians have children. Such children, like Jewish children under the old covenant, are included in the new covenant of grace. Further, as there was a sacrament for the old covenant (circumcision), so there is a sacrament for the new covenant (baptism).[38] Finally, as circumcision was given to infants to signal their membership in the covenant community, so baptism is appropriate for the infants of believing parents. Calvin states, "the children of believers are baptized not in order that they who were previously strangers to the church may then for the first time become children of God, but rather that, because by the blessing of the promise they already belonged to the body of Christ, they are received into the church with this solemn sign."[39] Baptists differ among themselves as to covenant theology, but even covenantal Baptists think the circumcision/baptism parallel breaks down for a number of reasons.[40]

First, some say the parallel fails to recognize that there are elements of discontinuity between the old covenant and the new covenant. The old covenant was ethnic, entered by physical ancestry, and signaled by a physical sign. The new covenant is spiritual, entered by the new birth, and signaled by a spiritual sign. The new covenant parallel to circumcision is spiritual circumcision, that of the heart (Rom. 2:28–29; Col. 2:11). Thus, the proper parallel to circumcision is regeneration.[41]

Others argue that the parallel is misapplied. As circumcision was applied to Abraham's physical seed under the old covenant, so baptism is to be applied to Abraham's spiritual seed under the new covenant. But the spiritual seed of Abraham are those of faith, which means that believers should be baptized, which, they would argue, excludes infants.[42]

But the most conclusive argument against infant baptism is the simple fact that infant baptism does not match the meaning of baptism reflected in

---

38. Calvin says, "whatever belongs to circumcision pertains likewise to baptism," and "what was circumcision for them was replaced for us by baptism." Ibid., 21:1327, 1329 (4.16.4, 6).

39. Ibid., 21:1323 (4.15.22).

40. Jewett, *Infant Baptism*, 233, asserts that covenantal theology, rightly understood, implies believer's baptism. Malone, *Baptism of Disciples Alone*, a former Presbyterian pastor, also argues that a proper covenant theology leads to believer's baptism.

41. Bridge and Phypers, *The Water That Divides*, 65.

42. Jewett, *Infant Baptism*, 236.

the New Testament. Infants cannot affirm their faith or make an oath of allegiance; they cannot proclaim their identification with Christ and his church. On the divine side, it is difficult to see how God can act in baptism to seal a decision that has not yet been made. A recurring problem for paedobaptists is making sense of the meaning of the baptism of infants who grow up and reject the faith of their parents. Might infant baptism even give a false sense of assurance to those who never make a personal decision of faith? By contrast, believer's baptism fits naturally into the consistent New Testament pattern in which faith precedes baptism.[43] It also naturally matches the Baptist view of the church as composed of believers only, a belief Baptists believe comes from the New Testament and is reflected in the limitation of baptism to believers.

The Timing of Baptism

Advocates of believer's baptism face two questions not germane to paedobaptists. First, they must ask, "At what age can a child exercise saving faith and thus meet the requirements for believer's baptism?" A second and related question is, "How soon after coming to faith should a young believer receive baptism?"

The first question is one regularly faced by Christian parents and their pastors. Parents are charged to raise their children "in the training and instruction of the Lord" (Eph. 6:4). As they do, quite often children at a tender age will make professions of faith. Parents will then frequently speak with their pastor. They want to do nothing to discourage their child's love for their Lord or act like they think the child is lying, yet they know that children's decisions can be made out of a desire to please parents or because their friends have made a similar decision. Also, they know that in other areas of life, they do not take a child's decision to be a firm commitment. A child may say at the age of seven that she has decided she wants to be a doctor or wants to marry the boy next door, but experience shows that such decisions are often modified over time. We believe that the Holy Spirit

---

43. One of the earliest presentations of this New Testament pattern was by the Anabaptist Balthasar Hubmaier, "On the Christian Baptism of Believers," in Balthasar Hubmaier, *Theologian of Anabaptism*, trans. and ed. H. Wayne Pipkin and John H. Yoder (Scottdale, Pa.: Herald Press, 1989), esp. 129–36, where Hubmaier systematically examines passages on baptism and finds the following consistent pattern: word, hearing, faith, baptism, works.

is involved in a decision to follow Christ in a way that may not be true of other decisions, but the question remains, at what age is a child competent to make a lifetime commitment to Jesus Christ? Or, to put it more precisely, what age does a child need to be to make a profession of faith that a church can accept as credible and thus grant believer's baptism? God can save a child whenever he chooses, but baptism is a decision of the church in which it endorses the reality of the child's decision.

Of course, the question is unanswerable in any definitive sense. Children mature at different rates, and God is free to act as he chooses in a child's life. But parents and churches are still faced with a decision: Do they affirm the reality of a child's profession of faith by administering baptism, or wait?

Some see the nature of conversion as raising serious questions about childhood decisions. William Hendricks and Dale Moody both assert that one must be lost before he can be saved; Hendricks doubts that children younger than nine can experience the radical separation from God that lostness involves.[44] Others argue that there is some New Testament support for the idea that twelve is the age of moral accountability, based on Paul's statement in Romans 7:9, which implies that he was not lost until "the commandment came," probably referring to his bar mitzvah. David Alan Black sees Paul's statement, along with the account of Jesus in the temple at age twelve (Luke 2:41–50), the common practice of confirmation at age twelve among groups that practice infant baptism, and the finding of secular developmental psychologists as indicating twelve as an age of important transitioning to adult responsibilities.[45]

Historically, Baptists prior to the twentieth century were slow to see childhood decisions as faith commitments warranting baptism. Dale Moody cites the Anabaptist requirement of adult repentance as questioning not only infant baptism but child baptism.[46] Any Baptist church of the eighteenth century that baptized those younger than mid to late teens could expect to be questioned by other Baptist churches in their association, and to this day childhood baptisms are very rare among Baptists outside the United States. But average baptismal ages have been dropping among Baptists in North America for decades. Grace Community Church, pastored by John MacArthur,

---

44. Hendricks, *A Theology for Children*, 249; and Dale Moody, *The Word of Truth* (Grand Rapids: Eerdmans, 1981), 462–63.

45. Black, *Myth of Adolescence*, 59–67.

46. Moody, *The Word of Truth*, 462–63.

delays the baptism of children until they show "evidence of regeneration that is independent of parental control"; in general, they wait until a child is twelve.[47]

An earlier chapter argued that a new Christian's class or new convert's class, to be taken prior to baptism, would be one way to add a safeguard to try to ensure that those baptized have made a valid profession of faith. Asking candidates for baptism to articulate their faith to the congregation or at least a representative group of the congregation prior to baptism should also help to separate those who have made a genuine, responsible decision from those who may have responded for other reasons or with limited understanding.

Such policies are challenged by those who say that baptism should immediately follow a profession of faith. Robert Saucy says, "It is significant that every baptism in Acts took place almost immediately following the confession of faith."[48] Others reflect the same idea in calling baptism "the initiatory rite of the church,"[49] and the widespread use of baptism as making official one's entrance into the church. Indeed, if baptism is to follow faith and serve as an act of declaring of one's allegiance, it would seem as if the sooner the better.

But there are two factors that qualify such an assessment. One is the fact that the baptisms in Acts, as far as we know, were of adults, and so there was not the need we have today to delay baptism of children. Second, despite what Saucy and others say, the biblical evidence for immediate baptism is not particularly strong. There is nothing resembling a command to baptize immediately, and while there are instances of immediate baptism, there are other instances where the time factor is not clear (Acts 18:7–8) and where conversions are reported without any mention of an immediate baptism (4:4; 13:48); in fact, conversions are spoken of as a daily occurrence, but not baptisms (2:47; 16:5). There is some deliberate openness as to the timing of baptism. The case for believer's baptism is much stronger than that for immediate baptism, and if the purpose for delay is to ascertain as much as possible that those to be baptized are believers, the delay seems commendable, rather than questionable.

---

47. "Evangelizing Children," A Grace Community Church Distinctive (Sun Valley, Calif.: Grace Community Church, 2003), 6.

48. Saucy, Church in God's Program, 195.

49. Erickson, Christian Theology, 1098.

The Mode of Baptism

By mode, we mean the manner in which baptism is administered. Is it by pouring or sprinkling water on the head, or by total immersion in water? Immersion was common in the early church, as is witnessed by large baptisteries still visible at many sites. Over the years, immersion was gradually replaced by pouring and sprinkling. Calvin acknowledged that the biblical word *baptizō* means to immerse, but thought the mode of baptism was "of no importance, but ought to be optional to churches according to the diversity of countries."[50] John Smyth and the General Baptists practiced baptism by pouring for the first three decades of Baptist life, until Particular Baptists in 1639 moved to restore immersion as the proper mode.[51] Immersion was endorsed by the 1644 London Confession and all major Baptist confessions thereafter. It soon became the standard mode for baptism among virtually all Baptists.

The reasons for supporting immersion are basically three. One is that, as widely recognized today, immersion is the meaning of the Greek word *baptizō*. Second is that immersion fits the New Testament descriptions of baptism, where individuals are described as "coming up out of the water" (Mark 1:10). Third is that immersion fits the symbolism of death and resurrection in Romans 6:3–4. Beasley-Murray believes that the reason why Paul says we are *buried* with Christ through baptism (v. 4), as opposed to being *crucified* with Christ (as in v. 6), is that burial better pictures immersion and shows that Paul thought of baptism in that way. He says, "The symbolism of immersion as representing burial is striking, and . . . not unimportant" for "the action suitably bodies forth the content of the *kerygma*," or gospel message.[52]

Nineteenth-century Baptists insisted on immersion as the only acceptable mode for valid baptism and offered detailed defenses of it.[53] Today, while Baptists continue to defend immersion as the mode that best suits the meaning of the word *baptizō* and the meaning of baptism as identification with Christ (in his death, burial, and resurrection) it is not a topic of intense debate. In

---

50. Calvin, *Institutes of the Christian Religion*, 21:1320 (4.15.19).

51. Dale Moody, "Baptism in Theology and Practice," in Basden and Dockery, eds., *The People of God*, 48, says it was Rom. 6:3–4 that convinced the Particular Baptists to adopt immersion as the proper mode of baptism.

52. Beasley-Murray, *Baptism in the New Testament*, 133.

53. Perhaps the best representative is Dagg, *Manual of Theology*, 21–68, where Dagg gives a forty-eight-page defense of immersion.

certain exceptional circumstances pouring or sprinkling may be acceptable,[54] but immersion is biblically, theologically, and symbolically preferable.

The Importance of Baptism in Contemporary Church Life

Baptism is one aspect of church life that many think about along these lines: "Is it really important? Does it really matter? After all, no evangelical claims that it is absolutely necessary for salvation. It's just a symbol." Admittedly, baptism is not a "first-order doctrine" involving an essential Christian belief, but a denominational doctrine, one that has separated denominations over the years. Today we live in a postdenominational era, when denominational distinctives are regarded as unfortunate, irrelevant, and hardly worth fussing over. It's reflected in the lack of care we give to baptism. For example, sermons on the importance of obeying Christ's command to be baptized are rare to nonexistent. Our baptismal services rarely show thoughtfulness or serve as occasions for articulate confession and joyful commitment to Christ and his church. Furthermore, some Baptists seem to doubt the value or validity of maintaining believer's baptism. Todd Wilson, while seeing believer's baptism as the ideal, maintains that Baptists "corrupt the symbol" when they require Christians baptized as infants to be rebaptized for membership in a Baptist church, because "baptizing a believer who has already been walking with God is a contradiction of the New Testament meaning of baptism."[55] But if believer's baptism is a matter of obedience, Wilson seems to prefer no obedience to the incomplete, imperfect delayed obedience of a later baptism. Baptist pastors and church members need to take baptism more seriously as an act of obedience, commitment, and worship. There are a number of way ways in which they can do so.

In terms of obedience, we simply need to note that baptism is in fact commanded. Many Christians eagerly talk of fulfilling the Great Commission, given by Christ in Matthew 28:19–20, but rarely note that baptizing is one of the activities that is to characterize the making of disciples.[56] We must

---

54. For example, I once had a student whose church voted to allow him to baptize a man who was terminally ill and in a critical care unit by sprinkling. I would make similar exceptions for someone who was pathologically afraid of water or someone so ill that immersion would be dangerous.

55. Wilson, "Why Baptists Should Not Rebaptize Christians from Other Denominations," 5:45, 43.

56. See the discussion in D. A. Carson, "Matthew," in *The Expositor's Bible Commentary*, 8:597. Carson says that baptizing should not be seen as the means of making disciples but as having a modal and imperative force as one of the activities that characterize disciple-making.

obey Christ in baptizing to fulfill the Great Commission. The sermon that marked the birth of the church concluded with the command, "Repent and be baptized" (Acts 2:38), a command the church obeyed as the gospel went forth. Ephesians 4:5 assumes that all Christians share in the "one baptism."[57] The New Testament has no conception of an unbaptized Christian. It is assumed to be a natural act of obedience, showing one's allegiance to Christ. It should also be an act of obedience required by the church, as the ordained way that a new member is incorporated into the local body. What Christ ordained and commanded should not be despised by his followers today. The fact that we cannot agree how baptism should be understood does not negate Christ's command.

Perhaps we would take baptism more seriously as an act of obedience if it was being done as a genuine symbol of commitment. Seeing young children nod assent to a pastor's question may be very precious or cute to parents, but it is not an adequate symbol of commitment. Churches must make a good faith effort to ensure they baptize only those who can make a credible profession of faith. Such baptismal candidates should be able to bear witness to the congregation that they are requesting baptism in order to testify obediently to their commitment to Christ. Then, while standing in the baptismal pool, candidates should be asked to make a profession of faith, not just answering a simple question, but stating their commitment.

If practiced in such a way, baptism could be a powerful means of worship. The very act pictures the transforming power of the gospel to put to death an old life and grant a new life, and may communicate the message in a more vivid way than words alone. For the one being baptized, it should be as memorable a day as a wedding, the day of public commitment to a life of love and union with the Lord. For the baptizing community, it should be an occasion as joyous as the birth of a new child into a family, with solemn dedication to the task of caring for this new member of the family. It should also be a time of renewal of the vows of allegiance and commitment taken by each member

---

57. Some may wonder if the "one baptism" is water baptism or Spirit baptism. In the context of Ephesians 4, water baptism seems most likely in view, as it is "a comprehensive, practical, public, binding, joyful confession of that 'one faith' in the 'one Lord.'" See Markus Barth, "Ephesians," in *The Anchor Bible*, ed. W. F. Albright and D. N. Freedman (Garden City, N.Y.: Doubleday, 1974), 34A:469–70. However, it is also possible to see Spirit baptism and water baptism as two forms or aspects of the one baptism; the former marks one's entrance into the invisible church (1 Cor. 12:13), the latter marks one's incorporation into a local church (Acts 2:41).

of the church at the time of her or his baptism. For all, it should be a high and joyous time of worship.

A helpful structure for such baptismal worship is suggested by Charles W. Deweese.[58] In addition to prayer, the reading of appropriate Scripture, and a statement on the meaning and purpose of baptism, this order of service would provide a time for the pastor to ask the baptismal candidates questions such as, What has God done to lead you to this point? What does believer's baptism mean to you? Why do you wish to become a member of this church? The candidates would be given time to answer, clarifying that their baptism is a time of obedience and commitment and a means of glorifying God for his work in their lives. The pastor would then put the church covenant into a series of questions to which they would answer, "I do," thus reflecting their baptism as a time of commitment to the church. Finally, the pastor would ask the congregation to enter into covenant with the new members and promise to support them. It would also be appropriate to preface baptism with a prayer, asking God to act in baptism, to bless, encourage, and seal the commitments made, to show that we believe we are not the only ones acting in baptism. These practices will help to make baptism a genuine act of worship.

THE LORD'S SUPPER: THE ORDINANCE OF RENEWAL

Baptism is a one-time initiatory rite, symbolizing and sealing our commitment to Christ and his church. The Lord's Supper is a continuing rite that churches observe repeatedly. In many denominations it is the central act of worship. While it is a multifaceted event, it may best be seen as a time of renewal. To carry further the analogy developed earlier in this chapter, if baptism is the wedding ceremony in which a believer publicly declares his or her commitment to Christ, the Lord's Supper is similar to an anniversary celebration in which the wedding vows are renewed. In fact, some Baptist churches in earlier times would recite their church covenant prior to observing the Lord's Supper, verbally renewing their commitment to the Lord and one another. Significantly, it is the only act of worship for which we are given specific instructions in the New Testament, and an act that almost all Christians have observed down through history. When we partake of the bread and drink of the cup, we join a band of untold millions. It is an act that deserves more attention than Baptists usually give it.

---

58. Deweese, *A Community of Believers*, app. C, 114–16.

An Act with Many Names

There are a variety of terms used for this ordinance, most with some biblical support. It is called communion in 1 Corinthians 10:16[59] and the Lord's Table in 1 Corinthians 10:21. The phrase "the breaking of bread" in Acts 2:42 and 20:7 probably refers to this rite as well. The term *Eucharist* is preferred by many, especially those in liturgical traditions. It is derived from the Greek word for thanksgiving, *eucharistia*, which is associated with this rite in 1 Corinthians 11:24 and in each of the Synoptic Gospel accounts (Matt. 26:26–27; Mark 14:22–23; Luke 22:17–19). Perhaps the most common term among Baptists is the *Lord's Supper* (1 Cor. 11:20), reminding us that originally this rite involved an actual meal.

One term not derived from Scripture is the older Catholic term, the *Mass*. It came from the Latin term *missa,* which meant dismissal, and was originally used as the closing blessing of any time of worship. Eventually it was applied only to the Lord's Supper.[60] It was the traditional term among Catholics for centuries, but many Catholics since Vatican II have been returning to the biblical term *Eucharist.*

The Debate over "This Is My Body"

The Gospels record Christ instituting what we call the Lord's Supper during an observance of Passover with his disciples (Matt. 26:17–30; Mark 14:12–26; Luke 22:7–30). As such, it was a celebration of God's redemption of Israel from slavery in Egypt. Part of that redemption involved the plague of the death of the firstborn of all the households of Egypt. Only those protected by the blood of a lamb were spared. The Lord's Supper was to signify the death of Christ, called by Paul "our Passover lamb" (1 Cor. 5:7). Interestingly, there is no record of the disciples celebrating Passover after the death of Christ. Passover celebrated the establishment of God's covenant with Israel. But in this observance with his disciples, Jesus described the cup as "the new covenant," established by his blood (Luke 22:20).[61]

---

59. This is the translation in the King James Version of *koinōnia* in this verse; most modern versions translate it as "participation" or "sharing."

60. McBrien, *Catholicism,* 823.

61. There are many intriguing aspects of the traditional Passover celebration that foreshadow Christian truths. These are explained in a presentation popularized by a number of messianic Jewish organizations called "Christ in the Passover" and published in book form by Moishe Rosen, *Christ in the Passover: Why Is This Night Different?* (Chicago: Moody, 1978).

Historically, the greatest controversy over the Lord's Supper has been over the words spoken by Jesus, called "the words of institution." Those words are "This is my body." There are four major interpretations of these words.

The traditional Catholic view is called transubstantiation. This view developed gradually and was not officially adopted until 1215, at the Fourth Lateran Council. Prior to then, there had been some who had made a careful distinction between the elements (the sign) and Christ's body and blood (the thing signified). There were some who used language that could imply the doctrine of real presence, but it could also have been simply figurative language. The issue was first debated explicitly in the ninth century between two otherwise obscure monks. Radbertus (785–860), "hankering for the mysterious and supernatural that characterized his time, taught that a miracle takes place at the words of institution in the supper: the elements are changed into the actual body and blood of Christ."[62] He was opposed by another monk, named Ratramnus (d. 868), who taught "the Augustinian position that Christ's presence in the supper is spiritual."[63] Official Catholic teaching came to follow Radbertus and affirm that when a properly ordained priest lifts the host (from the Latin word *hostia,* or "sacrificial victim," the term used to refer to the physical elements of bread and wine) and pronounces the words of institution *(Hoc est corpus meum)* a miracle occurs. The outward appearance, or accidents, of the bread and wine remain the same, but the inner reality, or substance, is changed (transubstantiated) into the actual physical body and blood of Christ. His body and blood are really, physically present in every wafer, every drop of wine.[64] Thus the celebration of the Mass involves a recrucifixion of Christ (an unbloody sacrifice), and grants to those who partake forgiveness of venial sins, an increase of grace, strength for preservation from mortal sin, and hope of ultimate salvation.[65]

All the Reformers objected to the idea that the priest had some power to deliver a miracle, to the idea of a recrucifixion of Christ, and to the idea that partaking provides grace and forgiveness of sins. But Luther did not object to the idea of Christ's physical presence. His view is called consubstantiation. It

---

62. M. E. Osterhaven, "Lord's Supper, Views of," in *Evangelical Dictionary of Theology,* 705.

63. Ibid.

64. The common people, not understanding the meaning of the Latin phrase, *Hoc est corpus meum* ("this is my body"), came to see it as a virtual magical incantation. It was eventually corrupted and passed into common usage as hocus-pocus, a phrase associated with the performance of magical tricks.

65. For more detail, see the discussion in McBrien, *Catholicism,* 820–33.

affirms that Christ's physical body is present in the Supper, not because of the words of a priest, but because Christ promised to be there. For Luther, the words, "This is my body," settle the question. He would not join forces with fellow Reformer Huldrych Zwingli because Zwingli argued that the word *is* means "signifies." Despite the fact that Zwingli could show several places in Scripture where *is* clearly means "signifies" Luther refused to consider Zwingli's view and regarded it as un-Christian. He said, "I have pressed them to show conclusive grounds why these words 'This is my body,' just as they are read, are false."[66] For Luther, the words had to be literal if they were true.

It is hard to understand why Luther was so adamant on this point, since he recognized figurative language elsewhere in Scripture. There are some hints of mysticism in his thinking, and he grew up among German peasants, whose religion often contained virtual superstition. Others think this was one aspect of his Catholic background he could not surrender, but in view of his attacks on the Catholic doctrine of the Mass, that seems unlikely. Whatever his reasons, he prized the presence of Christ in the Lord's Supper, and would not surrender the real and physical nature of that presence.

By contrast, Zwingli's name is associated with what is called the memorial view. Zwingli did not deny that Christ was spiritually present with believers when they gather in his name, but in his debate with Luther he emphasized that the word *is* in "This is my body" means "signifies," and was so concerned to deny physical presence that he said little about the idea of spiritual presence. The Lord's Supper is primarily done "in remembrance," as a memorial of what Christ did.

Calvin presents something of a mediating position. With Luther, he affirms Christ's presence in the Lord's Supper, but with Zwingli he denies that it can be a physical presence, since Christ's body ascended into heaven. He speaks of the Lord's Supper as a mystery whose purpose is "to nourish, refresh, strengthen, and gladden." In it, we receive Christ, but we do so by faith and by means of signs, which should neither be disdained nor "immoderately" extolled.[67] Calvin also helpfully brings in the work of the Spirit in the Lord's Supper. Christ's flesh is not dragged down out of heaven into the bread; rather, we are lifted to him, through "the secret working of the Spirit." He confesses, "if anyone should ask me how this takes place, I shall not be ashamed

---

66. Martin Luther, "Confession Concerning Christ's Supper," in Luther, *Basic Theological Writings*, 376.

67. Calvin, *Institutes of the Christian Religion*, 21:1363–65 (4.17.3, 5).

to confess that it is a secret too lofty for either my mind to comprehend or my words to declare. And, to speak more plainly, I rather experience than understand it."[68]

This view of the spiritual presence of Christ in the Lord's Supper has been the most widely held position since the Reformation, and has been affirmed by Baptists in at least one important confession. While Baptists are most commonly associated with the Zwinglian, memorial view, the Second London Confession incorporates the following paragraph, taken almost verbatim from the Westminster Confession:

> Worthy receivers, outwardly partaking of the visible Elements in this Ordinance, do then also inwardly by faith, really and indeed, yet not carnally, and corporally, but spiritually receive, and feed upon Christ crucified and all the benefits of his death: the Body and Blood of Christ, being then not corporally or carnally but spiritually, present to the faith of Believers, in that ordinance, as the Elements themselves are to their outward senses.[69]

However, this view is somewhat unusual in Baptist life. The view found most often with reference to the Lord's Supper is memorial.

The Significance of the Lord's Supper

In a sense, the debate over the nature of Christ's presence in the Lord's Supper is unfortunate, for it often detracts from a proper appreciation of what is offered to us at the Lord's Table. As many have noted, Baptists have been so concerned to deny Christ's physical presence that they have often in effect seemed to teach a doctrine of real absence. Wherever else Christ's presence may be found, don't look for it here!

The best word to describe the significance of the Lord's Supper is *renewal*. One of the criteria for an ordinance is that it must symbolize the gospel message. Baptism and the Lord's Supper do so, but in different ways. Baptism symbolizes the transformation effected by the gospel; it is thus the ordinance symbolizing our commitment to Christ, our new birth and justification. The Lord's Supper proclaims the gospel message of Christ's death as the sustenance

---

68. Ibid., 21:1403 (4.17.31, 32).
69. Lumpkin, *Baptist Confessions of Faith*, 293.

of the Christian life. The very elements of bread and wine speak of nourishment and refreshment. Thus, the Lord's Supper is the ordinance of ongoing sanctification, or the continual renewal and furthering of that initial commitment. By its very nature, baptism is a unique, singular occurrence, while the Lord's Supper must be regularly repeated.[70]

The first aspect of our renewal is to Christ. First Corinthians 11:24 gives the command to "do this in remembrance of me." The word *anamnēsis, remembrance*, is far richer than a mere recollection or commemoration. It is recalling an event with such vividness and power that it affects the present, bringing all the benefits of Christ's death to bear, remembering that his body was broken "for you" (1 Cor. 11:24). As we genuinely and biblically remember, we cannot help but renew our love, thanks, and worship of Christ. On the divine side, the Holy Spirit uses this occasion to nourish us spiritually as we come in faith. Faithful, believing remembrance has as its goal the renewing of our relationship with Christ.

But just as baptism serves to symbolize our commitment to Christ and his church, so the Lord's Supper serves as a renewal of our commitment to Christ and his church. First Corinthians 10:16–17 links the Lord's Supper to the unity of the body. As we partake of the one loaf, we renew our commitment to the one body. The horizontal significance of this ordinance is also seen in 1 Corinthians 11:29. We are warned not to eat or drink "without recognizing the body." Gordon Fee argues, convincingly, that the body here is not referring to the bread nor the fleshly body of Christ, but to the church.[71] It was the church as the body of Christ that was being abused by the way the Corinthians were partaking of the Lord's Supper. Their practice did not reflect their recognition of their unity as Christ's body in that place. Stanley Grenz reminds us that one place where we should always find Christ's presence in the Supper is in his body, gathered in his name (see Matt. 18:20).[72] But the Corinthian celebration did not manifest Christ's presence. Therefore, rather than bringing blessing, the Lord's Supper was calling forth judgment. The Lord's Supper should be the supreme occasion when the body renews its love for and unity with one another.

Not only do we renew our commitment to Christ and his body, we renew our commitment to his mission in the Lord's Supper. In it we "proclaim the

---

70. See the helpful comparison of baptism and the Lord's Supper in Strong, *Systematic Theology*, 964.

71. Fee, *First Epistle to the Corinthians*, 563–64.

72. Grenz, *Theology for the Community of God*, 701.

Lord's death until he comes" (1 Cor. 11:26). The note of his coming reminds us that there is a time limitation on the Lord's Supper. It is a rehearsal and foretaste of the messianic banquet to come at the marriage feast of the Lamb (Rev. 19:9). With that hope in sight, we renew our commitment to proclaim Christ's death until faith becomes sight and remembrance becomes reality.

The renewal called for by the Lord's Supper thus looks back to the past in remembrance, looks around in the present to the fellowship we experience with Christ and the body of believers, and looks ahead to the consummation, when Christ returns.[73]

Who May Partake? Open versus Closed Communion

One issue of special importance to Baptists has been the question of who may properly partake of the Lord's Supper. Both sides in the controversy believe that this ordinance is only for believers. They differ in what additional limitations there should be. The view called open communion affirms that the Lord's Supper should be open to all believers. The opposing view, called variously strict communion, close communion, closed communion, or restricted communion, believes that there is an additional limitation. Communion should be limited to baptized believers.[74]

Most denominations agree that baptism should normally precede participation in the Lord's Supper. For those that practice infant baptism, the order seems obvious. The problem is that Baptists do not see infant baptism as baptism at all. J. L. Dagg says the advocates of open and closed communion agree on the underlying principle, but not on how to apply it: "With them [advocates of open communion] we have no controversy as to the principle by which approach to the Lord's table should be regulated. We differ from them in practice, because we account nothing Christian baptism, but immersion on profession of faith, and we, therefore, exclude very many who they admit."[75]

---

73. Moody, *The Word of Truth*, 470–71, associates the past significance with the words *covenant* and *remembrance*, the present significance with *eucharistia* ("thanksgiving") and *koinōnia* ("fellowship"), and the future significance with the kingdom of God and the coming of Christ.

74. Strong, *Systematic Theology*, 971–73, adds two further prerequisites: church membership and "an orderly walk." However, since baptism is linked to church membership and most advocates of open communion would support the requirement of an orderly walk, requiring baptism prior to communion remains the key difference.

75. Dagg, *Manual of Theology*, 214.

Paedobaptists of course differ with Baptists on the propriety of baptizing infants and could welcome those baptized as infants or believers to the Lord's Supper. For them, open communion has never been that much of a question. Baptists who support open communion have done so based on the belief that the ordinance is the Lord's Supper, and therefore it is for all those who belong to the Lord, baptized or not. Furthermore, advocates of open communion think it is harsh, unloving, and offensive to exclude any true believers from the Lord's Table.[76] They may also point out that baptism is a secondary doctrine, not required for salvation, and that it has been widely disputed in the course of church history. They think it of insufficient importance to make the lack of it a barrier to the Lord's Supper.

Those who support strict communion offer three reasons for their position. First, it is a logical outgrowth of the Baptist view of the church. If the Lord's Supper is for the church, and the church is entered via believer's baptism, only baptized believers should come to the Lord's Table. The first part of this syllogism, that the Lord's Supper is for the church, is widely supported. First Corinthians 11 distinguishes between meals the members eat in their homes (1 Cor. 11:22) and the special occasion when they come together as a church to celebrate the Lord's Supper (v. 20). The text seems to regard it as a special observance just for the church. Therefore, it would be limited to the church's members, who, according to the overwhelming majority of Baptists, must receive believer's baptism to be members. Indeed, some object to open communion on the grounds that it leads logically to open membership, the idea that any believer should be accepted into church membership, whether baptized or not. The rationale is that if someone can partake of communion without baptism, she or he should also be able to become a church member without baptism. This is reflected in the essay by G. Todd Wilson. He objects to rebaptizing those who are already believers who come to Baptist life from other denominations. In support of this idea of open membership, he appeals to Baptist churches that practice open communion: "to practice open communion and then to deny a believer membership on the basis of closed baptism is inconsistent, if not contradictory."[77] Strong sees this path of open communion leading to open membership as resulting in "the complete de-

---

76. Ibid., 214–25. Dagg enumerates ten objections open communionists make against strict communion, but these two seem the most substantive.

77. Wilson, "Why Baptists Should Not Rebaptize Christians from Other Denominations," 5:45–46.

struction of both church and ordinances as Christ originally constituted them."[78]

Second, those who support strict communion argue that it is required by the horizontal dimension of the ordinance. In the Lord's Supper, we renew our commitment, not just to Christ, but also to the body of believers. But one who is not baptized, and therefore not a member of the church, cannot renew her or his unity with or commitment to the body. For this reason, some strict communionists limit communion to the members of the specific church in which the ordinance is celebrated, but most churches allow for transient communion, in which a baptized believer who is a member of one church but visiting in another church may be allowed to partake if her or his membership is in a church "of like faith and order," meaning a church that practices believer's baptism.

A third reason for supporting strict communion is that open communion denigrates baptism and the importance of obeying Christ's command to be baptized. Dagg asks "why should baptism be trodden under foot, to open the way of access to the eucharist?"[79] In fact, Mark Dever says the command to be baptized is so serious that if someone was admitted to church membership, but refused to obey such a clear command of Christ, such a person would have to be disciplined immediately.[80] Such discipline would involve exclusion from the Lord's Supper, for a member under discipline couldn't affirm a genuine unity with the body.

Until fairly recently, most Baptists have historically favored strict communion. There have been notable exceptions, such as John Bunyan, Robert Hall, and C. H. Spurgeon,[81] and historically the Free Will Baptists have always advocated open communion.[82] But most major Baptist confessions of faith, especially American Baptist confessions, have supported strict communion, as have their major theologians, such as J. L. Dagg and A. H. Strong. For example, the

---

78. Strong, *Systematic Theology*, 972–73.

79. Dagg, *Manual of Theology*, 225.

80. Dever, *A Display of God's Glory*, 52–53.

81. See the article by Timothy George, "Controversy and Communion: The Limits of Baptist Fellowship from Bunyan to Spurgeon," in *The Gospel in the World: International Baptist Studies,* ed. David Bebbington, Studies in Baptist History and Thought (Carlisle, U.K.; Waynesboro, Ga.: Paternoster, 2002), 1:38–58.

82. Lumpkin, *Baptist Confessions of Faith,* 369–76, gives the 1953 version of their *A Treatise of the Faith and Practices of the Original Free Will Baptists,* which states: "It is the privilege and duty of all who have spiritual union with Christ to commemorate His death, and no man has a right to forbid these tokens to the least of his disciples."

Principles of Faith of the Sandy Creek Association states, "the church has no right to admit any but regular baptized church members to communion at the Lord's table."[83] The New Hampshire Confession of Faith and all three versions of the *Baptist Faith and Message* have seen baptism as "prerequisite to the privileges of church membership and to the Lord's Supper."

In the twentieth century, there was movement away from strict communion toward open communion. By 1911, Northern Baptists had sufficiently relaxed their standards that they were able to merge with the historically open communion Free Will Baptists of the North, and, according to Leon McBeth, since the middle of the twentieth century, "one rarely hears of closed communion."[84] But while McBeth may accurately reflect a trend in Baptist churches, there are still defenders of strict communion. Stanley Grenz says, "baptism properly precedes participation in the Lord's Supper. . . . The reaffirmation of our personal loyalty to Christ inherent in the Lord's Supper presupposes our initial declaration of loyalty made in baptism."[85] Timothy George says that the defenders of strict communion who opposed Bunyan, Hall, and Spurgeon "were right to take seriously the covenantal and disciplinary dimensions of Baptist ecclesiology. The Lord's Supper, no less than baptism, is a mark of the true church, not a trivial ceremony or matter of indifference within the covenanted community." However, he also adds, "the open communionists were right to extend eucharistic hospitality in the spirit and love of Jesus."[86] The recent interest in recovery of meaningful church membership and redemptive church discipline could very well lead to a renewed interest in strict communion.[87]

I regard this as a difficult decision. Open communion certainly seems to be a more hospitable policy. Many Baptists have found that differences concerning baptism have not hampered their fellowship with non-Baptists in parachurch gatherings such as Promise Keepers or college groups like Campus Crusade for Christ. And Baptists themselves insist that baptism is sec-

---

83. Ibid., 358.

84. McBeth, *Baptist Heritage*, 697.

85. Grenz, *Theology for the Community of God*, 702.

86. George, "Controversy and Communion," 58.

87. If opposition is an index of interest, interest in closed communion may be growing. A full-length book (Tyler, *Baptism*) and three articles in a book from the moderate wing of Baptist life voice strong opposition to strict communion: Wilson, "Why Christians Should Not Rebaptize Christians from Other Denominations," 5:41–48; Thomas Clifton, "Fencing the Table," in Shurden, ed., *Proclaiming the Baptist Vision*, 67–72; and Humphreys, "A Baptist Theology of the Lord's Supper," 117–28. This much opposition implies that there are still supporters of closed communion among Baptists.

ondary, not essential to salvation. It seems reasonable to welcome all of the Lord's people to the Lord's Table.

But on balance, the case for strict communion seems stronger. The design and purpose of the Lord's Supper cannot be fully experienced apart from a commitment to those with whom one celebrates the ordinance. The horizontal dimension is missing in practice for many churches, Baptist and non-Baptist, but it seems an important element of New Testament teaching. This ordinance is primarily for the local church and its members. I even have some misgivings about extending transient communion to visiting members of other Baptist churches, but would do so in recognition of the fact that associations of churches bear witness to unity in truth in the larger body of Christ. Even so, those partaking as visitors could not experience communion in the same way as the members of the local body.

Furthermore, I support strict communion because I am not willing to follow the logic of open communion to open membership. The fact that baptism is not essential to salvation does not mean it is a matter indifferent (what has historically been called an *adiaphora*), on which obedience is a matter of personal choice. Believer's baptism has reflected the conscientious obedience of Baptists to what they have seen as Christ's command, and for most of their history it has served them well as one of the guardians of regenerate church membership. And since believer's baptism is required for church membership, and the Lord's Supper is for the church, believer's baptism is required to celebrate the Lord's Supper in unity and communion with other Baptists. To do otherwise is to denigrate baptism.

This position of strict communion need not be practiced in a harsh, unloving manner. Rather, prior to partaking of the Supper, it can be briefly explained that some matters pertain to those who are committed to the local body. Visitors would not expect, for example, to vote on decisions facing the local body. Likewise, one of the purposes of the ordinance of the Lord's Supper is to allow the members of the local body to renew their commitment to each other. Those who are not members of the body would be asked to refrain from partaking unless they do so as members of other churches associated with the local church. Fellowship with other believers across denominational lines can and should take place, but in contexts that do not require a de facto denial of an important article of faith (such as believer's baptism).

This rationale for strict communion will make little sense, however, if

Baptist church membership involves no genuine commitment to the body and if the Lord's Supper involves no genuine renewal of that commitment. Therefore, the recovery of meaningful church membership must proceed if the practice of strict communion is to be well grounded and credible.

A final prerequisite for participation in the Lord's Supper that is clear in Scripture but omitted in practice by many open and closed communionists is the requirement that those who partake be self-examined believers. First Corinthians 11:28 states this requirement clearly and attaches a most serious warning to it (see vv. 29–30). Yet, do we honor this prerequisite in our practice? Most of our members come to worship on any communion Sunday unaware and unprepared. Perhaps the preceding elements of worship provide some measure of preparation, but few Baptists expect or receive much in the way of spiritual nourishment from the Lord's Supper. The very poverty of our experience may be the judgment on us spoken of in 1 Corinthians 11:29. The final section of this chapter offers some practical suggestions for enriching the celebration of the Lord's Supper as an act of worship in Baptist churches.

The Lord's Supper in Worship: Practical Suggestions

Preparation for Participation

By far, the most important area in which Baptists can and should improve their celebration of the Lord's Supper is in providing help for their members in preparation. As mentioned above, it is clear that believers are to examine themselves before they participate, for unworthy participation is sin and may call forth divine chastisement. But what does such self-examination involve? How may churches guide their members into helpful self-examination and worthy participation?

My own thinking on these issues has been greatly stimulated by some of the practices reflected in the Anglican *Book of Common Prayer*. Those familiar with such worship will recognize its influence in the suggestions below.

The first and most obvious step is to announce the date for celebration of communion at least a week in advance and explicitly encourage members to prepare by examining themselves. The nature of this self-examination should be shaped by the meaning and significance of this ordinance. We have argued in this chapter that the Lord's Supper is the ordinance of renewal. Thus, self-examination should begin by focusing on the areas that need renewal in each member's life, leading to confession and repentance. But confession and repentance lead to forgiveness and renewal only because of Christ's death, which is proclaimed in the Lord's Supper. So a second part of preparation should be a genuine remembrance of Christ's death, leading to self-examination in the area of faith and an affirmation of trust in the broken body and shed blood of Christ as the only source of spiritual life. The Lord's Supper also involves a renewal of commitment to the body, so self-examination should include a consideration of relationships with other members. Are there grudges, unresolved hostility, divisions? Christ commanded reconciliation prior to acts of worship (Matt. 5:23–24); how much more so prior to celebrating the symbol of our forgiveness and the sacrament of our unity! First Corinthians 11:29 forbids participation without "recognizing the body." This is different from reflection on the meaning of the cross and Christ's broken body; it is recognition of the gathered body, the local church, Christ's body in that place.[88] Self-examination on this point should lead to forgiving one another and renewing of love for one another.

These three areas, renewal of repentance, faith, and love, seem in keeping with the meaning of the Lord's Supper and are the proper foci of self-examination. The *Book of Common Prayer* calls believers to the Lord's Table with these words: "repent ye truly for your sins past; have a lively and steadfast faith in Christ our Saviour; amend your lives and be in perfect charity with all men; so shall ye be meet partakers of those holy Mysteries."[89] But many will forget to make prior self-examination. However, time can be made for this in the course of the celebration of the ordinance, especially if the celebration is not tacked on as an afterthought, but made the focal point of that day's worship.

The *Book of Common Prayer* leads those participating in the Lord's Supper to renewal of repentance and confession by means of reading of the Ten Commandments, with the people responding after each commandment, "Lord, have mercy upon us, and incline our hearts to keep this law." As well, New Testament counterparts such as Jesus' statement of the Great Commandment (Matt. 22:37–40) may also be used. Renewal of faith can come in the recitation of the Apostles' or Nicene Creed, or in the reading of the precious promises of the gospel. Finally, renewal of love for the body can be expressed in reading texts dealing with our commitment to one another (such as Matt.

---

88. Fee, *First Epistle to the Corinthians*, 563–64.
89. *A Book of Common Prayer, and Administration of the Sacraments and Other Rites and Ceremonies of the Church* (Philadelphia: J. C. Pechin, 1835), 120.

7:12; Gal. 6:6–7, 10; 1 John 3:7, and others) and in taking an offering for the poor.[90] Here is how I have used these same basic ideas, with some revisions, in leading Baptist congregations in a time of preparation.

The Call to Preparation: 1 Corinthians 11:27–34

Scripture calls on us to examine ourselves before we partake of the bread and drink of the cup. Three areas of our lives call for special consideration and preparation, if we are to partake worthily. First, we must sincerely and humbly repent of our sins and intend by God's grace to lead a new life of obedience. Second, we must be trusting for the forgiveness of our sins wholly and only in Jesus Christ, who died for us and was raised from the dead. Third, we must be in love with and at peace with all men, especially those of this body of believers. If we receive the Lord's Supper thus, in penitence, faith, and love, we shall eat and drink to our great blessing. If not, it will be to our judgment. So let us seek to fulfill these conditions now, renewing our repentance before God, our faith in the Lord Jesus, and our love for the body.

Renewing Our Repentance[91]

Confession of Sin (repeat in unison)

"Most merciful God, we confess that we have sinned against you in thought, word, and deed, by what we have done and what we have left undone. We have not loved you with our whole heart; we have not loved our neighbor as ourselves. We are truly sorry and we humbly repent. For the sake of your Son Jesus Christ, have mercy on us and forgive us; that we may delight in your will, and walk in your ways, to the glory of your Name. Amen."

Hymn of confession: "Whiter Than Snow"

---

90. Ibid., 115–18.

91. Renewal of repentance could also be expressed in reading Scripture such as Psalm 51, a time of silent reflection, or a prayer of confession.

Renewing Our Faith[92]

Hearing the Gospel Promises

For God so loved the world that he gave his one and only Son, that whoever believes in him shall not perish but have eternal life. (John 3:16)

But God demonstrates his own love for us in this: While we were still sinners, Christ died for us. (Romans 5:8)

If we confess our sins, he is faithful and just and will forgive us our sins and purify us from all unrighteousness. (1 John 1:9)

Hymn of faith: "My Faith Has Found a Resting Place"

Renewing Our Love[93]

Responsive reading: "Love and Discipleship"

Sharing our love through prayer for one another.

Following this time of preparation comes the actual celebration of the Lord's Supper, with a brief explanation of the significance of the ordinance, prayers of thanksgiving, the distribution of the elements, the reading of the words of institution, and the partaking of the elements. This is fairly standard in many churches. Where most churches need help is in the preparation. The specific elements listed above can be easily varied, with the use of different verses of Scripture, other music, time for silent confession, or other media. What seems important is giving people some time and a way to renew their repentance, faith, and love for the body. In my own pastoral experience, I have found people very appreciative of such help in preparation; many have said they had never found the Lord's Supper so moving or meaningful.

---

92. Other ways of renewing our faith could be reading statements on the gospel from the church's confession of faith or reciting a statement such as the Nicene Creed or Apostles' Creed.

93. Renewing our love could be expressed in other ways, from greeting one another, to taking an offering to help those in need in the congregation, to singing a song of fellowship.

Frequency of Celebration

How often should a church observe the Lord's Supper? There is no command in Scripture, though there is at least a hint of weekly observance in Acts 20:7. Quarterly observance dates back to the Reformation and Huldrych Zwingli and seems to be most common among Baptists, though there are exceptions. There are two reasons why most Baptists seem satisfied with quarterly observance. The first is the fear that a too frequent observance would make the ordinance less special or significant and more routine and meaningless. However, it is worth noting that no Baptist pastor I know objects to weekly offerings and sermons. The second objection, while rarely articulated, is the concern that the time devoted to the preaching of the Word would be curtailed and that the preaching of the Word should have primacy. Perhaps a third reason would be that many Baptists do not find the Lord's Supper very meaningful, and four times a year seems more than enough to them.

In the absence of a scriptural command, it seems difficult to insist upon one pattern, though quarterly seems too infrequent to me, for it means that if one happens to be sick or out of town on the Sunday when communion is observed, six months could pass between times of participation. I do agree that weekly observance could involve some difficulties, and so I recommend monthly observance, alternating between morning and evening services, for churches that have services at both times. But this is a matter that can be left to the preference of individual churches.

The Proper Elements

Occasionally there is some discussion concerning how closely churches today should seek to replicate the exact elements of the Lord's Supper. For example, some younger Baptists question why we drink grape juice when the early church drank wine. The answer to that question has to do with Baptist support for the late nineteenth-century temperance movement. Inspired by that movement, Thomas Bramwell Welch developed a process for producing unfermented grape juice, and by the end of the nineteenth century most Baptists in America adopted it.[94] The use of a common cup has also been advo-

---

94. Welch's unfermented communion wine became widely popular later as Welch's grape juice. See G. Thomas Halbrooks, "Communion," in *A Baptist's Theology,* ed. R. Wayne Stacy (Macon, Ga.: Smyth & Helwys, 1999), 184.

cated by some as better symbolizing the unity of the body and fitting the circumstances of the original institution of the ordinance by Jesus.[95] But health concerns have led most Baptists to use the individual cups and trays invented by a rural preacher in Ohio in 1893.[96]

All these questions seem to miss the point. Jesus was simply using the most common food and drink of his day. Grape juice and bread cannot be mandatory, for the church exists in cultures where there are no grapes and wheat is not grown. The symbolism of nourishment should be expressed in the elements, and for that reason I prefer loaves of real bread to the prefabricated pellets that are distasteful in every sense of the word. Real loaves also fit the symbolism of a body being broken much better than tiny pellets or wafers.

But all these are issues to be left to the discretion of individual churches. Using real wine would cause more problems than it would be worth; individual cups are safer than a common cup; and loaves of bread are better symbolically and aesthetically than wafers, but all these are matters of taste and wisdom, not doctrine.

The Proper Atmosphere

I raise this issue because the observance of the Lord's Supper may be one of the next areas where differing conceptions of worship collide. Millard Erickson discusses whether the tone of the Lord's Supper service should be solemn or joyous and sees the answer to that question as shaped by underlying assumptions about the nature of worship. Particularly, he contrasts the traditional idea of worship, which he sees as focusing on the objective fact of what is being observed, to the more contemporary idea of worship, which he sees as more subjective and feeling oriented.[97]

I am not at all sure that Erickson treats contemporary worship fairly, but he does raise an important issue. For many people, the Lord's Supper is one of the most solemn occasions of the church's life. Yet both Erickson and A. H. Strong note that it should be a festive occasion. Strong's words are particularly interesting, since they were written about a century ago, long before contemporary worship was ever imagined: "Gloom and sadness are foreign to the spirit of the Lord's Supper. The wine is the symbol of the death of

---

95. Millard Erickson, "The Lord's Supper," in Basden and Dockery, eds., *The People of God,* 57.

96. Moody, *The Word of Truth,* 472.

97. Erickson, "The Lord's Supper," 59–60.

Christ, but of that death by which we live. It reminds us that he drank the cup of suffering in order that we might drink the wine of joy."[98]

In truth, the atmosphere in which we celebrate the Lord's Supper should be the same as that which marks all genuine Christian worship, one of both awe and praise. It is an awesome, unimaginable thing that Christ the eternal Son should give his body and blood for us, and only our familiarity with it blinds us to its awesomeness. Yet it was for us, and as we receive his blessing anew in the celebration of this ordinance, the only appropriate response is one of joyful praise.

CONCLUSION

For most of Christian history, the Eucharist or Lord's Supper has been the central act of Christian worship. Baptism, especially the baptism of infants, has been a major family occasion. Baptists saw, correctly I think, that both these ordinances had become distorted and proposed major reforms. They denied sacramentally transmitted grace and the necessity of the sacraments for salvation, and placed the preaching of the Word in the center of worship. But in the process we may have overreacted and lost some of the meaning these events are made to have for worship.

Baptism, when candidates are allowed to give testimony to what God has done in saving them, and when that work is powerfully symbolized, should be a time of blessing for the one baptized, as his or her commitment to Christ is celebrated and made into a time of joyful worship. The Lord's Supper, when celebrated by a body of believers who are committed to each other and come to the table to renew their confession, faith, and love for one another, should be another powerful expression of God's awesome grace, calling forth our grateful praise. If we take the time and effort to worship him aright in these ordinances, God will delight in receiving our worship, and respond with great blessing.

—————— STUDY QUESTIONS FOR PART 4 ——————

1. In what ways are the five ministries mentioned in chapter 9 provided in your church? Are some ministries more foundational or important than others? Why or why not?

---

98. Strong, *Systematic Theology*, 960; also Erickson, "The Lord's Supper," 59.

2. Does your church have a process or plan designed to help someone move from visitor to member to mature believer? What would need to be some of the elements of such a plan or process?

3. Are you familiar with contemporary worship? What are some of the objections raised to contemporary worship? To what degree are they valid? What criticisms can be made of traditional worship and to what degree are they valid?

4. Is evangelism the natural result of a healthy Christian life or the result of intentional efforts? What produces a church that ministers effectively to its community?

5. Why do most Baptists call baptism and the Lord's Supper ordinances rather than sacraments? Is the difference more than merely semantic?

6. Is baptism just a symbol of what happens in conversion, or is more involved? What, if anything, does God do in baptism?

7. Give the case for infant baptism as persuasively as possible, and then tell how you would respond to it from a Baptist perspective.

8. How old do you think someone must be to be baptized or participate in the Lord's Supper? Should it be immediately after conversion?

9. What do you think are the most important steps churches could take to improve their practice in the areas of baptism and the Lord's Supper?

———————— BOOKS FOR FURTHER STUDY ————————

Beasley-Murray, G. R. *Baptism in the New Testament*. Grand Rapids: Eerdmans, 1962. This is one of the classic books on baptism from a British Baptist, providing a detailed exegesis of virtually every New Testament text related to baptism.

Bridge, Donald, and David Phypers. *The Water that Divides: The Baptism Debate*. Downers Grove, Ill.: InterVarsity, 1977. An Anglican and Baptist combine in the writing of this book, which presents both perspectives fairly.

Carson, D. A., ed. *Worship by the Book*. Grand Rapids: Zondervan, 2002. This book consists of a wonderful essay by D. A. Carson, and reflections on worship from Anglican, Free Church, and Reformed perspectives. All three include sample orders of service and practical suggestions for worship planning, along with helpful overviews of the large literature on worship, including the contemporary worship wars.

Dagg, J. L. *Manual of Theology; Second Part: A Treatise on Church Order*. Philadelphia: American Baptist Publication Society, 1858; reprint, Harrisonburg, Va.: Gano Books, 1982. This book shows the intense interest and debate over the ordinances in the nineteenth century and gives responses to arguments for infant baptism and open communion still used today.

Jewett, Paul K. *Infant Baptism and the Covenant of Grace*. Grand Rapids: Eerdmans, 1978. Jewett gives a devastating treatment of the most common Presbyterian argument for infant baptism, namely, that as infants in Israel received the covenant sign of circumcision, so the children of Christian parents should receive the covenant sign of baptism. He shows that a proper understanding of covenant theology leads to believer's baptism.

Milne, Bruce. *We Belong Together: The Meaning of Fellowship*. Downers Grove, Ill.: InterVarsity, 1978. One of the few full book-length treatments of fellowship, Milne combines biblical knowledge, theological insight, and pastoral experience.

Ryken, Philip Graham, Derek W. H. Thomas, and J. Ligen Duncan III, eds. *Give Praise to God: A Vision for Reforming Worship*. Phillipsburg, N.J.: P & R Publishers, 2003. This anthology contains a number of essays giving guidance on issues like prayer and readings of Scripture in worship, and defending a more traditional view of worship.

Strong, A. H. *Systematic Theology*. Philadelphia: Judson Press, 1907. For decades, Strong's was the standard systematic theology text for Baptists. His section on the ordinances presents traditional Baptist positions with exceptional depth and detail.

Warren, Rick. *The Purpose Driven Church: Growth Without Compromising Your Mission and Message*. Grand Rapids: Zondervan, 1995. From one of the leading advocates of seeker-sensitive services, Warren's book is already something of a classic. It covers the five ministries of the church under the rubric of purposes, but does so drawing extensively on the methods Warren has used in building Saddleback Community Church into one of the largest and most vital churches in America. A very practical and valuable book.

PART 5

WHERE IS THE CHURCH GOING?

IN ALL DIRECTIONS

New Approaches for a Changing Landscape

IN THIS LAST PART OF THE BOOK, we ask a question looking to the future: Where is the church going? Chapter 11 answers this question from the North American context: "In all directions." The church in North America is taking on a variety of new shapes, forms, and approaches. We look at four of the most important of these new directions that churches are taking, and evaluate what forces are driving churches in these new directions. Chapter 12 broadens the focus to look at the church globally. This book has dealt primarily with issues most relevant to North Americans, especially Baptists in North America, but in today's global village, important trends and developments in the world will impact and be impacted by Baptists and Baptist churches.

THE CHANGING LANDSCAPE

There seems to be a fairly widespread acknowledgment that the cultural landscape in which churches function has changed significantly in the last fifty years. Leith Anderson says, "The last half of the twentieth century has been a transition time in history. We have moved out of a long era of comparative stability and predictability into a parenthesis of instability and unpredictability."[1] Certainly, the first half of the twentieth century faced some of the gravest political crises of history, with World War II the largest military

---

1. Leith Anderson, *Dying for Change* (Minneapolis, Minn: Bethany, 1990), 17.

conflict in our nation's history. Yet those crises occurred within a relative cultural unity, especially in North America. There was a fairly widely shared set of values about how one should live and what things were important. It is the disruption of that set of values that has precipitated the sense of instability characteristic of modern life. It is as if we are playing a game in which the rules are constantly changing.

The direction of that change has been most strongly influenced by the historical process called secularization, in which religion in general, and Christianity in particular, have been afforded an increasingly smaller role in defining societal norms. Large numbers of people are still religious, but religion is seen as a private matter, not as a source of universally valid and binding standards. Religious symbols such as the Ten Commandments are being removed from public life, and even widely shared cultural beliefs such as marriage being the union of one man and one woman are being challenged as based on religious beliefs that discriminate against homosexuals.

The forces of secularization have been strongest among the shapers of culture in America, those involved in the media, entertainment, and academic arenas. But they have not been without opposition. Large numbers of people of faith have made their voices heard in a variety of ways. The resulting conflict has been called the culture wars, or the struggle for America's soul.[2] American society seems polarized, almost half and half, between what may be called the cultural left and the cultural right.[3]

Those on the cultural left are characterized by the values of self-expression and self-fulfillment. They are the ones who most clearly reflect the changes of the last fifty years, with lifestyles representing "a fundamental alteration of the values and norms that shaped American life prior to 1960."[4] While this

---

2. For two accounts of the culture wars, see Robert Wuthnow, *The Struggle for America's Soul: Evangelicals, Liberals & Secularism* (Grand Rapids: Eerdmans, 1989) and James Davison Hunter, *Culture Wars: The Struggle to Define America* (New York: BasicBooks, 1991). For some of the effects of secularization on churches, see Bruce Shelley and Marshall Shelley, *Consumer Church: Can Evangelicals Win the World Without Losing Their Souls?* (Downers Grove, Ill.: InterVarsity Press, 1992), 18–22.

3. In the description of the cultural left and cultural right, I am drawing on the account of Shelley and Shelley, 26–35, who themselves are utilizing the research of Daniel Yankelovich, *New Rules: Searching for Self-Fulfillment in a World Turned Upside Down* (New York: Random House, 1981) and Robert Bellah, et al., *Habits of the Heart* (New York: Harper & Row, 1985). However, while Yankelovich sees a third group, called the cultural middle, I think that group has grown increasingly small since his 1981 work, and has largely blended into the two groups on the right and left.

4. Shelley and Shelley, *Consumer Church*, 28.

lifestyle began among the baby-boom generation, it has endured and been embraced by many in the following generations (variously called Gen-Xers, Busters, or Millennials). The cultural right is composed of those who live by an ethic of self-denial as opposed to an ethic of self-fulfillment. They are committed to traditional values, including hard work, respectability, and, in many cases, faith. These people are the loyal members of most churches and represent more than one-third of the adults in the United States.[5] As one might suspect from their commitment to traditional values, this group includes most of those born before 1945, and many of their children and grandchildren as well.

A second related but separate development on the cultural landscape of North America is represented by the amorphous term postmodernism. However, whereas secularization's effects began to appear in the baby-boom generation and have spread throughout American culture, postmodernism is more limited to the children of the baby-boom generation and has yet to spread as widely, but it too presents a challenge to churches operating in North America. As it has spread, postmodernism has proven increasingly diverse and difficult to define. In fact, Millard Erickson distinguishes between "soft" and "hard" postmodernism.[6] However, most discussions of postmodernity highlight its skepticism toward the power of reason, its doubts about the accessibility or existence of absolute, objective truth, and its belief in the socially constructed nature of reality.[7] D. A. Carson concurs. While acknowledging the diverse nature of postmodernism, he says, "The majority view . . . is that the fundamental issue in the move from modernism to postmodernism is *epistemology*—i.e., how we know things, or think we know things."[8]

Ed Stetzer helpfully notes that *"the shift to postmodernism has not happened everywhere,"* and that many evangelical churches are still effectively engaging many of the people around them.[9] In fact, Leith Anderson asserts, "Traditional churches will be one of the major growing segments of the

---

5. Ibid., 34.

6. Millard Erickson, *Postmodernizing the Faith: Evangelical Responses to the Challenge of Postmodernism* (Grand Rapids: Baker, 1998), 19.

7. The literature on postmodernism is huge and growing so rapidly that it is best tracked by searching the up to date bibliographies available on web sites such as http://www.newchurches.com, which has links to a number of related sites.

8. D. A. Carson, *Becoming Conversant with the Emerging Church: Understanding a Movement and its Implications* (Grand Rapids: Zondervan, 2005), 27. Emphasis in original.

9. Ed Stetzer, *Planting New Churches in a Postmodern Age* (Nashville: Broadman & Holman, 2003), 115. Emphasis in original.

twenty-first century to the surprise of many."[10] However, as the number of people heavily influenced by postmodernism is growing, there is a small but growing band of pioneers who believe that traditional churches, and even seeker oriented churches, will not effectively reach postmodern people, and that there is a need to engage this change in the culture in radically different, but what they see as radically biblical ways.

The church neither can nor should live in isolation from or in indifference to the surrounding culture. Christ sends his people into the world and calls them to be salt and light (Matt. 5:13-14; John 17:18). To do so, they must understand the culture and engage it. Paul even advocates accommodation to the culture on some issues, becoming like a Jew to reach Jews, like a Gentile to reach Gentiles: "I have become all things to all men so that by all possible means I might save some" (1 Cor. 9:22). Yet the church must not be of the world; the salt must not lose its distinctiveness. If it does, it becomes good for nothing. The church thus lives in tension. As the body of Christ, under his rule and authority, the church must be faithful to follow all that he commands. Some aspects of church life, order, and ministry are thus non-negotiable. However, the church is also entrusted with Christ's mission to the world, and that means understanding, seeking to influence, and where possible, to accommodate the cultural ways of the world.

The danger facing many traditional churches is defaulting on their mission. They risk preaching a message that is not intelligible to the culture around them, and preserving practices that unnecessarily alienate nonbelievers. The fact that most churches are making little inroads in their communities suggests that they may need to give more attention to the cultural landscape around them. In the remainder of this chapter, we sketch out some of the more prominent models of change that are seeking to be responsive to the culture. The danger they risk is losing faithfulness to biblical teaching. After we describe these new models, we raise questions as to the dangers they court in being, to some degree, culture driven.

MAJOR NEW DIRECTIONS

As the title of this chapter indicates, in responding to the changes taking place around them, churches in North America are going in all directions. A great number of churches in North America are undergoing radical changes

---

10. Leith Anderson, *A Church for the Twenty-First Century* (Minneapolis, Minn.: Bethany, 1992), 61.

as they take new forms and new approaches and move in new directions. But the new forms, approaches, and directions are anything but monolithic. Formerly, if a church identified itself as Baptist, or Presbyterian, or Methodist, one knew pretty much the stance of that church. Such labels are no longer sufficient, or even that helpful. Is the church traditional, contemporary, seeker driven, postmodern? Is it a megachurch, a house church, a cell church, a metachurch?

Some of these movements are still quite small and do not involve substantive changes in the understanding of what the church is, and a number of the models overlap, but at least four signal major new directions taken by a significant number of churches and call for closer examination.

To the Seekers

Perhaps the most widespread new direction being taken by many churches is toward those called "seekers." The seeker church movement is distinguished, not by any novel theological beliefs, but by innovative methodology, drawing upon the principles of marketing, designing services to attract those who do not attend church (those they call "seekers").[11] The two most well known such churches are Saddleback Community Church in southern California and Willow Creek Community Church in suburban Chicago, but their influence has spread across North America and beyond. Saddleback's pastor, Rick Warren, has popularized Saddleback's approach through two best-selling books, seminars, and electronic resources.[12] Willow Creek has been described by one church consultant as "the most influential church in North America and perhaps the world."[13] It too offers conferences, visited by more than seventy-five thousand in 1999 alone, and has formed the Willow Creek Association, a network of seeker churches that had grown to more than five thousand

---

11. Kimon Howland Sargeant, *Seeker Churches: Promoting Traditional Religion in a Nontraditional Way* (London, U.K. and New Brunswick, N.J.: Rutgers University Press, 2000), 7.

12. The books by Rick Warren are *The Purpose Driven Church* (Grand Rapids: Zondervan, 1995), which has sold more than a million copies in twenty languages, and *The Purpose Driven Life* (Grand Rapids: Zondervan, 2002), which was on the *New York Times* bestseller list for weeks and was used as the material for a forty day study course in thousands of churches. In seminars Warren has taught these same principles to more than 100,000 pastors and church leaders from more than 100 countries. He offers pastors a free weekly email called Rick Warren's Ministry Toolbox (contact toolbox@pastors.com).

13. The comment is attributed to Lyle Schaller as cited in G. A. Pritchard, *Willow Creek Seeker Services: Evaluating a New Way of Doing Church* (Grand Rapids: Baker, 1996), 12.

member churches by 2000, making it larger than 85 percent of the denominations in the United States.[14] While traditional churches may still dominate the American church scene numerically, the energy and momentum certainly seems to be with the seeker church movement. Among newer churches, it could be argued that the seeker church approach is the new norm.

What unifies and identifies the seeker church movement is their desire to attract those outside the church and their willingness to alter traditional Sunday services to do so. The very term "seeker" indicates their orientation; they are designing services for seekers, not members. Such services usually utilize contemporary music, casual dress, and messages that relate to what are believed to be the felt needs of seekers.

Beyond this common orientation to seekers, there is diversity in the seeker church movement. For example, Willow Creek emphasizes their desire to blend in with the surrounding culture. Their facilities, music, language, and use of technology are all designed to minimize any differences between the places and activities of seekers in their everyday life and those of the church.[15] But churches vary in the degree to which they believe they can or should alter their buildings, music, and so on. In fact, it may be possible to place seeker churches on a spectrum based on the completeness of their orientation to seekers, from seeker-friendly to seeker-sensitive to seeker-oriented to seeker-driven.[16] Even traditional churches may be becoming more seeker-aware.

This diversity in the degree of seeker orientation reflects the tension experienced in many seeker churches between services designed to attract seekers and services designed to edify members. Willow Creek, Saddleback and many other churches have concluded that it is best to have two separate services, one for seekers and another for members. Kimon Sargeant's survey of Willow Creek Association pastors indicates that this model of holding separate services is growing in popularity and is likely to become more prevalent in the seeker churches of the future.[17]

This pattern of believer services and seeker services suggests that seeker

---

14. Sargeant, *Seeker Churches*, 10, 22.

15. Ibid., 19.

16. James White observes that churches take one of five positions towards seekers. He calls them seeker hostile, seeker indifferent, seeker hopeful, seeker sensitive or seeker targeted. See James Emery White, *Rethinking the Church: A Challenge to Creative Redesign in an Age of Transition* (Grand Rapids: Baker, 1997), 44.

17. Sargeant, *Seeker Churches*, 25. At the time of his survey, Sargeant found that 37.8 percent of Willow Creek Association churches had separate seeker services.

churches are not so much beginning a new way to do church, as a new way to do evangelism. Rick Warren says, "Evangelistic services are nothing new; only the idea of using the Sunday morning time slot for an evangelistic service is a recent variation."[18] In fact, what is often criticized as seeker worship may be more properly evaluated as seeker evangelism. The problem is that the majority of seeker churches do not have separate services, raising the question of the appropriateness of orienting a service to evangelize seekers when the majority of those present are believers, who have come to worship God.

The size of the seeker church movement makes evaluation of it both difficult and necessary. As a large movement, it is undeniably diverse and so evaluation must be cautious. However, because it is so influential and has sparked such controversy, evaluation is imperative. This is especially so for Baptists, because many Baptist churches have been attracted to the seeker church movement, probably because many Baptist churches see growth and winning people to Christ as the highest priority. Sargeant notes that "Baptist churches are by far the most prevalent in the Willow Creek Association," numbering 31 percent of the Willow Creek Association churches, with two-thirds of these Baptist churches coming from the Southern Baptist Convention.[19]

On the positive side, several items must be noted as strengths the seeker church movement has brought to American Christianity. First, is should be noted that seeker church pastors seem to profess strongly traditional theological views. Sargeant's seeker church pastor survey found large majorities affirming conservative doctrine.

While many critics believe that in practice, seeker churches present a distorted gospel, such a charge is not in keeping with the theology professed by the pastors of such churches. They seek to present historic orthodox doctrine using contemporary media.

Second, it must be acknowledged that many seeker churches are reaching large numbers of people and bringing them to faith in Christ. Almost every

---

18. Warren, *Purpose Driven Church*, 246.
19. Ibid., 26. Sargeant's data is several years old; I suspect the percentage of Baptist churches adopting elements of the seeker church methodology may be even higher today. A survey or more than 700 Southern Baptist churches conducted in 2000 classified 12.8 percent as contemporary in their worship style and another 16.6 percent as blended in their worship, incorporating some aspects of contemporary worship. If the sample is representative of all Southern Baptist churches, it would indicate that more than 5000 Southern Baptist churches are contemporary and nearly 7000 are blended. See Philip Jones, "Research Report: Executive Summary of *Southern Baptist Congregations Today*" (Alpharetta, Ga.: North American Mission Board, SBC, n.d.), 4. The report is available at http://www.namb.net/research.

- 98 percent describe their theology as "evangelical."
- 99 percent say "the Bible is the inspired Word of God, true in all its teachings."
- 99.6 percent affirm "Jesus Christ is both fully God and fully man."
- 81 percent chose the statement "The only hope for heaven is through personal faith in Jesus Christ" as best expressing their view concerning salvation; the remaining 19 percent add the phrase, "except for those who have not had the opportunity to hear of Jesus Christ."
- 88 percent see human nature as perverse and corrupt.[20]

Figure 11.1 Theology of Seeker Church Pastors

account I have read of Bill Hybels or Rick Warren has noted their passion to reach people with the gospel of Christ. Sargeant says that one common conviction of seeker church leaders is that apart from radical change, American churches will become increasingly irrelevant to those outside their walls; those in the seeker church movement have made changes precisely to reach those people.[21] G. A. Pritchard says the church worldwide can learn from the Willow Creek model of developing services directed at seekers and from their model of biblical persuasion.[22] They have helped many churches share the gospel effectively, and member churches of the Willow Creek Association are, in large measure, growing. While 80 percent of American churches are stagnant or declining, 75 percent of Willow Creek Association churches are growing.[23]

Third, at least some seeker churches seem to maintain a healthy balance in their churches. For example, Rick Warren's book advocates that churches should be driven by five biblical purposes, not by the needs of seekers. His church has a careful plan to develop disciples, not just win converts.[24] Bill Hybels tells of learning from painful mistakes in the earlier years of Willow

---

20. Ibid., 20–21.
21. Ibid., 8–9.
22. Pritchard, *Willow Creek Seeker Services*, 204–05.
23. Sargeant, *Seeker Churches*, 23.
24. Almost one-fourth of Warren's *The Purpose Driven Church* is devoted to Part Five, which is entitled "Building Up the Church" (307–398). He specifically says churches must balance the purposes of outreach, worship, fellowship, discipleship, and service: "balancing the five New Testament purposes brings health to the body of Christ, the church" (129).

Creek and says, "We've set up all our leadership structures and goals to grow a full-functioning Acts 2 community, as opposed to just an evangelizing machine that doesn't drive the roots down deep and do all the other things it's supposed to do."[25] Many seeker churches are growing numerically because they are healthy in other ways as well, providing ministries that honor God, edify his people, and produce strong disciples.

But alongside these positive aspects there are causes for concern. One of the most often voiced criticisms has to do with the use of marketing by seeker churches. Sargeant identifies the need for marketing as one of the most common assumptions of seeker churches.[26] One of the most outspoken advocates of marketing the church, and one of the foremost authorities for many seeker church leaders, is George Barna, president of the Barna Research Group, a marketing company located in California. In *Marketing the Church*, Barna argues that there are many instances of marketing in the Bible, that it is just another word for church outreach or promotion, and that is absolutely essential if churches are to grow. In fact, he states: *"My contention, based on careful study of data and the activities of American churches, is that the major problem plaguing the Church is its failure to adopt a marketing orientation in what has become a marketing-driven environment."*[27] Perhaps the major exception to this lack of a marketing orientation is among seeker churches. Barna says, "If I had my way, there would be 100,000 Willow Creek Churches in this country."[28] He offers the following formal definition of marketing: "Marketing is the performance of business activities that direct the flow of goods and services from the producer to the consumer, to satisfy the needs and desires of the consumer *and* the goals and objectives of the producer."[29]

What problems do critics see with marketing the church? One thoughtful and thorough critique is given by G. A. Pritchard in his analysis of Willow Creek's marketing. He acknowledges that having an outward vision for the lost, being good stewards of resources, developing thoughtful strategies and being persuasive in communication are all biblical ideas and can be helpful to some extent. But he also thinks that marketing is anything but a neutral

---

25. Bill Hybels, as quoted in Verla Gillmor, "Community is Their Middle Name," *Christianity Today* 44, no. 11 (November 13, 2000), 50.

26. Sargeant, *Seeker Churches*, 7–8.

27. George Barna, *Marketing the Church* (Colorado Springs: NavPress, 1988), 23. Emphasis in original.

28. Ibid., 7–8.

29. Ibid., 41. Emphasis in original.

tool. Rather, he contends that marketing profoundly shapes and distorts both the communication and content of the gospel.[30] Douglas Webster specifies some of these distorting effects, saying that marketing the church will turn congregations into audiences, proclamation into performance, and worship into entertainment.[31] David Wells adds, "This marketing approach to church life raises questions of a most profound kind," including "Can the Church view people as consumers without inevitably forgetting that they are sinners? Can the Church promote the Gospel as a product and not forget that those who buy it must repent? Can the Church market itself and not forget that it does not belong to itself but to Christ?"[32] D. A. Carson does not deny the need to think through ways to make the gospel intelligible to modern secularists but warns that "The mentality that thinks in terms of marketing Jesus *inevitably* moves toward progressive distortion of him."[33]

There are two basic problems with Barna's definition of marketing. One involves the numerous problems raised when we look upon people as consumers.[34] Such a perception changes how church members see their relationship to one another in the church, and gives nonbelievers a mistaken view of their relationship to God. Even Alan Wolfe, not himself a Christian, observes, "This American propensity to reshape institutions to satisfy personal needs, while perhaps appropriate to consumer goods, seems to many observers to be out of place when matters of ultimate meaning are at issue."[35]

The second major problem with marketing, as defined by Barna, is that when applied to Christianity, the desire to "satisfy the needs and desires of consumers" will clash with a biblical understanding of the "goals and objectives of the producer." To his credit, Barna says that marketing seeks to satisfy both, but fails to recognize that the desire to satisfy the nonbeliever is fraught with danger for the church, for, according to Romans 3:11, these consumers are sinners more than they are seekers of God, and their desires are often hostile to God (Rom. 8:6–8). For marketing, the ultimate goal is growth in

---

30. Pritchard, *Willow Creek Seeker Services*, 242–44.

31. Douglas Webster, *Selling Jesus: What's Wrong With Marketing the Church* (Downers Grove, Ill.: InterVarsity Press, 1992), 16.

32. David Wells, *Losing Our Virtue: Why the Church Must Recover Its Moral Vision* (Grand Rapids and Cambridge, U.K.: Eerdmans, 1998), 202.

33. D. A. Carson, *The Gagging of God* (Grand Rapids: Zondervan, 1996), 508. Emphasis in original.

34. The problems raised by thinking in consumer terms are discussed at length in Shelley and Shelley, *Consumer Church*.

35. Alan Wolfe, *Transformation of American Religion*, 65.

numbers. That is how the success of marketing is measured, but do we really think the health of a church can be adequately judged solely by the response of unbelievers to the gospel? If so, Jesus' earthly ministry was a colossal failure, for he left behind only 120 followers (see Acts 1:15), and his model of speaking in parables seems decidedly un-seeker-friendly, by design (see Mark 3:11-12).

Moreover, the desire to satisfy the needs and desires of consumers places an enormous pressure on the church to make its message more appealing. From his study of the messages preached in the seeker services of Willow Creek Community Church from June 1989 to May 1990, G. A. Pritchard concluded that Willow Creek's use of marketing had led to a distortion of the gospel due to their desire to appeal to the felt needs and desires of the audience. The result is what Pritchard calls "a fulfillment theology." The message at Willow Creek is that Christianity brings personal fulfillment. Pritchard acknowledges that the Willow Creek staff have no desire to alter the gospel, but his analysis showed that "The difficult or unpopular elements of the Christian message get shaved off by a marketing method."[36] For example, Pritchard found that only 4 messages over the course of a year, or 7 percent, emphasized God's holiness, while ten times that amount or 70 percent of the messages emphasized God's love.[37]

Such unintentional distortion is by no means limited to Willow Creek. Jonathan Wilson notes that while Rick Warren's book *The Purpose Driven Life* begins with the words, "It's not about you," in the end, personal fulfillment looms large: "The ecclesiology implied in this book is fully expressed in the earlier book [*The Purpose Driven Church*], where the church is instrumental to the fulfillment of individuals."[38] Concern for the consumer exercises a shaping influence, even when the conscious intention is faithfulness to the biblical message.

Alan Wolfe says that growth-oriented churches tend to downplay the offensiveness of sin to a holy God and rarely mention the prospect of hell for nonbelievers.[39] Claims that churches need to emphasize God's love, because that is what seekers need to hear and believe, seem to be unfounded. Pritchard's

---

36. Pritchard, *Willow Creek Seeker Services*, 251.

37. Ibid., 259.

38. Jonathan R. Wilson, "Practicing Church: Evangelical Ecclesiologies at the End of Modernity," in *The Community of the Word: Toward An Evangelical Ecclesiology*, eds. Mark Husbands and Daniel J. Treier (Downers Grove: InterVarsity, 2005), 68.

39. Wolfe, *Transformation of American Religion*, 166–67.

research reveals that almost all the seekers he interviewed believed God loved them before ever attending Willow Creek. What they did not believe, and did not hear, was that sin arouses the wrath of a holy God.[40] From his study, Alan Wolfe's conclusion is that growth-oriented churches seem to owe much of their growth to their willingness to tell people what they want to hear.[41]

We noted above that seeker church pastors are overwhelmingly orthodox and conservative in their theology. They have no desire to alter the message of the gospel, and many no doubt do preach the Bible faithfully. George Barna himself seeks to honor Christ and recognizes that marketing can be misused. Why then are the dangers discussed above still so real and threatening in the seeker church movement?

This situation is due to a second weakness that is a perennial problem in American evangelicalism, but is especially prominent in the seeker church movement. It is an inadequate analysis of American culture from a biblical worldview. Jonathan Wilson notes that Rick Warren's works lack "any critical examination of culture" and show "a cultural and historical naiveté."[42] Wilson acknowledges the popularity of Warren but suggests that it might be "a reflection of how well his work reflects back to our culture its aspirations and 'values.'"[43] For example, seeker church leaders encourage churches to alter their buildings architecturally so that they feel no more threatening to enter than a shopping mall, without ever pondering if there may not be a good reason for a church building to have a different feel than a mall. They think from the perspective of the American consumer, unchurched Harry, without ever subjecting his perspective to a biblical analysis. In fact, the Bible seems to question the assumption that we should regard the typical unbeliever as a seeker of God. In Romans 3:11, Paul says there are none who seek God, and goes even further in Romans 8:7, saying that the sinful mind is "hostile to God." In 2 Timothy 3:4, he speaks of a time when some even in the church will be "lovers of pleasure rather than lovers of God." That is why trying to satisfy the needs and desires of the unchurched is so perilous. Much of Christianity is counter-cultural, but seeker churches, by their desire to be culturally adaptive, can mute the counter-cultural aspects of the gospel before they even fully recognize them.

---

40. Pritchard, *Willow Creek Seeker Services*, 263–64.
41. Wolfe, *Transformation of American Religion*, 36.
42. Wilson, "Practicing Church," 68.
43. Ibid., 69.

Marketing, without a careful, biblical appraisal of American culture, will lead to the incorporation of American cultural norms and practices in churches that conscientiously practice marketing. For example, we noted above that George Barna's conviction of the need for a marketing orientation among American churches, was borne from "careful study of data and the activities of American churches,"[44] not from a study of Scripture and theology, or even from a study of American culture from a biblical perspective. Indeed, most of the advocates for the seeker church movement have little patience for such analysis. Pritchard says a "serious critique of American culture from a Christian perspective is generally absent at Willow Creek" because "Creekers do not think critically with the categories and content of Christian theology."[45] He notes that there is no theological education requirement for Willow Creek staff members, even for the main teaching pastors. As a result, they lack the resources to analyze from a Christian worldview psychological concepts like codependence and boundaries, even though such concepts form major aspects of many of their messages.[46]

At the root of this aversion to critical thinking seems to be a prior commitment to pragmatism. David Wells concurs with Pritchard's analysis, saying that the seeker church movement's "most prominent advocates rarely show any cultural acuity at all. What they usually have is an eye for what might work. The raw pragmatism that is foundational to their thinking is embraced as if it were part and parcel of the divine revelation; the serious questions that need to be asked about how this process of adaptation might affect the content of faith simply go unanswered,"[47] or even more sadly, the serious questions are never asked, because they are not even seen as serious questions. After all, if people are coming, what could be wrong? Rick Warren says, "we should never criticize any method that God is blessing" without asking if the presence of people alone is evidence of God's blessing.[48] In fact, it matters not just that people come; it is vital to know what they come to and why they come.

I think it is likely that the seeker church movement will become a larger and larger part of American evangelicalism, including Baptists, for the foreseeable

---

44. Barna, *Marketing the Church*, 23.
45. Pritchard, *Willow Creek Seeker Services*, 272.
46. Ibid., 273–74.
47. Wells, *Losing Our Virtue*, 202.
48. Warren, *Purpose Driven Life*, 156.

future. I applaud much of what they do and worship myself in a church with many aspects of seeker methodology. But I am concerned that there is little theological, cultural, or historical awareness among the most visible leaders of the movement. They seem ready to allow the church's methods to be determined by the shifting preferences of nonbelieving consumers, as discovered through market analysis. But how far can the church's methods be changed without affecting the church's message? For example, if the church treats seekers as consumers before they join the church, will the dangers which accompany a consumer mindset disappear when they join the church? Will consumers become members or continue as consumers? Current examples suggest the latter is more likely. Without giving more serious attention to questions such as these, the seeker movement is at the mercy of the currents of contemporary culture, currents which rarely run in godly directions.

To Extremes of Size

We mentioned in an earlier chapter the rise of megachurches as a unique feature of late twentieth century American Christianity, a feature that is continuing in the current century. Along with the rise of larger and larger churches, there is also an emphasis on small groups, sometimes as a constituent part of a larger church, and sometimes existing more independently. Often, these two extremes in size, the megachurch and the microchurch, are found together, in churches that emphasize equally involvement in large group worship services and small group meetings. In fact, some use the term metachurch to refer to "the dynamics of growing larger through small groups—Sunday School and/or home cell groups."[49]

Many of these churches overlap with the subject of the previous discussion, as they incorporate aspects of seeker methodology. Many of the most well known seeker churches are also megachurches. But a significant number of megachurches are traditional in their style of worship and programs, and a few megachurches would call themselves postmodern more than seeker oriented. Our discussion in this section is limited to the questions raised by their common feature, their size.

First, a few words of definition and description are in order. Megachurches

---

49. John N. Vaughan, *Megachurches & America's Cities: How Churches Grow* (Grand Rapids: Baker, 1993), 57. However, Vaughan also notes that some use the term metachurch for churches with 10,000 or more in attendance (53–55).

are usually defined as those having 2000 or more attending their weekly worship services. While there have been a few such large churches in the past,[50] they never became numerous or a widespread feature of church life until relatively recently. But in the 1960s and 1970s, megachurches began to proliferate, first in countries outside the United States and then within the United States. One of the largest and most well known is the Yoido Full Gospel Church in Seoul, Korea, called by John Vaughan "the largest Christian congregation in recorded history," with more than 780,000 members,[51] but there are also megachurches in Brazil, Africa, China, Russia, and Australia.

In the United States, megachurches are an increasingly prominent part of American church life. In 1993, John Vaughan stated, "In the United States, a new congregation breaks the 2,000-worship attendance barrier nearly every two weeks,"[52] but even that figure may underestimate the growth of megachurches. A Web site devoted to studying megachurches lists nearly eight hundred in the United States, but makes no claim to be exhaustive.[53]

What are these megachurches like? Scott Thumma gives two very helpful reports, drawing upon his own research on megachurches, and on a survey of six hundred megachurches conducted by the Faith Communities Today Project.[54] While their most obvious common characteristic is their size, there are other important similarities and differences among megachurches. In

---

50. John N. Vaughan, *The Large Church: A Twentieth-Century Expression of the First-Century Church* (Grand Rapids: Baker, 1985), 39–64, gives a history of large churches. He notes several historical precedents for megachurches. For example, in the fourth and fifth centuries Constantinople had several church buildings with seating for up to 5,000 with one capable of holding 20,000. From the eleventh to the sixteenth century Europe experienced an era of large cathedral building. More recently, C. H. Spurgeon's Metropolitan Tabernacle in Victorian England held more than 5000.

51. Vaughan, *Megachurches*, 18. Vaughan gives the membership as more than 600,000, but his numbers are pre-1993. Since 1993, the church has emphasized planting satellite churches throughout Seoul, in part because of space limitations. Their goal is to plant 5000 satellite churches by 2010. Even with that emphasis, membership at the home church had grown to 780,000 by 2003. See the history of Yoido Full Gospel Church at http://www.nationmaster.com/encyclopedia/Yoido-Full-Gospel-Church, accessed 15 October 2004.

52. Vaughan, *Megachurches*, 41.

53. The Web site is operated by the Hartford Institute for Religion Research, and was updated May 2004. See http://hirr.hartsem.edu/org/faith _megachurches_database_html, accessed 15 October 2004.

54. The two reports by Scott Thumma are entitled "Megachurches Today: Summary of Data From the Faith Communities Today Project" and "Exploring the Megachurch Phenomena: Their Characteristics and Cultural Context." Both are available on the Web site http://www.hirr.hartsem.edu. The latter report is drawn from Thumma's dissertation, "The Kingdom, the Power, and the Glory: Megachurches in Modern American Society" (Ph.D. diss., Emory University, 1996).

addition to being large, most megachurches have not plateaued, but are continuing to grow. Three-fourths of those surveyed had grown by 10 percent or more in the past five years. They are located largely in the Sunbelt states, especially California, Texas, Florida, and Georgia, and predominantly in the suburbs of large cities. Theologically, the most common word these churches use to describe themselves is "evangelical."[55]

However, all megachurches are not alike. Perhaps the largest number are nontraditional like the seeker churches discussed earlier, but a good number are traditional or a blend (what Thumma calls "conventional" and "composite").[56] This diversity is reflected in their worship practices. Of the 600 megachurches surveyed, while all include preaching in their worship, nearly three-fourths use visual projection equipment and electronic keyboards, guitars and drums in their music, 60 percent feature altar calls, and 22 percent use dance or drama quite often. One-fourth identify themselves as Pentecostal or charismatic, and approve of speaking in tongues in worship. Perhaps reflecting the growing influence of seeker methodology, 21 percent report significant change in their worship in the past five years.[57]

The relatively recent nature of megachurches is also reflected in the survey. While more than half of the six hundred megachurches surveyed were founded before 1961, most became megachurches much more recently. Two-thirds had moved to their current locations after 1970, and the majority reported their tremendous growth as having taken place in the past twenty-five years.[58] This suggests that megachurches are "a particular and distinctive response" to contemporary society, with "definitive traits [that] are uniquely modern, fashioned in reaction to and patterned after modern society."[59] This seems especially true of seeker churches, which have sought deliberately to blend in with contemporary society. In fact, one factor in their growth has

---

55. According to the survey data reported in Thumma, "Megachurches Today," (available at http://www.hirr.hartsem.edu/org/faith_megachurches_FACTsummary.html, accessed 15 October 2004), 5, 40 percent of megachurches are found in the South, 32 percent in the West, 21 percent in the Midwest, but only 6 percent in the Northeast. Three-fourths are located in the suburbs of cities of 50,000 or more. 88 percent name the Bible as the one most important source of authority for their church.

56. Scott Thumma, "Exploring the Megachurch Phenomena: Their Characteristics and Cultural Context," available at http://www.hirr.hartsem.edu/bookshelf/thumma_article2.html, accessed 15 October 2004, 2.

57. Thumma, "Megachurches Today," 7.

58. Ibid, 5–6.

59. Thumma, "Exploring the Megachurch Phenomena," 2.

been the way they fit with the culture of the predominantly middle class Baby Boomers that are the major constituency of megachurches. The dangers in such cultural conformity we have discussed above. However, there are other dangers specific to megachurches.

The difficulties of practicing genuine congregational polity in a large church like a megachurch was mentioned in chapter six and should be a concern for Baptists, who are among the leaders in developing megachurches.[60] Still, congregationalism is not impossible for megachurches, and can be preserved, if it is valued, though more authority naturally flows to leaders as churches grow.

Another question associated with megachurches is raised by the common practice of multiple worship services. Of the six hundred megachurches surveyed, 93 percent offer at least two Sunday morning worship services; 48 percent have three or more.[61] John Vaughan sees a direct relationship between a church's ability to grow and its willingness to offer multiple services.[62] But do multiple services undermine or threaten the unity of a church? In fact, if all the members never assemble, is it even valid to call the people involved a church?[63] This question is posed in an even sharper form by some megachurches which have services in two or more locations. Can such disparate groups be one church?

Of course, there can be a spiritual unity in the common affirmation of the gospel, a common devotion to Christ, and a common commitment to the mission of the local church without physically assembling, but the type of unity affirmed by a common gathering is lost in such situations. The New Testament offers only slight support for speaking of large groups of believers as a church, if they do not actually assemble. Of course there are a dozen or so texts that use the word *ekklēsia* for the universal church, which never visibly assembles. But aside from those references, the evidence is sparse. Acts 9:31 refers to the church (singular) throughout Judea, Galilee, and Samaria, which covers a region far too large to allow a common meeting. But usually the New Testament speaks of *churches* (plural) in larger geographical regions

---

60. Vaughan, *Megachurches*, 53–55.

61. Thumma, "Megachurches Today."

62. Vaughan, *Megachurches*, 82.

63. Mark Dever and Paul Alexander, *The Deliberate Church: Building Biblically in a Haphazard Age* (forthcoming), 43–44. While recognizing the weighty pragmatic reasons for multiple services, Dever and Alexander oppose them, based on the importance of the church's assembling. However, they do not think it is an issue over which a pastor should split a church.

such as Galatia (1 Cor. 16:1), Asia (1 Cor. 16:19), or Macedonia (2 Cor. 8:1), and speaks of *church* (in the singular) when referring to a city like Jerusalem (Acts 5:11), Antioch (Acts 13:1), Caeserea (Acts 18:22), Ephesus (Acts 20:17), Cenchrea (Rom. 16:1), or Corinth (1 Cor. 1:2).

Part of the reason for this differentiation in usage may be the reservation of the term church for a group that actually assembles, though the church in Jerusalem, being composed of more than 5000 believers (see Acts 4:4), may not have been able to meet together regularly. On the whole, however, it seems that one of the ideas implicit in the word *ekklēsia*, and in the predominant usage of the term, is the idea of actually assembling.[64] Certainly the church need not have all its meetings together; the early church met house to house as well as in the temple (Acts 2:46). But if the whole church never assembles, I think it can undermine its unity and create potential problems. For example, suppose the early service attenders vote one way on a congregational decision, but the later service attenders vote contrarily. Does the larger congregation trump the smaller or do the services have any degree of autonomy? Something important is lost if the whole church never assembles, and some megachurches may do well to rent out a larger facility for occasional gatherings of the whole church.

Those megachurches who meet in multiple locations face this same problem in an even greater degree. Members of churches with multiple services at one location at least still have the potential of contact with one another in passing or in other church functions, but different locations seem to involve genuinely different churches. The only common factor is often the pastor. But in the New Testament each church had its own elder or elders (Acts 14:23). A pastor overseeing more than one church seems more like a bishop. There is some historical precedent in Methodist circuit riders who would oversee several small congregations. But that seems different than present situations where a pastor's only contact with some of his congregations is preaching to them. A New Testament elder does more than preach to his flock; he shepherds them. Even if he has fellow elders to help shepherd the flock, he faces the responsibility of giving an account to God for those under his leadership. But how can anyone account for a scattered flock of several thousand in a variety of locations? Multiple services and especially multiple locations raise ecclesiological questions not often considered, when the pragmatic advan-

---

64. See the earlier discussion in chapter three for the idea of assembling as important to the essence of the church.

tages seem so clear. But, at our best, Baptists, and other evangelicals, have sought to base their practice on sound biblical theology, not simple pragmatism. These questions deserve more thorough and thoughtful consideration than megachurch advocates have thus far given them.

Another problem inherent in a megachurch is the difficulty in functioning as a genuinely New Testament church. We argued earlier that one mark of a church is the possession of a full range of ministries, including intimate fellowship with other believers in living a life of service and ministry to one another. Can megachurches provide this and other ministries that seem more suited to smaller groups? Many have looked again at the New Testament picture of the church and concluded, for a variety of reasons, that intimate fellowship, effective nurturing, personal discipling, and genuine community can only happen in smaller groups of believers. Thus, the megachurch movement has arisen side by side with and may have provoked what we may call a microchurch movement.[65] I see this movement toward small groups as taking three forms: church based small groups (Sunday School classes, home groups), cell churches, and house churches.

The most common type of small group in most churches, including megachurches, is a Sunday School class. Almost all (95 percent) of the megachurches surveyed had Sunday School classes for adults and children; 94 percent utilize other types of small groups, with 50 percent saying such small groups are "central to their strategy for Christian nurture and formation."[66] John Vaughan notes, "Large churches tend to function paradoxically and simultaneously as minidenominations and macrocosms of small groups."[67] Willow Creek church leaders describe their church "not just as a church *with* small groups but a church *of* small groups."[68] But in general, in these types of small groups, there is a clear subordination of the small group to the church; the large group is the church and is the focal point. The other two forms of the microchurch movement place much more focus on the importance and independence of the small group.

Ralph Neighbour Jr. has been one of the most vocal advocates for the second form of small group, the model of church life called the cell church.

---

65. Microchurch is Leonard Sweet's term for house churches and similar small groups. Leonard Sweet, *Faithquakes* (Nashville: Abingdon Press, 1994), 76.

66. Thumma, "Megachurches Today."

67. Vaughan, *The Large Church*, 13.

68. Verla Gillmor, "Community Is Their Middle Name," *Christianity Today* 44, no. 13 (Nov. 13, 2000), 50. Emphasis in original.

He argues, "*Cell churches are the only way that true community can be experienced by all Christians. . . .* The cell group is not just a *portion* of church life . . . . *It is church life; and when it properly exists, all other competing structures are neither needed nor valid.*"[69] In this model, Christians meet in groups no larger than fifteen, multiplying as they grow, for the purposes of edification, community, and serving and supporting one another. The cell is the center and focal point of the individual believer's Christian life, but a single cell is not meant to live in isolation. Cells join together with other cells to form a congregation, which meets for equipping and evangelism events, and in some cases for worship. Alongside the cell and congregation there are, in this model, mass meetings, which Neighbour calls "celebration," for praise, worship, teaching, preaching, evangelism, and public worship. But of these three levels (cell, congregation, and celebration), the cell is the most important. It is the focal point of the church, and the place that "meets all the basic needs of the believer."[70]

The third form of the microchurch movement is the formation of house churches. These differ from cell group churches in a number of ways. Organizationally, they see less necessity of grouping in the levels of congregation or celebration. In many cases, house churches may grow out of more traditional churches, may cluster or associate with other house churches, or may form a house-church based congregation, but they see no one form as biblically required.[71] House churches can exist alone. Functionally, house churches seem to be more intentionally holistic and fully ecclesial. By that, I mean that whereas Neighbour's cell group model envisions cells rapidly multiplying and membership changing every few months, the house church values its members staying together and deepening relationships. In this, the cell model may reflect Neighbour's passion for evangelism and the spread of the gospel to all the world. While he speaks in a very complimentary fashion of Robert and Julia Banks and their work in the house church movement, he also says

---

69. Ralph Neighbour, Jr., *Where Do We Go From Here? A Guidebook for the Cell Group Church* (Houston, Tex.: Touch Publications, 1990), 112–113. Emphasis in original.

70. Ibid., 198. Neighbour gives a surprisingly specific outline of this model, saying that five cell groups should be guided by a "zone servant," that 25 cells should form a regional congregation, and that all the cells in a city should form the celebration (194–196). This model resembles that of the Yoido Full Gospel Church in Seoul, South Korea, but I do not know of any significant North American examples.

71. Robert & Julia Banks, *The Church Comes Home* (Peabody, Mass.: Hendrickson, 1998), 106. The Banks specifically cite their differences with Ralph Neighbour's model, and give several possible alternative models (127–156).

that many, but not all house churches, "simply do not possess a vision for aggressively reaching the unevangelized, either in their own communities or abroad."[72] Theologically, the house church differs from the cell group in that the house church "seeks to embody all aspects of a New Testament church"[73] while the cell church, though able to function alone, sees an assembly of cells (congregation) as at the very least desirable and assigns certain functions of the church (worship, teaching, equipping) to the larger levels (congregation and celebration).

The microchurch movement, especially in the cell church and house church forms, raises some questions for megachurches. Ralph Neighbour argues, "A cell group is the true Body of Christ, not five thousand sitting in rows observing one man's charismatic activity." Therefore, he continues, megachurches need to ask, "How small must we become to become the authentic church of the New Testament?"[74] Robert and Julia Banks plead, "For the sake of the vitality of the church as a whole, for the sake of those who are feeling marginal in it, and with a view to those most open to the gospel, we need to rediscover that *small is beautiful* and then restructure our congregational life accordingly."[75]

In terms of evaluation, Banks in particular does a good job in pointing out that much of Paul's description of the church assumes a small-group, family-like aspect of the church,[76] but the New Testament allows and reflects both large and small group meetings. From the very beginning of the church, Acts 2 says the early church met both in the temple and in their homes (v. 46). Acts 15:22 seems to assume that the church in Jerusalem, though composed of thousands, met together in some sense and yet Acts 12:12–17 describes a house meeting of a portion of that church. We have already noted how Paul consistently referred to all the believers in a city as a single church, and yet could also speak of a house-sized gathering as a church. The New Testament seems to allow for both megachurches and microchurches. Of the two, however, I think the microchurch is more able to function healthily alone

---

72. Neighbour, *Where Do We Go?* 203.

73. C. Kirk Hadaway, Francis M. DuBose and Stuart A. Wright, *Home Cell Groups and House Churches* (Nashville: Broadman Press, 1987), 13.

74. Ralph Neighbour, "About Megachurches," available at http://www.cellchurchinfo/Articles/Ralph%20Neighbour/Megachurches/htm, accessed 15 October 2004.

75. Banks, 98. Emphasis in original.

76. Ibid., 30–41. They note Paul's use of family language for the church, the integration of worship and fellowship, the assumption of widespread participation, and the spread of the gospel in homes as arguing for home based churches.

than the megachurch. By this I mean that in contexts such as persecution, house churches may be the only safe way for Christians to assemble. In such cases, I think house churches can provide worship, teaching, fellowship, and all that Christians would need to grow. Indeed, many mission leaders see house churches as the best way to start churches in mission contexts.[77] On the other hand, I do not think a Christian whose only participation was in a megachurch worship service could experience fellowship and fullness of life in Christ; she or he needs a small group. Happily, as we noted above, most megachurches seem to recognize this and are providing small groups. Megachurches and microchurches belong together.

This is especially so in terms of shepherding. Another difficulty megachurches face is providing adequate oversight for thousands of members. Paul Yonggi Cho, pastor of the huge Yoido Full Gospel Church, has said that he could not pastor more than 500 people by himself. The only way his megachurch can function is with thousands of cell leaders, who shepherd their small groups.[78] As churches grow larger, there are more and more possibilities of individuals falling between the cracks or simply never getting noticed. Megachurch elders should place high priority on getting their members into small groups, and developing those who can help them shepherd those small groups, for their calling includes the awesome charge to "watch over" their flock "as men who must give an account" (Heb. 13:17).

Megachurches seem likely to continue to play an increasingly important role in American church life for the foreseeable future. Many are vital and growing, and their size alone gives them visibility and allows them to be "the trendsetters of the contemporary Christian world."[79] In many cases, their fit with contemporary culture adds to their attractiveness, but, as we mentioned in the case of seeker churches, a cultural fit carries with it the danger of cultural conformity, calling for a more thoughtful analysis and critique of culture than has been common. Megachurches that meet in different locations and megachurches that have multiple services raise ecclesiological questions and potential dangers that need more careful consideration than megachurch leaders have given them. Yet, at the same time, I see nothing in the New Testament that calls megachurches per se into question, as long as they couple their large group meetings with smaller

---

77. Hadaway, DuBose, and Wright, *Home Cell Groups*, 26.

78. Paul Yonggi Cho with Harold Hostetler, *Successful Home Cell Groups* (Plainfield, N.J.: Logos International, 1981), 65–66, cited in Vaughan, *The Large Church*, 24.

79. Thumma, "Megachurches Today," 2.

groups where individual believers can experience intimate fellowship, personal instruction and pastoral oversight.

To the Postmodern Generation

In the opening pages of this chapter we noted that the mindset or worldview called postmodernism is part of the changing landscape in which North American churches minister. Postmodernism has been the subject of an immense literature discussing its origin, features, characteristics, and challenges, and has called forth widely divergent responses from evangelical scholars and churches.[80]

Some suspect that all the debate over postmodernism may be much ado about nothing. Andy Crouch observes, "The 'emerging church' movement has generated a lot of excitement but only a handful of congregations. Is it the wave of the future or a passing fancy?"[81] Michael Horton seems unsure if postmodernism is even that radical of a change from what preceded it. He says, "Call me dismissive, but I cannot get beyond the notion that postmodernism in the popular sense is little more than the triumph of popular culture, with its obsessions with technology, mass communications, mass marketing, the therapeutic orientations, and consumption."[82]

For many churches in many areas, postmodernism is not yet a pressing concern, for as Ed Stetzer notes, "*the shift to postmodernism has not happened everywhere.* . . . There are still large pockets in North America where people live out their lives in much the same manner as their parents before them," but Stetzer also believes that the shift is coming and is already affecting the next generation.[83]

Others think we must oppose postmodernism as necessarily destructive of truth, absolutes, orthodox theology, and healthy spirituality. In a series of books, David Wells has keenly examined the influence of contemporary culture on Christianity and the church and offers advice summarized by Millard

---

80. See, for example, Erickson, *Postmodernizing the Faith*, in which he presents six varying responses to postmodernism by evangelicals.

81. Andy Crouch, "The Emergent Mystique," *Christianity Today* 48, no. 11 (November 2004): 37.

82. Michael Horton, "Better Homes and Gardens," in *The Church in Emerging Culture: Five Perspectives*, ed. Leonard Sweet (El Cajon, CA: emergentYS, 2003), 108. Horton believes that much of what is called postmodern should be seen as ultramodern or hypermodern.

83. Ed Stetzer, *Planting New Churches in a Postmodern Age* (Nashville: Broadman & Holman, 2003), 115. Emphasis in original.

Erickson as, "Just Say 'No.'"[84] Erickson himself distinguishes between hard postmodernism, which he sees as a threat to Christianity, and soft postmodernism, which he says may actually be an encouraging development from the standpoint of Christian faith.[85]

But the perspective we want to examine in this section is that represented by what is called "the emerging church." They believe that postmodernism is a real and powerful influence in contemporary culture, and that it is imperative for churches to "learn the vernacular" of the postmodern world, so that they can "speak the gospel within the culture, and minister to postmodern people."[86] Otherwise, they believe the message of the church will be unintelligible to a growing number of North Americans.

It is important to note that those in this movement believe that ministry to postmoderns requires a more radical change in mindset than that required by changing to contemporary or seeker sensitive worship. One representative narrates his journey from seeker-sensitive to what he calls post-seeker-sensitive as originating when he began to realize that non-Christian youth and young adults were not responding to contemporary, seeker services as they had just a few years earlier. As he experimented and talked with youth and young adults, he found that "many of the things we had brought into our church to make the services contemporary and relevant were the very things young adults didn't like."[87] D. A. Carson includes protest against seeker-sensitive churches as part of the overall protest that he sees as characteristic of those in the emerging church. They are "against what is perceived to be a personally stifling cultural conservatism, against modernism and its incarnation in modern churchmanship, and against modernism's incarnation in seeker-sensitive churches."[88]

---

84. Erickson, *Postmodernizing the Faith*, 23. The three books by David Wells are *No Place for Truth; or, Whatever Happened to Evangelical Theology?* (Grand Rapids: Eerdmans, 1993), *God in the Wasteland: The Reality of Truth in a World of Fading Dreams* (Grand Rapids: Eerdmans, 1994), and *Losing Our Virtue: Why the Church Must Recover Its Moral Vision* (Grand Rapids: Eerdmans, 1998). Curiously, however, in these books he uses the term modernity to refer to characteristics of contemporary culture that are usually seen as postmodern.

85. Erickson, *Postmodernizing the Faith*, 20.

86. The literature of the emerging church, with a few exceptions, is largely found on web sites. The quote above is from http://www.emergingchurch.org/churches~ns4.html, accessed 14 October 2004. Other important Web sites for this movement are www.emergentvillage.com, www.newchurches.com and www.theooze.com.

87. Dan Kimball, *The Emerging Church: Vintage Christianity for New Generations* (Grand Rapids: Zondervan, 2003), 36.

88. Carson, *Becoming Conversant*, 41.

Whereas seeker oriented churches have drawn their members predominantly from the baby boom generation, the emerging church is targeting those younger and those who may be older but have been so influenced by postmodernism that even seeker churches seem foreign to them. Supporting their efforts are the findings of George Barna that young adults ages eighteen to thirty-two are those least likely to describe themselves as committed Christians and that church attendance is declining by generation, with church attendance of teenagers living independent of their parents lower than at any time in the past twenty years.[89]

What is this thing called postmodernism that calls for such radical change? Definitions abound, but with little unanimity. Most theologians have highlighted the changing view of truth and knowledge as defining motifs of postmodern thought. Millard Erickson's delineation of seven postmodern tenets includes items such as a denial of the objectivity, certainty, and goodness of knowledge, rejection of progress and meta-narratives, and a view of truth as community defined.[90] Stanley Grenz likewise describes postmodern thought as characterized by the rejection of trust in reason, rejection of the goodness of knowledge, and rejection of human ability to solve all our problems.[91] One church planter working with postmoderns sees them as having adopted "a new epistemology."[92]

How do those in the emerging church movement see postmodernity? The definition given by the emerging church Web site lists four key characteristics of postmodernity: (1) the rejection of enlightenment assumptions such as the power of science and the inevitability of progress, (2) the rise of globalization and pluralism, (3) a reduced role for experts and gatekeepers, reflecting a new perspective on authority and knowledge, and (4) truth is seen as customized and subjective, as opposed to universal and objective.[93]

---

89. Kimball, *Emerging Church*, 48, citing findings by George Barna, "How Americans See Themselves," *Barna Research Online* (28 May 1998), "Adults Who Attended Church As Children Show Lifelong Effects," *Barna Research Online* (5 November 2001) and "The Year's Most Intriguing Findings, from Barna Research Studies," *Barna Research Online* (17 December 2001), all available at www.barna.org.

90. Erickson, *Postmodernizing the Faith*, 18–19. A helpful paraphrase of the meaning of phrases like denial of personal objectivity and uncertainty of knowledge is given in Stetzer, 118.

91. Stanley Grenz, "The Community of God: A Vision of the Church in the Postmodern Age," *Crux* 28 (June 1992): 19.

92. Stetzer, *Planting New Churches*, 115.

93. "What Is Postmodernism?" available at http://www.emergingchurch.org/postmodern~ns4.html, accessed 14 October 2004. I have paraphrased some of their more obscure expressions. For example, they phrase the third characteristic as "the 'gnutellafication' of authority and knowledge," referring to the digital music platform called "gnutella" which cuts out middlemen and central servers.

A more thorough and helpful presentation is that given by Dan Kimball, who contrasts the "nutrients" in the soil of the modern era with those of the post-Christian, postmodern era.[94]

Modern Era	Post-Christian Era
Monotheism	Pluralism
Rational	Experiential
Religion	Mystical
Propositional	Narrative
Systematic	Fluid
Local	Global
Individualistic	Communal/Tribal
Truth	Preference

Figure 11.2 Key Characteristics of Modern and Postmodern Eras

Brian McLaren, perhaps the leading spokesman for this movement, associates postmodernism with a host of other "posts" he believes we must leave behind. He writes, "In the postmodern world, we become postconquest, postmechanistic, postanalytical, postsecular, postobjective, postcritical, postorganizational, postindividualistic, post-Protestant, and postconsumerist."[95] Such an approach produces *A New Kind of Christian,* which is the title of one of McLaren's influential books. In fact, those in the emerging church believe the postmodern world requires new approaches to church, worship, leadership, evangelism, and spiritual formation. For the most part, they do not recommend any one worship style, but offer a variety of examples to allow others to get a feel for the ethos underlying the variety of approaches taken by those in this movement.

D. A. Carson describes that ethos, which he says is true of "almost every-

---

94. Kimball, *Emerging Churches,* 61.

95. Brian D. McLaren, *A New Kind of Christian: A Tale of Two Friends on a Spiritual Journey* (San Francisco: Jossey-Bass, 2001), 19.

one within the movement," in these words: "an emphasis on feelings and affections over against linear thought and rationality; on experience over against truth; on inclusion over against exclusion; on participation over against individualism and the heroic loner."[96] How is that ethos expressed in worship and church life?

Dan Kimball lists twelve differences between the approach to worship in modern, seeker-sensitive churches and emerging, postmodern churches. Postmodern worship is experiential, spiritual-mystical, uses the arts, is multisensory, with space utilizing crosses, symbols, and darkness to communicate reverence and organized to promote community.[97] Leonard Sweet shortens the key characteristics of postmodern worship to four: experiential, participatory, image-driven, and connected (the last referring to motifs such as community, globalization, the desire to connect with what is ancient, and the role of technology in postmodern life).[98]

What type of church is produced by this new approach to worship and church life as a whole? From his research and observations, Ed Stetzer gives "the ten most frequent traits of successful postmodern churches" as they are expressed "in their key values."[99] Those values are as follows: (1) they are unashamedly spiritual (as opposed to primarily rational); (2) they promote incarnational ministry, and (3) engage in service; (4) they value experiential praise and (5) preach narrative expository messages (showing their distrust of reason and logic); (6) they appreciate participating in ancient patterns and practices (because they don't see our age as having all truth); (7) they make use of the arts and multiple senses in worship (their world is image driven); (8) technology is an assumed aspect of church life (reflected in the fact that most information on emerging churches circulates via websites rather than books); (9) they highly value being part of a living community (as opposed to modern individualism); and (10) their leaders work as a team with

---

96. Carson, *Becoming Conversant*, 29.

97. Kimball, *Emerging Churches,* 185. For those who want specific examples, Kimball gives a detailed layout of the postmodern worship at his church, both the elements of worship and the physical organization of the room (248–49).

98. Leonard Sweet, *Postmodern Pilgrims: First Century Passion for the Twenty-first Century World* (Nashville: Broadman & Holman, 2000). Sweet uses the acronym EPIC for postmodern worship.

99. Stetzer, *Planting New Churches,* 137. Stetzer doesn't define what he sees as a "successful" postmodern church. Presumably, it is a church that is effective in actually reaching postmodern individuals. Interestingly, I'm not sure that all postmoderns would endorse such a view of what makes a church successful, but I do think Stetzer's list includes items that seem consonant with the ideas of all the postmodern advocates I have read.

a concern for transparency or authenticity. Stetzer acknowledges that not all of these are unique to postmodern churches, but he does think that as a whole they are not characteristic of modern churches.

It is difficult for anyone to evaluate such a diverse and still developing movement as the emerging church, more so for one who is a member of the baby boom generation and has not personally experienced a postmodern church. Nevertheless, I will venture some observations based on the resources I have researched, and put them in the form of answers to three questions.

Is all the talk about this shift to a postmodern world overblown hype, and much ado about nothing? While I agree with Michael Horton and Andy Crouch that part of what is called postmodernity is really ultramodernity or just the world being the world, there does seem good evidence that there is a shift taking place in our culture, and that it does involve a significant change in the way many (not nearly all) people approach the world. At the very least, I think it is obvious that we have entered a post-Christian era in North America. In such a situation, it is important to learn to speak in a way that others can understand. This will mean that churches will need to take care to explain their vocabulary and justify their assumptions.

However, it is equally important to recognize that there are still many people, young and old, who do not see the world through postmodern lenses, and that there are a disproportionate number of these people in evangelical churches. In their zeal to reach the postmodern generation, some in the emerging church have tended to view more traditional churches and their modernist mindset with an unbecoming measure of disdain. Postmodernism is viewed, not just as the cultural context in which they have to work, not just as something of a necessary evil, but as a positive good. Postmodernism is a preferable cultural context, one that leads people into a more authentic Christian life. The idea that comes through in much emerging church literature is that modernism is bad and postmodernism is good. Correspondingly, traditional churches that minister in the context of modernism to people with a modern mindset are rarely seen in a positive light. Carson notes, "It is difficult to find a paragraph in any of the emergent writings that says anything positive and grateful about modernism or about the Christian churches that went around the world under modernism."[100] Certainly there are features in postmodernism that Christians may applaud, such as the challenge to the omnicompetence of reason and American individualism, but there are also

---

100. Carson, *Becoming Conversant*, 65.

serious weaknesses in postmodern thought that have not been carefully critiqued by those in the emerging church movement. Likewise, there are features in traditional churches that merit critique, but there are also many
traditional churches that are ministering faithfully and making authentic disciples of Christ even though they approach life with a primarily modern
mindset. In fact, such churches can be a friend and aid to emerging churches
in helping them recognize elements of postmodern culture that are inescap-
ably anti-Christian. Too often, many in the emerging church movement seem
to be recovering from painful childhood experiences in traditional churches
that leave them unable to view such churches as valued partners.

To return to the question, "Is all the talk about postmodernism overblown
hype?" The answer is "probably not." Postmodernism is certainly stronger in
some areas than others, but some of its effects are likely to be enduring, and
churches will need to respond to those changes, while those in the emerging
church movement need to recognize, respect, and learn from faithful churches
who minister in more traditional ways to the significant number of those less
affected by postmodernism.

This leads to the second evaluative question that may be asked of the
emerging church movement. What of the changes proposed by those in the
emerging church? In many cases, their proposals are laudable and should be
applied, but not just in churches seeking to reach postmoderns. Many of their
proposals seem to be New Testament correctives to modern distortions. Their
critique of the modern consumer church is accurate, and mirrors some of
my own concerns for seeker churches and megachurches. Moreover, as I
looked at Stetzer's list of the ten traits and values of successful postmodern
churches, I could not help but note that almost all would be true of any successful church, and most have solid New Testament backing. I'm very glad,
for example, that Dan Kimball insists that worship services are times for believers to worship God and be instructed and encouraged.[101] Nonbelievers
can come and be evangelized simply by observing genuine Christian worship. There is no need for the service to be adjusted to the consumer preferences of seekers, especially nonbelieving seekers. And as Kimball notes, the
evangelistic power of God-centered worship is reflected in Paul's teaching
that corporate worship in Corinth would cause nonbelievers to recognize
God's presence and fall down in conviction (1 Cor. 14:23–25).

A biblical case can be made for the importance of community, for the use

---

101. Kimball, *Emerging Church*, 115–16.

of the arts in the life of the church, for multi-sensory worship, and living a life of corporate mission. Other aspects, such as the appreciation for ancient patterns and sacred space and the use of technology, are more matters of preference than doctrine, but many of the proposed changes in these areas seem positive.

Other changes they call for do not seem to be new at all. For instance, when Brian McLaren says the gospel is primarily relational and missional more than informational, that the church is a community more than a place, that the church should welcome sinners rather than keep its members safely secluded, is he saying anything that evangelicals have not been saying for years? Duane Liftin says evangelicals have been discussing these issues and trying to "get the salt out of the saltshaker" for nearly half a century, and that "the emergent emphasis on 'salvation within history from sin by grace' need not be set against 'salvation beyond history from hell by grace.'"[102]

Still, there is much to be learned from the emerging church response to postmodernism. D. A. Carson sees five major strengths in this movement that all churches should seek to emulate. Those in this movement are skilled at understanding the culture in which they live (which is a skill every missionary should develop), they emphasize authenticity in their churches and in their lives, they recognize the influence of social location on interpretation of Scripture (and thus they value diverse viewpoints), they have been interested and at least somewhat effective in reaching those usually overlooked by or uninterested in the church, and at least some have shown an interest in connecting with elements drawn from the larger history of the church.[103]

But postmodern culture also holds dangers for churches and the Christian faith as a whole. Some elements of the culture may serve as a bridge for the gospel, some may be transformed and become serviceable to the cause of Christ, but some elements must be opposed. The emerging church has been so concerned to respond to postmodernism that it has yet to produce a serious critique of postmodern culture. Lacking that critique, some of their responses and proposed changes seem to weaken the gospel in serious ways. For example, one of the ideas commonly associated with postmodern thought is a questioning of the idea of truth. According to the emerging church Web site, truth in postmodernism is seen as personal, plural, and relative, rather

---

102. See the discussion of the views of Brian McLaren and Duane Liftin in "Emergent Evangelism," *Christianity Today* 48, no. 11 (November 2004): 42–43.

103. Carson, *Becoming Conversant*, 45–55.

than universal, absolute, and objective.[104] But if truth is not seen as absolute and universal, what of the claim of the gospel that Jesus is the only way, truth, and life that leads to God? In reviewing Brian McLaren's *A Generous Orthodoxy*, D. A. Carson notes that McLaren tries to avoid both absolutism and relativism, but in doing so finds it hard to say why someone should be a follower of Jesus rather than follow any other religion. He observes, "Here McLaren does not say that one [who follows Jesus] is closer to the truth, or anything of that sort."[105] In seeming deference to postmodern sensibilities, McLaren and many (not all) in the emerging church movement simply avoid the tough questions regarding the truth claims of Christianity.

Accommodation to postmodern culture also seems to have affected how some see sin, wrath, and God's character, all of which affect how one sees the cross. The substitutionary theory of the atonement is dismissed by both Brian McLaren and Steve Chalke as "a form of cosmic child abuse," and replaced by a view of sin, repentance, and atonement that leads Carson to say, "If words mean anything, both McLaren and Chalke have largely abandoned the gospel."[106]

Fortunately, many in the emerging church have not moved as far as McLaren and Chalke, but they are among the movement's most influential leaders. But the movement's very premise is also a weakness, for unlike the 16th century Reformation, this movement did not begin with a call to change to be faithful to Scripture, but a call to change to be responsive to the culture.

Restructuring worship simply to appeal to postmoderns strikes me as opening emerging churches to the same error they criticize in seeker-churches, that of fostering consumerism, the idea that the church must adjust to the preferences of the consumer. We need a renewed recognition, among all churches, that worship is not first of all for believers or seekers, but for God. We need continued discussion as to the merits of the regulative principle (the idea that worship should include only elements clearly taught or implied by Scripture) versus the normative principle (the idea that whatever is not prohibited is allowable in worship) and how both apply to how we worship God today.[107]

Finally, what should churches do in response to the rising tide of

---

104. "What Is Postmodernism?" available at http://www.emergingchurch.org/postmodern~ns4.html, accessed 14 October 2004.

105. Carson, *Becoming Conversant*, 134. The book to which he refers is Brian D. McLaren, *A Generous Orthodoxy* (El Cajon, Calif.: emergentYS/ Grand Rapids: Zondervan, 2004).

106. Ibid., 186.

107. For more on this issue, see the discussion in chapter nine.

postmodernism? Is responding "something that churches of *all denomina-tions are called* to do"?[108] Perhaps in some sense, but certainly not all churches are called to respond to postmodernism in the same way. All can be aware of the changes in our culture, and be careful to explain their terms and assumptions, and to take pains that the gospel is communicated fully and clearly to our post-Christian culture. Churches should also be aware of the threat that some aspects of postmodern thought are to biblical theology. But not all churches are yet surrounded by lost postmoderns. Even those that are should take care that their worship and church life are governed primarily by biblical principles and only secondarily by the desire to be responsive to postmodern preferences.

Moreover, I am not convinced that all the changes proposed by even some of the more conservative in the emerging church are necessary to win postmoderns. In a recent visit to Washington D.C., I was struck by the fact that the church I was visiting, decidedly not a part of the emerging church, was composed overwhelmingly of those under 30, and located in a city that would be about as deeply influenced by postmodern thought as any in America. It embodied some of the traits Stetzer lists for successful postmodern churches (it is very spiritual, strong on incarnational ministry, service, community, technology, and team ministry), but its worship was not in keeping with most postmodern approaches. This church is not alone in winning postmodern young people without adopting radical changes.

Andy Crouch notes that Manhattan's Redeemer Presbyterian Church is winning thousands of postmodern young people with Reformed preaching and worship, and churches following its example are thriving on both coasts. He cites Colleen Carroll Campbell's study of "the new faithful," young, postmodern Americans who are embracing traditional orthodoxy without postmodern modifications.[109] This suggests that there is something more than a new style of worship or alterations in our vocabulary or other changes involved in winning postmoderns to Christ. What is crucial is the gospel, ex-

---

108. "Churches," available at http://www.emergingchurch.org/churches~ns4.html, accessed 14 October 2004. Emphasis in original.

109. Crouch, "The Emergent Mystique," 41. The reference is to Colleen Carroll, *The New Faithful: Why Young People Are Embracing Christian Orthodoxy* (Chicago: Loyola Press, 2002). Her study finds a strong return to traditional theology and morality among the post baby-boom generation. Her study deals mainly with Catholic young people, but includes some evangelical and Orthodox young believers. Her findings dovetail with those in the emerging church on one issue. She too notes the appreciation for mystery, symbolism and liturgy among the young people she studied.

pressed clearly in the preaching of the word and the lives of those in the church, communicated lovingly and patiently in worship and witness, and reflected in the lives of disciples who are growing in Christlikeness. D. A. Carson sees Redeemer Presbyterian as an example of a church that *"displays all the strengths of the emerging church movement while avoiding most of its weaknesses."*[110]

So churches should be aware of what is happening in the culture, how those around them are thinking, and how best to communicate to them. That is simply part of loving our neighbor and being all things to all men (1 Cor. 9:22). They should consider if they are making the gospel clear and intelligible, and if their worship and life together honor Christ. If those things are in place, I think they have responded as they need to. Some churches may make more radical changes, but they should do so cautiously, weighing all changes more in terms of biblical fidelity than postmodern affinity, lest they simply exchange the conformity to modern culture, so apparent in many traditional and seeker churches, for conformity to postmodern culture, which has some aspects antithetical to genuine Christianity.

To the Past

The final direction to be traced in this chapter does not involve a distinct group of churches as much as an impulse evident in a variety of churches, ranging from traditional to seeker to megachurch and perhaps some in the emerging, postmodern church movement as well. It is an impulse to recover some of the practices and approaches to church life of those in the past. Thus it seems appropriate to refer to these churches as historic churches.

In Baptist life it is seen in the growing number of churches utilizing practices that were common in the nineteenth century and earlier in Baptist churches in North America, and are still common in Baptist churches in many parts of the world. Some are practices that involve taking church membership seriously, such as exercising care in the admission of members (reflected in the growing number of churches with new member classes), renewing the practice of church discipline, and adopting church covenants to express the commitment members make to each other.[111] Others involve a renewed

---

110. Carson, *Becoming Conversant*, 56. Emphasis in original.

111. The centrality of such practices to Baptist ecclesiology in the past, their disappearance in the twentieth century, and the prospects for their recovery today were discussed in chapters four and five.

examination of the practice of polity, and have led a number of Baptist churches to renew the practice of a plurality of elders.[112]

In the larger evangelical world, this same impulse to recover something from the past can be seen in an organization like the Alliance of Confessing Evangelicals, whose identifying statement, the Cambridge Declaration, begins with these words: "Evangelical churches today are increasingly dominated by the spirit of this age rather than by the Spirit of Christ. As evangelicals, we call ourselves to repent of this sin and to recover the historic Christian faith."[113]

While the Alliance of Confessing Evangelicals has been generally critical of seeker churches and many megachurches, some of the practices central to historic Baptist ecclesiology are being embraced by a wide variety of churches, including some megachurches and seeker churches. Capitol Hill Baptist Church in Washington, D.C. has been one of the leading churches in this regard, both in adopting a number of historic practices and in publicizing them, in books like *Polity*, containing a reprint of ten "historic Baptist documents" concerning "how to conduct church life."[114] But numerous seeker churches and megachurches, quite different from Capitol Hill Baptist, are adopting similar practices. For example, more than three-fourths of the six hundred megachurches surveyed by the Faith Communities Today Project utilize required new members' classes, and megachurch members are notable for their high rates of participation and involvement.[115] Seeker churches, some of which are megachurches, share this concern for meaningful membership. Willow Creek requires members to renew their commitment each year or they are dropped from the membership list; Saddleback requires new members to sign a membership covenant, and the church has practiced church discipline since its inception. And while I have no data, it seems that a return to past practices would fit with the postmodern trait of "appreciating and participating in ancient patterns."[116]

It is not clear what has prompted the interest in and return to earlier

---

112. There have been at least half a dozen books in the past decade discussing polity, especially the issue of elders. See the discussion in chapter seven.

113. The Cambridge Declaration is available at the Web site of the Alliance of Confessing Evangelicals. See http://www.alliancenet.org.

114. Mark Dever, ed., *Polity: Biblical Arguments on How to Conduct Church Life* (Washington, D.C.: Center for Church Reform, 2001).

115. Thumma, "Megachurches Today," 11, and Thumma, "Exploring the Megachurch."

116. Stetzer, *Planting New Churches*, 137.

practices among such a diverse range of churches. Many would say they simply found these practices in the Bible. Perhaps their presence in the Bible was highlighted by the sense of failure and dead end reached by many churches following twentieth century practices. Perhaps the accelerating rate of change has produced a desire for practices rooted in something more substantial than shifting cultural preferences. Whatever the source, I applaud the presence of this impulse, for it is a helpful guard against what I think is the greatest danger facing evangelical churches today, the danger of uncritical cultural accommodation.

If traditional churches are open to the charge of being culturally irrelevant and unintelligible, seeker churches, megachurches, and perhaps even postmodern churches run the risk of cultural conformity. And as these contemporary innovative churches dominate more and more of American evangelicalism, this risk of cultural conformity becomes the dominant threat. In fact, this has been perhaps the besetting threat to Christianity in America. Alan Wolfe, speaking especially of the relationship of Christianity to American culture in the past fifty years, says, "In every aspect of the religious life, American faith has met American culture—and American culture has triumphed."[117]

One of the major resources available to churches to help them avoid cultural captivity is history. Virtually all the contemporary evangelical innovators seek to remain biblical. Their motto is, changing methods but the same message. And overwhelmingly these churches are evangelical churches, who desire to bring people to Jesus Christ and teach them the truths of the Bible. But the medium can powerfully affect the message, and as the history of interpretation makes painfully clear, the Bible is always interpreted within a cultural framework that can dramatically shape the message found within the Bible. In such a situation, history affords us a vantage point from which we can see how the message of the Bible looked to others who were not laboring in the same cultural framework and thus not subject to the same shaping influences.

The turn to the past, of course, does not solve all problems. The past was not of one mind on many subjects and was subject to the distorting influences of the culture of the times. But since we cannot learn from the future, the only alternative is to learn from the past, believing that God's Spirit did not begin his ministry of illuminating his word for his people with this generation,

---

117. Wolfe, *Transformation*, 3.

but that because of his ministry in the past there may be wisdom for us in the words of our forbears. Many of the churches we see as innovators have in fact been drawn to practices from the past. I believe they could profit from a more thorough examination of their practices in the light of Scripture as seen by earlier generations.

There is, however, one other resource we have not yet mentioned. In addition to traveling to the past historically, we can travel to other cultures geographically and see how God's Spirit has led his people in other cultures to understand Scripture and practice their life together. In the next chapter, we look at the spread of the church around the world and consider some insights and questions raised by the church in other cultures.

CHAPTER 12

INTO ALL THE WORLD

The Future of the Global Church

WHILE THIS BOOK IS PRIMARILY addressed to churches in North America, the question attended to in this part of the book ("Where is the church going?") cannot be answered without broadening the focus to include a global view. As technology shrinks the world and we become more and more a global village, important trends and developments in the church around the world have the potential to affect churches in America. Moreover, since all Christians share in the one universal body of Christ and thus in the communion of saints, it is only right that they care about the health and welfare of the larger body. Further, since all Christians also share in the mandate to make disciples of all nations (Matt. 28:19–20), it is appropriate that they evaluate their progress in terms of their corporate obedience to that mandate. Finally, since the church has received Christ's promise that he will build his church, despite all the opposition of the forces of evil (Matt. 16:18), it is edifying to survey the progress of the church around the world and marvel at what Christ has built.

THE AMAZING STORY

Although little recognized by secular historians, the progress of the church around the world, especially in the past two hundred years, is an amazing story. Andrew Walls compares how a visitor from Mars would have seen Christianity in 1789 and then two hundred years later. In 1789, "he might well have assumed Christianity to be the tribal religion of the white peoples," while two centuries later "he would find Christianity a world religion . . . firmly

established in every continent, among people of the most diverse and disparate origins and cultures," and "receding only among the Caucasians—to whom
200 years before it seemed confined."[1] Justo González states categorically,
"there is little doubt that, from the point of view of the history of Christianity, the most important event of the nineteenth century was the founding of
a truly universal church, in which peoples of all races and nations had a part."[2]
Peter Jenkins chides fellow historians who ignore the importance of the religious changes that have taken place in the past century, calling such neglect
"comically myopic, on a par with a review of the eighteenth century that
managed to miss the French Revolution."[3]

This book is not a history of missions; that task has been more than ably
accomplished by others.[4] But we cannot discern where the church is going if
we do not know from whence it has come, and thus a brief review of history
is in order.

While there were certainly many heroic missionaries involved in the spread
of Christianity across Europe in the first millennium of the church's history,
and others who took the gospel to the lands colonized by European nations
in the post-Reformation era, the modern missionary movement is usually
seen as beginning in the late eighteenth century and exploding in the nineteenth century.

One who is often called the father of that movement is the Baptist William Carey, whose 1792 work, "An Enquiry into the Obligations of Christians, to use Means for the Conversion of the Heathens," is a landmark in
the history of missions.[5] Carey argued, contrary to the interpretation common since the Reformation, that Christ's command to make disciples of all
nations (Matt. 28:19–20) was not limited to the apostles, but was binding
on all Christians. Christians were thus obligated to use "means" to obey
Christ's command. The specific means Carey proposed was the formation

---

1. A. F. Walls, "Outposts of Empire," in *Introduction to the History of Christianity,* ed. Tim Dowley
   (Minneapolis, Minn.: Fortress Press, 2002), 557.
2. Justo González, *The Story of Christianity* (Peabody, Mass.: Prince Press, 2001), 2:303.
3. Jenkins, *The Next Christendom,* 1.
4. The classic history of missions is the seven-volume work by Kenneth Scott Latourette, *A History of
   the Expansion of Christianity* (Grand Rapids: Zondervan, 1937–1945). Neill, *History of Christian
   Missions,* is a more succinct account. Ruth Tucker, *From Jerusalem to Irian Jaya: A Biographical
   History of Christian Missions* (Grand Rapids: Academie Books, 1983) is a fascinating approach to
   the same topic, as she gives a history in the form of ninety-nine short biographies.
5. The full text of Carey's work, along with a biography of Carey's life, is found in Timothy George,
   Faithful Witness: The Life and Mission of William Carey (Birmingham, Ala.: New Hope, 1991).

of a society composed of all those willing to support the sending of missionaries to seek the conversion of the heathen. At Carey's prompting, a small group of Baptists in England formed such a society in 1792 and sent Carey to India as their first missionary. Almost immediately, other denominations in England and North America followed suit. In the nineteenth century, called the "great century" of missions by the foremost historian of missions, Kenneth Scott Latourette, Christianity became the first and only truly worldwide religion, as thousands of missionaries fanned out into every continent. Many died, especially in Central Africa, but when one fell, another would step forward. It is truly an amazing story of courage and love, one that changed the face of the world in ways far more profound than those accomplished by the more well-known political leaders of the era.

The advance continued in the twentieth century, though interrupted by two World Wars. Yet even that stimulated more progress, as some of those who saw the world in the course of World War II came back to the United States only to find that they could not stay home. They had seen firsthand the needs of the world and felt compelled to respond. The post–World War II era saw the emergence of a new wave of missionary activity, primarily from evangelical North American churches, leading Ralph Winter to write of this period as *The Twenty-five Unbelievable Years, 1945 to 1969*.[6]

Winter is also largely responsible for reshaping how mission leaders began to see the task of missions. He noted that the Great Commission tells us to make disciples of all nations, or *ethnē*. He called for Christians not just to seek to reach every person with the gospel, but to focus their efforts especially on reaching unreached peoples. Those who already had Christians within their own ethno-linguistic grouping should be reached by those Christians; missionaries should focus their attention on genuinely unreached people groups, those who had no Christians in their ethnic group or no Christian who spoke their language.[7] Thus, a motto adopted by some in the missions community was no longer just "The Gospel for Every Person," but also "A Church for Every People," a motto that shows the centrality of churches in the ongoing task of missions.

---

6. Ralph D. Winter, *The Twenty-five Unbelievable Years, 1945 to 1969* (Pasadena, Calif.: William Carey Library, 1970).

7. Winter's important address on this topic was initially given at the 1974 Lausanne Congress on World Evangelization. See Ralph Winter, "The New Macedonia: A Revolutionary New Era in Mission Begins," in *Perspectives on the World Christian Movement: A Reader*, ed. Ralph Winter and Steven Hawthorne (Pasadena, Calif.: William Carey Library, 1981), 293–311.

THE GLOBAL FUTURE OF THE CHURCH

This brief review of the history of missions leads us to our central concern in this chapter. What lies ahead for the church globally? No doubt there are many trends that emerge from the historical trajectory of the past two hundred years. Three seem relevant to the focus of this book, the doctrine of the church.

The first statement we can make about the future of the church is that it seems clear the church will continue to be planted globally, especially among unreached peoples. Indeed, church planting seems to be the priority task for many missionaries. For example, the 2000 and Beyond Movement has adopted as their goal the motto mentioned above: "A Church for Every People and the Gospel for Every Person." As of the year 2000, they had identified 1,117 ethnolinguistic groups with populations in excess of 10,000 with less than 100 believers. Those groups are the ones they are especially interested in targeting.[8]

Another recent development in missions emphasizes not just the initial planting of a few churches among a people, but the development of what is called a church planting movement (CPM). This methodology is central to the vision statement adopted by the Southern Baptist International Mission Board in 1998: "We will facilitate the lost coming to saving faith in Jesus Christ by beginning and nurturing Church Planting Movements among all peoples."[9] David Garrison, author of a booklet explaining this strategy, defines a Church Planting Movement as "a rapid and multiplicative increase of indigenous churches planting churches within a given people group or population segment."[10] Such churches are deliberately small. House churches or cell churches (between ten and thirty members) are lay-led and designed to multiply rapidly. In fact, rapid reproduction is an underlying imperative. In describing some of the universal elements of Church Planting Movements, Garrison reports, "when reproduction rates slow down, the Church Planting Movement falters. Rapid reproduction communicates the urgency and importance of coming to faith in Christ. When rapid reproduction is taking place, you

---

8. Luis Bush, "Where Are We Now? Evaluating Progress on the Great Commission," *Mission Frontiers* 22, no. 3 (June 2000): 18.

9. David Garrison, "Church Planting Movements," available via http://www.imb.org/CPM, chap. 1, p. 1, accessed October 25, 2004. The Web site numbers each chapter beginning at page 1, and so references in footnotes will include chapter and page number.

10. Ibid.

can be assured that the churches are unencumbered by nonessential elements and the laity are fully empowered to participate in this work of God."[11]

This emphasis on church planting reflects the New Testament teaching that God's Spirit works through the church to accomplish his merciful purposes on the earth. Howard Snyder says that the church is uniquely empowered to be "God's healing force throughout the earth," and thus, "church planting is the number one priority of gospel globalization."[12] However, Snyder also adds, "it is not enough merely to plant churches. It makes all the difference in the world—all the difference for the kingdom—what *kind* of church is planted."[13] Some have raised questions about the kind of churches being produced in missions settings, ecclesiological questions that require careful consideration. We will return to those questions shortly.

A second major trend emerging from the past that will continue into the future for the church globally is the incredible vitality of the Pentecostal/charismatic branch of Christianity. Pentecostalism is usually seen as originating out of the holiness churches of the late nineteenth century. Holiness churches saw the baptism of the Spirit as a second work of grace, subsequent to salvation, and essential to a deeper Christian life. Pentecostalism was distinguished from the holiness churches by its stress on speaking in tongues as the normative manifestation of one's reception of the baptism of the Spirit. Thus, all Christians were to experience something like what happened on the day of Pentecost recorded in Acts 2. The movement's origin is associated with tongue-speaking among the students of Charles Fox Parham at the Topeka Bible College in January 1901, but was popularized by the 1906 Azusa Street Revival in Los Angeles.[14]

A related but separate form of the movement began in a different context among a different audience in 1960, when Dennis Bennett, an Episcopalian rector in California, shared with his congregation the news that he had been experiencing the Holy Spirit in a new way in his life. This movement quickly spread across the United States and beyond. It has at times been called neo-Pentecostalism but more often the charismatic movement. It differed from the Pentecostal movement in that it found its adherents among the members

11. Ibid., chap. 3, p. 5.
12. Howard Snyder with Daniel V. Runyon, *Decoding the Church: Mapping the DNA of Christ's Body* (Grand Rapids: Baker, 2002), 161.
13. Ibid.
14. For more on the origins and historical development of Pentecostalism, see Walter J. Hollenweger, *Pentecostalism: Origins and Developments Worldwide* (Peabody, Mass.: Hendrickson, 1998).

of established mainline churches and did not issue in new charismatic denominations. Rather, these charismatics sought to renew their own churches
and denominations, though that pattern seems to be changing, as more and
more independent charismatic churches are being born. In common with
the Pentecostals, they have emphasized the ministry of the Holy Spirit, including the baptism and gifts of the Spirit.

Their importance for this chapter lies in their explosive growth, especially
in missions contexts. In one century, those identified as Pentecostals or
charismatics have grown from zero to an estimated 523.7 million. Of these,
about 126 million are in Africa, 135 million in Asia, and 141 million in Latin
America. The great majority are found in what one source calls neocharismatic,
nonwhite indigenous movements.[15] They are the dominant church model in
many mission settings.

In terms of ecclesiology, there is little written about this area of Pentecostal doctrine. Most discussion has focused on their distinctive doctrines concerning the Holy Spirit. Yet their emphasis on the Spirit seems to be shaping
their ecclesiology as it develops. One of the earliest formulations of a Pentecostal view of the church describes the church as a fellowship involving a
common experience of the Spirit and mutual edification. Without excluding
the importance of preaching or the sacraments, they emphasize the importance of the mutual ministry of members of the church, as instruments of
the Spirit, employing the charismata (spiritual gifts) given by the Spirit in
service to the members of the body. One summary describes the essence of
Pentecostal ecclesiology in these words: "The dynamic of the fellowship is
concretely lived out through the charismata."[16] In general, charismatic
ecclesiology agrees with the Pentecostal emphasis on fellowship, but, in keeping with their origin within established denominations, they seek to link their
experience of the Spirit with the faith handed down in their churches, and
see the Spirit working through tradition and sacrament.[17]

Several of the emphases of Pentecostal ecclesiology seem well-founded in

---

15. These numbers are from Barrett, ed., *World Christian Encyclopedia*, 1:19–20. For more on one
    segment of these neocharismatic, nonwhite indigenous church movements, see "African Indepen-
    dent Churches' Ecclesiology," in Veli-Matti Kärkkäinen, *An Introduction to Ecclesiology: Ecumeni-
    cal, Historical and Global Perspectives* (Downers Grove, Ill.: InterVarsity, 2002), 194–201.
16. Kärkkäinen, *Introduction to Ecclesiology*, 75. Kärkkäinen draws upon an unpublished paper by
    Peter Kuzmic and Miroslav Volf, "Communio Sanctorum: Toward a Theology of the Church as a
    Fellowship of Persons" (Riano, Italy: International Roman Catholic-Pentecostal Dialogue, 1985).
17. Ibid., 76–77.

Scripture. Baptists agree with Pentecostals in seeing the New Testament as portraying the importance of participation by the whole assembly in the life of the church and a belief in the importance of the local church. In recent years, their emphasis on the importance on the charismata for equipping believers has been adopted by many Baptists and most evangelicals, though there are still differences on the so-called miraculous gifts.[18] Beyond those emphases, the greatest contributions of the Pentecostal/charismatic movement to the larger evangelical world may be (1) as a reminder of the importance of the power of the Spirit in empowering believers and churches, (2) as examples of zeal in evangelism, and (3) as leaders in the ability to instill indigenous principles in planting new churches in some Third World countries.[19]

However, the almost ubiquitous presence of Pentecostal/charismatic Christians in missions contexts also raises some questions for missionaries from other perspectives. In most missions settings, close cooperation among evangelical missionaries is fairly common. Southern Baptist missionaries, for example, partner extensively with other evangelical groups they call "Great Commission Christians." But how far can partnership go with Pentecostal or charismatic groups? Baptists do have some concerns about certain aspects of Pentecostal theology. Those aspects are not central in the same way the gospel is, but they do affect the type of church one plants, especially in terms of what practices are accepted as part of worship. Some Southern Baptist leaders have expressed concern that Southern Baptist missionaries are planting churches that are "often neo-charismatic leaning and quasi Biblical."[20] How far Baptists can go in cooperating with Pentecostal and charismatic churches and how far they can adopt aspects of Pentecostal and charismatic church life is an ongoing and open question.

---

18. For a fuller listing of their emphases, see the list of seven "salient features" of Pentecostal ecclesiology by Michael Harper, "The Holy Spirit Acts in the Church, Its Structures, Its Sacramentality, Its Worship and Sacraments," *One in Christ* 12 (1976): 323, as cited in Kärkkäinen, *Introduction to Ecclesiology*, 77–78, n. 44. For the differing views on the miraculous gifts, see Wayne Grudem, ed., *Are Miraculous Gifts for Today?* (Grand Rapids: Zondervan, 1999).

19. Harper suggests that one reason behind the remarkable growth of Pentecostalism is that whereas other denominations' efforts were often associated with "empire-building and the westernizing of other cultures, Pentecostal outreach has very largely been free from such taints." Michael Harper, "The Holy Spirit Acts in the Church, Its Structures, Its Sacramentality, Its Worship and Sacraments," *One in Christ* 12 (1976): 323, as cited in Kärkkäinen, *Introduction to Ecclesiology*, 78.

20. An unpublished paper by Paige Patterson, Keith Eitel, and Robin Hadaway expresses this concern. The paper is informally titled "Points of Discussion," and was prepared for a February 2004 meeting of the trustees of the Southern Baptist International Mission Board with International Board Administration staff and Patterson, Eitel, and Hadaway.

The third major trend affecting the global future of the church is the on-going movement of the weight of the church from the Northern to the Southern Hemisphere. This shift is the theme of Peter Jenkins's important work, *The Next Christendom: The Coming of Global Christianity.* He notes that while some in the West have seen the growth of secularization as indicating that Christianity is on its death bed, the story is quite different outside of Europe and the Northern Hemisphere. He says, "Over the past century, however, the center of gravity in the Christian world has shifted inexorably southward, to Africa, Asia, and Latin America." Moreover, he adds, "This trend will continue apace in coming years. . . . Christianity should enjoy a worldwide boom in the new century, but the vast majority of believers will be neither white nor European, nor Euro-American."[21]

He notes that some important differences between the newer and older churches are already becoming apparent. For example, it is clear that the newer churches, even those that are associated with older, traditional denominations, are overwhelmingly conservative in their moral and theological orientation. In the 1998 Lambeth Conference of the world's Anglican bishops, a liberal statement concerning homosexuality was defeated, due to the votes of Asian and African bishops.[22] Even more recently, the decision of American Episcopalians to ordain a practicing homosexual as a bishop has threatened to rend the worldwide Anglican communion, as Anglican bishops in Africa have considered withdrawing. If they do so, it will have enormous consequences, for of the seventy million Anglicans worldwide, more than twenty million live in Nigeria alone. By 2050, while there may be 150 million Anglicans worldwide, "only a tiny minority will be White Europeans."[23] If Southern Hemisphere Christians are able to exercise influence in keeping with their numbers, the positions of several mainline denominations may change radically, for the leading churches in Africa are Catholic, Anglican, Methodist, and other traditional denominations.[24]

A more ominous impact looms when the rise of southern Christianity is charted alongside the growth of Islam. Jenkins suspects that as Christianity expands its influence, many countries in the Southern Hemisphere may de-

---

21. Jenkins, *The Next Christendom,* 2.

22. Ibid., 7, 121.

23. Ibid., 59.

24. Ibid., 57–58. Despite all the attention given to the growth of Pentecostal and independent churches, Jenkins notes the continuing presence in even greater number of Roman Catholics in Africa, Latin America, and parts of Asia.

velop "a powerful Christian identity," one with potential political implications.[25] The problem is that many of the growing Christian communities are developing alongside strong Muslim groups in the same country or area, and there have already been a number of situations (Nigeria, Indonesia, the Sudan, Philippines) where radical Islam has shown resistance to the toleration of Christians in their midst. If they grow in power, Christians might similarly oppress Muslims. Jenkins says, "a worst-case scenario would include a wave of religious conflicts reminiscent of the Middle Ages, a new age of Christian crusades and Muslim jihads."[26]

In such a situation, there is a need for a renewed emphasis on some principles historically associated with Baptist ecclesiology, namely, religious liberty and the separation of church and state. The former does not imply that all religions are equally true or valid, but simply recognizes that faith decisions must be made on bases other than governmental decree. The latter does not mean that religion has no place in the public life of a people, but that the church does not seek to use coercive power to accomplish its purposes. As one Baptist confession of faith puts it, "The church should not resort to the civil power to carry on its work. The gospel of Christ contemplates spiritual means alone for the pursuit of its ends."[27]

QUESTIONS RAISED BY THE CHURCH IN OTHER CULTURES

For most of its history, the church has enjoyed a relatively homogeneous cultural background. Initially, that background was Greco-Roman, which was the foundation for much of Western or European culture. But the movement of the church into all the world has brought the church into a variety of new cultures, raising a number of important questions. This section examines the questions raised by the presence and planting of the church in other cultures.

We noted in the previous chapter the struggle evangelical churches face in America of excessive identification with the culture, or cultural conformity. Indeed, we suggested that one of the major dangers with seeker churches and possibly postmodern churches is that, in seeking to be culturally relevant and attractive, they may become disobedient to biblical patterns of church life.

---

25. This is the reason why the title of Jenkins's book is *The Next Christendom*. He sees the potential for some nations to become religiously unified as in medieval Europe.

26. Ibid., 13.

27. These statements are found in the article titled "Religious Liberty" in all three versions of the *Baptist Faith and Message* (1925, 1963, and 2000).

The opposite danger, the lack of a proper adaptation to culture, has been the challenge of missionaries in planting the church in other cultures. Missionaries have struggled to bring the gospel without also bringing in parts of Western culture. Churches in some contexts met in buildings and sang songs that were alien to the culture. As a result, Christianity was rejected in some cases as a foreign, Western religion.

In addition, the Bible itself was written within a culture that is not always easily transferable to another culture. This involves a variety of challenges. For example, the New Testament requirements for an elder include that he be the husband of but one wife and a good manager of his household (1 Tim. 3:2, 4–5). But in some cultures, those two requirements seem contradictory. For the Higi of Nigeria or the Kru of Liberia, a man could be judged an effective manager of his household only if that household included at least two wives. According to Charles Kraft, the Kru say, "You cannot trust a man with only one wife."[28]

Churches in Islamic contexts have struggled with how far a believer in Christ can retain his or her Muslim identity. Can he or she still attend the mosque or say Muslim prayers? Or for churches originating in Muslim cultures, is it acceptable to worship on Thursday evenings? Is there any reason why women cannot sit on one side and men on the other side of a room during a worship service? Can Christians adopt lying prostrate as a normal posture for prayer?[29]

All these are examples of what is called contextualization, the attempt to communicate across cultures by putting one's message into the thought forms and worldview of those to whom it is addressed. While some aspects of a given culture may be incompatible with Christian faith and thus call for opposition (e.g., polygamy), other aspects may be adaptable. In the area of ecclesiology, the goal of contextualization is usually seen as a "dynamic equivalence" church, in which New Testament principles for church life are put in culturally appropriate forms.[30] But this assumes a knowledge of the relevant

---

28. Charles H. Kraft, *Christianity in Culture: A Study in Dynamic Biblical Theologizing in Cross-Cultural Perspective* (Maryknoll, N.Y.: Orbis, 1979), 324–25.

29. Don Newman, "Keys to Unlocking Muslim Strongholds," in Winter and Hawthorne, eds., *Perspectives on the World Christian Movement*, D-152. Newman advocates the formation of "messianic mosques," in which "followers of Jesus do not leave their culture but continue to appear as Muslims while worshipping Jesus." For more suggestions, see Phil Parshall, *Beyond the Mosque* (Grand Rapids: Baker, 1985).

30. See Lausanne Committee for World Evangelization, "The Willowbank Report," in Winter and Hawthorne, eds., *Perspectives on the World Christian Movement*, C-182. This report characterizes the dynamic equivalent model as "helpful and suggestive," while acknowledging that questions remain as to whether it is adequate in itself to provide all the guidance needed.

New Testament principles, the ability to separate those principles from our cultural forms, and the ability to put them in forms appropriate to another culture, without allowing the form to distort the message. Such a task has proven difficult for North American church leaders operating in their own context; it is proving to be a challenge for missionaries as well.

For example, Phil Parshall, one of the leading advocates of contextualizing the church in Islamic culture, has recently written of the danger of context-ualization crossing a line and becoming syncretism, a harmful blending of Christianity with other teachings. He examines the strategy of a Christian missionary joining a Muslim mosque for the purpose of becoming a Muslim to reach Muslims, and concludes that the practice is open "to the charge of un-ethical and sub-Christian activity."[31] It crosses the line from contextualization to syncretism. Proper contextualization without falling into syncretism will require missionaries with strong biblical, cultural, and theological knowledge, and the ability to do theological and cultural analysis.

Thus, the presence of the church in other cultures raises numerous questions of ecclesiology and calls for renewed study of the issues considered in part 1 of this book—those relating to the nature, marks, and essence of the church. Missiologist Darrell Guder states, "It is widely acknowledged that the planting of new churches in previously unevangelized cultures was undertaken with a very inadequate ecclesiology."[32] This inadequacy in the area of ecclesiology remains today. In a recent interview, mission leader C. Douglas McConnell was asked to name the greatest challenge facing the global evangelical missions movement today. He responded, "There is a critical need for frontier mission types to develop an ecclesiology. We are church planters but in some cases we do not understand what a church is either theologically and even to a lesser extent in practice."[33] The complexity of questions surrounding contextualization argues strongly for providing missionaries with the theological training that will give them the tools to analyze the issues adequately and develop a contextual, but biblical, ecclesiology.[34]

---

31. Phil Parshall, "Danger! New Directions in Contextualization," *Evangelical Missions Quarterly* 34, no. 4 (October 1998): 409.

32. Darrell L. Guder, "The Church as Missional Community," in *The Community of the Word: Toward an Evangelical Ecclesiology*, eds. Mark Husbands and Daniel J. Treier (Downers Grove: InterVarsity and Leicester, U.K.: Apollos, 2005), 123.

33. "Looking Back . . . Looking Forward," *Mission Frontiers* 22, no. 3 (January 2000): 9–10.

34. In view of this, the movement of some missionary agencies, including the Southern Baptist International Mission Board, to reduce educational requirements for missionaries seems unwarranted and may prove dangerous to the health of the churches these missionaries will develop.

Moreover, if planting churches is at the heart of the task of missions, then issues of ecclesiology deserve more careful consideration than is often given. For example, we mentioned that the Southern Baptist International Mission Board has adopted as a major part of its strategy the development of Church Planting Movements, which involve the rapid production of a large number of churches. But relatively little is said about what kind of churches such movements are to produce. The major concern seems to be that these churches continue to rapidly reproduce. But eventually, these churches must face the questions that determine what kind of a church these churches will be. For example, will they be composed of regenerate individuals only? Will they baptize believers only? How will they decide if someone's profession of faith is credible and thus a proper basis for baptism? How will the church be governed? How will an individual church relate to other churches? How a church answers these questions is part of what determines what kind of a church it is and will be.

This emphasis on rapid reproduction itself raises problems. Some would say that this emphasis "does not foster maturation of the church, leadership development nor establishment of long-term vision or stability for the church. It seems to rely almost exclusively on the early sections of Acts as a foundation for this model while ignoring the patterns of maturation found in the Pastorals and General Epistles."[35] For example, 1 Timothy 3:6 says that an elder, one who is to provide leadership and oversight for a church, "must not be a recent convert," but in a rapidly multiplying movement, how can the use of relatively new converts in leadership roles be avoided? Titus 1:9 speaks of the elder's ability to encourage others in doctrine and defend sound doctrine against those who oppose it. How quickly can that be developed? Alongside the concern for rapid reproduction, there needs to be a concern for healthy babies. Multiplication can be desired, planned for, and encouraged, but if what is multiplied is unhealthy, all we have done is multiply problems. All these questions simply underscore the importance of a thorough understanding of the doctrine of the church, not just for North American pastors but for missionaries who seek to plant churches in other cultures.

Handing the Bible to new believers and telling them to answer these questions for themselves may seem to reflect a trust in the Scripture and the Spirit, but it seems a bit arrogant to suppose that the Spirit was not at work among believers in earlier times. Baptists have a strong heritage of reflection on Scrip-

---

35. Patterson, Eitel, and Hadaway, "Points of Discussion," 2.

ture with regard to the doctrine of the church, a heritage modern-day Baptist missionaries and the churches they help develop would do well to consult.

Happily, such consultation is beginning to happen. Among Southern Baptists, formal discussions have taken place in their International Mission Board and North American Mission Board concerning the development of ecclesiological guidelines for church planters that address some of the issues of the nature and mark of the church. In addition, faculty members at two Southern Baptist seminaries have contributed to these discussions with formal statements on Guidelines for Church planters.[36] In the larger evangelical world, the April 2004 theology conference at Wheaton College was devoted to the theme of ecclesiology.[37] All these are encouraging developments that need to be continued as the expansion of the church into new cultures continues.

But there is one final, more positive, hopeful and even eschatological question raised by the presence of the church in other cultures. It arises from Christ's statement in Matthew 24:14: "And this gospel of the kingdom will be preached in the whole world as a testimony to all nations, and then the end will come." As the church is planted around the world, and the gospel is preached in more and more of the *ethnē*, or nations, the end seems to be drawing near. Could we be the generation that sees the fulfillment of this promise? Second Peter 3:11–12 tells us "to live holy and godly lives as you look forward to the day of God and speed its coming." It seems then that part of living a holy and godly life is having a part in the spread of the gospel to all nations, for then the end will come. Our hearts echo Paul's cry, *Maranatha,* "Come, O Lord!" (1 Cor. 16:22).

──────────── STUDY QUESTIONS FOR PART 5 ────────────

1. What do you see as the most important changes in American culture affecting churches in the past twenty years? How have those changes affected churches you know?

---

36. Statements have been adopted by the Southern Baptist International Mission Board and by portions of the faculties of Southwestern Baptist Theological Seminary and Southeastern Baptist Theological Seminary. All three draw upon Baptist heritage, especially as reflected in Baptist confessions of faith, and address many of the issues raised in this book.

37. The papers from this conference are available in Mark Husbands and Daniel J. Treier, eds., *The Community of the Word: Toward an Evangelical Ecclesiology* (Downers Grove: InterVarsity and Leicester, U.K.: Apollos, 2005).

2. Is marketing the church a valid and vital practice for contemporary churches? Why or why not?

3. What are some of the elements of the worldview called postmodernism? How should churches respond to it?

4. What do you see as the strengths and weaknesses of each of the models mentioned in chapter 11 (seeker churches, megachurches, cell churches, postmodern churches, historic churches)? Which model is most appealing to you? Why?

5. What are some of the major differences between the state of the church worldwide in 1800 and the state of the church worldwide today?

6. Why is church planting the major emphasis of many missionary agencies?

7. Chapter 12 noted three important trends in the church worldwide: the continuation of church planting, the explosive growth of Pentecostals/charismatics, and the move of Christianity to the Southern Hemisphere. Which of these three did you find most interesting or enlightening? Do you see any one of the three as being of special importance? If so, why?

8. Describe what is meant by the term *contextualization* in missions. What elements of the church can and cannot be contextualized?

———— BOOKS AND WEB SITES FOR FURTHER STUDY ————

Carson, D. A. *Becoming Conversant with the Emergent Church: Understanding a Movement and its Implications.* Grand Rapids: Zondervan, 2005. This is the most thorough and thoughtful critique I have read of the emerging church movement, by one of the leading scholars of evangelicalism. Carson's treatment is fair and gracious, but uncovers causes for serious concern in the writings of Brian McLaren and Steve Chalke, two of the most influential voices in the emerging church movement.

Hadaway, C. Kirk, Francis DuBose, and Stuart A. Wright. *Home Cell Groups and House Churches.* Nashville: Broadman, 1987. Though somewhat dated, this book provides a good overview of both home cell groups and house churches, giving some historical background, theological rationale, and various models.

Jenkins, Philip. *The Next Christendom: The Coming of Global Christianity.* Oxford, U.K.; New York: Oxford University Press, 2002. Jenkins gives a fascinating account of how the center of the world Christian movement has shifted to the Southern Hemisphere and the implications that shift may have for the future.

Pritchard, G. A. *Willow Creek Seeker Services: Evaluating a New Way of Doing Church.* Grand Rapids: Baker, 1996. This book, based on the author's doctoral dissertation, gives a fair, sympathetic, and yet incisive critique of the seeker services of Willow Creek Community Church. It is a model in that its tone is irenic, its basis is careful, thorough research, and its commentary is insightful.

Ryken, Philip Graham, Derek W. H. Thomas, and J. Ligon Duncan III, eds. *Give Praise to God: A Vision for Reforming Worship.* Phillipsburg, N.J.: P & R Publishing, 2003. This collection of essays presents some of the concerns of those who are calling the church to recover some of the emphases from worship in the past.

Sargeant, Kimon Howland. *Seeker Churches: Promoting Traditional Religion in a Nontraditional Way.* London, U.K.; New Brunswick, N.J.: Rutgers University Press, 2000. In many ways, this book is similar to the one by Pritchard; it differs in that it broadens the scope of study beyond Willow Creek to churches in the Willow Creek Association, it utilizes data gathered from a survey of six hundred seeker church pastors, and it approaches issues from more of a sociological than a theological perspective.

http://www.emergingchurch.org. One of the characteristics of postmoderns is their utilization of technology. In keeping with that characteristic, the most current literature on ministry to postmoderns is on Web sites. This one is sponsored by a loose fellowship of churches linked mainly by their commitment to using new approaches to reach postmodern people.

http://www.hirr.hartsem.edu. This Web site is operated by the Hartford Institute for Religion Research and contains, among other things, two very interesting reports on megachurches.

http://www.newchurches.com. This Web site carries research and scholarly articles by authors such as Ed Stetzer on a variety of types of new churches, from house churches to seeker churches to postmodern churches to new churches overseas. It also provides helpful links to a number of related Web sites, such as theooze.com and LenSweet.com.

A CALL FOR FAITHFUL CHURCHES

I LOVE PASTORS. I THINK PASTORAL ministry is a high calling, yet one that is made increasingly difficult by the widespread assumption that the only criterion of success in pastoral ministry is numerical growth. But very few churches in stable or declining areas of population experience significant numerical growth. In many cases, pastors of churches in such areas suffer agony of spirit, both because they desire to see people come to Christ and because they feel themselves a failure when years go by and the numbers stay the same or grow very slowly. Even pastors in growing churches feel the pressure to continue to grow. Some pastors may know that they can gather a crowd but be uneasy about the means they use to draw people in.

No doubt there are many cases where pastors should feel a sense of guilt over a lack of growth, because they have not sufficiently modeled or taught evangelism, or because the worship, teaching, and fellowship are so lackluster as to repel rather than attract prospective new members. But some nongrowing churches may be among rich, self-satisfied Americans, and Jesus spoke clearly of the difficulty to getting such people into the kingdom of heaven (Matt. 19:23–24). Other churches may be located in areas where there is an abundance of churches and a scarcity of residents, or in an area where the young people are moving away and all that is left are the older folks.

Part of the reason for writing this book was to help pastors, especially Baptist pastors, who may be struggling with questions concerning success in pastoral ministry, for one of the implicit themes of this book is that a successful church and a successful pastoral ministry is one that pleases Christ by honoring God's Word and his design for the church. I cannot promise that adopting a church covenant, renewing church discipline, exercising care in baptism, and following all the other suggestions in this book will produce great growth. It is likely to produce some numerical growth in most cases, and spiritual growth in almost all cases, but that is not the point. If God has given us instruction in his Word concerning his people, he is honored and a church is successful to the degree that it follows his instruction. Thus, the successful church is the faithful church.

Even the major metaphors for the church give hints that numerical growth is not the point. It may be desired, but churches are nowhere commanded to grow in numbers or chided because they haven't added more members lately. For example, the church is the people of God, but the people of God throughout the Old Testament were always a minority and often a remnant. They were not chosen because of their large numbers; on the contrary, Israel was among the "fewest of all peoples" (Deut. 7:7). Similarly, the church is the body of Christ, but it need not follow the pattern of most Americans and grow obese; the goal is health. As the temple of the Spirit, the chief treasure of the church is not the size of its temple but that which dwells within. Even the metaphor of the church as family reinforces this point. Is a family with eight kids necessarily healthier or more successful than a family with four kids?

The criterion every pastor and every church member should adopt as defining success is faithfulness. If a church is faithful to be and do what Scripture calls it to do and be—to be God's people, showing forth his gospel in their corporate life; to be a temple energized by the Spirit's ministry among them; to be a building composed of living stones; to be a society governed as members of the body seek the direction of their Head, with the leadership of godly shepherds; to be Christ's body, ministering his love in the world and honoring his presence as they worship and observe his ordinances—such a church is a faithful church and a successful church. Numerical growth is desirable, because we desire to see people come to Christ, but it is not the only manifestation of the blessing of God.

In the end, the one we seek to please in our churches must not be the seekers, nor the postmoderns, nor the traditionalists, nor the members, but the Lord of the church, and we please him by honoring his design for the church. This book has presented how most Baptists have historically understood that design, from what the church is to be, to who composes it, to how it is governed, to what it is to do, to where it is headed. Much of what has been written is the common teaching of evangelical Christians, and I rejoice in the common ground we share. My special concern has been to present a Baptist perspective on these issues, not because I believe Baptists are infallible (the evidence to the contrary is incontrovertible). Rather, I present this perspective for three reasons: first, because Baptists today seem to have lost their way on many of these issues and a larger historical perspective can be of great help; second, because there is no similar perspective available in print; third, because, in the end, I do think Baptists have gotten these matters of ecclesiology right. Otherwise, I would not be a Baptist. I invite readers to place the perspective in these pages alongside that of Scripture and compare for themselves.

In the midst of the difficulties of day-to-day ministry in our churches, it is all too easy to lose sight of the glorious destiny of the church. What we see looks far less hopeful. But the whole Christian life is lived by faith, not sight. And so I call pastors, and all those concerned for the welfare of Christ's body, to see again the vision of what Christ's love will make of his body. He will "make her holy, cleansing her by the washing with water through the word, and . . . present her to himself as a radiant church, without stain or wrinkle or any other blemish, but holy and blameless" (Eph. 5:26–27). Our joyful privilege is to be fellow workers with God in moving his church toward that glorious destiny. I call upon pastors and leaders in all the local assemblies where that bride is being prepared to give themselves to the high calling of presenting to Christ a faithful bride.

Scripture Index

GENESIS
2:18 .173
12:1–3 13

EXODUS
18:19–22 . . . . 182n
19:5–6 32
28–29 204
28:41 204

LEVITICUS
27:30 129

NUMBERS
8:5–22 204
8:10 207
27:18–23 204

DEUTERONOMY
4:20 32
7:6 .32
7:7 .352

2 CHRONICLES
7:15–16 46

NEHEMIAH
8–10 118
9:38 118
10:28–39 119

PSALMS
19:1 45

29:2 239
51 . . . . 290n
96:9–12 45
148 45
150:6 45

ISAIAH
56:7 45

JEREMIAH
7:11 45
31:33 33

HOSEA
1:10 32
2:23 32

ZECHARIAH
4:6 .76

MATTHEW
1:21 33
4:4 .163
4:19 73
5:13–14 . . . . 250, 302
5:23–24 289
5:48 166
7:12 290
9:35 228
10:42 194
13:24–30 . . . . 56, 89
16:18 . . . 13, 28, 43, 47, 70, 335
16:19 . . . . . . 75, 106, 147, 148n

18:15–17 147
18:15–18 34
18:15–20 . . . . . . 46, 125n, 146
18:17 . . . . 28, 28n
18:18 . . . . 75, 106
18:20 282
19:13–15 . . . . 205, 269
19:21 251
19:23 111
19:23–24 351
21:13 45
22:37–39 34
22:37–40 . . . . 220, 289
24:14 347
26:17–30 278
26:26–27 278
28:19 59
28:19–20 . . . 94, 220, 226, 253,
261, 275, 335, 336
28:20 . . . . 94, 228

MARK
1:10 274
1:15 265
3:11–12 309
3:14 204
6:5 205
10:13–16 269
10:16 205
10:41–45 140
10:45 226
14:12–26 278
16:16 94

LUKE

2:41–50 .... 123, 272
4:16–21 238
6:12–13 204
12:42 164
14:23 .... 89, 90, 129
18:15–17 269
22:7–30 278

JOHN

1:12 35
1:14 46
3:5–8 225
3:16 291
4:24 239
6:63 225
7:39 .... 74, 233
10:11 162
10:11–13 163
13:15 42
13:34–35 34
14:6 224–25
16:13 225
17:18 302

ACTS

1:8 73
1:15 309
1:21–22 60
2 .... 13, 30, 33, 35,
  69, 73, 74, 245, 248, 252,
  266, 307, 319, 339
2:38 .... 94, 263, 263n,
  265, 265n, 276
2:41 .... 28, 68, 72, 84, 94,
  122, 261, 264, 276n
2:42 .... 35, 59, 227,
  228, 233, 238, 278
2:42–47 .... 7, 17, 220,
  220n, 221, 227
2:43 248
2:44 .... 35, 36
2:45 249
2:46 .... 238, 316, 319
2:47 .... 73, 84, 227,
  248, 250, 252, 273
4 ....162n
4:4 .... 28, 68, 72, 84,
  122, 273, 316
5:11 .... 30, 316
5:12–14 248
5:14 122

6 ....159, 162n, 192, 193,
  194, 195, 198, 200, 204
6:1–2 192
6:1–4 202
6:1–6 .... 148, 204
6:2 194
6:2–4 191
6:3 .... 146, 192, 205
6:6 204
6:7 .... 72, 253
8:2–4 29
8:12 .... 94, 122, 261
8:16 263
8:17–18 205
8:36–38 122
8:36–39 ....261n
8:48 122
9 72
9:12 205
9:17 205
9:31 .... 28, 72, 253, 315
10:42 254
10:44–48 269
10:48 263
11:18 253
11:21 84
11:22 30
11:23 253
11:26 35
11:30 .... 162n, 178n
12:1–2 160
12:5 .... 28, 30
12:12–17 319
12:17 181
13 .... 142, 205
13–14 266
13:1 316
13:1–3 .... 148, 206
13:2–3 .... 28, 29, 146
13:3 204
13:15–42 238
13:48 .... 122, 273
13:49 253
14:1 122
14:21 122
14:21–23 84
14:23 ...28, 68, 148, 159, 162n,
  178, 180, 186, 204, 205, 316
14:27 .... 148, 253
15 .... 142, 144, 146, 159
15:2 .... 162n, 178n
15:4 .... 28, 148, 178n
15:6 .... 178n

15:9 264
15:12 148
15:13 181
15:22 .... 28, 30, 146, 148,
  159, 319
15:22–23 .... 162n, 178n
15:28–29 146
15:41 180
16:4 .... 162n, 178n
16:5 .... 28, 72, 273
16:14 84
16:15 261
16:33 122
16:33–34 269
18:3–4 176
18:5 176
18:7–8 273
18:8 .... 122, 269
18:22 316
19:5 263
19:6 205
19:32, 39 .... 26n
20 162
20:7 .... 278, 292
20:17 .... 162, 178, 316
20:21 265
20:28 .... 28, 34n, 162, 163
20:28–31 .... 29, 163
20:30 74
21:8 160
21:18 .... 162n, 178n, 181
22:16 .... 263, 265n
28:8 205

ROMANS

1:6–7 .... 27, 175
1:16 225
2:28–29 270
3:11 .... 308, 310
4:19 129
5:8 291
6 264
6:3–4 .... 263, 274
6:4 .... 264, 274
6:6 274
7 34
7:9 .... 123, 272
8:6–8 308
8:7 310
8:9 47
8:29 166
11:29 175
12:1 .... 45, 239

12:4–5 38
12:5 .... 39, 40, 83
12:8 .... 163, 164n
12:9–21 .... 72, 253
12:13 234
12:16 234
13:4 201
13:8 250
15:7 .... 129, 234
15:26–27 234
16:1 .... 29, 192, 200, 201,
    203, 316
16:2 201
16:4 180
16:5 .... 29, 180
16:16 .... 29, 34
16:23 30

1 CORINTHIANS
1:2 .... 27, 29, 34, 56, 84,
    175, 316
1:13 55
1:16 269
3:5 201
3:7 .... 71, 73
3:9 .... 44, 71
3:10–11 47
3:11–16 44
4:2 164
5:1–13 .... 125n
5:2 146
5:4 47
5:7 278
5:9–13 147
5:11 84
5:12–13 .... 68, 135
5:13 34
6:11 .... 47, 265n
6:19 44
9:22 .... 248, 302, 331
10:16 .... 104, 278
10:16–17 .... 37, 282
10:21 278
10:32 ....34n
11 284
11:1 155
11:3 173
11:16 ....34n
11:17–33 104
11:17–34 261
11:18 .... 30, 104
11:18ff 29
11:20 .... 278, 284

11:22 .... 34n, 284
11:24 .... 278, 282
11:26 .... 47, 240, 283
11:27–34 290
11:28 288
11:29 ...... 104, 282, 288, 289
11:29–30 288
12:12–13 .... 175n
12:13 .... 38, 264, 276n
12:14–20 38
12:16–17 37
12:18 47
12:25–26 40
12:26 .... 69, 250
12:27 37
14:23 30
14:23ff 28
14:23–25 327
14:24–25 248
14:26 .... 239, 240, 242
14:33 .... 34, 68
14:40 .... 68, 207
15:9 .... 29, 34n
16:1 .... 29, 316
16:2 129
16:19 .... 29, 180, 316
16:22 347

2 CORINTHIANS
1:1 ....34n
2:6 .... 146, 148
6:16 44
8:1 .... 29, 316
9:13 234
13:14 .... 36, 225

GALATIANS
1:8 155
1:8–9 .... 74, 147
1:13 .... 29, 34n
1:18 .... 74, 181
1:19 181
1:22 180
2:10 250
2:12 181
3:2 264
3:26 .... 35, 59
3:27 .... 265n
3:28 .... 48, 59, 224
4:4–5 35
5:13 250
6:1 .... 125n
6:6–7 290

6:10 .... 250, 290

EPHESIANS
1:1 .... 35, 84
1:13 264
1:22–23 41
2:20 .... 28n, 60, 159, 225
2:21 47
2:21–22 .... 14, 44, 47
2:22 75
3:10 .... 13, 29
3:20–21 126
3:21 .... 13, 29, 70
4:3 225
4:4 .... 53, 55
4:4–5 .... 35, 39
4:5 .... 38, 39, 276
4:5–6 83
4:11 ..28, 29, 43, 160, 162, 163,
    178, 224, 228
4:11–12 .... 129, 159
4:11–16 163
4:12 .... 41, 160, 250
4:13–16 42
4:15 .... 41, 73
4:16 .... 42, 43, 47, 115
4:29 129
5:18–21 240
5:22–33 .... 42, 171
5:23 41
5:23–24 173
5:23–27 29
5:25 70
5:25–27 .... 13, 57, 116
5:26–27 353
5:29–30 41
6:4 271
6:21 201

PHILLIPIANS
1:1 .... 28, 84, 162n, 178,
    191, 200
1:18 74
1:27 129
2:3–4 129
2:7 129
3:6 29
4:8 .... 244, 247
4:15 29
4:18 45

COLOSSIANS
1:2 .... 35, 84

1:15–17 42
1:18 .... 41, 42
1:24 41
2:10 42
2:11 270
2:11–12 264
2:12 263
2:19 .... 41, 42, 43, 115
3:16 ... 163, 224, 228, 234, 240
4:7 291
4:15 .... 29, 180
4:16 .... 28, 30, 61

1 THESSALONIANS
1:1 .... 29, 35, 84
1:1–2 129
2:14 ....34n
5:11 234
5:12 ..... 163, 164n, 165, 178
5:12–13 207
5:12–22 .... 72, 253

2 THESSALONIANS
1:1 35
1:2 84
1:4 ....34n
3:14 61
3:14–15 .... 125n

1 TIMOTHY
1:20 .... 125n
2 242
2:9–15 171
2:12 .... 200, 203
2:13 173
3 ..166, 192, 193, 194, 199, 205
3:1 .... 162n, 176
3:1–2 178
3:1–7 .... 163, 253
3:2 .... 29, 143, 162n,
    163, 167, 169, 181, 193,
    199n, 224, 228, 344
3:2–7 .... 166, 192
3:4 168
3:4–5 .... 164n, 165, 344
3:5 .... 34n, 193
3:6 .... 167, 169, 193
3:8 .... 28, 196, 199
3:8–13 .... 191, 192, 196, 200
3:9 192
3:10 .... 193, 196
3:11 ... 193, 199, 201, 203, 213
3:12 .... 164n, 193, 196

3:15 .... 225, 232
4:13 .... 28, 241
4:14 205
5:1–2 35
5:9–16 200
5:16 29
5:17 ......142, 142n, 143, 155,
    161, 162n, 163, 164n, 165,
    176, 185
5:19 .... 162n, 178
5:19–20 .... 125n, 148
5:22 205
6:18 234

2 TIMOTHY
1:6 205
3:4 310
4:5 160

TITUS
1 .... 166, 205
1:5 ....148, 159, 162n,
    180, 186, 204, 205
1:5–9 .... 163, 192
1:6 .... 167, 168, 193
1:6–9 .... 166, 253
1:7 ... 162n, 164, 178, 181, 193
1:8 167
1:9 ..... 74, 163, 169, 192, 193

HEBREWS
5:1 205
7:28 205
8:1 205
10:24 234
10:25 .... 12, 129
12:22–23 57
13:7 ...... 163, 164, 166, 178
13:15–16 45
13:16 234
13:17 .... 129, 155,
    163, 164, 165, 178, 207, 320
13:20 162
13:24 .... 164, 178

JAMES
2:2 27
5:14 .. 162n, 164, 178, 181, 207

1 PETER
1:22 129
2:2 163
2:4 47

2:5 .... 45, 47, 71, 225
2:9 .... 45, 160
2:9–10 .... 32, 238
2:25 162
3:21 265
4:8 126
4:10 .... 129, 160, 175
5 162
5:1 .... 162, 178
5:1–4 163
5:2 .... 162, 163, 176
5:2–4 166
5:3 .... 140, 166
5:4 162
5:5 .... 162n

2 PETER
3:11–12 347

I JOHN
1:3 36
1:5–7 234
1:7 237
1:9 291
2:9 234
2:9–10 34
3:10 .... 34, 234
3:14 .... 34, 234
3:16–18 250
3:17 .... 226, 290
4:7–8 .... 34, 234
4:11–12 234
4:19–20 34
4:19–21 234

2 JOHN
1 .... 162n, 178

3 JOHN
1 .... 162n, 178

JUDE
3 60

REVELATION
1:6 .... 45, 160
2–3 .... 181, 182n
5:9 59
5:10 45
19:9 283
21:3 .... 13, 33

SUBJECT INDEX

A

Abraham, 13, 33

accountability, age of. *See* age for believer baptism.

Adam, 173

African church, 112

age for believer baptism, 111–13, 122–24, 271–73

Akin, Daniel, 146n, 165, 174, 181n, 182, 213

Alexander, Paul, 116n, 315n

Alliance of Confessing Evangelicals, 247, 332

American Baptist Convention. *See* Northern (American) Baptists.

Anabaptists, 21, 64, 83, 85, 90–91, 124, 268–69, 271n, 272

Anderson, Justice, 82, 98

Anderson, Leith, 299, 301–2

"angel of the church," 181

Anglican Church, 91–93, 95, 138, 342

apostles, 59–61, 159–60, 204
    succession, 60, 160
    teaching, 60–61, 63, 227–28

Apostles' Creed. *See* Creed.

apostolicity of church, 59–61, 63, 234

archbishops, 138

Arminian theological tradition, 92–93

Arminius, Jakob, 91–93n

Arnold, Clinton, 121n

Asian church 112

association, Baptist, 143–45
    Charleston, 97, 144, 205
    Philadelphia, 96, 144, 154, 156, 205, 241
    Sandy Creek, 161n, 286

atonement, 329

Augustine of Hippo, 55–56, 75, 85–86, 89, 258, 259, 268–69, 279

authority. *See also* pastor.
    apostolic, 60, 139, 146
    Christ's headship, 41–42, 101, 143
    congregational, 101, 106, 125, 143–44, 146–48, 152, 154, 316

autonomy of church. *See* authority.

Azusa Street Revival, 339

B

baby boom generation, 301, 315, 323

Banks, Julia, 318–19

Banks, Robert, 35, 76, 318–19

baptism, 263–77
    believer, 85, 93, 95, 96, 99–100, 111–13, 121, 122–24, 264, 271–73, 275, 283, 284, 287, 346
    command of, 285, 287
    Lord's supper and, 283–88
    meaning of, 38, 85, 89, 263–67
    membership and, 94–95, 102–3, 116, 120–24, 284, 286

mode of, 263, 274–75, 283
sacramental understanding of, 57, 62–66, 85, 89, 99, 201–2, 264–65, 267–71, 284
spirit, 38, 276n
worship through, 276–77
Baptist Faith and Message, 96, 103, 104, 144, 170, 286
Baptists. *See also* baptism.
 confessions of, 39–40, 93–98, 162, 194, 285–86, 347n. *See also Baptist Faith and Message,* New Hampshire Confession of Faith, Second London Confession.
 distinctives of, 12, 18–21, 21, 61, 82, 97 98, 136, 143, 274
 ecclesiastical movements of 17–18, 305
 English, 92–96, 144, 264–65
 heritage, 346–47
 Landmark, 64
 North American, 92–95, 109, 111–12, 138n, 150, 202, 229, 243n, 251–52, 255, 272–73, 274, 285–86, 305n, 338, 341, 346
 particular, 93, 95–96, 202, 274
 Romanian, 112
 trends among, 109–14, 121, 138, 254, 272–73, 351–53
 worship, 228, 241, 242, 251
Barna, George, 307, 308, 311, 323
Barrett, David, 75n
Bartchy, Scott, 147, 173–74
Beasley–Murray, G. R., 265, 269, 274, 295
believers' church. *See* membership.
Bennett, Dennis, 339
Berkouwer, G. C., 61
Bible. *See* Scripture.
Bilezikian, Gilbert, 170n
bishop, 28, 52, 138–140, 161–62, 164, 194. *See also* elder; overseer.
Black, David Alan, 123n, 272
Boa, Kenneth, 235
body of Christ, 37–43, 71, 224–25, 236, 250, 282, 302, 352, 353
Book of Common Prayer, 288–289
Boyce, J. P., 32n
Brand, Chad, 213
Brazilian church, 113, 121

bride of Christ, 13, 116, 353
Bridge, Donald, 295
building, church as, 33, 43–49, 71, 75, 225, 352
Bunyan, John, 285

C
call to ministry, 174–77
called-out people, 26–36, 52, 55, 69, 70, 74, 83, 146, 175, 225, 315–16
Calvin, John, 12, 63, 85n, 90, 161, 176, 194, 269–270, 274, 280. *See also* Calvinism.
Calvinism, 92–93
Campbell, Colleen Carroll, 330
Campus Crusade for Christ, 222–23, 286
Capitol Hill Baptist Church, 114, 129, 231, 332
Carey, William, 255, 336–337
Carroll, B. H., 202
Carson, D. A., 77, 140, 147n, 166, 240n, 275n, 295, 301, 308, 309, 325–26, 328, 329, 331, 348
catechism, 86, 121–22
Catholic Church, Roman. *See* Roman Catholic Church.
catholicity, 57–59, 139, 234.
cell church, 18, 317–19, 338. *See also* house church; microchurch.
Chalke, Steve, 329
charismatic movements, 339–41. *See also* Pentecostal church.
children, 111, 122–24, 168, 193, 269, 271–72
Cho, Paul Yonggi, 320
Christ
 atoning death of, 33, 233, 262, 263, 281–83, 289, 294, 329
 headship of, 29, 41–43, 148–49, 352
 love of, 250, 252, 353
 resurrection of, 33, 233, 263
 return of, 282–83, 347
 union with, 57, 260, 263, 264
church. *See also* covenant, church membership; deacon; discipline, church; elder; membership; pastor.
 apostolicity of, 59–61, 63, 234
 authority in, 41–42, 60, 101, 139, 143–44, 146–48, 152, 154, 316
 catholicity of, 57–59, 139, 234

Christ and, 13, 37–43, 71, 116, 224–25,
236, 250, 282, 302, 352, 353
competence, 102, 120
composition of, 67–76, 81–87, 96, 315–16
congregational, 17, 46, 71, 100–2, 114,
135–138, 143–57, 165, 208, 209,
211, 315
creation of, 15, 225
culture and, 11, 110–11, 300n, 302, 304,
314–315, 330–31, 333, 343–345
denominational traditions of, 18–20,
25, 30, 54, 111, 275
destiny of, 347, 353
doctrine of, 11, 14–18.
episcopal, 137–40
essence of, 64, 67–76
family, 35, 174, 236, 319, 340, 352
growth, 41–43, 48, 71–73, 153–54, 238,
246, 254–55, 306, 314, 335–36, 351
health of, 115, 150, 224, 254–55, 306n
history, 15, 86, 139–40, 170–71, 324,
328, 331–34;
holiness of, 34, 55–57, 89, 234, 353
local, 28–31, 37, 53, 70–71, 83–85, 140,
143–46, 261
marks of, 16, 51–76, 221–24, 234, 286
metaphors for, 13–14, 31–49, 71, 75,
147, 225, 339, 250, 302, 352
nature of, 25–49, 64–65, 224–27
order in, 28, 136
people of God in, 13, 32–36, 67–68,
224, 225, 352
persecution of, 14
planting, 338–39, 341, 346–47
polity, 17–19, 68, 125, 135–57, 184, 188,
346
presbyterian, 137–38, 140–43
state and, 88–91, 267, 343
traditional, 301–2, 304, 314, 326–27,
331, 333
unity of, 30, 37–39, 52–55, 83, 234, 282,
315
universal, 28, 29, 41, 52, 53–54, 55, 57,
83, 105, 315, 335, 336
visible/invisible, 53
work of, 17, 68, 219–56, 317, 338–39,
341, 346–47
world events and, 32–33

Church of England. See Anglican Church.
"church power," 101, 106, 144. See also
competence, doctrine of.
Clark, Stephen, 172
Clowney, Edmund, 77, 219
Colson, Charles, 243–44
commitment, 230, 235–36, 261–63, 267, 272,
276, 277, 282, 285, 289
communion. See Lord's supper.
community, 48, 235, 237, 245, 261, 317–18,
325, 327, 328, 330
competence, doctrine of, 102, 120
complementarian, 170–174
confession. See also creed.
of faith, 291n
of sin, 289–90
congregational polity
case for, 17, 45–46, 135–57, 165
challenges facing, 151–57, 315
ideal, 71–76, 209, 211
models of, 145–46
regenerate membership and, 100–2
consistory, 140
Constantine, 17, 52, 87–88, 90
constitution/by-laws, 125, 184, 188
consumer attitude, 72, 156–57, 236, 300n,
307–12, 327, 329. See also marketing.
contemporary worship. See worship.
contextualization, 344–45
conversion, 88–89, 122–24. See also
regeneration; salvation.
corpus permixtum, 56, 87–91
covenant
church membership, 40, 96, 114, 116–
20, 125, 127–29, 230, 237, 331–32
old/new, 32–33, 269–70, 278
theology, 32, 270n
Cowan, Steven, 213
Cowen, Gerald, 136n, 174n, 175n, 180, 197,
213
Creed
Apostles', 289, 291n
Nicene, 51–52, 289, 291n
Criswell, W. A., 33n, 174
Crosby, David, 153–54
cross of Christ, 33, 233
Crouch, Andy, 321, 330
Culpepper, R. Alan, 204n, 207n

culture
  contemporary, 30, 72, 171–72, 299–
    302, 304, 322, 324, 326–27, 331
  Greco–Roman, 173–74, 343
  North American, 30, 71–72, , 110–11,
    236, 326, 333
  postmodern, 301–2, 314–15, 321–33,
    330–34
  reaching out to, 15, 343–47
  "wars," 300–1
Cyprian, 12, 52
Cyril of Jerusalem, 58

D

Dagg, John L., 32n, 125, 136, 174, 274n, 283,
  284n, 285, 296
Dargan, E. C., 178
Dawn, Marva, 244
Deacon Family Ministry Plan, 197
deacon, 191–212. *See also* deaconess;
  ordination.
    ordination of, 204
    origin, of, 148, 192
    qualifications of, 192–93
    role and responsibilities of, 71, 191–92,
      193–97, 145
    selection of, 197–98
    two-office view of, 17, 160, 179–80
    wives of, 199–200, 210
deaconess, 198–204
death of Christ, 33, 233, 262, 263, 281–83,
  289, 294, 329
democracy, ideal of, 138, 145, 149, 152, 165
denominations, 18–20, 25, 30, 54, 111, 275
Depression, U.S., 251
Dever, Mark, 58, 59, 77, 100, 115, 116n, 130,
  150, 154n, 178n, 179, 183n, 203, 214,
  228–29, 254, 285, 315n
Deweese, Charles, 40n, 94, 98, 102, 105, 112,
  117–18, 121n, 125n, 131, 202, 277
diocese in episcopal polity, 137
discipleship, 224, 226, 228–32, 235, 275,
  305–6, 317, 336–37
discipline, church
  basis for, 34, 84, 106
  mark of, 63, 147–48
  practice of, 105–7, 110–16, 124–26,
    285, 331–32

discipling class, 113–14, 121–22, 237, 273,
  331, 332
dispensationalism, 32
distinctives, Baptist, 21, 61, 82, 97–98, 136, 143
Donatists, 52, 55, 89
DuBose, Francis, 319n, 320n, 348
Duncan, J. Ligon III, 241–42, 243n, 296, 349
Durnbaugh, Donald, 87n

E

edification, 239, 240, 242, 340
egalitarianism, 170–74
Eitel, Keith, 341n
ekklēsia. See called-out people.
elder, 17, 28, 140–46, 160–89, 209, 332. *See
  also* overseer; pastor.
    deacon and, 194–95, 203, 211–12
    distinctions among, 140, 143, 154,
      161–62
    ordination of, 187, 205
    pastor and, 185
    plurality of, 140, 146, 154, 177–83, 211
    qualifications of, 166–77, 344, 346
    responsibilities of, 140, 163–66, 185,
      224
    rule by, 102, 137, 142, 154–57, 211
    selection of, 186–88
    terms of, 188
    transition to, 183–89
emergentvillage.com, 322n
emerging church, 18, 322, 333, 343. *See also*
  postmodern culture.
    characteristics of, 322–28
    evaluation of, 326–31
    strengths of, 328
    weaknesses of, 328–31
    worship, 325–26, 327.
emergingchurch.org, 322n, 349
Episcopal Church. 137–40. *See also* Anglican
  Church.
episkopos. See bishop; elder.
epistemology, 301, 323
equality, 172–74
Erickson, Millard, 62n, 101, 103, 136, 149,
  152, 219, 221, 261, 301, 322, 323
eucharist. *See* Lord's supper.
evangelicalism, 310–11, 314, 326, 332, 333,
  341, 347, 353

evangelism. *See also* evangelist; missions; witness.
  ministry of, 72–73, 221, 226, 235, 252–56, 318
  postmodern, 302, 322–24, 330–31
  "seeker," 228–29, 245–47, 305, 306, 341
  worship purpose of, 239, 240, 242
evangelist, 160
Eve, 173
ex opere operato, 258, 262, 268
experientialism, 324–25. *See also* worship.
expository preaching. *See* preaching.

F

faith, 35, 122, 224, 258, 262, 264–73, 289, 291, 301
Faith Communities Today Project, 332
faithfulness, 351–53
fatherhood of God, 35
family, church as, 35, 174, 236, 319, 340, 352
Fee, Gordon, 38, 44n, 104, 167n, 264n, 282
fellowship, 35–36, 48, 69, 221, 225, 232–38, 317, 321, 340
feminism, 170–71
foot-washing, 260
forgiveness, 264–65, 279, 289
free will Baptists, 285–86
freedom, religious. *See* religious liberty.
Freeman, J. D., 82
Furman, Richard, 111

G

Garrett, James Leo Jr., 97n, 111n, 126, 131, 142, 146, 149, 151, 153, 155–56, 213
Garrison, David, 338
gathered church, 81
general Baptists, 92–95, 202, 274
George, Timothy, 45n, 77, 285n, 286, 336n
globalism, 255, 324, 335–47
glossolalia. *See* tongues, speaking in.
God
  fatherhood of, 35
  holiness of, 34, 55, 248–49, 309–10
  love of, 34, 248–49, 309–10
  worship of, 244, 246–49, 329
  wrath of, 310, 329
González, Justo, 336
gospel

centrality of, 59, 73–74, 224–27, 330–31, 337, 343, 347
  mark of, 62–66, 73–74, 221
  postmodern, 328–29
  unity in, 53–55
grace, 258–59, 262, 264, 271, 279, 294, 328
Graham, Billy, 53
Graves, J. R., 202
Great Commission, 220, 226, 253, 254, 275–76, 335–37
Green, Michael, 35, 235, 253
Gregory I (the Great), 251
Grenz, Stanley, 64n, 99, 101, 104, 149, 152, 155, 219, 261, 267n, 282, 286, 323
Griffith, Benjamin, 106, 144n, 148n
growth, church, 41–43, 48, 71–73, 153–54, 238, 246, 254–55, 306, 314, 335–36, 351
Grudem, Wayne, 41n, 145, 170n, 177n, 215, 265n, 266, 341n
Guder, Darrell, 345

H

Hadaway, C. Kirk, 319n, 320n, 348
Hadaway, Robin, 341n
Haines, Stephen, 113, 131
Hammett, John, 207n, 222n., 223n, 253n..
Harper, Michael, 341n
headship of Christ, 29, 41–43, 148–49, 352
heaven, 115, 309, 328
hell, 115, 309, 328
Helwys, Thomas, 92–93, 202
Hendricks, William, 123, 272
heresy, 65, 74, 147
Heyrman, Christine Leigh, 111
Hinson, E. Glenn, 52n, 206
hirr.hartsem.edu, 313n, 314n, 349
historical developments, 15, 86, 139–40, 170–71, 324, 328, 331–34, 346–47
holiness
  of church, 34, 55–57, 89, 234, 353
  of God, 34, 55, 248–49, 309–10
Holiness Church, 339
Hollenweger, Walter J., 339n
Holy Spirit
  baptism of, 35–36, 38, 264n, 276n, 339
  coming of, 33, 35, 233
  ministry of, 47–48, 69, 74–76, 225, 239, 333–34, 340, 341, 346, 352

Pentecostal view of, 340–41
temple of, 43–49, 71, 225, 352
homosexuality, 300, 342
Horton, Michael, 321
house church, 18, 29–30, 180, 182, 317–20, 338. *See also* cell church, microchurch.
household baptism, 269
Howell, R. B. C., 194–95, 202
Hubmaier, Balthasar, 271n
Hudson, Winthrop, 143
Hughes, R. Kent, 242n
Hybles, Bill, 245, 306–7
hymns. *See* worship.

I

Ignatius of Antioch, 161
image of God, 233
immersion. *See* baptism.
individualism, 69, 113, 236, 324, 326
infant baptism, 57, 85, 89, 99, 201–2, 267–71, 284
International Mission Board, 255, 338, 341, 345n, 346–47
Internet, 11
invisible church, 53. *See also* universal church.
Irenaeus, 60, 75
Islam, 342–45
Israel, 32–34

J

James the Just, 181
Jenkins, Philip, 14, 256, 336, 342–43, 348–49
Jerusalem church, 30, 84, 162, 180, 197, 200
Jerusalem Council, 142, 144, 146
Jesus. *See* Christ.
Jewett, Paul, 32n, 170n, 296
Johnson, Terry, 241–42
Johnson, W. B., 179
Justification, 57, 281

K

Kärkkäinen, Veli–Matti, 340n, 341n
Keach, Benjamin, 106n, 194, 241
keys of the kingdom, 75, 106, 147
Kimball, Dan, 322–25, 327
kingdom, church and, 75, 95, 106, 147, 347
knowledge, 323

Koinōnia, 36, 69, 104, 232–35. *See* fellowship.
Kraft, Charles, 344
Küng, Hans 61, 77

L

landmarkism, 64
Latourette, Kenneth Scott, 336n, 337
leadership, 163–64, 179, 182, 184, 194, 207, 209, 211–12
Lee, Jason, 92n
Leonard, Bill, 155, 207n
Littell, Franklin, 85n
liturgy. *See* worship.
local church, 28–31, 37, 53, 70–71, 83–85, 140, 143–46, 261
Longenecker, Richard, 205n, 220n, 252–53, 263n, 265
Lord's supper, 29, 37–38, 47, 63, 65, 194–95, 238, 277–94
closed, 102–5, 114, 283–88
consubstantiation, 279–80
elements of, 195, 279, 282, 292–93
frequency of celebrating, 292
Holy Spirit in, 279–81
institution of, 278
meaning of, 102–5, 281–83
memorial view of, 280–81
preparation for, 288–91
renewal in, 277, 281–83, 288–91
terms for, 278
transubstantiation, 260, 279
worship and, 241, 277, 288–94
love, 34–35, 234, 250, 252, 253, 289, 291, 337. *See also* Christ.
Lumpkin, William L., 94n, 131, 205n, 285n
Luther, Martin, 45, 63, 83n, 86–87, 90, 91, 175n, 260, 268–69, 279–80

M

MacArthur, John, 123, 155, 273
McBeth, Leon, 85n, 93, 286
McBrien, Richard, 52n, 140, 258–59
McConnell, C. Douglas, 345
McLaren, Brian, 324, 328–29
Malone, Fred, 32n
Marcellino, Jerry, 243–44
Maring, Norman, 143
marketing, 303, 307–12

marks of the church, 16, 51–76, 221–24, 234, 286
Mass. *See* Lord's supper; Roman Catholic Church.
maturity, spiritual, 151, 169, 196, 211, 230–31, 346
means of grace, 234, 262, 265, 267
megachurches, 18, 152–53, 312–17, 319–20, 327, 332–33
    around the world, 313
    characteristics, 313–15
    difficulties and dangers of, 315–17
membership
    baptism and, 94–95, 102–3, 116, 120–24, 284, 286
    covenants and 117–20, 127–29, 331
    discipline and, 114–16, 124–26
    "open," 257n
    partaking Lord's supper and, 283–88
    participation and, 230–31, 237–38
    regenerate, 17, 32–36, 57, 81–108, 110–16, 120–24, 151–52, 156, 209, 287, 346
    weakness of, 109–14, 156–57
metachurch, 312
metaphors for church, 13–14, 31–49, 71, 75, 147, 225, 339, 250, 302, 352
Methodist church tradition, 138
microchurch, 18, 312, 317–20. *See also* cell church; house church.
Milne, Bruce, 225n, 234–35, 237, 296
Minear, Paul, 31n, 77
ministry, 138, 160, 191, 230
    congregational, 210, 212, 220, 317, 340–41
    diaconal, 194–97, 203
    individual, 176–77
    pastoral, 163, 175–77, 194
missions, 230, 255, 282–83
    catholicity and, 59, 65
    ecclesiology of, 328, 345–47
    expansion of church in, 88, 335–39
    future of, 338
    history of, 336–37
    ministry of, 227
modernity. *See* culture.
monasticism, 90
Moody, Dale, 272, 274n, 283n

Morris, Leon, 148–49
music. *See* worship.

N

nature of church, 25–49, 64–65, 224–27
Neighbour, Ralph Jr., 317–19.
Neill, Stephen, 88, 336n
Nelson, David, 239n, 240
new covenant. *See* covenant.
New Hampshire Confession of Faith, 96, 104, 286
newchurches.com, 301n, 322n, 349
Newton, Phil, 183n, 214.
Nicene Creed. *See* Creed.
Noll, Mark, 179n, 254n
Norman, R. Stanton, 136, 213
North American Baptists, 64, 109–11, 114, 138, 254
North American Mission Board, 14, 112, 124, 305n, 347
Northern (American) Baptist tradition, 286
Novatians, 52, 55

O

obedience, 103, 253–54, 275, 276, 285, 287
offerings, 45
"open" membership, 257n
order in church, 28, 136. *See also* discipline.
ordinances, 37–38, 64, 103–4, 249, 257–63, 352. *See also* baptism; Lord's supper.
    administrator of, 260–61
    criteria for, 260
    local church, 261–62, 282, 284–85, 287, 289
    meaning of, 261–63
    number of, 259–60
    terms for, 258–59
ordination, 204–8
Origen, 268
Orthodox Church, 53
overseer, 28, 160–63. *See also* bishop.

P

paedobaptism. *See* baptism.
papacy. *See* Roman Catholic Church.
parachurch organizations, 19, 53, 65, 70, 222–23, 261–62, 286
Parham, Charles Fox, 339

Parshall, Phil, 344n, 345
particular Baptists, 93, 95–96, 202, 274
Passover, 278
pastor, 28, 71, 144, 160–63, 209, 351–53. *See also* elder; overseer.
    authority of, 143, 144, 146, 164–65
    leadership, 146, 153–54
    teaching ministry of, 43, 224, 228–29, 250
pastoral oversight, 316, 320
Patterson, Paige, 26, 146n, 165n, 182, 213, 341n
Pendleton, J. M., 20n, 97
Pentecost, 14, 33, 339
Pentecostal church, 75, 314, 339–41
people of God, 13, 32–36, 67–68, 224, 225, 352
persecution, 14
"personal fulfillment," theology of, 309
Peterson, David, 239–40
Phillips, Richard, 53n, 54, 77
Phoebe of Cenchrea, 200–1, 203–4
Phypers, David, 295
Piper, John, 167n, 170n, 183n, 185, 195, 201, 203, 214, 215
planting, church, 338–39, 341, 346–47
plurality of elders. *See* elder.
polity, church. *See* church; congregational polity; constitution/by-laws; deacon; elder.
pope. *See* Roman Catholic Church.
post-Christian, 324, 326
postdenominationalism, 11, 18, 275
postmodern culture, 321–34
power, 74–76
pragmatism, 14, 144, 311
prayer, 242, 344
preaching
    elder role of, 163
    expository, 228
    mark of, 62–66
    worship and, 241, 242, 292, 294
presbyter, 45, 161. *See also* elder.
Presbyteros. See elder.
presbyterian polity, 140–43
priesthood
    modern, 138–39, 260
    of believers, 45–46, 101, 149, 160, 175, 260

Pritchard, G. A., 303n, 306–11, 349
Promise Keepers, 19, 223, 286
prophet, 160
Puritans, 91–92.

R
racism, 59.
Radbertus, Paschasius, 279
Rainer, Thom, 254n
Ratramnus, 279
Rauschenbusch, Walter, 251
reason, 301, 323–26
Reformation
    Anabaptist, 90–91
    marks of church in, 62–65
    theology of, 161, 279–80
    unity of church in 52–53, 58, 70
regenerate church members. *See* membership; regeneration.
regeneration, 105–6, 156, 270, 273. *See also* conversion; salvation.
regulative principle. *See* worship.
relativism, 329
religious liberty, 343
remembrance, 282–83. *See also* Lord's supper.
repentance, 272, 276, 289–90, 329
resurrection of Christ, 33, 233, 263
return of Christ, 282–83, 347
Reymond, Robert, 142
Robinson, John, 71
rock, Peter as, 28, 43
Roman Catholic Church, 28, 43, 52–53, 58, 60, 63, 65, 138, 258–60, 279
Romanian church, 112
Rome, bishop of. *See* Roman Catholic Church.
Ryken, Philip, 77, 296, 349

S
sacraments, 37, 62–66, 249, 258, 264–65, 340. *See also* ordinances.
Saddleback Community Church, 128, 230, 246, 303–4, 332
saints, 34, 83, 84, 106
salvation, 115–16, 123, 264–67, 272–73, 279, 294, 328, 329. *See also* conversion; regeneration.

sanctification, 57, 282
Sargeant, Kimon, 243, 245–46, 248, 303–7, 349
Saucy, Robert, 77, 192n, 238, 260, 263, 266, 273
Scripture
    authority of, 15–16, 61, 86–87, 90, 306
    fidelity to, 329, 331, 334, 343, 345, 352
    mark of church, 62–66
    ministry of, 60–61, 228–29, 163, 194, 228–29, 241
    worship and, 228–29, 241–42
Second London Confession, 96, 102, 104, 205, 242, 281
sects, 110
secular culture, 72, 113, 300–1, 342
"seeker" ecclesiology
    culture and, 71–72, 310–12, 322–23, 329, 331, 343
    evangelism through, 308–12, 322
    membership in, 332–33
    movement, 17, 303–12
    worship in, 228–29, 243–49, 304–6, 309, 314, 327
separatists, 21, 91–93.
Septuagint, 26–27
serving others, 221, 226, 249–52
session, 140–42
Shelley, Bruce, 72n, 156, 300n, 308n
Shelley, Marshall, 72n, 156, 300n, 308n
singing. See worship.
small groups, 232, 237, 238, 252, 317–20. See also cell church; house church; microchurch.
Smyth, John, 92, 194, 274
Snyder, Howard, 62, 235, 339
social gospel, 250–52. See also serving others.
sola Scriptura, 63, 90
soul competence, 46
Southern Baptist Convention, 109, 111–12, 150, 229, 243n, 251–252, 255, 305n, 338, 341, 346.
spiritual gifts. See Holy Spirit.
Spurgeon, C. H., 32n, 174, 206, 285
Stafford, Tim, 12
Stark, Rodney, 88–89, 90n, 110, 235
state, secular, 88–91, 267, 343

Stetzer, Ed, 64n, 224, 244, 301, 321
stewardship, 164, 196
Stott, John, 223
Strauch, Alexander, 164n, 199n, 200, 215
Strong, A. H., 99, 136, 181, 259, 282n, 283n, 285, 293–94, 296
Summary of Church Discipline, 97, 106, 112, 116
Sunday school, 229–30, 232, 312, 317
Sutton, Jerry, 150n
Sweet, Leonard, 325
synagogue, 162, 182, 238
syncretism, 344–45
synod, 141

T
tabernacle, 46, 239
teaching, 163, 169, 209, 221, 224–25, 227–32, 237
technology, 325, 328, 335
temple, 43–49, 71, 225, 238–39, 352
Ten Commandments, 289, 300
Tertullian, 35
theology, 15–16
    covenant 32, 270n
    "personal fulfillment," 309
    Reformation, 161, 279–80
    "seeker," 305–6
theooze.com, 322n, 349
Third World, 341
Thomas, Derek W. H., 296, 349
Thumma, Scott, 313–15
tongues, speaking in, 314, 339
Toon, Peter, 139, 213
Towns, Elmer, 64n, 224, 244
tradition, 340
transubstantiation. See Lord's supper.
Trent, Council of, 258, 260
Trinity, 233
Troeltsch, Ernst, 110
truth, 239, 301, 323–24, 328–29
Tucker, Ruth, 336n
Tyler, John, 100n, 286n

U
union with Christ, 57, 260, 263, 264
unity in body, 30, 37–39, 52–55, 83, 234, 282, 315

universal church, 28, 29, 41, 52, 53–54, 55,
    57, 83, 105, 315, 335, 336

V

Van Gelder, Craig, 54, 57, 59n, 77
Vaughan, John, 152n, 153, 312n, 313, 315,
    317
visible church, 53
Volf, Miroslav, 64, 250, 340n

W

Waldron, Samuel, 165n, 213
Walls, Andrew, 335–36
Warren, Rick, 115, 219–20, 222–23, 228–30,
    237, 238, 243, 245, 254, 296, 303, 305,
    306, 309–11
Webster, Douglas, 308
Wells, David, 308, 311, 321–22
Westminster Confession of Faith, 281
Wheaton College, 347
White, James Emery, 304n
White, James R., 179
Willimon, Will, 238
Willow Creek Association, 48, 245–46, 249,
    303–7, 309–11, 332
Willow Creek Community Church
Wills, Greg, 107, 113, 115, 131, 162n, 178n,
    180n
Wilson, G. Todd, 257n, 275, 284, 286n
Wilson, Jonathan, 61, 309

Winter, Ralph, 337
witness, 115–16, 124
Wolfe, Alan, 72, 308–310
women, roles of, 137, 170–74, 201, 203–4,
    212
Word of God. *See* Scripture.
work of church, 17, 68, 219–56, 317, 338–39,
    341, 346–47
world. *See* globalism.
worship, 44–46, 221, 225, 234, 238–49, 329.
    See also baptism, Lord's supper;
    ordinances; preaching.
    arts in, 325, 328
    characteristics of, 239–40
    dimensions of, 240
    elements of, 226, 238, 242, 243
    multiple services, 315
    music in, 241, 243–44, 314
    purpose of, 244–47
    regulative principle of, 242–43, 329
    styles of, 243–49, 293–94, 324–25
    Word of God in, 226
Wright, Stuart, 319n, 320n, 348

Y

Yoder, John, 87n
youth, 322–324, 330–31

Z

Zwingli, Huldrych, 63, 90, 280–81, 292